NEW LIGHT ON NIMRUD

Proceedings of the Nimrud Conference
11th–13th March 2002

edited by

J.E. Curtis, H. McCall, D. Collon and L. al-Gailani Werr

This volume is dedicated to the memory of

Rabi'a al-Qaissi
Jeremy Black
Manhal Jabr
David Oates

NEW LIGHT ON NIMRUD

Proceedings of the Nimrud Conference
11th–13th March 2002

edited by

J.E. Curtis, H. McCall, D. Collon and L. al-Gailani Werr

Jointly organised by the British School of Archaeology in Iraq and the British Museum
and supported by a grant from the British Academy

British Institute for the Study of Iraq in association with The British Museum 2008

LONDON

British Library Cataloguing in Publication Data
A catalogue record for this book is available from the British Library
ISBN 978-0-903472-24-1

Designed and typeset by Meeks & Middleton
Printed by Short Run Press in Exeter

CONTENTS

FIGURES, PLATES AND PLANS

Figures

Colour Plates

(a) The crown with the lapis-lazuli grapes hanging down on the interior.

(b) The top of the crown.

(c) The interior of the crown.

Plate VI

(a–b) Details of the crown shown on Plate V.

Plate VII

The gold jug (height 13 cm) from Tomb III.

Plate VIII

(a–b) Some of the many necklaces made of semi-precious stones, from Tomb III.

(c) Gold necklace with eye-stone pendants, from Tomb III.

(d) Strap work dress ornament from Tomb III.

(e) Gold finger rings, inlaid with semi-precious stones, from Tomb III.

Plans

INTRODUCTION

Nimrud in Northern Iraq is one of the greatest sites in the Ancient Near East. It was the capital city of the Assyrian king Ashurnasirpal II (883–859 BC) and boasted a series of richly decorated palaces and temples. The excavations there by Sir Henry Layard in the middle of the 19th century uncovered stone bas reliefs and winged bulls and lions, some of which are now in the British Museum, and the excavations of Sir Max Mallowan and Professor David Oates between 1949 and 1963, on behalf of the British School of Archaeology in Iraq, produced many outstanding finds, particularly large numbers of beautifully carved ivories. Iraqi excavations in 1988–1990 revealed the tombs of a number of Assyrian queens containing astonishing quantities of gold objects and jewellery on a scale to match the discovery of the tomb of Tutankhamun. Following the 1st Gulf War in 1991 and the imposition of sanctions, further archaeological work in Iraq, at least for foreign missions, became impossible, and scholars more and more turned their thoughts towards publishing and evaluating previous work. It was in this climate that the idea of organising a joint British School — British Museum conference about Nimrud was conceived. The intention was to review the results of the many different excavations at the site, and to put Nimrud and the remarkable objects found there into a broader Near Eastern context.

The suggestion of organising an academic conference about Nimrud was first mooted at a meeting of the Governing Council of the British School of Archaeology in Iraq, and to take the proposal forward a working party was established consisting of John Curtis, Jeremy Black, Georgina Herrmann and Lamia al-Gailani Werr. This group met three times in the course of 1999, and in November 2000 Dominique Collon and Henrietta McCall were co-opted onto the working party. They were later joined by Sam Moorhead, then of the British Museum's Education Department. Although it had not been the original intention, it was decided that the conference should be timed to coincide with a special exhibition at the British Museum on 'Agatha Christie and Archaeology: Mystery in Mesopotamia', conceived by Charlotte Trümpler of the Ruhrlandmuseum in Essen. Part of the rationale for this was that participants would then have an opportunity to see the exhibition while attending the conference, which would be particularly convenient if they were coming from abroad. As the exhibition was scheduled to be shown at the British Museum from 8 November 2001–24 March 2002, the conference was planned for the period 21–23 November 2001. Following the destruction of the World Trade Centre in New York on 11 September 2001, however, it was decided to postpone the conference for four months, as many colleagues around the world were understandably reluctant to travel in the weeks following this disaster. The conference eventually took place at the British Museum from 11–13 March 2002. Over 30 leading scholars from Iraq, the United States, Poland, Italy and Germany joined colleagues in Britain for a wide-ranging survey of Nimrud and it is pleasing that 34 papers are published here.

The conference would not of course have been worthwhile or credible without the participation of Iraqi scholars, and it is gratifying that in the end six Iraqi colleagues were able to join us, namely Rabi'a al-Qaissi (State Board of Antiquities and Heritage), Dr Donny George Youkhanna (State Board of Antiquities and Heritage), Dr Muayyad Sa'id Damerji (Ministry of Information), Manhal Jabr Ismail (Director of the Northern Region), Muzahim Mahmud Hussein (Department of Antiquities, Mosul) and Dr Ali Yaseen al-Jabory (University of Mosul). Owing to the uncertain political situation at that time we were worried that it might be difficult to obtain visas for these Iraqi colleagues, but in the event, the British Consulate in Amman became as committed to finding ways for these academics to travel to Britain, as we were determined to have them here. We would like to record our gratitude to the staff at the Consulate, especially Jayne Singleton, for all their patience and assistance. The presence of these Iraqi scholars was invaluable. Apart from giving us important information and an insight into the fabulous gold jewellery discovered at Nimrud, they were able to address a wider world through the press, radio and television. The opportunity was also taken to invite two of the Iraqi scholars to give lectures at the British Museum on Thursday 14 March. Donny George spoke about his excavations at Umm al Agarib and Muzahim Mahmud lectured on 'Recent excavations at Nimrud'.

The first day of the Conference was devoted to a review of the archaeological excavations at Nimrud, starting with its first excavator, Austen Henry Layard, in the mid-nineteenth century, and coming up almost to the present day. It is worth pointing out here that although the proposals of David Thomas for creating a Nimrud database have not in the event been adopted, we have decided to include his paper as an indication of work in progress at that time. The afternoon session ended with a talk by Charlotte Trümpler introducing the exhibition, which delegates had an opportunity to visit. They were then revived after a very full day with refreshments in the Assyrian Basement.

The second day was devoted to the Nimrud Tombs. The topic was introduced by Dr Muayyad Damerji and Dr Donny George, and their colleague Muzahim Mahmud Hussein described the discoveries in detail. A packed lecture theatre then saw photographs of the magnificent collections of gold jewellery, the workmanship of which was described by our Iraqi colleagues. A group discussion followed on the methods of gold-working. Other papers that day addressed topics such as the inscriptions from the tombs, the textiles, the seals and beads, the bronze coffins, and the identity of the royal occupants. Professor Nicholas Postgate summed up the significance of the tombs in the final paper of the afternoon. In the evening the London Centre for the Ancient Near East (LANES) organised a public lecture by Dr Sam Paley on 'New research on the North-West Palace at Nimrud' in which he described his computer-generated reconstruction programme.

In the course of the second day, the following resolutions were reached by the participants in the Nimrud Conference:-

1.   The Conference notes and confirms the continuing importance of the historic site of Nimrud and the associated archaeological material held in museums in Iraq for the development of international scholarship and understanding of our common cultural heritage. Bearing in mind the damage to sites and artefacts occasioned by the events of 1991 and their aftermath, the Conference calls on all individuals and organisations to use their best endeavours to safeguard, and ensure the continued conservation of, archaeological sites and artefacts in Iraq and minimize any threats to them from whatever cause.

2.   The Conference notes with concern the serious situation in Iraq caused by the continued reduction in the flow of the River Tigris, and the resultant plans for the Makhul dam which would submerge the Assyrian capital at Ashur. The Conference urges all concerned parties, both within Iraq and internationally, to explore every possible means of preserving the site of Ashur which is of unique importance in the history of Iraq in particular and world civilisation in general.

The final day of the Conference focused on 'Art and Literacy at Nimrud'. The three sessions dealt with the public buildings (their form, decoration and role); the minor arts (ivories, seals, bronzes and pottery); and finally, literary matters (scribes and tablets). The Conference concluded with a lecture by Dr Joan Oates (who first dug there in 1952) on 'The changing role of Nimrud'. An enjoyable end-of-conference dinner was held at SOFRA in Covent Garden.

On the day after the Conference the British School of Archaeology in Iraq organised a lecture by Professor Alan Millard on 'From cuneiform to Kufic: writing in early Iraq', following which the Iraqi ambassador Mudafar al-Amin invited all the participants in the Nimrud Conference to a reception at his residence in Holland Park Villas.

It is a tragedy that since the Conference two of the six Iraqi delegates have passed away. Rabi'a al-Qaissi, by then Director of the State Board of Antiquities and Heritage, was killed in a car accident in Jordan on 3rd November 2003, while on his way to attend the opening of a new Mesopotamia gallery in the Louvre in Paris. Shortly after this, Manhal Jabr, Chief Archaeological Inspector for Nineveh Governorate, died in hospital in Mosul on 24th December 2003 from a heart attack. He was a chronic diabetic who suffered greatly during the period of sanctions from lack of medication. The editors of this volume also record with sadness the death of Professor David Oates on 22nd March 2004, but we feel proud that his last public lecture was the one he gave on the first day of the Conference on the subject of the long association of the British School of Archaeology in Iraq with Nimrud. The death at only 52 of Dr Jeremy Black, one of the co-organisers of the Conference, is particularly sad. Jeremy readily undertook all matters relating to the literary papers. He was wonderfully efficient and reliable and his premature passing is a great loss. This volume is dedicated to the memory of these four scholars.

The Conference was a genuinely collaborative effort between the British School of Archaeology in Iraq and the British Museum, and was made possible by a generous grant from the British Academy. We are also grateful to the British Museum Volunteers who helped throughout the Conference and also arranged the reception held on the first evening. Three of the editors owe a particular debt of gratitude to Henrietta McCall who has borne the brunt of the editing and without whom this publication might not have seen the light of day.

A news release for the conference stated that it would be a landmark in the continuing attempt to maintain cultural relations with Iraq. Since that was written, and just over a year after the conference was held, Iraq was invaded by coalition forces with disastrous results for the Iraqi cultural heritage. In the subsequent looting of the Iraq Museum many Nimrud ivories were smashed and broken, and it is feared that those remaining intact are in dire need of conservation. Small crumbs of comfort can be drawn from the fact that some of the most precious ivories and the gold treasures from the Nimrud tombs were stored in the Central Bank, and thus escaped the looting, added to which the site of Nimrud itself appears to have fared better than many others. However the overall picture remains gloomy, and all of us who care about Iraq have a clear responsibility to draw the attention of the world to the problems currently afflicting cultural heritage in Iraq and to provide as much help and assistance as we can to our Iraqi colleagues.

The editors

Top
Speakers at the Nimrud Conference in the BP Lecture Theatre, British Museum, 13th March 2002
Back Row, from left: Muzahim Mahmud Hussein; Manhal Jabr; Rabi'a al-Qaissi; Muayyad Said Damerji; Donn
George Youkhanna; John Curtis
Front Row, from left: Lamia al-Gailani Werr; Dominique Collon; Jeremy Black; Henrietta McCall; Farouk al-Ra

Bottom
Participants at the Nimrud Conference, including front row from left: Muayyad Said Damerji; David Oates;
Rabi'a al-Qaissi; Manhal Jabr; Muzahim Mahmud Hussein

1   NINETEENTH-CENTURY NIMRUD: MOTIVATION, ORIENTATION, CONSERVATION

Julian Reade

Nimrud, as I recall it from the early 1960s, could be paradise. In spring, for a month or two, after the first rains had come and before the moisture from the last rains evaporated, there were flowers and lush vegetation, a succession of species cramming their growth and germination into lancets of time, changing the colour of the countryside from week to week. To the west there was the gleam of the Tigris river, and the low browner hills beyond, on the fringe of the Mesopotamian desert. Snow glistened from a different world in the mountains of Kurdistan to the north. There were beetles and butterflies and birds, and eventually there was the migration of the storks. They flew very high, following the course of the Tigris from the south, and when they arrived at Nimrud they circled for a while and then split, one group following the same river northward and a second group diverging east to follow the course of the Greater Zab. I imagined the storks circling like this in 613 BC, after the first Median invasion, when they realized that the hospitable roofs of Kalah were no longer there to welcome their nests and their young.

This kind of idyllic vision appears repeatedly in old books mentioning Nimrud. For the workmen of the hereditary provincial governor Ahmed Pasha Jalili in the early nineteenth century, however, Nimrud had a more practical use, as a source of ready-cut stone conveniently sited between his city of Mosul and the tomb of the saint Sultan Abdullah further down the Tigris (fig. 1-a). Henry Layard (fig. 1-b), the first great archaeological excavator of Nimrud, on starting work in 1845, encountered in the North-West Palace a wall-panel upon which was 'rudely inscribed, in Arabic characters, the name of Ahmed Pasha', and someone remembered how workmen had

'uncovered this slab; but being unable to move it, they cut upon it the name of their employer... My informant further stated that, in another part of the mound, he had forgotten the precise spot, they had found sculptured figures, which they broke in pieces, the fragments being used in the reparation of the tomb' (Layard 1849a: I, 28–29). This was well before the first Ottoman Antiquities Law, which was to be introduced in 1874. Such things were not wanted in Stamboul (Constantinople, Istanbul) until they began to make headlines in Europe, so that only large-scale archaeological work seems to have attracted official attention. Layard himself operated throughout by maintaining good relations with the local governors and people, but was supported from 1846 onwards by a letter from the Grand Vizier, obtained by Sir Stratford Canning, the influential British ambassador at Stamboul, which set the precedent for British archaeological work until 1864. Layard was permitted to excavate and export material in view of 'the sincere friendship which exists firmly between the two governments', Ottoman and British (Layard 1849a: I, 130; translation quoted from Larsen 1996: 99).

Layard was aged twenty-eight when he began his excavations. He seems to have had at least two motives, or rather two sets of motives, and since reasons for digging Nimrud have changed over time and continue to do so, following private and public agenda, it is worth considering what they really were at the start. The prime motive which he himself judiciously describes is curiosity, an altruistic love of knowledge for its own sake, accompanied implicitly by the sober desire that success might bring him personal distinction. Layard was familiar with the beautiful Graeco-Roman sites of the

---

The illustrations for this paper are reproduced by courtesy of the Deutsche Orient-Gesellschaft, kindly supplied to me some years ago by Dr Eva Strommenger (figs 1-a 1-g, 1-j), and of the British Museum (figs 1-b–f, 1-h–i, k–p). The largely unpublished nineteenth-century archives in the British Library (BL) and British Museum (BM) consist of notebooks, diaries, letters, and official reports and documents, with a great jumble of information. Most of the surviving drawings and cuneiform copies from the actual excavations are in the BM Department of the Middle East (ME). Layard himself seems to have kept virtually all his documents, but someone, surely Lady Layard, systematically crossed out indelicate passages before the documents were presented to the BL, and presumably destroyed some of them which one might have expected to find, including a full diary of his first season. This paper uses the following abbreviations:

AE = BM Central Archive, volume on Assyrian Excavations
BL = BL Additional Manuscript
BLO = BL Oriental and India Office
Corr and Corr NS = ME volumes of correspondence (numbered by volume before 1868, thereafter by year)
Minutes = BM Central Archive, Trustees Committee Minutes
OP = BM Central Archive, volumes of Original Letters and Papers (Volumes 1–100 = 1742–869, with the volume numbers starting anew in 1870)
RAS = Royal Asiatic Society, Rawlinson Papers
Reports = Departmental Reports to Trustees, in ME or BM Central Archive
Returns = BM's published Annual Parliamentary Returns
Transcripts = ME volume of 'Transcripts of letters relating to excavations', taken from originals often in the BM Central Archive

Fig. 1-a. Nimrud as a ruin: a winged lion in the throne room façade of the North-West Palace, with the ziggurat beyond, 1906. (Assur photograph 2084, taken by Walter Andrae, Deutsche Orient-Gesellschaft).

Mediterranean, but on visiting Mesopotamia in 1840 he had found there a civilization represented, as he put it, 'by the stern shapeless mound rising like a hill from the scorched plain, the fragments of pottery, and the stupendous mass of brickwork occasionally laid bare by the winter rains... These huge mounds of Assyria made a deeper impression upon me, gave rise to more serious thought and more earnest reflection, than the temples of Baalbec or the theatres of Ionia'. He listened to legends of the remote past told him by the Arabs. 'My curiosity had been greatly excited, and from that time I formed the design of thoroughly examining, whenever it might be in my power, these singular ruins.' That altruism and disin-terested curiosity were true incentives is shown by the enthusiasm with which, before he himself was able to work at Nimrud, and even before the discovery of Khorsabad, he had urged others to do so: not only the British businessmen, Mr Sterling of Sheffield and Alexander Hector of Baghdad, to whom he could suggest that 'the objects of antiquity to be discovered would amply repay the expense', but also the French antiquari-ans Pascal Coste and Paul-Émile Botta (Layard 1849a: I, 6–10; 1887: II, 368). Before his second expedition, when he was conscious of possible French or Prussian competition, he suggested that it should become a joint British-Ottoman project, to provide material both for

Fig. 1-b. Detail from a watercolour portrait of Layard, 1843, by Amadeo Preziosi. (British Museum photograph, PD 1976-9-25,9, presented by Miss Phyllis Layard).

London and for a new museum which the Ottoman authorities were thinking of creating at Stamboul (OP 41: 5.ii.1849).

A deeper motive, however, which shines through everything he wrote and did at the time and through his lifelong support for the underdog, was his love of freedom. 'How I long for a black tent, a horse, a flock of sheep, and a wife in the solitary mountains of Luristan, where I may do as I like and say what I like. This is the only life worthy of an independent man' (quoted from Waterfield 1963: 102). He already knew the wilds of Luristan and was then living insecurely but comfortably in Stamboul. A return home to London would have meant at best a cool reception and a dusty office. He had prospects of a diplomatic career, but Nimrud offered more. It was situated in one of the most chaotic and misgoverned provinces of the Ottoman Empire, where he could act almost as a free agent, with the power to control his own destiny. He acquired his own country estate: while this did entail social responsibilities, he could also indulge in pursuits proper to a young gentleman abroad, such as pigsticking and coursing gazelle. The older reminiscences of expatriate Englishmen, whether as archaeologists or as imperial administrators, often give the impression that what they valued above all else were the opportunities to hunt and shoot. It was surely Layard who

Fig. 1-c. South gate of the citadel, April 1878, with Rassam on the right. (Rassam 1897: facing p. 222) (British Museum photograph of original print by Mosul photographer).

contributed an authoritative and almost lyrical description of such sports in the countryside near Nimrud to the *Handbook for Travellers in Turkey in Asia*, produced by his publisher and friend, John Murray (p. 441 of the 4th edition, 1878); the *Handbook* has very little about ancient mounds. Similarly, many years afterwards, Hormuzd Rassam, while not interested in hunting, could still present himself as an English gentleman when excavating at Nimrud, a status unattainable in the England he had adopted as home (Reade 1993): in April 1878 he was wearing top hat and morning coat on site (fig. 1-c), the uniform of respectability still expected of some British Museum staff into the early twentieth century (Miller 1973: 259).

Sir Stratford Canning, who paid for the first excavations at Nimrud, also had mixed motives. He was rewarding Layard for unofficial diplomatic services. He was interested by the potential scientific results, since Botta's discoveries at Khorsabad had reinforced the significance of reports on Nimrud made by Claudius Rich (1836: II, 129–33), the Revd George Badger (1852: I, 86–93) and Layard himself. Canning's main discernible motive, however, seems to have been a characteristic vanity. He did not wish to be remembered only as an ambassador (Lane-Poole 1888: II, 148–49). 'I am quite proud of my public spirit in the cause of antiquity and fine art': he wanted his name, like that of Lord Elgin, to be associated with the recovery of Marbles, and he successfully got another lot from Halicarnassus too. As a politician he was to express the hope that Layard's discoveries, transferred to London, would 'beat the Louvre hollow'.

Once Marbles had been found at Nimrud, Canning succeeded in handing over financial responsibility to the Trustees of the British Museum, who had in turn to satisfy the British government Treasury. The motives of the Trustees, unpaid representatives of the ruling class, were similar to those which had led their grandfathers, sent abroad on the Grand Tour to sow wild oats and acquire polish, to return home laden with the curiosities, pictures and Marbles that can still be seen in some of their stately homes. What the Trustees were doing with the British Museum was create an equivalent stately home for the nation, indulging their own interests while patronizing the universal 'cultivation of learning and taste... leading to the general concord and prosperity of the human race' (BL 39077: 14–17; 21.ix.1846). Marbles were the best education of all. The Trustees had previously taken no action on a proposal to excavate at Nimrud, made in early 1844 by Hormuzd Rassam's elder brother Christian, the British Vice-Consul in Mosul, to the Earl of Aberdeen, Foreign Secretary, keen antiquarian and Trustee (OP 32: 14.ii.1845). Since Christian was an entrepreneur, his real motive may have been financial (e.g. Larsen 1996: 74–75, 311–12), and he carried no weight in London, but Canning's success was an ample recommendation. Soon the more adventurous travellers, on the extended Grand

Fig. 1-d. Colossal figures in doorway of Ninurta shrine, 1850. (Clive 1852: pl. 11) (British Museum photograph of watercolour, made by courtesy of Ann Searight; original now in the Searight collection, Victoria & Albert Museum).

Tour of the eastern Mediterranean, would be adding Nimrud to their itineraries; in 1850 at least two of them, the Hon. Robert Clive (1852) and the Revd Solomon Malan (Gadd 1938), made drawings which are still helpful records of the excavations (fig. 1-d).

So there was the romantic Layard, renouncing city life for a rustic idyll, supported by a vain diplomat and remote Trustees, excavating a ruin whose only previous use had been as a quarry, in a region where the religious establishment generally regarded academic research and suchlike endeavours as 'difficult and useless' (Layard 1853a: 663). His workmen and the governor of Mosul naturally thought he was looking for gold (Layard 1849a: I, 32), rather than the less immediate but sometimes pecuniary reward of a golden reputation: I occasionally wonder what would have happened if chance had led Layard to the rich royal tombs of Nimrud. It was also thought, given the weakness of the Ottoman Empire and the presence of western missionaries, that foreign archaeologists were another subversive influence: they were even accused of digging military trenches and of seeking evidence to justify territorial claims. This was nonsense, but they were certainly looking for intellectual territory, on the assumption that all research was legitimate, and Layard seems to have treated all his workers, regardless of their background and status, with a degree of even-handed respect which must itself have been viewed as subversive.

All these attitudes had a lasting effect on the progress of the excavations. Records of the Trustees' deliberations, however, while justifying contemporary criticisms of them and the system they had inherited, nonetheless show them doing their utmost to be constructive, at a time when they had other serious problems (Layard 1853a: ix; Miller 1973: 167–223). It was with their keen support, and hence mainly with money from the Treasury, that the more impersonal motives prevailed and the work proceeded.

Government expenditure on excavations at Nimrud and elsewhere in Assyria reflected public enthusiasm, which was also expressed later by private subscriptions. Expectations which continued to drive the work were the straightforward acquisition of Marbles for the Museum, the recording and anticipated decipherment of cuneiform inscriptions, the discovery of remains relevant to Biblical history, the supposed national interest in outdoing the French, and the excitement which is regularly generated by explorations of a Lost World.

As for the standards of excavation, Layard (1849a: I, 326–27) described what he had to do in his first season, largely alone since he had only Hormuzd Rassam to help him manage the dig, and because 'there was no inclination to send an artist to assist me... I had therefore to superintend the excavations; to draw all the bas-reliefs discovered; to copy and compare the innumerable inscriptions; to take casts of them; and to preside over the moving and packing of the sculptures'. He had to do delicate excavation work in person, and 'felt that I was far from qualified to undertake these multifarious occupations. I knew, however, that if persons equal to the task, and sufficiently well acquainted with the various languages... were sent out expressly from England, the whole sum granted would be expended before the excavations could be commenced'. It is a classic statement of the dilemma all archaeologists have faced at Nimrud and elsewhere, how to choose priorities, how to allocate time and resources, how to cut corners.

All the same, Layard did not feel obliged to stay permanently on site. He happily set off during his first season of 1845–47, with a Jebour escort, for an exploration of Ashur (Qal'a Shergat); he describes the place as 'notoriously dangerous, being a place of rendezvous for all plundering parties, whether of the Shammar, the Aneyza, or the Obeid' (Layard 1849a: II, 44–45). During his second season of 1849–51, when he should have been overseeing the excavation of the Nimrud temples, he slipped away with Shammar and Jebour friends and about sixty workmen for a two-month archaeological trip through the Jezira to the Khabur. His account of this is the best section of his second popular book (Layard 1853a: 234–336), because he had enjoyed it so much. The Trustees, who had not been consulted, hastened to insist that his Khabur expenses were not to be charged against the grant for excavations. Layard paid for this, and for some other work, from his own modest resources.

Otherwise, for nearly all the nineteenth century, Nimrud was a quiet place, grazed by sheep and turned by the plough when the countryside was secure. Besides Layard, with Rassam as his assistant, members of archaeological expeditions funded by the British Museum worked there for parts of seven years (references: Postgate and Reade 1980: 304–5). Henry Rawlinson was there briefly in 1852 with Felix Jones, and was formally responsible for further work by Rassam in 1852–54, and by William Loftus and William Boutcher in 1854–55. George Smith excavated briefly in 1873. Rassam was back in 1878–79, working with an Ottoman representative under the new legislation. There were a few visits by other antiquarians and entre-preneurs, including in 1862 the French consul at Baghdad, Henri-Pacifique Delaporte (Chevalier 1995: 92); he acquired a few Marbles there, and sent them to the Louvre through the agency of the Swiss businessman, Julius Weber, who went to Nimrud himself for more Marbles in 1864 (Green, this volume). The subsequent appearance of Nimrud on 15 or 16 December 1906 is recorded in photographs by the German archaeologist, Walter Andrae (1907: 17) (figs 1-a, 1-g, 1-j). The site was photographed by Gertrude Bell in April 1909 (www.gerty.ncl.ac.uk).

James Felix Jones (1813–78) deserves special mention, because he is little known and because he was the first exponent of landscape archaeology in Iraq. He was captain of the *Nitocris*, the Hon. East India Company's paddle-steamer on the Tigris, and must have been trained to make coastal charts. In 1852 he mapped the cities of Nimrud and Nineveh and their surroundings, and the Assyrian plain between the Tigris and Jebel Maglub, with details unmentioned by many later archaeologists. The three maps were printed by the Company at the Trustees' request (OP 49: 6.viii.1853), and were perhaps intended for distribution with a published paper (Jones 1855); there are copies in the British Museum (ME) and the Royal Asiatic Society, but they are seldom seen for sale. In 1854 Jones made a map of Ashur and its surroundings, which was also printed, although only one copy is known to me, in the British Library (Reade 1981: 147, fig. 1), and he prepared another of Babylon and its surroundings, the notes for which were 'mislaid' (Loftus 1857: 18, 45; Selby 1859: 6; Rawlinson 1865: III, 338). His reports of 1844–55 on the Nahrawan canal and other parts of the

province of Baghdad were published in the Transactions of the Bombay Geographical Society (1849, 1850, 1852, 1856), and virtually all his work was later collected in a single book (Jones 1857), but these are rare volumes. His Nimrud map (Plan 2) includes the city, the upper Awai dam across the Tigris though not the lower 'artificial impediment' observed by Rich (1836: II, 133), and the nearby site of Selamiyah, which is hardly mentioned in academic studies but looks suspiciously like Nimrud's twin, prominent in periods when Nimrud was not, having Sasanian and Islamic settlement inside a city-wall which may go back to the third or early second millennium BC. Jones included the Fort Shalmaneser arsenal at Nimrud; he misinterpreted its relationship with the city-wall, but his version is indeed what the contours suggested.

Rawlinson's visit was more of a study season than an excavation. He looked at inscriptions of which Layard's outstanding copies, together with a full set of squeezes, had already reached London the previous year (Reade 2002: 204–10). Smith found little except one important inscription. Loftus, while he dug widely and recovered a major hoard of ivories, did not publish a proper account of his Assyrian excavations and died prematurely; as a nineteenth-century traveller he probably recorded his activities in a diary, which may survive somewhere, but subsequent researchers have not yet found it. By far the most significant discoveries were made by Layard who published fully and by Rassam, and they fall into four main groups.

First, there was the architecture. Layard himself (1849a: II, 119–20) describes how easy it was to find this, once the principle had been recognized. 'The Assyrians, when about to build a palace or public edifice, appear to have first constructed a platform, or solid compact mass of sun-dried bricks, about thirty or forty feet above the level of the plain. Upon it they raised the monument... Consequently, in digging for remains, the first step is to search for the platform of sun-dried bricks. When this is discovered, the trenches must be opened to the level of it and not deeper; they should then be continued in opposite directions, care being always taken to keep upon the platform. By these means, if there are any ruins they must necessarily be discovered, supposing the trenches to be long enough; for the chambers of the Assyrian edifices are generally narrow, and their walls, or the slabs which cased them if fallen, must sooner or later be reached.' Excavation continued by following the walls; the interiors of rooms were often left unexcavated.

Planning the buildings accurately was difficult, especially in underground tunnels. Layard had learnt basic surveying before he left London in 1839, but his ground-plans mostly seem to have been made by stretching a tape between points and along walls, and treating all corners as true right-angles, without triangulation. For his second expedition Layard hoped to achieve better results,

Fig. 1-f. Excavation of the Kidmuri shrine, April 1878. (Rassam 1897: facing p. 226)
(British Museum photograph of original print by Mosul photographer).

recording both archaeology and weather. Items he requested from London included '3 thermometers, and 1 for measuring height; 1 aneroid barometer; a good telescope; 1 prismatic compass; 2 magnifying glasses—spectacles etc.; an adjusting stand for his camera lucida; 1 foot rule and 1 measuring tape; compasses etc etc', besides plenty of drawing books and equipment (OP 42: 14.vii.1849). Some of these things must have been in his 'most important case', containing 'reliable instruments' and fishing tackle, but he told his friend Henry Ross that it had failed to arrive (BL 38941: 45–46; 2.ix.1850; BL 38979: 305; 30.ix.1850). So he could not add fishing to his recreations, and was obliged to measure the height of the Nimrud ziggurrat by pocket sextant and barometer (BL 39089 F: 4). Because, about two years after Layard's final departure, Rawlinson was trying to pay him for fishing tackle (BL 38981: 283–84; 15.iv.1853), the missing case does seem to have reached Baghdad in the end. The fullest and most accurate nineteenth-century plan of the Nimrud citadel mound, including much of what is now known to be the Nabu Temple, is that drawn for Loftus by Boutcher (Barnett and Falkner 1962: end-plate), who probably brought his own instruments. There are no Nimrud plans from Rawlinson, and little from Smith and Rassam. Renewed British Museum interest in scientific planning of Assyrian sites only emerges in a letter written by Leonard King at Nineveh to Wallis Budge, then Keeper of the Department, on 30.xii.1903 (D'Andrea 1981: 231). King had visited the German excavations at Ashur, had been deeply impressed by Andrae's tachymeter, and wanted one like it; he even asked permission to use the metric system in the field, with the reassurance that 'we can afterwards give a foot-scale to the plans and reduce any measurement we give to feet and inches.'

Layard's two great palace plans, those of the North-West Palace at Nimrud and the South-West Palace at Nineveh,

consist largely of rooms panelled in stone (Layard 1849a: I, facing p. 62; 1853a: facing p. 67). He recognized that both palaces extended far beyond these quarters, and he did plan and excavate some plastered walls, especially those identified during his second season in the northern temple area at Nimrud (Layard 1853a: facing p. 123; *cf.* Reade 2002: 137, fig. 2), but panelled walls were his prime objective, just as they had been for Botta. The difficulty of identifying plastered walls in poor condition close to the surface is evident in an 1878 photograph of excavations in the Nimrud shrine of Ishtar Kidmuri (fig. 1-f). Rassam commented on the utter ruin of the building, but the stone fittings are present, and he must have dug the walls away. The credit for recovering an almost complete Assyrian ground-plan, and for serious consideration of how such buildings functioned, goes to Victor Place and Félix Thomas (1867–70), who worked at Khorsabad during 1852–53, followed by Andrae at Ashur and by Gordon Loud at Khorsabad (Andrae 1938; Andrae and Boehmer 1992: 122–25; Loud and Altman 1938: 10–50). Buildings dug by the British at Nimrud began to make better sense under Max Mallowan and David Oates in the 1950s.

Alien features of Assyrian architecture presented Layard with special problems. The best-known public buildings in Europe, both ancient and modern, had grand exterior façades. It was assumed that Assyrian grand façades too were on the exterior of buildings, rather than being located as they often in fact were, like many Islamic façades, overlooking interior paved courtyards. This assumption is the more understandable because it had often happened that rainwater, collecting in a ruined Assyrian courtyard from which it was once drained through a channel or culvert, had eventually tended to undermine the walling on one side and create a ravine. Each of the ravines dramatically breaking the sides of

Fig. 1-g. The ruins of the throne room façade, North-West Palace, with the ravine to its north-west, 1906. (Assur photograph 2083, taken by Walter Andrae, Deutsche Orient-Gesellschaft).

the mound at Nimrud looked like the remains of an approach from the plain below, leading up to an open paved area. There was just such an arrangement at Persepolis, the one ancient Near Eastern palace complex then visible above ground. At Nimrud, correspondingly, Layard observed one ravine in front of the North-West Palace throne room façade, which for him confirmed that this was an external feature (fig. 1-g), and another in between the shrines of Ninurta and Sharrat-niphi, which were therefore separate buildings. When Layard (1853a: 653–56) came to discuss the general architectural lay-out, he made a fulsome acknowledgement of his debt to

the architectural restorations of James Fergusson (1851), and wrote of nine distinct buildings on the citadel, and of seven great flights of steps or inclined ways. He was not altogether comfortable with this scheme, however, noting that it left the citadel on the Tigris side 'apparently defenceless'. Although he was mistaken in this blanket identification of ravines with entrances, the throne room block of the North-West Palace with its grand façade was indeed built by Ashurnasirpal well before the rooms on the opposite northern side of the courtyard, which were built by his son (Mallowan 1966: I, 86–87), so that it does seem to

Fig. 1-h. John Martin's The Fall of Nineveh, *1829–30, presented by the artist in 1833. (British Museum photograph, PD Mm, 10.5, mezzotint with etching).*

have stood for a time in relative isolation, much as Layard envisaged it.

A second Assyrian anomaly was the absence of columns, which were a standard feature of much Graeco-Roman, Egyptian, Persepolitan, and medieval and recent Christian and Islamic architecture in the Near East. Columns had naturally been prominent in John Martin's dramatic image of the Fall of Nineveh (fig. 1-h), published in 1830. But where were the columns at Nimrud? Layard (1853a: 647–50), again with reference to Fergusson, though not without reservation, made them of wood and placed them in upper storeys, which accounted for their disappearance. The composition of Fergusson's own image of *Nimrud Restored* (fig. 1-i), suggests a deliberate translation of Martin's vision of Nineveh (combined with Martin's related image of Babylon, which includes a river) into the calmer idiom of Claude and Canaletto, adapted to fit the archaeological findings but still dominated by columns. It may be thought that this columniation of Assyrian architecture was a deliberate attempt to domesticate it, to make it more acceptable, just as the phrase 'Assyrian Empire' implied a familiar type of political structure. It must have had this effect on western eyes: similarly, when Layard's cousin Charlotte Guest had a special building made at Canford, to house the collection of Assyrian sculpture he had given her, it was in another familiar style, the Gothic (Russell 1997: 95–112). Nonetheless Fergusson's architectural fantasy was a reasoned hypothesis, given the information available at the time.

Physical conservation of mudbrick architecture, including walls that were sometimes decorated with painted plaster, would have been even more difficult in the nineteenth century than it is today. It was unimaginable at Nimrud, since there was not yet local interest, let alone reliable guards. Even in England the conservation

of historic buildings was a novelty. For instance, a letter was written in 1844 to the newly formed British Archaeological Association (1845: 163) about the Prior's House at Wenlock, 'an interesting monastic house, almost the only one remaining habitable which has not been altered or modernized. The Abbey... is not preserved as it should be. The farm-servants are permitted to disfigure the remains of the church in the most wanton manner, making a practice of tearing asunder the beautiful clustered piers, a few only of which are now left, with crow-bars for mere amusement. Mr Fisher solicits the kind interference of some member of the Association with Sir W.W. Wynne, the owner of the property, to put a stop to such Vandalism.' This kind of behaviour was as common in England as in the Orient. The Trustees of the British Museum worried about the conservation of ancient stone structures from which portions were removed. 'I cannot indeed say that the individual stone will be missed, but I fear from the precedent', wrote the Marquess of Northampton about Karnak in Egypt to his 'brother Trustees' (OP 43: 5.iii.1850); there were similar concerns about Lycia (Jenkins 1992: 143–44). The Trustees did what they could for Nimrud by instructing that all the trenches should be refilled after excavation (fig. 1-j).

Layard and Boutcher made coloured drawings of the better wall-paintings, but seldom specified their exact positions. They tended rather to treat them out of context as individual designs. Much the same principle was applied to many of the alabaster wall-panels carved in low relief which, together with a few free-standing sculptures and monuments, formed the second major group of discoveries. This was natural in the case of the very first carved wall-panels found by Layard, in the South-West Palace at Nimrud, since they had themselves been removed from other buildings in antiquity and reused at

Fig. 1-i. James Fergusson's Nimrud Restored. *(Layard 1853b: pl. 1) (British Museum photograph from engraving).*

Fig. 1-j. Winged lion and wall-panels reburied at Nimrud, with handling slots visible on their upper edges, 1906. (Assur photograph 2085, taken by Walter Andrae, Deutsche Orient-Gesellschaft).

random. It was not appropriate in the North-West Palace, where during his first season Layard found about 300 alabaster panels, over 2 m high and up to 2 m wide, mostly complete, standing in or close to their original positions, together with larger human-headed winged lions and bulls. These were the very Marbles that Canning and the Trustees wanted, they were even made of a stone sometimes known as marble, and comprehensive recording of where they all stood seems an elementary requirement.

One reason for the failure to do this systematically is that the resources were not available. Layard could hardly have recorded the first Nimrud discoveries adequately in the time at his disposal, even if he had been willing to sacrifice all his other interests and pursuits. He did in fact record a great deal more than many later archaeologists,[1] which is why the provenance of most wall-panels can be re-established, but the Trustees themselves wanted original objects far more than records. So they instructed Layard to draw everything worth drawing; later, if shipwreck were discounted, the Marbles themselves

would soon be in London. The need to pay for an additional artist cannot at first have been obvious to the Trustees; and, since at this stage they knew almost as little about Layard's abilities as they did about the Marbles he was uncovering, it is not surprising that the Treasury, through them, was far from generous with money. Indeed, after the Marbles began to arrive in London, there was to be much debate about whether sculptures in a style which seemed so primitive in comparison with the Greek were worth possessing at all (e.g. Bohrer 1998: 345). This argument played a part in restricting the total number of wall-panels finally accepted, from both Nimrud and Nineveh.

For Layard's second season, however, beginning in 1849, the Trustees while never open-handed did pay for an artist, Frederick Cooper, and even a medical doctor, Humphry Sandwith. It was hoped that Sandwith would act as a naturalist too; years later he did indeed send the Museum an aye-aye from Madagascar (Minutes: 23.vii.1859), but his main occupation in Assyria was shooting more familiar types of animal. Sir Henry Ellis, Principal Librarian and senior official at the Museum, once wrote in person that he had dispatched sheets of silver paper requested to protect Cooper's drawings (BL 38979: 167; 16.iii.1850). While the drawings are good, however, and Cooper seems to have done what was asked of him conscientiously, his diary (ME) shows him as a townsman, dreadfully homesick, who

---

[1] Layard was the first (and for a long time the last) archaeologist to take the trouble to draw a serious section at Nimrud. It records deposits against the face of the ziggurat (BL 39089 G:2: distorted schematic copy in Layard 1853a: plan 2 facing p. 123).

much preferred taking tea, playing cards and attending divine service in Mosul with Christian Rassam and his English wife Matilda, to the privations of Nimrud. Cooper went home early with a certificate of ill-health (rheumatism, congestion of the liver, and other complications) provided by Sandwith who left at the same time with similar symptoms. 'Neither of these gentlemen were at all qualified for an expedition of this kind & I have received little or no assistance from them', wrote Layard to Ross (BL 38941: 45; 2.viii.1850); this was unjust to Cooper, but Layard had not chosen him, and was himself feverish with malaria when he wrote. It was not easy to find a substitute. Requisite equipment included a brace of pistols besides a sun umbrella with swivel (OP 44: 24.x.1850). According to William Brockedon, the artist and inventor, an old family friend of Layard, 'Skilful men with the promise or prospect of employment here will not go... I think your best chance is to excite a young man, who can draw, to enter into your glorious pursuits' (BL 38979: 367; 26.xi.1850). As Layard wrote to Samuel Birch, then an Assistant at the Museum (Corr 8: 3158; 16.ix.1850), what he wanted was 'a man of some energy and discrimination whom I can trust', someone who would share the fun as well as the grind, someone like himself. The best drawings were eventually made by Boutcher in 1854, three years after Layard's departure; he too had a camera lucida (Corr NS 8: 3071; Loftus to Jones, 9.iv.1855). By then there was much more to do at Nineveh than at Nimrud.

Cooper's immediate replacement, Thomas Bell, a freshly qualified Silver Medal student from the Government School of Design, chosen for the Trustees by their ageing sculptor and artistic adviser, Sir Richard Westmacott, had unsurprisingly none of the appropriate qualities. As Ellis announced, however, Bell was bringing with him a Calotype or Talbotype, and had been trained in its use (BL 38979: 359; 18.xi.1850). The Calotype was a photographic camera, perhaps even provided by William Fox Talbot, inventor of the negative-positive process, who had previously tried to persuade the Trustees to give Charles Fellows a Calotype for his final expedition in search of Lycian sculptures (Corr 13: 5209; 1.viii.1843); Talbot later became an expert on cuneiform, with permission to photograph tablets at the British Museum (Minutes: 12.vi.1852). While the Frenchman Gabriel Tranchand, however, made magnificent use of a Calotype at Khorsabad in 1852–54 (Chevalier and Lavédrine 1994), the British attempts at photography in the field were abortive.

Bell himself was drowned soon after reaching Mosul in 1851. In 1852 Westmacott, apparently unaware that three experienced artists had written to the Museum to volunteer their services, found the Trustees another unsuitable young man, Charles Hodder; Layard, then in London, was astonished by the choice (Gadd 1936: 78). Presumably Hodder was also trained to use the Calotype;

it is doubtful whether he did so, however, though this may have been because the wall-panels still at Nimrud had been reburied, and he was doing most of his recording in poorly lit tunnels at Nineveh. He left early in 1854, very sick, and the Calotype was eventually auctioned in Baghdad in July 1855, fetching 66.50 kerans, slightly over £3 in English currency (OP 60: Jones to Rawlinson, 3.ix.1855). It may have been used briefly beforehand, however, as in 1854 Dr J. McA. Hyslop, Assistant Surgeon at the British Residency, took photographs of Baghdad (Jones 1857: 310–11, with figures, cf. BLO Album 21: 2053–58, 4096–98); Jones refers to the deteriorating 'collodion' on Hyslop's photographs, as if his camera had been of the fast new wet-plate type, but that could be a mistake. Whoever bought the Calotype became perhaps the first Baghdadi photographer.

Boutcher in 1854 also had a photographic apparatus, the property of Dickenson Bros, the publishers, who were involved in employing him: in the spring he took photographs in Babylonia, now lost, but there survive four faint sepia prints of wall-panels which he photographed at Nineveh in the summer (Barnett 1976: 72, pls XX, XXXVI). Loftus then wrote from Mosul, however, to tell Rawlinson that photography was impracticable (RAS, D 13: 31.vii.1854): it was impossible to 'apply the Photograph... in the trenches' (OP 51: 28.ix.1854). Subsequently Rawlinson also informed Ellis that Boutcher's 'photographic apparatus seems to be useless for want of a better camera and fresh chemicals' (OP 52: 5.ii.1855); this device is last heard of in the Residency at Baghdad, awaiting Dickensons' instructions on its disposal (OP 60: Jones to Rawlinson, 3.ix.1855).

There was yet another camera (Transcripts: 361; Rawlinson to Loftus, 21.ii.1855), which was not used on the excavations because it did not even reach Mosul. In September 1854 Loftus had written to Rawlinson that 'Mr Boutcher daily expects a new instrument from Paris adapted to the waxed paper process which he finds to answer best in this climate' (OP 51: 28.ix.1854): one advantage of the process, a French invention perhaps recommended by Tranchand or Place, was that negatives did not deteriorate so rapidly. Boutcher was later to explain to Rawlinson how this camera, 'manufactured expressly for me', had been detained for five months at the Mediterranean port of Skanderoun (Alexandretta, Iskanderun), where he discovered it while on his way home (OP 53: 2.vii.1855). Over twenty years later, when Rassam wanted photographs of new excavations at Nimrud (figs 1-c and 1-f), he was obliged to commission them from a professional in Mosul (Corr: 5290; 15.iv.1878). He then urged the Museum to buy him a camera (AE: 24.vii.1878), but this was apparently not thought necessary, since he was now expected to be digging for cuneiform tablets rather than wall-panels, and the objects would be travelling back to London anyway.

The other reason for inadequate recording is simply that archaeological techniques, procedures and proprieties were still at an early stage of their development. In particular, Layard was faced at both Nimrud and Nineveh with a high proportion of 'duplicate' wall-panels. The Trustees, while periodically concerned over questions of ownership to which there was no easy answer, did not want duplicates, and the summary fashion in which Layard described 'duplicate' sequences of figures implies sympathy with this view. The many sculptures which he was sending to Canford in 1851 (now mostly in the Metropolitan Museum, New York) aroused the suspicion of the British Museum but were then acknowledged as 'duplicates', though Layard refrained from mentioning their acquisition in his 1853 book. I myself in 2002 heard a visitor to the Nimrud Gallery of the British Museum apply the same term even to many of the panels now on display. As Layard wrote to Ellis (BL 38942: 18; 30.xii.1850), 'Mere sculptures in case of loss might be replaced, but the collection [of bronzes] which I propose to send overland is, I believe, unique, and could perhaps never be replaced'. He accordingly dispatched to the Museum the entire main sequence of narrative wall-panels from the North-West Palace throne room, although a few fragments went astray. From the remaining rooms, on the other hand, he mostly sent single examples of panels showing magical figures, and groups of two or three panels which could be regarded as individual works of art, like panels plucked by a collector from an Italian altar-piece: they were not treated as parts of broader decorative schemes.

There were therefore plenty of panels, at both Nimrud and Nineveh, which were surplus to British Museum requirements but which might have been (and sometimes were) damaged or destroyed if left on site. Once Layard had gone, the Trustees entrusted the disposal of them to Rawlinson's discretion (Barnett 1976: 20–21; Reade 2000a). Some were given to missionaries in Mosul, for dispatch back to their colleges in America, where they were valued as demonstrating the wickedness of paganism and the truth of Scripture (Stearns 1961: 2–3); some went to the French, to various British institutions, and to the Crystal Palace Company (thence to Berlin); some went to individuals as souvenirs. A letter to Layard from Henry Danby Seymour, MP, who must have been given a small figure from Room I of the North-West Palace, expresses the viewpoint of the collector or connoisseur: 'Gruner [cf. Russell 1997: 85–90] is designing me a frame for the hawk-headed sculpture—the border to be taken from some Assyrian pattern. I want a cast taken of the sculpture, and to have the cast coloured as it is supposed the sculpture was. It will stand like a firescreen with the sculpture on one side and the painted cast on the other' (BL 38979: 231; 18.v.1850). The attitude of people on the spot, at a time when carved fragments were abundant, is exemplified by a letter to Layard from Christian Rassam, probably writing about Nineveh (BL 38979: 369–71; 28.xi.1850): 'The Honble Mr Coke MP arrived here two days ago from Persia... I hope you will not be annoyed as I consented to his taking a piece of sculpture that was knocking about the mound which I fancied was of no use'. While it was also known that the Marbles like smaller antiquities could have commercial value as works of art, that does not seem to have been very much more in the nineteenth century than the cost of removal and shipment. Nonetheless Alexander Hector, who in June 1847 had sold the Museum some pieces taken from Khorsabad, was always interested in superfluous panels (Minutes: 22.vii.1848): several from the North-West Palace now in the Brooklyn Museum were plainly acquired as an investment (Stearns 1961: 15–16). Christian Rassam, the Vice-Consul whom Rawlinson described to Layard as 'quite incorrigible as

Fig. 1-k. Removal of the first winged bull from its position at Nimrud, March 1847. (Layard 1849b, I: frontispiece).
(British Museum photograph).

regards money' (BL 38981: 117; 5.ix.1852), seems to have been particularly enterprising. Clive (1852: title-page; Barnett and Falkner 1962: pl. LXXXV) describes his own Tiglath-pileser panel from Nimrud as 'obtained from H.B.M. Vice Consul at Moosul, 1850', which suggests that he had paid for it. In June 1853 Christian was trying to sell North-West Palace panels at £100 apiece (Franck 1980: 44), and he was able to continue such activities after the archaeologists had gone. Bainan or Bihnan (Behnam?), 'a skilful marble-cutter and a very intelligent man' employed by Layard (1849a: I, 328), must have known exactly what he was doing when in 1853 he 'forgot' where the finest remaining panels in the North-West Palace were buried (BL 38982: 28–29; H. Rassam to Layard, 18.vii.1853); many of these stayed at Nimrud.

Transport was organized in two ways. First, the panels and colossal figures had to be removed from position (fig. 1-k). They were mostly in good condition, and did not present the kind of problems faced at Nineveh, where on one occasion Loftus had to cover some inscribed surfaces with bitumen in order to keep the fragments together (Barnett 1976: 20). They were very heavy, however, and so their backs were usually sawn off, in order to reduce the total weight. Layard also removed the duplicate inscriptions which separated the upper and lower registers of the narrative panels from the North-West Palace throne room. The panels then had to reach the sea. One option was to send them overland by mule or camel via Aleppo to Skanderoun; this route was adopted by the missionaries, but they had to cut each panel into about three pieces, which were wrapped in wool and fitted into wooden cases of manageable size (Stearns 1961: 7). The commoner method of transport, which required larger cases but no additional cutting, was by raft (*kelek*) down the Tigris to Basra. Rafts also carried the colossal figures, which could not be cased (figs 1-l and 1-m); accounts for packing

materials refer to mats and felts (OP 44: 8.vii.1850), and the mats sometimes left their impression on the backs of panels which had been soaked. Layard wrote bitterly to Edward Hawkins, Keeper of Antiquities at the Museum, how 'the Trustees would seem to think that anything can be done for nothing here, as if I were old Merlin himself who had only to wave his hand and send colossal lions flying over the four quarters of the globe' (OP 44: 10.vi.1850), but he later took pleasure in describing the difficulties he had surmounted in moving them from the mound to the river (Layard 1849a: II, 79–97; 1853a: 202–4).

The British shipments, because of their official status, were exempt from the Ottoman taxes on transportation, but the river passed through tribal territory, entailing some risk of robbery and destruction. One of Layard's shipments was attacked unsuccessfully in November 1850, and another, sent by Rassam from Nineveh, was destroyed near Shergat in July 1851; in May 1855, in a famous disaster, most of the French finds from Assyria and Babylonia were lost near Qurnah, together with some panels from Nimrud and Nineveh. The most remarkable episode, however, which occurred in April 1850 when the two largest winged lions from Nimrud were afloat, was caused by a defective embankment. It was described to Layard by the indomitable Felix Jones (BL 38979: 237–40; 22.v.1850),

'Your *kelleks* with the two lions arrived here [Baghdad] about the 20th of last month and were despatched on the 22nd, as soon indeed as I could prepare our boat to accompany them. Three of my own people went with them also for their greater security, and Kemball and myself thought that nothing could happen to them after their departure. You will readily therefore imagine my surprise and annoyance on reaching Busrah to find but the larger raft there with a lion and 17 Nineveh slabs, the

Fig. 1-l. Transport of the first winged bull from Nimrud to the river, March 1847.
(Layard 1849b, II: frontispiece). (British Museum photograph).

Fig. 1-m. Winged colossus loaded on a raft, c. 1850. (British Museum photograph of watercolour by Frederick Cooper (?) now in the Searight Collection, Victoria & Albert Museum).

smaller one with the broken lion, six slabs and two cases having been swept by the force of the stream into a large and new opening that the Tigris a few days previously had made in the right bank at Um al Hamed about 20 miles in a straight line between Kut and Amareh. Passing it at night on our way down we were nearly meeting the same fate; for, ignorant of the irruption, we were steaming along as usual and were nearly drawn into the influx, though steaming certainly at 11 miles an hour allowing for the current. It was not surprising to me therefore when I heard one of the rafts had been swept in against the efforts of the *kellekchi's*, and the other was only kept from a similar accident by the boat and the whole of the people making every exertion to prevent it. It was while so engaged that the smaller one with only two men at the oars came within the vortex and, unmanageable as these machines are, was quickly hurried into the gut by the impetuous stream that carried it a mile into Mesopotamia before it could be brought to the bank, where I found it on my way up deserted by its people, who were compelled to beat a retreat with starvation staring them in the face and no chance of doing anything had they remained. I pulled into the marsh and found the *kellek*, with one broken lion, six slabs(?) and two cases aground on the right bank of the torrent about 3/4 mile from the Tigris... The *kellek* was aground with most of the skins burst, the water having fallen, but was surrounded by mud and swamp. Could I have refloated it, it could not have been towed against the torrent that was sweeping across the country, for these shallow things when anchored even, in a stream, at once dip forward and the body of water then rushes over them. Towing therefore would have been out of the question. I was obliged to leave it to its present fate, but had a *Seyid* of the people, who are located in the neighbourhood, whom I created a temporary *wakeel*,

promising him a reward if he prevented the disfigurement of the stones. Lynch's boat proceeds today with the stones lately arrived from Mosul, and will remain on the spot till I reach Um al Hamed about Tuesday next. 1 shall start immediately after the Damascus post and hope to give you a good account of some of your pets, if not all, on my return to this city about 10th June. 1 have some doubts as to the recovery of the lion this time; for I fear its weight, surrounded as it is with mud and water, will prevent our acting efficiently. Al Allah, as the Arabs say. It will entail a little more expense on the nation, but if it is to have its hobby it must pay for it. In the great show for the Industry of all Nations in 1851, I doubt much their having such specimens of industry as the Assyrian marbles for the public to gaze upon, whether we look upon the sculptures themselves or on the labor and energy of the excavation.'

Jones' use of the word 'hobby' to describe the collecting of antiquities expresses a view that must have been widely held but is seldom quoted. He did rescue this lion, but it and its fellow still had to be loaded on to a ship at Basra, and this too involved rough handling, as the hatches of the vessel were too small and the colossal figures had to be levered into place (OP 44: 6.xi.1850; Larsen 1996: 129, fig. 15.3). Once on board, the loads might seem safe from anything but shipwreck, but this was not so. There had been a fearful row in 1848 after cases from Nimrud were opened for repacking during transhipment at Bombay; some objects put on display were stolen (Gadd 1936: 48–50), although the two Sargon vases specified in Layard's letter of protest (OP 41: 24.x.1848) are now in the Museum; at least one of them had surfaced in the possession of an English clergyman (Barag 1985: 28). Birch later wrote to Layard (BL 38979: 178; 28.iii.1850): 'No trader would consign a bale of his rotten handkerchiefs in such a manner as a great nation does its most valuable treasures of ancient art.' In the same year Hawkins wrote after receiving the *Urania* load (BL 38979: 319–22; 18.x.1850): 'Pray give instructions to Mr Lynch not to allow the quid tallow to be shipped in the same vessel with the sculptures, or that it be stowed away where it cannot have access to them. The last fragments which came over were embedded in tallow, which in the hot climate at Busrah was of the consistency of castor oil; the skins burst, and when the hatches were opened in England, the tallow was in bulk and had to be dug out with spades and pickaxes. Our fragments are not injured as I expected but they are discoloured.' Layard complained vigorously that almost every piece shipped on the *Fortitude* had been injured, with loose animal bones used as dunnage in the ship's hold (OP 46: 13.ix.1851); he had also been told that, on the *Apprentice*, some smaller Nimrud sculptures had been placed in the hold underneath a colossal lion and bull, so that nearly all had been broken, and many fragments lost. On one occasion, either in Basra or London, a case dropped into the water and was not recovered (Reports: 11.ix.1851). In 1854 Rawlinson was still explaining that loads 'should not be subjected to movement from the rolling of the vessel or to damage from leakage. If placed in the hold, good dunnage must be provided' (Transcripts: 199; 25.iii.1854). The essential problem was diffusion of responsibility. Many people were involved in what happened between the moment when the cases of antiquities arrived on rafts at the harbour of Ma'qil just above Basra, where they were entrusted to the British Vice-Consul and kept in the East India Company's storage area (Minutes: 23.x.1847; 8.i.1848), and the moment when they were unloaded, in London or Liverpool, from ships usually organized by the Trustees. The sailors knew how to handle ships, but the secure stowage of freight depended on good will and good luck.

Once the Marbles were in London, an immediate requirement was to find space for them (Jenkins 1992: 157–62). They had to be mended and mounted for display (Reade 2000b: 617–18), with cement and adhesives less obtrusive than the bitumen used by Loftus in the field (Harbottle 1973: 211); Westmacott chose Penrhyn slate as the backing for broken pieces (Minutes: 27.i.1849). It was desirable to provide casts for sale, as was regularly done for many Greek sculptures. The panels had to be kept clean, and they had to be protected, since vandalism was always a possibility (Minutes: 26.vii.1879). These were conservation issues. As in all matters concerning the care of the collections, both the Trustees and their senior staff were extremely cautious. Following Birch's recommendation, for instance, the Trustees had even authorized covering the granodiorite Rosetta Stone with glass, for fear that handling by the public would wear it away (Minutes: 13.xi.1847). There was not yet any tradition, however, of maintaining detailed conservation records, and information about the treatment of Nimrud material is

hard to track. The Museum's annual *Parliamentary Returns* of the nineteenth century often say how many objects were treated, but little about what was actually done: so, while we know that the Ashurnasirpal statue found by Layard at Nimrud was reconstructed in 1914 with copper plugs (*Return*, 1915: 64), we do not know what had happened to it beforehand.

Soon after the Nimrud Marbles began to arrive, Hawkins wrote to Birch: 'The Nimroud stone appears to be so soft and liable to injury that I would not consent to anything being done to them without the entire consent of [Michael] Faraday or some *most* able chymist' (Corr 7: 2525; 21.viii.1847). Nonetheless casts of the smaller narrative panels did begin to be made in 1847, according to the Museum *Synopsis* of 1852 (cast catalogue at end, with dates of manufacture), and work continued for over a year, until the Trustees noted with displeasure a mark left by a workman on the small human-headed lion, and ruled that no more moulds should be made without their express permission (Minutes: 10.ii.1849). One application to mould some of the larger Nimrud wall-panels emphasized that there could be 'no possible stain' (OP 44: 5.xi.1850), but was refused. After a similar request from the Louvre, the Trustees instructed that experiments should be made, by moulding some of the 'less valuable' pieces (Minutes: 11.x.1851). Faraday wrote to Hawkins: 'Those who make casts do it so often from sulphate of lime in the form of plaster that they ought to be better practical judges than I am, but I should be inclined to avoid the use of plaster against the slabs. There would however be no difficulty I suppose in taking wax impressions from the slabs and then making plaster casts in these. In a small way the process is common enough' (Corr 5: 1722; 11.x.1851). The Prussian government wanted casts, as did the Crystal Palace Company, represented by Fergusson who claimed that plaster of Paris had done no harm in the past; he proposed after consulting 'several persons skilled in such operations' that as an extra insurance 'merely squeezes of clay' should be taken: 'Mr Layard and your formatore Mr Pink are both perfectly certain that no damage would be done' (OP 49: 8.viii.1853).

Hawkins continued to resist, since he was worried about damage both to surviving paint and to the finest details carved 'upon so soft and soluble a material... The Trustees are to this day charged with having irreparably injured the Parthenon sculptures by the removal of colour which, it is said, they retained when they were brought to the Museum. It is vain to deny the charge, it is reasserted, and as the Marbles have been cast and cleaned they cannot be appealed to in proof one way or the other. It is desirable that these Assyrian slabs should remain as they are, that any charge which may be hereafter brought may be answered by appeal to the slabs themselves' (OP 50: 7.xii.1853). He argued that there must be a slight change every time they were moulded, but was unable to produce evidence that there had so far been any perceptible damage from the process. So the Trustees, worn down by three years of persistent applications, eventually agreed that the large panels 'should be moulded, being protected wherever colour appeared, either by tin-foil, or by any other best means of protection' (Minutes: 10.xii.1853); the fine incised details are not mentioned. It is unclear whether clay was indeed used for moulding, though it remained an option (OP 82: Birch, 25.xi.1865). According to the 1855 *Synopsis*, casts of almost all the Nimrud sculptures were by then available for sale: a small winged bull and lion cost £15 each. Soon afterwards the Museum's Nimrud moulds were transferred to the care of Messrs Brucciani, and were nearly all recorded as being in good condition (OP 58: 10.x.1857), but after thirty years several moulds had been 'damaged by time and wear' and replaced by duplicates (Reports: Renouf, 6.vi.1888). Lazarus Fletcher of the Museum's Department of Mineralogy then presented a report which, while dealing primarily with a limestone stela of Shalmaneser, discussed the conservation of all the alabaster panels and the possible dangers of moulding them: he was against the use of both plaster of Paris and tin-foil (OP 84: 6.vii.1888), and an application from Edward Robinson of the Boston Museum of Fine Arts for the lion and bull, the moulds of which were 'exhausted', was refused (Corr: 174; 31.vii.1889).

While moulding only happened occasionally, the work of cleaning the Museum was routine. The building had some open stoves, and needed heat to counteract damp (e.g. Corr NS 6: 2783; Birch to Hawkins, 17.xi.1851; OP 58: Sydney Smirke, 27.xi,1857). Areas where sculptures were kept might suffer the occasional mishap, such as smoke from spontaneous combustion when packaging of straw, sawdust, and pitch or tar, combined with shavings from a carpenter's work, was left in contact with hot pipes and began to smoulder (OP 43: 9.i.1850), but condensation and straightforward air-pollution were unavoidable before air-conditioning had been invented: in one winter the Museum used 200 tons of coal and 700 chaldrons of coke (OP 43: 21.i.1850). Hawkins had told Birch that 'very few of the [limestone Egyptian] tablets have suffered from anything bad wiping off London dust' (Corr 7: 2525; 21.viii.1847), a job performed as in a stately home by the Museum housemaids, but there had been complaints both about overzealous treatment, such as the use of acid water to wash marble (OP 32: John Henning, 1.i.1845), and about damage caused directly by dirt (Minutes: 8.iii.1845). In Hawkins' opinion, covering the limestone tablets with glass would 'do more good than all the chymists together' (Corr 7: 2525; 21.viii.1847). Eventually Birch was to ask for technical advice on 'the best means of preserving the Assyrian Sculptures from discolouration and decay' (Minutes: 28.ii.1863). The best advice he got, if conservation was the only issue, was that he should glaze them (OP 75: Mr Richard Westmacott, 9.iv.1863); Fletcher, who was better qualified, was to say

the same (OP 84: 6.vii.1888). A long-term project to do this was approved by the Trustees (Minutes: 1.vii.1865), but took many years to implement. Since the main problem seems to have been in the damp Assyrian Basement, the Nimrud Gallery was the last to be done. The wall-panels there were finally covered by glass in the late 1880s, and the arrangement had long-term value, since it seems to have been reinstated after the air-raid precautions of 1918 and 1939–45, and will have offered some protection against the Great London Smog of December 1952. The present arrangement, with open access, was suggested in the same year, when Cyril Gadd was Keeper of the Department, and was supported by the Keeper of the Museum's Research Laboratory (Reports: letter from H. J. Plenderleith, 1.x.1952).

The traces of colour seen by Layard were particularly vulnerable. He had been surprised not to find as much colour on the Nimrud panels as on those at Khorsabad, but black, white or red did sometimes survive 'on the hair, beards and eyes... on the sandals and bows... on the tongues of the eagle-headed figures... very faintly on a garland round the head of a winged priest [ME 124582], and on the representation of fire in the bas-relief of a siege [ME 124554];' he published a coloured illustration of the head (Layard 1849a: I, 64; II, 306–7; 1849b: pl. 92).[2] Several of his field drawings include paint (fig. 1-n) (cf. also Curtis and Reade 1995: 219, no. 248), although clearly omitting some repetitive features such as the blackness of hair. Some panels may have suffered in shipment, but there is still plenty of black and red on a king's head now in Cambridge (Kinnier-Wilson 1962: 91–92, pl. XXXI).

Because there is generally so little colour on panels in both Europe and America, maybe some owners did scrub figures deliberately in order to make them look more like classical marbles. The Trustees were strongly opposed to the removal of colour, however, and took the exceptional step, in response to a complaint by Layard about loss of paint on the head he had published, of ordering 'That Sir Henry Ellis be instructed to enquire and ascertain when and by whom the Head at the West end of the first Assyrian gallery was washed; by what authority it was done; and whether any report has been made to any Officer of the Museum on the subject' (Minutes: 13.viii.1853). Perhaps because academic staff did not always supervise menial duties (several letters from

---

[2] A notebook from Layard's first season (BL 39090 B:23) lists the following colours: 'Bracelets on arms painted black/crossing with red edging/Mace handle red/Tiara of king, horse reins and/ornament above red/Handle of dagger below head of/animal—blue/the head a reddish brown/ornament all black pecked with red/The knob or rope near leg, blue/Bracelets red. Tassels ditto [i.e. blue?]'. The site is not named, but this may be a record of paint seen on panels at Khorsabad rather than Nimrud (cf. Layard 1849a: II, 306–7).

Fig. 1-n. Two North-West Palace panels with surviving paint, drawn by Layard. (Original Drawings III, NW 43, British Museum photograph, ME 124564-5).

Hawkins protest about things happening in the galleries without his knowledge), no adequate response to this complaint has been traced.

Hawkins retired in 1860, and his Assyrian responsibilities passed to Birch. The two had been custodians of the Department's corporate memory, aware of long-standing issues such as conservation. When Birch died in office in December1885, the classicist Sir Charles Newton was put in overall charge until the Egyptologist, Peter Renouf, a newcomer to the Museum, was appointed Keeper in April 1886. In this period Theophilus Pinches the Assyriologist, who had been appointed in 1878, was heavily involved with cuneiform studies, and the ambitious young Wallis Budge, appointed in 1883, must have acquired substantial responsibilities: during 1886 the Assyrian sculptures were 'dusted and washed' (*Return*, 1887: 37). The Nimrud wall-panels, which had been exposed on open display since the 1850s, will have been among those treated, which may explain why, while the Museum *Guide* of 1884 (pp. 74–76) discusses the traces of paint on sandals, bows, eyes and hair in the large panels, later editions from 1892 onward say much less on this subject. Photographs taken in 1913 (*Return*, 1914: 71; Budge 1914) indicate that the panels looked then much as they do now: paint survives on some sandals standing at ground-level, on the bases of bows, and in corners of eyes, which will have been the most awkward areas for cleaners to reach. Comparison between Layard's drawing and the present state of at least one large Nimrud panel (ME 124565), as shown in prints published by Canby (1971: pl. XIX), indicates that the fine details too were at some stage affected, and something comparable seems to have happened to the carvings on the limestone White Obelisk from Nineveh, which was displayed nearby and must have been equally dirty.

Another Nimrud monument whose conservation history is unclear has been known, since 1875 or earlier, as the Black Obelisk (Birch 1875: 25). This is inscribed with the annals of Shalmaneser III and was described by the Museum *Synopsis* of 1855 (p. 147) as 'the most important historical monument as yet recovered from Assyria'. From 1849 onwards it was almost continually on open display, and was remounted in 1904 (*Return*, 1905: 54). It is made of a dense black limestone with white veining, originally described by the English as black marble (e.g. Layard 1849a: I, 345; *Guide to the Nimroud Central Saloon* 1886: 26), and by the French as black basalt (Oppert 1865: 107; Ménant 1874: 97). The correct identification as limestone, given by Olmstead (1923: 151) who probably first saw the obelisk in 1904, may well go back to the nineteenth century. The Museum *Guide* of 1892 (p. 84), however, edited by Budge (Corr 1892: 141), no longer defines the material, while editions of the *Guide* from 1900 (p. 24) to 1922 (p. 46) describe it as 'black alabaster'. Because cleaning in 2001 revealed that much of the actual surface of the stone, including broken areas, is not dense black but distinctly grey in tone, it would seem that the original appearance had been affected by pollution, moulding or washing, but was then skilfully restored in the late nineteenth or the early twentieth century. The obelisk had first been moulded in 1848 at Bombay (Gadd 1936: 49), for the city's leading scientist, Dr George Buist. When the artist Edwin Landseer requested a cast, Hawkins saw no objection because it was a 'hard stone' (OP 41: 5.ii.1849); the work was duly authorized (Minutes: 10.ii.1849), and the cast seems to have been a popular item, as by 1888 Brucciani had two moulds, one of which was worn out (Reports: Renouf, 20.vi.1888). Catalogues to hand give the price of a cast as £3 in 1852–55, £17 in 1953, and £30 in 1961; it was 'price on application' by 1963, and is no longer available.

The physical problem of where to display the Nimrud Marbles had been solved by a series of expedients which still define part of the Museum ground-plan. The acquisition of these bulky things, and of other major collections, had been conveniently timed from the Trustees' viewpoint, because the Museum was being rebuilt. They or the Treasury had declined an expensive proposal, made by Hawkins, to expand by acquiring and gradually demolishing all the perimeter properties surrounding the Museum: 'But', as he wrote to Layard, 'this is taking a prospective view of affairs and not suitable for persons who scarcely venture to look before them beyond the length of their noses' (BL 38979: 319–22; 18.x.1850); the purchase was finally made in the 1890s, although most of the perimeter properties still stand, protected now by their own historic status. The new acquisitions were very inconvenient for the architect Smirke, however, since he was repeatedly obliged to alter his careful plans and accommodate additional galleries. Despite these difficulties, and the concomitant costs which always had to be justified, the Trustees patiently continued to accept Assyrian sculptures, from both Nimrud and Nineveh, and even demand more when they seemed of particular interest. It was on 14.xi.1854, when money was short, the excavations were ending, and the problems of space in the Museum were becoming intolerable, that a letter was finally written to Rawlinson in Baghdad saying that 'The Trustees consequently recommend you to limit your collection of slabs, or other objects, to those which either from superiority of workmanship, or from historical connection, or from elucidation of the peculiar manners of the age are most remarkable... The Trustees are anxious to secure whatever is superior to that which they at present possess, and anything merely equal or inferior had better not be sent to us. They are however desirous to have Drawings or Photographs of all' (BM Central Archive: *Letterbook*).

Once the Nimrud Marbles were being displayed, sometimes temporarily in inconvenient corners, they attracted huge public interest both as startling images and as monuments of Biblical significance. They featured in many journals and books, and naturally came to be included in histories of ancient art. While the Trustees intended to publish them fully, however, they needed government money to do so; private enterprise, in the shape of Layard (1849a, 1849b, 1853a, 1853b) through his publisher John Murray, relieved them of the immediate obligation, but publication was left incomplete. The first official book on Nimrud sculptures only appeared in the early twentieth century (Budge 1914). The men by then in charge at the Museum were apt to denigrate Layard and his achievements, and there was no attempt to relate the panels to the original contexts in which he had found them, or to include records of panels not in London. The situation finally changed when, from 1935 onwards, Ernst Weidner began to publish the scattered Assyrian carvings in *Archiv für Orientforschung*, and Gadd (1936) revealed

the wealth of information kept in the Museum and Library archives. It was over a century before a catalogue of all recorded wall-panels from Tiglath-pileser's Nimrud palace appeared (Barnett and Falkner 1962), and later still that the character of the North-West Palace and its extraordinary scheme of architectural decoration began to receive proper attention.

The third group of major finds from Nimrud consisted of inscriptions. Above all there were the two long annalistic texts on the Black Obelisk and on the Great Monolith of Ashurnasirpal II (not to be confused with the Ashurnasirpal stela, to which Rawlinson and others have sometimes applied the same name). They were found during Layard's first and second seasons respectively. The Great Monolith was left at Nimrud in fragments, but both inscriptions had a relatively satisfactory history, because they were copied by Layard. The Trustees, encouraged by popular and scholarly interest, and conscious of the magnificent libraries in their own mansions, recognized an obligation to publish new inscriptions promptly. Those from the first season appeared in a cuneiform font (Layard 1851: pls 87–98). Publication of those from the second season was also authorized (Minutes: 10.vii.1852), and was making good progress until thwarted by Rawlinson, whose pride, social skills and years of devoted work and self-sacrifice had convinced himself and others that he was the leading expert on cuneiform (Larsen 1996: 334–35). 'It would be a mere waste of money now as I have told the Trustees to publish Layard's last batch of inscriptions in their present state. His Sennacherib annals were too faulty to be of use and the big monolith of Assarakhpal [Ashurnasirpal] would be only valuable in the event of his being able to connect the fragments & restore the missing parts, which rather I suspect to be out of his power. In the mean time I am getting all the historical matter into a presentable form for publication' (Corr 11: 4481; Rawlinson to Birch, 2.viii.1852). Layard, however, who knew perfectly well how the fragments were connected, had already shown his copies to the Revd Edward Hincks of Killyleagh. They and other texts enabled Hincks to decipher the Akkadian script (cf. Larsen 1996: 179, 213–14, 297–303), and this achievement might have taken far longer without them. The Great Monolith eventually appeared in 1861 in the first of a series of British Museum volumes, *The Cuneiform Inscriptions of Western Asia* (pls 17–26), edited by Edwin Norris under Rawlinson's nominal supervision.

The last group of discoveries from Nimrud consisted of the smaller objects. In particular, in his first season Layard found a collection of fragments of ivory furniture (fig. 1-o), to which Loftus was to make a substantial addition, and in his second season he found an enormous hoard of bronzes, both furniture and vessels. Layard was thrilled by these finds, many of which are now recognized as fundamental to the study of the evolution

Fig. 1-o. Ivory panel with still undeciphered cartouche in Levantine hieroglyphic script, from North-West Palace. (ME 118120, British Museum photograph).

of Greek and European art. At the time they provided the Ottoman government with yet another reason to wonder what treasures it might be losing. Hawkins became 'very irate at the mention which has been made of your proceedings, in various newspapers... It has been announced over and over again that you have found a splendid throne composed of ivory and gold' (BL 38979: 169; 27.iii.1850). Canning, when reporting to the Prime Minister on his negotiations for another Ottoman letter of support, which was less favourable and does not seem to have been used, ascribed the obstacles he was encountering to 'an incipient desire at the Porte to collect materials for establishing a museum of its own. To this may be added the rival solicitations of other antiquarians, particularly of the French, and a general feeling of jealousy excited by Mr Layard's success, and the frequent exaggerations respecting it which have figured in the public journals of Europe' (BL 38979: 411; 18.x.1850). In letters which he wrote to Mosul (BL 38979: 335, 372; 30.x. and 30.xi.1850), Canning also implicates Layard's outspoken first book (1849a): 'Fathi Mahomet Pasha, who has a voice in the matter, appears to have taken umbrage at your hostility to that system of corruption by which he thrives at the expense of his benefactor's empire'... 'You may remember my admonitions on this subject were more frequent than welcome. In all times and places the evil eye is worth neutralizing by silence and modesty. In the east it cannot be defied without danger.' Yet, despite the publicity and its ramifications, and although Layard himself illustrated a selection of his ivories and bronzes, they were relatively neglected by scholars for a long time afterwards. A catalogue of the principal Nimrud ivories appeared in 1975 (=Barnett 1975). It has only been much more recently, with the extensive new collections excavated by Mallowan and Oates and published by Georgina Herrmann (e.g. 1986; 1992), that work on Nimrud ivories has really flourished. John Curtis is currently preparing a catalogue of the bronzes.

One reason for this neglect was technical. It consisted in the sheer difficulty of lifting, packing, handling and

conserving small unstable antiquities, since the expertise did not yet exist and treatments were speculative. The description of early conservation methods given by Budge (1925: 147–57), although no more reliable in detail than anything else he wrote, draws a reasonably convincing picture of the degree of confusion possible. There is despair, for instance, in the tone of a letter written by Joseph Bonomi to Birch, about Egyptian stone stelas exfoliating (Corr 2: 295; 7.v.1847), but the Trustees were able to call on famous scientists, such as Sir John Herschel on that occasion (OP 38: 14.vii.1847). He warned against a suggested process that might compound the damage, identified salts and variable humidity as likely causes of decay, and recommended an experiment with soaking in pure water; if a varnish was then wanted, it should be a waterproof resin that would 'dry with a certain cohesion or glutinousness'. Mercifully salts are seldom an intractable problem in Assyria, but Layard (1853a: 564) recorded how some clay tablets from alluvial Babylonia, disintegrating through efflorescence, 'have been partly restored by the same process as the ivories from Nimroud... They have been boiled in a glutinous substance, which has penetrated into the very heart of the clay, and is expected to prevent its further decay'. Layard's acceptance that a single treatment might suit both clay and ivory from different environments is disconcerting. The method eventually adopted to clean and conserve clay tablets in the 1890s, as recommended by Sir William Flower, was partial baking in sand heated to about 150°C, which was in principle the same technique as that already used by Rassam at Babylon (Reports: Budge, 25.ix.1895; Reade 1986: xxi, xxxi); dilute hydrochloric acid was applied to the more stubborn deposits.

A special committee of three Trustees had considered the conservation of ivories from Layard's first season. They consulted Hawkins, the naturalist Professor William Owen, and Mr H. (or J.) Flower, 'who has much experience in cementing and preserving decayed bone', i.e. natural history specimens. Flower had excellent results with one piece, and was duly entrusted with another eighteen panels (OP 39: 15.i.1848, 8.ii.1848), before they were drawn by Edward Prentice (Layard 1849b: pls 88–91). Flower does not seem to have revealed his technique immediately, since in his first book Layard (1849a: II, 9) only described it as an 'ingenious process' of replacing the lost 'glutinous matter'. There was still doubt about how to treat ivories in the field, and Layard must have had the same practical problems as those we encountered, in much more comfortable circumstances, in the 1960s (Reade 1982: 108–9). Hawkins wrote to Layard (BL 38979: 170; 27.iii.1850): 'I have spoken to the man who repairs the ivories, he is a mysterious gentleman, and ill willing to disclose his own method of working or giving information which may interfere with his own work at some future time. He is quite averse to your steeping any of the ivories in isinglass, but recommends that you tie them round with *abundance* of fine thread and then with a camel's hair pencil putting a very thin layer of isinglass, then wrapping them up in tissue paper and putting an external coat of isinglass upon that... Those ivories, which came embedded in the mud in which they were found, bore their journey very well [a tribute to Layard's good sense when he first encountered this material], and I think if you found any more such, their preservation may be further assured by a coating of isinglass or glue round the whole of the outside.' Ivories found later by Rawlinson and Loftus, at Sherifkhan and Nimrud respectively, were boiled in gelatine at once (Transcripts: 83; 21.iv.1852; OP 52: 11.ii.1855); in this period gelatine was also the material used in making moulds of European ivories (OP 54: A. Nesbit; 4.vii.1855). According to Budge (1925: 151), Assyrian ivories still needed to be conserved by Robert Ready, approved as the Museum's part-time Repairer on 12.vii.1859, who used 'one of his secret methods'. Two 'Assyrian ivory busts' and other unspecified ivories are mentioned in lists of some of the items, possibly from several Museum departments, treated by Ready during 1860–67 (Corr NS 11: 5046–121); the annual *Returns* also say how many items were conserved. While Ready's treatment for wood involved turpentine and camphor (ibid.: 5079), his treatment for ivory was still saturation with gelatine, just as it was for bone and bread (ibid.: 5093); the method he used for saturating is not described. The long-term results of the gluten or gelatine treatments of the Nimrud ivories seem to have been reasonably satisfactory.

There were comparable worries over the Nimrud bronzes. 'How to pack these treasures and to send them safe to England after the fate of the last cargo of small objects', wrote Layard (Corr 8: 3158; 7.i.1850) 'I am at a loss to devise. Owing to decomposition of the metal these beautiful relics are so fragile that the least movement breaks them. I have been employed for hours in removing them. I must do my best with cotton and sawdust, but I really feel afraid of sending them by raft to Busrah, and then trusting them to the sea-captain's merciless paws. I can conceive the amazement with which you will contemplate them should they ever reach the B.M. unsmashed. Oh that sea-captains could have a little regard to "Glass, fragile, this side up!" From what you say the last cargo of marbles must have been sadly ill-treated, but it is on a piece with the rest, and I am heartily disgusted at the shabby way in which the whole thing has been managed.' A fortnight later Layard was using 'cotton and chopped straw' (BL 38942: 12; 21.i.1850). Hawkins advised (BL 38979: 172; 27.iii.1850), 'I do not think you can do better than you have done; only I should not put cotton next to the rough oxidated metal as it is troublesome and dangerous to remove. Wrap them in soft paper, then in cotton wool, and then as tight as they will bear in chopped hay not too fine; not in sawdust, as it is apt to shift and give unequal pressure which is dangerous. Each box might be covered with coarse cloth well tarred, on both sides... and it would then defy all danger from water; but have you the means of doing this? Perhaps more greased cloth might answer the purpose, and I know that you have plenty of tallow.' Jones (BL 38979: 237–38; 22.v.1850) describes how one of the crates he recovered from the wrecked raft was 'saturated with water and alive with maggots... It contained two pieces of an old copper utensil (Ninus's footbath?) which I have carefully dried and repacked, in the same way exactly as you did it, in fresh chopped straw.' Layard himself (1853a: 199), describing part of what he thought to be a bronze throne, states that 'I succeeded, after much trouble, in moving and packing two of these legs; but they appear to have since fallen to pieces'.. One problem will have been use of the overland route to Skanderoun for transporting the finest bronzes. Stephen Lynch & Co., trading with Baghdad, had given the route up because camels had to be unloaded every night, and the jolting caused too much damage to goods; Layard had ascertained this (BL 38979: 329; 12.x.1850), but still preferred a land journey, under his own supervision, to a sea journey round the Cape.

Long-term conservation of the bronzes was a problem still to be confronted. While it was possible to investigate the ancient technology (Percy, *apud* Layard 1853a: 670–72), it was by no means easy to separate and clean decayed fragments while preventing rather than precipitating further decay. Nothing seems to have come of Birch's proposal to consult a foreign curator, J. Dubois at the Louvre, who in 1843 had already written about cleaning a bronze statue (Corr NS 6: 2772; undated). Instead, samples were sent to the distinguished chemist William Brande at the Royal Mint, who observed that 'Those which are *least corroded*... are covered with a green and mottled incrustation, consisting chiefly of sub-carbonate of copper, suboxide of copper, and oxide of tin: it dissolves with effervescence in muriatic [hydrochloric] and in nitric acids (diluted) and may be removed so as to leave the metal clean underneath, by the careful application of such acids, as the accompanying

Fig. 1-p. Bronze bowl from North-West Palace. (ME N17, British Museum photograph of engraving of watercolour by E. Prentice, Layard 1853b: pl. 74).

specimens shew. The thinner flat-bottomed, and most corroded vessel, is partly changed through and through into oxide, and in such places is perfectly brittle, as the broken portion of the edge shews' (OP 46: 30.vii.1851). Layard was at first satisfied with Brande's results and recommended that he continue to work on the 'engraved and embossed dishes and vases' (OP 46: 1.viii.1851), but Brande, on returning the next two vessels sent to him, stated that 'Their extreme state of corrosion has prevented my saving any of those portions which are oxidized *throughout*, but... those parts which are only obscured or covered by oxide and carbonate of copper, admit of tolerably perfect cleansing. Under these circumstances it is a matter of doubt to me how far it may be advisable to meddle with any of those which are in the same predicament' (OP 46: 7.viii.1851). The danger of fresh corrosion is not mentioned, and Brande must have been unaware that original surfaces sometimes survive between separable layers of corrosion. A month later, however, Layard had found that the vessels 'which had been cleaned by Mr Brande, were suffering much injury, apparently from the use of some strong acid in removing the oxidation... The process of oxidation progressing daily and threatening to destroy the beautiful designs graven upon the metal' (OP 46: 13.ix.1851). He had therefore consulted John Doubleday, the Museum's Repairer during 1836–56, who had previously rebuilt the Portland Vase, and who 'by a very simple process and without employing acids succeeded most completely in restoring the vessels and in bringing out the designs and embossing upon them... [and] in detaching those which adhered together'. Doubleday was then given more

pieces, although Prentice was to draw them first, in case of 'any accident hereafter' (Minutes: 20.ix.1851; Layard 1853b: pls 63–67) (fig. 1-p). I have not traced a description of Doubleday's technique: perhaps it involved warm water and soap, which Eric Miller tells me can be surprisingly effective. Doubleday, like Mr Flower, was reluctant to divulge the tricks of his trade. His successor Robert Ready also liked to keep such information within the family (OP 82: Franks, 2.x.1886); the legitimacy of this secretive attitude was discussed and accepted by the Keepers of Antiquities when Ready's son, Augustus, was being appointed as the Museum's electrotypist (Minutes: 9.x.1886). R. Ready's own lists record the cleaning and repairing of many, usually unspecified, Assyrian bronzes (Corr NS 11: 5046–121). He was thought to use dilute acid on some objects of this material (OP 82: Renouf, 4.x.1886); there is no mention of oil, with which he was accustomed to saturate iron, nor of varnish, which he applied to some Egyptian bronzes (Corr NS 11: 5093, 5110). How best to conserve items like the Nimrud bronzes continued to be discussed throughout the twentieth century too.

These quantities of fragile material were not the kind of thing that an aristocrat brought back from the Grand Tour. They were an archaeological archive, uncomfortably deposited in a Department of Artistic Antiquities. How were these objects to be numbered and stored, and who was to attend to them? They were neither Greek nor Egyptian, and specialists had plenty of things in far better condition to absorb their interest. So most of the small Nimrud objects drifted out of the limelight, and their significance was submerged by academic politics. Layard, disenchanted with the archaeological world, put them into his past. He was moving on to the more serious activities made possible by his youthful successes at Nimrud. His 1849 book about the first discoveries made his name, and remains good reading. While repeatedly disadvantaged by his habits of looking ahead, telling the truth, and being proved right, he became over the years one of the country's most distinguished politicians. He helped found and manage the Ottoman Bank. He was an effective Trustee of the National Gallery. He helped revive the glass mosaic industry of Venice. He was a fine ambassador in difficult circumstances in both Madrid and Stamboul. His reputation grows with time (Waterfield 1963; Fales and Hickey 1987).

It is appropriate that a paper about nineteenth-century Nimrud should end as an encomium of Layard. He demonstrated the importance of the site, and everything done since has built on foundations laid by him. He would have been pleased to find the British Museum in 2002 hosting a conference about the place he loved. And as a man who spoke Arabic and who had as I do many happy memories of Iraq, he would have been delighted to see, present at the conference, archaeologists from that country who are continuing his research at Nimrud.

2   JULIUS WEBER (1838–1906) AND THE SWISS EXCAVATIONS AT NIMRUD IN *c.* 1860, TOGETHER WITH RECORDS OF OTHER NINETEENTH-CENTURY ANTIQUARIAN RESEARCHES AT THE SITE

Anthony Green

Abstract

The Zurich businessman Julius Weber conducted excavations at Nimrud at an early stage during his 1860–68 period of residence in Baghdad. Here I give a brief account of his life and work, including what little is known about his archaeological activities in Nimrud. In the course of the narrative, I also review the record of early nineteenth century European visitors to the site, together with their antiquarian explorations. Apart from a few minor corrections and additions in light of comments by participants at the Nimrud Conference, and some subsequent research, the text follows that of my paper delivered to the Conference in March 2002.

The excavations at Nimrud of Julius Weber-Locher in about 1860[1] have all but been forgotten. In his *Rise and Progress of Assyriology,* E.A.W. Budge devotes a single sentence to these excavations, and to the fact that Weber sent Assyrian bas reliefs to Zurich (Budge 1925: 220), while R. D. Barnett in a catalogue of the Nimrud ivories refers only to 'the clandestine burrowings of natives, such as that which enriched the sculptures and collections of M. Weber and M. Pacifique Delaporte'.[2] It is particularly ironic that this reference comes immediately after an account of the excavations of Loftus at the site in 1854–55 in which Barnett laments the 'unjust silence' concerning that work, and berates Layard for writing that practically nothing of importance had been found there by Loftus (Barnett 1975: 24). For the rest, both specialist works on Nimrud and Assyria, and general accounts of archaeological exploration in Mesopotamia and the Near East such as those of Hilprecht, Lloyd and Larsen, give no mention of Weber's work (Hilprecht 1903; Lloyd 1980; Larsen 1996).

Julius Weber, Swiss businessman and amateur antiquarian (fig. 2-a), was born on 8th August 1838 and died aged 67 on 30th March 1906. From 1860 to 1868, he lived in Baghdad, where he headed the Schweizerische Exportgesellschaft Zürich, and carried out excavations at Nimrud some time between 1860 and 1863. There are various sources from which details of his life history can

be ascertained. Those I have used so far include private correspondence, local government archives for the cantons of Zurich and Zug, company records of the Zurich Insurance Company, several published company histories, records of the Antiquarian Society of Zurich (Antiquarische Gesellschaft in Zürich), a privately commissioned and privately published Weber family history (Strickler 1922) and notices in the local press, especially in the *Neue Zürcher Zeitung.*

Weber was born to a wealthy and locally important family in the village of Bubikon in the rural outskirts of the city of Zurich, the second of three brothers. His elder brother Wilhelm was born in 1828, and his younger brother Hermann in 1835. The house in which all three children were born is still a famous landmark in the area.

The Ritterhaus or Johanniterhaus Bubikon, as it is known (fig. 2-c), is a medieval building, itself having associations with the Middle East. It was built in 1192 as a stopover for Crusaders on their way to the Holy Land, as a school for young crusading brothers, and as a retirement home and hospital for old or invalid Crusaders. It was built and run by the crusading Order of St John, the Knights Hospitaller, who, on the Crusader conquest of Jerusalem in 1099, having occupied the site of the hospital, situated close by the church of St John the Baptist, took upon themselves the particular role of caring for the Christian sick. After their expulsion from Jerusalem (by the armies of Saladin) in 1187, and then from Acre and the Holy Land in 1291, they in turn occupied the islands of Cyprus, Rhodes (1310–1522) and then Malta (from 1530, until its conquest by Napoleon in 1798). They are still known as the Knights of Malta and their device is today named the Maltese Cross. With their headquarters in Rome, they still exist today as the *Johanniter* or Order of St John and operate hospitals, retirement homes and the St John's Ambulance Service.

The house in Bubikon, which today is a Crusader museum, had passed into private ownership in 1789 and to the Weber family in the early nineteenth century. Although it is not mentioned in surviving correspondence, I cannot help feeling that the history of the house in which he was born and spent his early life would have been a factor in stimulating Julius Weber's interest in the antiquities of the Ancient Near East.

---

[1] On the question of the year, see below.

[2] Barnett 1975: 24. cf. Al-Haik 1968: 62: 'Excavations made through native clandestine diggings'. Also Gadd 1936: 121: 'a good deal of grubbing... either by local inhabitants or by native speculators'.

Fig. 2-a. Julius Weber-Locher. (Copyright Staatsarchiv des Kantons Zürich).

Fig. 2-b. Elise Weber-Locher. (Copyright Staatsarchiv des Kantons Zürich).

Fig. 2-c. The Ritterhaus at Bubikon. (Copyright Staatsarchiv des Kantons Zürich).

The stimulus which he himself cites, however, and of which he was conscious, was the widespread excitement generated all over Europe by the French and British excavations of Paul-Emile Botta at Khorsabad and Austen Henry Layard at Nimrud. The Musée des Antiquités Orientales at the Louvre, the first museum of Near Eastern antiquities in the world, was inaugurated by King Louis-Philippe on 1st May 1847, while the antiquities sent by Layard to London formed the core of the Mesopotamian collections of the British Museum. The discoveries stimulated the so-called 'Assyrian revival movement' in European art, especially after the display at London's Great Exhibition in 1851, and were used (and misused) as important evidence on both sides of the current debate in Europe over the veracity of the Bible.[3] As for Weber, his interest focused in particular on Nimrud, which had been so productive for Layard (Layard 1849a; 1849b; 1853a; 1853b, Green 2000b).

After his schooling in Bubikon and Zurich, Julius Weber studied for a time in Geneva, and it was while he was there, we are told, that he decided to make a career in the Near East. He travelled to Aleppo, where he became a partner in the business firm of Zollinger and Streiff, then in 1860 he proceeded to Baghdad. From there he arranged to take over, on his own behalf, the trading company of the Volkart Brothers in Winterthur, still to this day a big international trading corporation, and refounded it in Baghdad as the Schweizerische Exportgesellschaft.

After three years he returned briefly to Switzerland in order to marry Elise Locher from a prominent local family of Trogen (born in 1840) (fig. 2-b). The wedding took place in St Peter's church in Zurich, after which, in

line with Swiss custom, the couple adopted the double surname of Weber-Locher.

Soon after marriage, the couple travelled via Syria and, passing through Mosul, to Baghdad. On 15th May 1864, in Baghdad, their daughter Lisa was born. The family purchased and lived in a house on the left bank of the Tigris, which stood immediately next to the British Embassy, and was later to become the residence of the Russian consul.

Following the mysterious illness of baby Lisa, and advised by their British physician, one Dr Wood, that the baby would not, in his opinion, long survive the hot climate of Baghdad, Frau Weber returned with her daughter and servants to Zurich at the beginning of 1866. On the way home, a son Julius was born in Marseilles on 17th March 1866. Mother and children then moved on to Zurich and settled in Flintern near Zurich, in the house of Frau Weber's brother-in-law who was a Member of the Swiss Federal Parliament, and did not return to the Middle East. Julius Weber joined his family in Zurich for Christmas of 1867, but in the early spring of the following year he returned to Baghdad. A second son, Oscar, was born to Elise on the 25th November 1868.

Julius Weber's rapid return to Baghdad had been occasioned by the murder of his chief assistant in Mesopotamia. After 1868, however, he again left the business in the hands of his employees, though technically remaining head of the company until its liquidation in 1877.

After his final return to Switzerland, Julius Weber was involved in a number of different business ventures. He became respectively Vice-President and President of the insurance companies Zurich and Schweiz: the former is

---

[3] Cf. Green 2000a; 2000b; with key references.

still a major player in the insurance market. However, the wealth he had accumulated through his involvement in the Ottoman trade with Iraq, he mostly used to found the Zug-based metalworking company Metallwerkfabrik Zug, of which he was the senior partner and President of the Board of Directors. In this capacity, he is often mentioned in press reports as an important local employer in Zug. In the 1880s, he became a member of the Zurich City Council.

The family spent much time not only in and around Zurich, but also in France, especially on the French Riviera, where Weber is said to have had many friends and to have sought relief from his sufferings. This clearly refers to some aspect of ill health, but I have not yet found any more specific reference to his ailment. His obituary refers only to his death in the night following a 'long illness'.[4]

By the time Weber went there, Nimrud had been visited and investigated by a number of Europeans. In their recent book on Nimrud, Joan and David Oates attribute the first modern mention of the site to Claudius James Rich.[5] In fact there is a record of an earlier visit by a westerner to the site, the British traveller, James Silk Buckingham (1786–1855), on 8th September 1816. He refers to two *tells,* which he calls 'mounds' and 'heaps' and which he names as Nimrod-Tuppé and Shah-Tuppé, probably Tell Nimrud (the main mound) and Tulul al 'Azar or Fort Shalmaneser. He says that his party passed by the sites 'without seeing any thing remarkable in them, more than common mounds of earth; though they probably might have shown vestiges of former buildings had they been carefully examined, a task which I could not now step aside from the road to execute' (Buckingham 1830: I, 54–55 (=1829: 31)).

Claudius James Rich (1787–1821), Baghdad Resident of the (British) East India Company, visited Nimrud on 4th March 1821, shortly before his death, accompanied by his wife and a group of friends. He noted the ziggurat mound and the site of Tulul al 'Azar in Fort Shalmaneser, which he calls 'Tell Seikh'. He also recovered from the surface and from a local village a number of inscribed brick fragments (Rich 1836: II, 129–33).

Some members of the British government-sponsored Euphrates Expedition of 1835–37, led by Colonel Francis Rawdon Chesney (1789–1872), were at Nimrud during 1837. Two independent records are preserved, the first by

William Francis Ainsworth (1807–96), surgeon and geologist to the Expedition, who visited the site on 9th March (Ainsworth 1888: II, 320). As with Rich, he noted the ziggurat mound and also the density of antiquities on the surface, which included inscribed bricks, glazed tiles and potsherds (Ainsworth 1844: 137–39). Writing later, after Layard's world-famous discoveries of monumental sculpture, he also recalls that 'the only structure at this time visible above the surface was a huge mass of limestone at the north-west corner of the mound, hewn into the shape of two parallelopipeds, the larger 2 feet 7 inches on each side, the smaller 2 feet 2 inches, with a basin cut out in the centre. There had manifestly been an inscription, now illegible, on the larger block'. Alluding to the discoveries of Layard, he adds, however, that 'it was never dreamt what colossal sculptures were concealed within so small a space' (Ainsworth 1888: II, 320).

A second account comes from Alexander Hector (died 1875), storekeeper and purser of the *Euphrates,* the surviving steamboat of the Expedition, who was at Nimrud on 3rd June. He also observed the ziggurat mound, as well as the indications of the ancient city wall, and saw Assyrian reliefs and inscribed bricks. Tempted to make excavations, he desisted at this time on account of its being 'so dreadfully hot'.[6] Nevertheless, according to a certain interpretation of Hector's correspondence, 'despite Layard's later claim that he had it in mind since 1840 to excavate at Nimrud, Hector, who had been closely acquainted with Layard since at least 1841, writes as though recognition of the importance of this site was his own idea. Whilst he and Layard had obviously discussed archaeological topics in relation to the Mosul area, there is the clear implication that Hector had never heard Layard express interest specifically in Nimrud. This suggests that the first recognition of the importance of Nimrud as a site was due to Hector rather than Layard' (Saggs 1970: 41–42). It should be admitted, however, that even if this interpretation should prove correct, we cannot be sure that the impression given by Hector, Layard's later rival for the prize of excavating at Nimrud, was necessarily accurate. In a letter to T. Stirling, dated as late as 20th April 1845, Hector tried to persuade his correspondent to sponsor excavations at the site, which he identified as Biblical Rezen (Saggs 1970: 41).

Another Briton to claim his prior recognition of the site's archaeological potential, and would-be contender to

---

[4] *Neue Zürcher Zeitung* 3rd April 1906, early evening edition.

[5] Oates and Oates 2001: 1, also wrongly attributing Rich's visit to Nimrud to the year 1820. According to Richardson 1995, the first mention of the site under the name of Nimrud is that of Niebuhr, who was travelling in the area in 1766 (not 1776 as misprinted in Richardson 1995).

[6] Letter of Hector to T. Stirling, June 1845, quoted by Chesney 1850: 137–38, note. Hector's position with the Expedition is stated in Ainsworth 1888: I, xv. He was married to a famous Dublin-born British novelist Annie French Hector (1825–1902), who published under the pseudonym Mrs Alexander. Her works include the semi-autobiographical *Kitty Costello* (1902). Hector is said to have disapproved of his wife's writing career, and most of her novels were published after his death.

conduct excavations at Nimrud, was the missionary, the Revd George Percy Badger (1815–88), later (from 1845) to be official government Chaplain of Bombay. The brother-in-law of Christian Rassam—Christian was married to Badger's sister Matilda (cf. Saggs 1970: 74, note 2)—Badger made missionary tours in Mesopotamia in 1842–44 and again in 1850. In March 1844, the year before the commencement of full-scale excavations at the site, he visited Nimrud together with a Russian travelling companion whom he names Ditell. They explored the remains, surveyed and measured the mounds, and made notes on the ziggurat, referred to as 'the cone'.[7] After visiting Sir Stratford Canning (1786–1880), the British ambassador in Istanbul, Badger sent him a report[8] and promoted himself as a possible future excavator of the site,[9] a move which heightened tensions between himself and Layard (Waterfield 1963: 115, 213). According to Budge, Badger's 'report was the clearest and fullest account of Nimrûd possible at that time, and there can be little doubt that it induced Stratford Canning to start excavations' (Budge 1920: II, 96). Certainly Badger himself sought to claim so (Badger 1852: I, 86). Others did, and do, doubt it.[10]

John Curtis has referred to Badger's work as 'the first recorded excavations at Nimrud' (Curtis 1997a: 141). However, local excavations on behalf of Ahmed Pasha of the Jalili family are recorded as early as about 1815,[11] and in any case, Badger does not say that he excavated, although he wanted to do so. The first recorded European excavations at the site, therefore, were apparently those conducted by the British missionary the Revd James Phillips Fletcher,[12] and his party, who also arrived at Nimrud in 1844. Fletcher was accompanied by a Russian travelling companion, whose name he does not give, and a couple of local guides. Once again the impressive ziggurat mound was noted. Finding fragments of inscribed bricks on the surface, the party was inspired to conduct the first recorded, though admittedly rather minor, European excavations at the site. 'The infection of investigation seized us all', says Fletcher. 'Swords and a

spear or two, which we borrowed from some of the local villagers, were put into requisition, and we were soon busily engaged in turning over the soil. A few bricks were the reward of our labours, but as we shortly became fatigued with such desultory work, we left off and returned to the village' (Fletcher 1850: II, 74–75).

As is well known, these rather feeble efforts were followed by Layard's full-scale excavations in 1845–47, and 1849–51, those of Rassam in 1853–54, and of Loftus in 1854–55.[13] These excavations, especially those of Layard, which were popularized in books and exhibitions, inspired Europeans interested in antiquity, including Julius Weber. The local Zurich press tended to compare Weber to Heinrich Schliemann, the German excavator of Troy, probably because he too combined a career in business with archaeology, and financed his own excavations. Weber himself however refers to his wish to emulate the British and the French.

Weber's excavations at Nimrud took place in about 1860 or 1861.[14] The exact year is unknown to me, since the only reference I have found to the date is in a letter dated 14th September 1864 referring to the excavations of 'a few years ago'. This letter, sent from Baghdad, is addressed to one Dr Ferdinand Keller, who was Chairman of the Antiquarian Society of Zurich (Antiquarische Gesellschaft in Zürich) and is preserved in the archives of that Society.[15] It reads:

Bagdad den 14 Sept 1864
Herrn Dr Ferdinand Keller
zuhanden der Antiquarischen Gesellschaft
Zürich
Hochgeehrtester Herr.
    Letzen Winter verschifften undere Agenten in
Bassora auf unser(em) Segelschiff 'Pamentur' eine Anzahl
Steinplatten, die ich vor einigen Jahren in den
Ruinen von Nimrod einige Stunden südwärts von
Mossul habe ausgraben lassen.
    Diese zum größten Theil ausgezeichnet erhaltenen
Stücke sollten Jhnen gewiß sehr werth sein & Freunde

---

[7] The following year Badger's travelling companion in the Near East was, somewhat improperly it is suggested, the unchaperoned fourteen-year-old Anna Harriet Edwards, later Leonowens, who was subsequently to travel to Siam (Thailand) and become the Anna of *The King and I* fame: cf. Bristowe 1976.

[8] Later quoted by Badger 1852: I, 87–91, together with his letter to Canning, ibid: 91–92.

[9] See his letter to Canning in Badger 1852: I, 92.

[10] Cf Saggs 1970: 42, note 1, quoting Hector and Canning. We should bear in mind, however, that Hector was himself a contender to excavate at Nimrud, and Canning also had his own agenda for the site.

[11] Reade 1965: 120, cites Layard 1849a: 28–29. See also J. Reade, this volume: 1–21.

[12] I have not so far had access to his autobiography (Fletcher 1853), and his years of birth and death are unknown to me.

[13] The last listed wrongly in Postgate and Reade 1980: 305, under '1854' only; cf., however, Barnett 1987: 103.

[14] Al-Haik 1968: 62, lists the excavations under '1860–63', but this is the full period of Weber's first residence in Baghdad, and it is clear that his work at Nimrud occupied only a short time during this period.

[15] Archiv der Antiquarischen Gesellschaft in Zürich, now housed in the Schweizerisches Landesmuseum, Zurich, Briefe an Private Bd. 24 (1862–64, T–Z), Letter no. 83. Single sheet of blue paper with two page letter written front and back. I am grateful to Dr Lucas Wüthrich, current President of the Society, for photographs and for his transcription. An earlier transcription, published by Strickler 1922: 71, has some variants on that of Dr Wüthrich, and the German text given here attempts to represent as far as possible the forms, and retains the line divisions, of the original document.

machen & möchten Sie außer London und Paris wohl
kaum zu finden sein.

    Darauf gestützt erlaube ich mir, Jhnen diese
Platten anzubieten, franco Dünkirchen oder London,
wo sie unser Schiff ausgeladen hat und wo Jhnen solche
auf Jhnen Wunsch hin durch die gef(ällege) Vermittlung
der Schweiz(erischen) Export Gesellschaft in Zürich, der ich
darüber geschrieben, ausgeliefert würden.

    Diese Platten hätten eigentlich erst diesen Winter
(S.2)
verreisen sollen & kam es mir dieser
Tage zu Ohren, daß unser Bassora-Agent schon letzten
Winter diese Steine verladen habe, ohne Ordres &
ohne mit etwas mitzutheilen.

    Jm Ungewissen darüber habe ich gleich nach
Bassora geschrieben, kann aber erst in einigen
Tagen die Antwort haben & so zeige ich Jhnen
denn dieses nun an (*oder:* den dieses nur an), um damit (*oder:*
um daß) Sie gleich die
nötigen (*oder:* richtigen) Maßregeln treffen können, indem
zur Stunde die 'Pamentur' längst angekommen
& ausgeladen haben muß, & behalte mir vor
Jhnen mit Vorgehendem mit nächster Post zu bestätigen oder
berichtigen.

    Mit ganz besonderer Hochachtung & Ergebenheit
Julius Weber[16]

The Assyrian bas reliefs sent by Weber to Zurich were
thus acquired by the Antiquarian Society of Zurich and
are today in the possession of Zurich University, and
exhibited in that institution's Archäologische Sammlung.

---

[16] To Herr Dr Ferdinand Keller, for the attention of the
Antiquarian Society.
Highly Honoured Sir,

    Last winter our agents in Basra shipped a number of
stone slabs on our sailing vessel 'Pamentur', which I had
excavated a few years ago in the ruins of Nimrud, a few hours
south of Mosul. These, for the most part excellently preserved
pieces, should be most valuable to you and bring great joy,
and most probably you cannot find their like anywhere
outside London and Paris.

    In this regard I would like to offer you these reliefs
franco (trading language for 'free of carriage' or 'transport
included') to Dunkirk or London, where our ship will have
docked and where our vessel will have had them unloaded,
delivered on your request by the Swiss Export Society in
Zurich, which I have informed.

    These reliefs should actually have been shipped only this
coming winter, but it has come to my attention only recently
that our Basra agent had shipped these reliefs already last
winter without my direction and without informing me. Not
knowing anything about it, I immediately wrote to Basra but
I will get the answer only in a few days, and so I now inform
you about that, so that you can take the necessary measures—
because in the meantime the 'Pamentur' must have, quite a
while ago arrived and unloaded, and I intend to confirm the
above information in my next letter.

    With very special high esteem and utmost humility,
Julius Weber.

There are five slabs from the North-West Palace of
Ashurnasirpal II showing genies and stylized trees and, on
one, just the Standard Inscription,[17] while seven slabs
from the Central Palace of Tiglath-Pileser III show
narrative scenes from military campaigns. These reliefs
were clearly the pride of Weber and the main purpose of
his excavations. I do not here propose to say much about
them, however, because they have been fully published by
Julia Asher-Greve and Gebhard Selz in their book *Genien
und Krieger aus Nimrūd* (Asher-Greve and Selz 1980).
Moreover, they are not so interesting with regard to
Weber's archaeological work at the site, since they would
seem to have been originally excavated by Layard or
Rassam and then left in position and simply removed or
perhaps re-excavated from Layard's trenches by Weber.
For some of these reliefs this is confirmed by the fact that
drawings of them can be found among Layard's illustrations.[18] In the period between the closing-down of British
Museum excavations in 1855 and the opening of *The
Daily Telegraph* excavations of 1873, and renewed
British Museum excavations from 1877, there were
hordes of amateur antiquarians visiting Nimrud and
removing reliefs from the old trenches. In his book *Reliefs
from the Palace of Ashurnasirpal II*, J.B. Stearns has used
biographies, college histories and articles in the college
journals to reconstruct some of the stories of those
Americans, mostly missionaries, who removed and
shipped to the United States reliefs from the North-West
Palace.[19] Many more such tales remain to be told (or not
told, where no written accounts have been left) and have
resulted in the wide distribution of Nimrud bas reliefs
across European and North American collections.[20]
Weber seems to have been in this general tradition of
travellers who removed reliefs from existing excavations.

Perhaps more interestingly, from the point of view of the
history of archaeological work at the site, however, is the
implication that Weber and some of his employees
conducted their own excavations in another area of the
main mound. Weber published an article about these
excavations in the 19th number of the Journal of the
Antiquarian Society of Zurich, the volume for November
1862 to December 1863.[21]

---

[17] See now Meuszyński 1981: 70, nos L-33, L-34 (Zurich nos
1910, 1911); Paley and Sobolewski 1987: 52, no. T-2 (Zurich
no. 1912).
[18] Cf. Barnett and Falkner 1962: pls XXXV–XXXVI (Zurich
no. 1916 = British Museum Original Drawings III, Central I),
pls XLVIII–XLIX (Zurich no. 1919 = Original Drawing III,
Central XXIX), and pls L–LI (Zurich no. 1920 = Original
Drawing III, Central XXVIII).
[19] Stearns 1961: 1–4. See Englund 2003.
[20] Cf. the distribution lists in Meuszyński 1981: 881–85; Paley
and Sobolewski 1987: 88–90.
[21] *Neunzehnter Bericht über die Verrichtungen der
Antiquarischen Gesellschaft in Zürich* (vom November 1862
bis December 1863).

This rare volume is no longer readily available, and is not even to be found among the present works in the collection of the Antiquarian Society of Zurich itself. To date I have not succeeded in tracing an extant copy of this issue, and consequently have not seen Weber's report. From a secondary notice, however, it seems likely that the report gives little precise detail about the excavations, and may have consisted of little more than a list of finds presented to the Antiquarian Society (Strickler 1922: 71–71). Moreover, as reproduced in this secondary notice, the list does not distinguish between finds from 'Niniveh' i.e. Nimrud, and others said to have been found, presumably on the surface, at 'Babylon'— probably also including material from other sites in southern Mesopotamia which were conveniently close to Weber's base in Baghdad; and Weber may well also have purchased some pieces.[22] Some items listed, however, can definitely or plausibly be identified with pieces preserved in the Archaeological Collection of Zurich University, and in several cases are clearly of Assyrian or Babylonian origin.[23] The material includes a number of clay figurines which are in a style which could be Neo-Assyrian, but are perhaps more likely Neo-Babylonian, and so should probably be assigned to southern Mesopotamia.

At Nimrud, Weber's expedition seems to have found a number of objects, probably including cylinder seals, tablets and clay figurines, and possibly also fragments of sculpture, vessels of pottery and/or glass, and maybe a figurine of bronze. It is difficult to be more precise, because of the mixing in the published list of finds presented to the Antiquarian Society of material from Nimrud with that of Babylon and/or other southern Mesopotamian sites. Therefore, while a large number of objects in the present museum can be definitely attributed to the Weber collection on account of their accession numbers, we do not, on the whole, know which of these came from Nimrud. The published list of finds presented to the Antiquarian Society gives 54 objects, not including the bas reliefs, but characterizes them simply as from the ruins of 'Nineveh and Babylon'. One Hellenistic clay figurine in the collection has 'Babylon' written on it in black ink, but for the rest we can only guess for each item whether it should be assigned to Nimrud or Babylon, or

indeed another site, since the published descriptions are usually not detailed enough to be identified beyond doubt with specific items in the collection.

From the large number of alabaster figurines in a Parthian style in the Zurich collection one might theorize that Weber's excavations at Nimrud were carried out somewhere near the south-east edge of the main mound, where possible evidence of Parthian-period settlement has been observed in later excavations.[24] However, it could equally be that the Parthian-style clay figurines come not from these excavations but are a part of the material from 'Babylon'.

The reception of Weber's antiquities in Zurich was rather mixed. Dr Keller, the Chairman of the Antiquarian Society, does not seem to have been particularly grateful for the gift and complained about the trouble it put him to in finding space to house the reliefs. In an article in the 20th number of the Society's Journal, he thanked Weber and praised him richly. Nevertheless, all the antiquities including the reliefs, were immediately donated by the Society to the University of Zurich.

The records of the Antiquarian Society of Zurich record that on 30th January 1864, an assistant of Weber gave a lecture presenting a general overview of the Nimrud excavations and general information about the state of Assyrian research.[25] What a pity that this lecture was not published.

In September 1867, the German Assyriologist Jules Oppert visited Zurich and studied the inscriptions in Weber's collection. He then read a paper to the Antiquarian Society in which the minutes record, 'he read from the inscriptions so fluently that everyone was astonished'. Always the arch-cynic, the Chairman of the Society, Dr Keller, is recorded as having commented, 'We don't know if it is all true' (cf. Boissier 1912: 11). Other scholars from Germany, France and Switzerland gave lectures at the Society about the collections in subsequent years, and Alfred Boissier thereafter published a small book discussing some of the most interesting finds (Boissier 1912), but without discussing the excavations.

---

[22] Strickler 1922: 71–72.
[23] One piece is a prehistoric (Early Dynastic?) anthropomorphic stone statuette: Müller 1976.

[24] Full publication of the Mesopotamian material in this collection is in preparation by the present author. The inscriptional material was initially assigned to Jeremy Black, who was kind enough to fly to Zurich at a moment's notice during the course of my study period, and we intended to prepare a joint publication in due course. Dr Black died suddenly in April 2004, aged 52.
[25] Cf. Boissier 1912: 10–11.

3 THE EXCAVATIONS OF THE BRITISH SCHOOL OF ARCHAEOLOGY IN IRAQ

David Oates

First of all may I say what a particular pleasure it is to Joan and to me to see our Iraqi friends and colleagues with us for this conference. We owe them so much. Whatever we have done in Iraq has always been with their extraordinarily friendly co-operation. We thank you, and we are glad to be able in some small way to return your hospitality.

I cannot possibly in half an hour give an account of thirteen seasons of excavation by the British School of Archaeology at Nimrud. Since most of the papers to follow will be concerned with the objects of art, with the sculptures, with the ivories, indeed all the objects of beauty and interest, I shall leave these to others who know more about them anyway. What I would like to do is to show you a few buildings and give you some idea of the setting in which all these things were found, the setting in which that extraordinary phenomenon, the Assyrian imperial monarchy, operated.

The site of Nimrud consists of a large citadel mound together with an even larger, walled outer town (fig. 3-a). In Assyrian times, the river actually flowed at the western foot of the tell itself, thereby providing water transport and easy access for the stone coming from upstream which

was used for building and particularly for the famous reliefs. The town wall, some 7.5 km in length, ran up to and along the western edge of the river terrace. On the west side of the citadel overlooking the river were, at the northern corner, the ziggurat together with the Ninurta temple which was actually attached to it in the northern manner, south of which was the largest of all the palaces, the palace of Ashurnasirpal, the founder of the Late Assyrian capital city, from which come the most famous of the reliefs. Further south was the so-called Central Palace and, finally, the South-West Palace, probably built in the seventh century (Plan 3 and 3-c). Since Mallowan's time the Iraqis have of course also identified a palace of Adad-nirari III, just south of the North-West Palace. On the eastern side of the citadel we worked in the Governor's Palace and one of the largest temples, the temple of Nabu known as Ezida (see below), and the little palace across the road from it, the so-called Burnt Palace.

I wish to turn first to the northern outer courtyard of the North-West Palace, because that was the centre of the administration; this is the area that is most easily accessible from the citadel itself and it was here that the government offices were located (Plans 4a and 4b). In

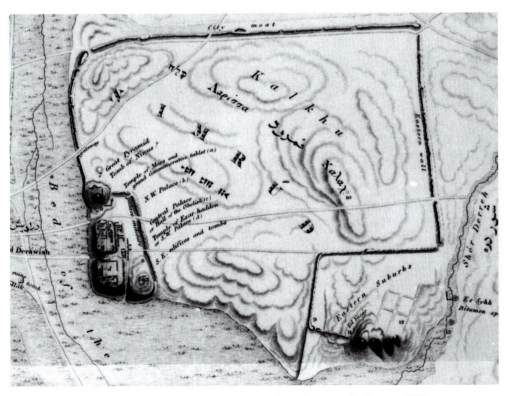

Fig. 3-a. The walls of Nimrud as surveyed by Captain Felix Jones in 1852.

32 *The excavations of the BSAI*

Fig. 3-b. View of the citadel at Nimrud looking south.

these were found many administrative letters, the well-known 'Nimrud letters' which provide unparalleled information about foreign affairs in the late seventh century. For me these are the most interesting tablets found at Nimrud. Tablets were in fact recovered from several rooms along the north side of the courtyard. Here we could identify in the north-east corner a reception suite with a miniature version of the royal throne room (plans 4a and 4b, rooms 21, 25–27), and associated with it a number of smaller rooms which were obviously offices. Adjacent to this were the palace oil store and perhaps the wine cellar (30, 31). In the heavily eroded north-west corner of the courtyard there was part of a similar reception suite (1, 19) and set of offices (3–5) which quite clearly also belonged to an important department of state, but these had gone out of use when Nimrud itself ceased to be the capital about 700 BC. This was obviously the office of another high official and the associated rooms those in which his juniors worked and wrote and kept their archives. Indeed Room 4 seems to have been the archive room in which the tablets were stored (the actual filing boxes can be seen in Oates and Oates 2001: fig. 120). These tablets tell us that one of the departments in this wing dealt almost entirely with external relations, reports to the king from his governors and commanders on the northern and western frontiers (the letters I mentioned earlier). In a sense this was the ancient equivalent of the Foreign and Commonwealth Office. In the seventh century BC, when the capital had moved to Khorsabad and then Nineveh, the preserved records concerned largely local administration within the province of which Nimrud remained the capital, but the

size of reception room 21, still in use in 612 BC, suggests the presence still of officials of high standing.

To the south was the great throne room, the focal point of an Assyrian palace. This area has been magnificently restored by the Directorate General of Antiquities. The façade was restored as early as 1956, and to the west in an adjoining alcove was found the famous stele of Ashurnasirpal II, which Layard must have missed by a foot or two and which was one of Max Mallowan's greatest treasures (Mallowan 1966: I, fig. 27). The inscription records the foundation and completion of the palace in about 878 BC, and a vast celebration, a great feast, lasting ten days, which was given to some 70,000 people, including 47,000 who had worked on the building of the new city, 5000 high officials from abroad or from the provinces, 1500 palace officials and another 16,000 or so who had been the occupants of the original town on this site. This earlier town was founded by Shalmaneser I in the thirteenth century, when Nimrud was obviously quite a small place. All that is visible today is of the ninth and eighth centuries with restoration at later dates in the seventh.

To turn to Ezida, the temple of Nabu (fig. 3-c), the plan shows the main entrance from the north from 'Shalmaneser Street' through the so-called 'Fish Gate' (owing to the presence of limestone 'mermen' on either side (Mallowan 1966: I, fig. 198)). In Ezida itself, the outer northern courtyard housed the offices dealing with the ordinary business of the temple, and on the south side there is a rather impressive façade leading to an inner courtyard with the main shrines of Nabu and his wife

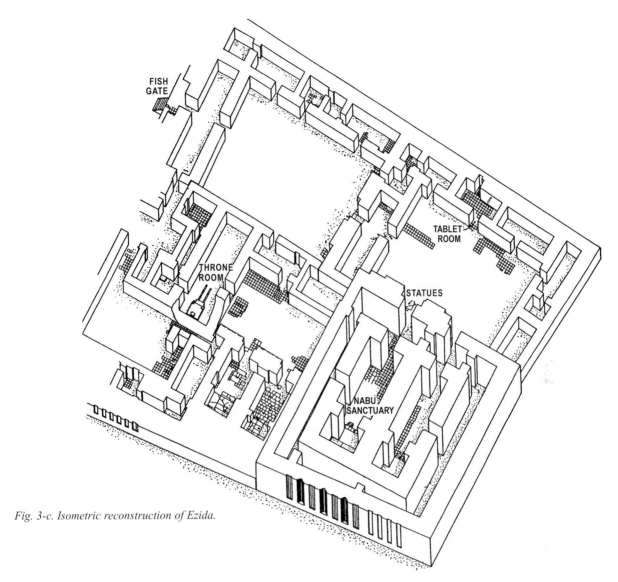

Fig. 3-c. Isometric reconstruction of Ezida.

Tashmetum. In this south-east quadrant is a room with a wide doorway and a little well in the back wall (NT12), which contained a number of tablets. We believe that it was used as the scriptorium or writing room. Nabu was of course the god of writing whose symbol was the stylus, and he became the custodian of a great many important documents by virtue of that office. Many tablets were both inscribed and kept here, including copies of earlier texts that were the equivalent of books in a modern library. Some of these temple library tablets were found here by us and others more recently by our Iraqi colleagues who are restoring the whole building.

In the north-west quadrant there was a second pair of shrines, identical with those of Nabu and Tashmetum but on a very much smaller scale. Next to the smaller shrines and opening off a small internal courtyard is what is obviously a throne room, identified by its stone dais and the tramlines in the floor in front. Such tramlines are characteristic of important reception rooms and were used to carry a sort of trolley brazier which could be advanced or retired according to the taste of the gentleman sitting at the

end (a colour illustration can be seen in Oates and Oates 2001: pl. 12c). The shrines had little foundation boxes let into the floor and sealed by small slabs of stone which made their presence quite obvious to the excavator. One of the entertaining ways of passing half an hour after work was to see whether there was anything in a box. Fig. 3-d shows the 1956 dig staff ranged around the room, watching one of our Sherqati workmen opening a box in which of course nothing was found. But it gives me a chance to illustrate Max Mallowan himself, the great man, together with his wife enjoying the scene from above.

The purpose of this curious pair of small shrines and the throne room which opened off the same courtyard is of some interest. We have tablets which describe a festival called the *akitu* festival conducted at Nimrud and reported by the responsible priest to the king who was then in Nineveh. These describe in some detail the course of events. The statue of Nabu was taken out of his own shrine, presumably the larger of the two at the southern end of the temple, in order to go hunting. He was then brought back to the bedchamber of the palace and his

Fig. 3-d. The 1956 expedition staff watch the excavation of a ritual deposit in one of the small shrines of Ezida. Agatha Christie reclines at the top of the trench, Max Mallowan is on the left of the picture, and Tariq Madhloom and David Oates are in the foreground. (Photograph J. Oates).

marriage was celebrated. In the Nabu temple itself, moreover, we found a tablet referring to a number of rooms in the building including a bedchamber. It is our belief that the ceremonies associated with the *akitu* festival were specifically provided for by this separate suite of rooms with its own small courtyard, the bedchamber, perhaps the throne room and the two twin shrines which reproduce the plan of the major temples and which were obviously for some special ceremony (see further discussion in Oates and Oates 2001: 119–23).

In the throne room were found a great many fragments of a group of unusually large tablets which proved to be the text of agreements, in fact, 'treaties', between Esarhaddon and various minor rulers on the Persian frontier to the south-east of Assyria, who agreed thereby to support the accession of Esarhaddon's son, Ashurbanipal. This in itself is a very interesting historical piece of evidence, and I do not think that it is entirely coincidental that these tablets were deliberately broken by the Medes (who sacked the place in 612 BC) on the throne base associated with the *akitu* festival, because it was by tradition, at least in Babylon, that it was at the New Year *akitu* festival that royal authority was confirmed formally by the god of the city.

Before we leave the Nabu temple I should mention that it was here on this site that we found almost the only good sequence of later occupation overlying the Assyrian buildings. First of all, in many of the Assyrian buildings all over the tell and indeed in Fort Shalmaneser also there was a layer of what we called squatter occupation, that is people who crept back into the buildings after the sack of Nimrud in 612, and appear to have eked out a miserable existence there. After them there came, at least on the evidence that we have found, a brief and probably not very extensive Achaemenid occupation in the sixth century, and after that, between 250 and 150 BC, a succession of small village houses, which fortunately we were able to date by those beautiful things—coins, which actually tell you the dates of the levels you are dealing with. A number of coins were found in the graves, enabling us to define the occupation as lasting from about 250 down to 150 BC which is roughly the date when the Parthians came into Mesopotamia. The graves and houses also provided very useful information in what I think remains the only well-stratified sequence of Hellenistic pottery known from northern Mesopotamia. Such well-dated information of course enables us to date many other sites which contain comparable material.

Just to the north of Ezida, the stone-paved roadway known as 'Shalmaneser Street' owing to the presence of stone lions bearing an inscription of Shalmaneser III, who completed much of the building work of his father, leads through the east gate into the outer town, an area of some 330 ha (nearly 820 acres), in the south-east corner of which are the two mounds known as Tulul al 'Azar. The overall plan (fig. 3-a) reveals both inner walls and an outer wall some 400 m to the west and 200 m to the north, shown by Felix Jones as part of the city wall. This constituted the outer defence of the *ekal mašarti* or arsenal, which Mallowan called Fort Shalmaneser owing to the Shalmaneser bricks found at the north gate. The outer walls on the west enclosed a very large parade or exercise ground (fig. 3-e). A small area of the northern outer wall has been excavated only in comparatively recent years by our Italian colleagues. We were never able to work there because it was all cultivated land, and in any case there was more than enough to do in excavating the main part of the building, which covered an area of about 300 × 200 m.

The northern part of the building is divided into four quadrants, two large outer courtyards, which were the ones more easily accessible from outside, and which were used principally for storerooms and particularly for workshops, and then to the south, a third quadrant which is subdivided with smaller courtyards. This was used for the storage of much more precious materials and it was in this area that we and the Italian expedition have found most of the vast quantity of ivories from this building. The fourth quadrant consists of a very large open parade ground with barrack rooms, each with an ablution room

Fig. 3-e. Reconstruction of Fort Shalmaneser (courtesy ILN *picture library).*

adjoining it, together with a residence which, from tablets found within it, we know to have been that of the *rab ekalli*, the chief officer of the whole establishment (rooms SE1–3, 6, 10, SW6). To the south is the throne room (T1) and further formal reception rooms as in the North-West Palace, to the west of which are domestic quarters (Area S).

The west outer wall stood to a height of over 3 m, but we were in fact able to count the individual courses in the adjacent fallen wall, enabling us to demonstrate that the original height of the walls was at least 7 m. From the west outer gate we managed to derive a small piece of history. Here the gateway and the antechamber had been paved with stone slabs covered with bitumen. But we noticed that although the slabs were apparently in good condition the

marks on the bitumen made by the passage of vehicles were not consistently in one direction. It followed that these bitumen-covered slabs had been relaid. In fact the whole roadway had been taken up and rebuilt.

I should mention that two attacks on Assyria were recorded in history: by the Medes in 614 and by the Medes together with the Babylonians in 612, and it is clear that in the interval the Assyrians felt a quite unjustified confidence attested not only in their lack of haste in repairing the gates of the arsenal but also because they campaigned in the south in 613. It is to that interval that we ascribe the repairs that we have noticed in Fort Shalmaneser. Moreover, on the outside of the same gateway, in the wall of a projecting tower, we observed a very deliberate hole. Here was an illustration in the flesh,

Fig. 3-f. Alabaster statue of Shalmaneser III in workshop NE 50, in situ where it had been brought for repair, ht. 1.03 m.

Fig. 3-g and 3-h. The Shalmaneser III throne base, in situ and detail of the central decoration.

as it were, of exactly the technique that the Assyrians can be seen on their reliefs to be employing to bring down the wall of a city that they are attacking. If you go to the Assyrian gallery you can find reliefs of the Assyrians attacking a city and with their picks in their hands digging away the base of the wall so the upper material would collapse. In fact at Nimrud the Assyrians at this point were hoist with their own petard.

Near the doorway between the north-east and south-east courtyards was found further evidence of the unprepared state in which the fortress was found at the time of the second attack in 612, because there was found a whole pile of the capstones which had been used to protect the sockets of the great outer and inner doors of the building (Oates and Oates 2001: fig. 97), so it was quite clear that the Assyrians were not in the least expecting a sudden attack. They were proceeding in quite a leisurely fashion to rebuild and repair the damage done by the first attack.

I mentioned that the northern two courtyards were devoted very largely to workshops. Several had benches along one of the walls which is exactly the same sort of bench that we used in the dig house to work at, with the same holes in the walls to hang things on and support racks. In Fort Shalmaneser the floor in front of the bench is paved, presumably because they were using liquids of some sort and didn't want to make the floor a morass of mud. One of the workshops yielded a statue of Shalmaneser III himself which had quite obviously been broken and brought in for repair (fig. 3-f). In the same room we found a very long (about 1.20 m) iron saw of the type that masons used for cutting blocks of stone. In fact when we found the statue the two parts of its broken corner had already been drilled with dowel holes running diagonally through, ready for repair. But the repair was obviously interrupted by the final sack.

Among the other objects from the storerooms of the outer two courtyards was a large piece of furniture originally encased partly in bronze with ivory defining the long seat and the armrest at one end encased in copper or bronze. The seat itself was decorated with shell inlay which we were able to recover because much of it was still lying in its original position although the wood had rotted away (Oates and Oates 2001: fig. 145).

Moving to the southern part of the *ekal mašarti,* to the house of the *rab ekalli* (Oates and Oates 2001: 164), we found not only his wine cellar (SW6) but other historical evidence of considerable interest. Obviously this was a store under the direct supervision of the superintendent of the building, and in among the wine jars we found tablets which recorded the rations of wine that were issued not just to individuals but to whole establishments, whole departments of government. A very large quantity for instance went to the Egyptian scribe. It didn't reflect his personal capacity, it reflected the number of people he had in his department and thereby its importance. So even from these ration issues, apparently so ordinary, one begins to get a picture of the underlying administration. One set of wine jars actually had on the top of them, perhaps fallen from the upper rooms, great lumps of a substance known as Egyptian blue which was actually used for the inlay in some of the more elaborate ivories. This must have been a precious material, kept under the *rab ekalli*'s supervision, but it also implies that at least some work on the ivories was being executed here at Nimrud.

At the very southern edge of the Fortress the later, seventh century king Esarhaddon had built an extension to the outer wall (represented by the whole of the shaded area on the plan). This included a massive stone façade at its base, and in particular a new stone postern gate which gave access both to the domestic area courtyard in the south-west of the building and to the parade ground outside, the exercise ground (but note that the latter doorway, which was found in 1963, is not shown on the reconstruction, fig. 3-e).

The whole of the south-west corner was cut off from the rest of the building by barred doors. This constituted the domestic or harem area, within which was a small throne room (S5) decorated with a procession of eunuch officers of the court, almost the only fresco of which we could recover any substantial design (Oates and Oates 2001: fig. 113). It is of interest that the figures entered the room from the south door, making a complete circuit around the room before approaching the throne at the other end, clearly a formal ritual that explains the positions of the doors in the larger throne rooms.

External decoration was carried out in the more durable material of glazed brick, and outside the doorway that led from the southern terrace into the southern part of the throne room suite we found a vast pile of broken glazed bricks which was put together largely by Julian Reade, first of all by working out the pattern on the dig and then by a long period of hard work in the Iraq Museum. The result was an enormous panel, now displayed in the Iraq Museum, with an inscription of Shalmaneser III, two representations of the king himself facing a sacred tree in the middle, two horned animals rampant on either side of another tree, and a frieze of targets and kneeling animals all the way around the outside (Oates and Oates 2001: fig. 112). Going through the doorway bearing this great decoration, one came into first an antechamber (T3) and then to the great throne room itself (T1). At the east end—all that we ever excavated—was an enormous throne base set in a niche in the east wall, and beside it the ablution slab which is a routine part of the furnishings of a room of that sort. The two large holes in the floor are secondary and were probably postholes needed to support the roof beams, probably after damage in the 614 attack.

The throne base makes a suitable piece with which to conclude (figs 3-g and 3-h). It consisted of two large limestone slabs, and was decorated all the way around with friezes of relief sculpture 25–30 cm high, depicting subject peoples from the provinces bringing in the various forms of tribute which went to support all this grandeur. On the front of the throne base is the most important scene which shows the meeting of the king of Assyria, Shalmaneser himself, and the king of Babylon, Marduk-zakir-shumi, through whom Shalmaneser had achieved considerable prestige by restoring him to the throne of Babylon. This scene is the demonstration of perhaps the highest peak of Shalmaneser's political career. Also depicted are the royal escort and long lines of bearers of tribute to the Assyrian king. One scene depicts a foreign ruler, with an attendant bearing his staff of office and

Fig. 3-i. The great raising of the throne base for transport to the Iraq Museum, with the very welcome assistance of the Iraq Petroleum Company, 1962.

another bearing a model of his city, and accompanied by a little boy who is obviously the ruler's son, whose fate would have been to be educated as a hostage at the Assyrian court. Among the tribute are elephants' tusks, great logs of cedar, jewellery, ingots and metal cauldrons.

I'm afraid I've overrun my time but I'll just show you one more scene, which represents one of the most alarming moments of my life (fig. 3-i). I won't tell you any more

about it but I think you can see the implications. We had terrible trouble with our epigraphist who was convinced there was an inscription on the underside of the slabs and insisted on standing underneath while this great (eight ton) weight was being hoisted up the 6 m height of the throne room walls. He was prevented from doing so in the end, and the throne base was safely dispatched to Baghdad. And for now that must be my last tribute to the Iraq Museum.

4   THE NIMRUD DATABASE PROJECT[1]

David Thomas

Introduction

Archaeologists most frequently use computers as sophisticated word-processors, yet this is an under-exploitation of the many potential uses of computing within archaeology: from analysing data to manipulating images and building virtual models of ancient buildings, as Professor Paley describes in his paper.

The Nimrud Database Project aimed to create a computerized database of the objects from Nimrud, focusing initially on excavated data arising from the BSAI excavations from 1949–63 and related post-excavation studies. Objects from Nimrud are scattered around the world, in over 60 museums, institutions and collections, which inhibits their study. By collating data on the objects in one database, and making it easily accessible to researchers, we hope to facilitate further work on these important finds and that some of the inevitable gaps in the records will be filled, errors and omissions corrected, and missing data and objects located.

Collaborative Work

It must be stressed from the outset that the Nimrud Database Project is a collaborative project, and as such, it is reliant on the hard work of many people. It was initiated and is being co-ordinated by Dr John Curtis and the computing work I have been doing is highly dependent on the work of people such as Dr Jeremy Black, Dr Georgina Herrmann, Helen McDonald, Jenny Oates and Christopher Walker, to name but a few. My part in the project has been funded by two grants from the British School of Archaeology in Iraq (BSAI), and we are grateful for their continuing support.

A Brief Introduction to the Computing Part of the Project

A database is an organized collection of related information, such as that derived from an excavation. The Nimrud Database was created using Microsoft ACCESS 2000, which is a powerful relational database available on PCs. As Andersen states:

'The principle behind a relational database is that the information is divided into separate stacks of logically-related data, each of which is stored in a separate table... Once the information is arranged in separate tables, you can view, edit, add and delete information with on-line forms; search for and retrieve some or all the information with queries; and print information as customized reports' (1999: 52).

The main advantages of storing data in several related tables, rather than one large unspecific table are:

- Reduced data redundancy and increased efficiency, which speeds up searches and queries and means that the database requires less disk space.
- Simpler storage of data in smaller, more specific tables.
- Greater consistency and accuracy when making changes or corrections, because you only need to make the change in one place.

The increased efficiency and simpler tables can be illustrated by comparing the following tables.

Table 1, a single large table is how many projects without a proper relational database record their data, but you will

Table 1

ND No.	Object	Material	Base Diam.	Rim Diam.	BM Acc. No.	BM Acc. Date	Drawing No.
ND-00189	Pot	Clay	8.5	18.2			1949/7
ND-08823	Bead	Carnelian					
ND-09122	Buckle	Gold			100324	12/1/59	1958/21
ND-12009	Pot	Clay	12.5	16.1			1963/18
ND-13220	Ring	Copper			110991	23/9/65	

---

[1] The database proposed in this paper remains at the formative stage. A 'stage two' funding proposal was prepared for BSAI to submit to the British Academy, but it was not adopted. Nevertheless, this paper is included here as a record of work being undertaken at the time of the conference.

notice that 14 of the 40 cells contain no data/are irrelevant. This amounts to 35% of the table, which is not significant with so few entries, but will become a potential problem as more data are added.

It is better to sub-divide this large table into four smaller, more specific tables (note that these 4 tables require 31 cells and do not have any empty/irrelevant cells):

Pots

ND No.	Object	Material	Base Diam.	Rim Diam.
ND-00189	Pot	Clay	8.5	18.2
ND-12009	Pot	Clay	12.5	16.1

10 cells

Nimrud Objects in the BM

ND No.	BM Acc. No.	BM Acc. Date
ND-09122	100324	12/1/59
ND-13220	110991	23/9/65

6 cells

Drawings

ND No.	Drawing No.
ND-00189	1949/7
ND-09122	1958/21
ND-12009	1963/18

6 cells

Miscellaneous Objects

ND No.	Object	Material
ND-08823	Bead	Clay
ND-09122	Buckle	Gold
ND-13220	Ring	Copper

9 cells

One of the central tenets of Relational Database design is that each record in a table must be unique in some respect. In these examples, the Nimrud Number field is the unique, or Primary Key field.

All the small tables can be related to each other because they all have a common field—Nimrud Number. It is therefore possible to create a query that will combine information from several different tables—for example, you could easily find out the accession number and type of drawn objects in the BM, by selecting the relevant information from the different tables:

ND No.	Object	Drawing No.	BM Acc. No.
ND-09122	Buckle	1958/21	100324

Query 1: Drawn Nimrud Objects in the BM

The Structure of the Nimrud Database

The way the different tables of the Nimrud database relate to each other, and their contents, are shown in an Entity Relationship (or ER) Diagram (Appendix I). Although this ER Diagram may seem dauntingly complex at first, it will hopefully become more comprehensible when its characteristics are explained and groups of tables are looked at in detail.

Each box represents a table; the caption in the black band at the top of each box is the name of the table, while the subsequent list contains the table's field names. The field names are abbreviated but hopefully relatively intuitive. The lines between the boxes show which fields link to each other, while the 1 or 00 indicate the type of link.

Most links or relationships between tables are either one-to-one (where a record appears once in one table and only once in another table, such as in most cases with Nimrud Numbers) or one-to-many relationships (where a record in one table can appear many times in another table, such as in the Room Register table, where one Building Abbreviation can appear numerous times in association with different Room Numbers).

Object Tables—ND Number, ND Ceramics, ND Sealings, ND Small Finds, ND Tablets, Corr Ceramics and Corr Small Finds
Central to these tables, and to the database in general, is the Nimrud Number table. This core table contains basic information about an object, its provenance and current location, and useful summary information in the form of tick-boxes, such was whether it has been published, photographed, details checked and corrected.

Different types of objects yield different types of data, so I have created separate tables for Ceramics, Sealings, Tablets and other Small Finds. The data recorded include a mixture of measurements and descriptive text. The 'Corr' tables allow researchers to record corrected measurements, where they find that the original records include a mistake.

The Rogue Object Numbers Table is considered in detail below.

Object Location Tables—BM Acc Obj, Non BM Acc, Location, ND Obj Moves, Missing Obj and ND BM Catalogue
As stated in the introduction, part of the reason for creating the Nimrud database is that so many of the objects from

Nimrud are now scattered around the world. The database aims to provide an up-to-date record of where objects are thought to be, or where they were last seen. This will enable specialists to search the database to find out, for example, where all the beads from Nimrud are and whom they would need to contact to gain access to them.

This part of the project is heavily reliant on people volunteering information as to exactly what is held in the collections they are responsible for. It is hoped that by collating this information, we will be able to relocate some of the objects whose precise whereabouts are currently somewhat vague.

At the moment, much of the data in the Nimrud database relates to objects in the British Museum, but we hope that other institutions will provide any additional data they have, allowing us to import their data and/or modify the design of the database to incorporate them.

Drawings and Photos Tables
The ND Neg, Building Abbrev, Room Reg and ND Plans tables relate to photographs taken on site and building plans. As such, they focus on the buildings rather than the objects, and thus cannot be linked to the central Nimrud Number table.

Data on the object drawings and photos are included in the ND Drawings, ND Obj Neg and ND Obj Prints tables, and linking or Junction Tables ND-Obj Neg and ND Obj Print. These Junction Tables are required because it is possible for a photograph to contain several different objects, and for an object to appear in several different photographs, thus creating a many-to-many relationship. ACCESS cannot cope with many-to-many relationships, because the Nimrud Number field no longer contains unique, single pieces of data.

ND No.	Season	Obj. Neg. No.
ND-01119, ND-11087	1949	12
ND-01119	1949	13

The way around this problem is to create a Junction Table that lists each unique piece of information. Although this results in a marginal increase in the size of the table, it means that the data can be sorted and queried properly.

ND No.	Season	Obj. Neg. No.
ND-01119	1949	12
ND-11087	1949	12
ND-01119	1949	13

References Tables—Book Bibliog, Journal Bibliog and WWW Ref
The final group of tables include information about published data from the Nimrud excavations and post-

excavation studies. Although these tables are not currently related to the other tables, we feel that they provide a potentially useful additional resource to researchers, especially because the Nimrud database is initially concentrating on unpublished material.[2]

The WWW Ref table includes links to websites containing information about Nimrud. As funding of libraries is cut back, the World Wide Web is becoming an increasingly useful and important resource for researchers—just typing 'Nimrud' into the Goggle search engine in Yahoo yields 2,340 web page matches!

It should be remembered, however, that the content of many websites is often less rigorously peer-reviewed and sometimes inaccurate or misleading, which is why this table includes a check-box to show whether the web page has been visited or not.

Forms — User-friendly data viewing and data entry

The tables at the core of ACCESS databases are not a particularly convenient format in which to either view or enter data, so we have created a series of forms to ease these processes (Appendix II). The forms, like the tables, have drop-down lists, where appropriate. These lists allow the person doing data entry to select an option from a pre-defined list, although they are not restricted to items on the lists. The advantages of drop-down lists are that they help to standardize and speed up data entry. Several fields, such as ND No. are also formatted so that the data can only be entered in a standardized and consistent way.

We have also designed what is known as a 'switchboard' or user-friendly front page (Appendix III). The switchboard allows the user to chose from a series of option buttons, which link to forms. The user can thus avoid becoming immersed in the structure of the database, which might seem a bit daunting to someone unfamiliar with ACCESS. That said, it is very beneficial if the user has some understanding of how the database is structured and why.

Problems Encountered During the Database Design and Data Entry

Database Design
There is no such thing as 'the perfect database design' and some of you may well think of improvements that could

2 We are very grateful to Joan and David Oates for supplying us with a copy on disk of the bibliography from their recent book on Nimrud; this bibliography has formed the basis for these tables.

be made to this one. Where possible, we will try to incorporate feedback, so that the database is efficient and user-friendly—for example, we are currently in the process of designing forms specifically for people entering data about ivories and duck weights.

I am aware of some compromises that have been made between the theory and practice of database design, especially considering that ACCESS is primarily designed for business rather than archaeology. I feel, however, that these compromises are relatively minor and that they could be modified later, if necessary.

Ideally, you design the database before a project starts collecting data and you tailor your paper recording system to fit the database and to ease data entry. In reality, however, it is still difficult to persuade some projects to do this in the year 2002, and it is obviously impossible to do this for projects that took place half a century ago. The result has to be a compromise between how the data were recorded and how a modern database can deal with such data.

Data Entry

Trials have shown that it is not practical to scan the archive of registers, using character recognition software, because the pages are old, include blemishes and contain unusual characters which the software has difficulty recognizing. Much of the paper archive that has already been computerized has been entered as lists in Word documents or Excel spreadsheets, or into Mr Walker's Apple Macintosh database. A large part of the project, therefore, after the design and refinement of the database, has been to 'massage' these data into the appropriate tables in the Nimrud Database.

This is an on-going process and requires time-consuming and fiddly editing and formatting, before the data can be imported into the database. The imported data then need to be cross-checked and often modified, so that they appear in the most appropriate and logical part of the database.

The following table indicates the amount of data currently entered or imported into the database:

Type of Data	Number of Records in the Database
ND Numbers (Objects)	> 3,000
Site Photograph Nos	750
Object Photo Negative Nos	225
Object Print Nos	400
BM Accessioned Objects	750
Non-BM Accessioned Objects	800

Rogue Numbers

The Rogue Object Numbers table, which was mentioned in passing earlier, caters for some of the anomalies that

the Nimrud records have thrown up. As has already been explained, each table must consist of a series of unique records, otherwise the database will not function properly.

We all know, however, than when you are in the field, it is often tempting to assign a, b, c, etc. rather than a new object number to a collection of objects. Similarly, some objects are never numbered, or lose their numbers.

These objects, of which there are currently over 1000, violate the requirements of the database and are thus recorded in the Rogue Object Number table, where they have been assigned an arbitrary running number until they can be given a new ND Number and fitted back into the database.

Potential Future Work

The amount of potential future work for the Nimrud Database Project is obviously enormous. The project has initially concentrated on the unpublished material from BSAI excavations; we are still adding data from the archives, and from the many post-excavation studies and publications, such as those on the ivories and tablets.

There have, of course, also been many other excavations, ranging from Layard's in the 1840s to the on-going work of the Iraqi Department of Antiquities. No Nimrud database would be truly complete without including data from these other sources, although incorporating different projects' recording systems within the one database would be challenging, to say the least.

The continual updating of the database presents a significant dilemma as to how best to make it available to interested scholars. One option would be to issue the database on CDs periodically, or to deposit it as a downloadable file with the Archaeological Data Service in York, for example; another is to adapt the design of the database to make it available directly over the Internet and to persuade an institution to host it on their website.

We are also considering how to provide information to people who are not familiar with Access, or who do not have the required computer resources. One option is to export the relevant data as delimited text or Excel files.

The original object registers and project archives are also of obvious interest and academic value. We hope to scan these and make them available on CD, since they are unchanging and thus better suited to being distributed in this way. Scanning the Object Registers would have the additional benefit of conserving the paper records, which obviously deteriorate over time. Similarly, it would be beneficial to scan all the project photographs and drawings, if resources allowed.

Conclusion

This paper has aimed to provide an outline of the Nimrud Database Project, demonstrate its worth and the potential for future collaboration and information exchange, without submerging the reader in a sea of computing jargon. We are sure that a lot of Nimrud data exists that we are currently unaware of and we hope that through increased publicity and the expansion of the Nimrud Database Project, these data will become more accessible and useful as a basis for the further study of the objects from Nimrud.

Appendix I: Nimrud Database Entity Relationship Diagram

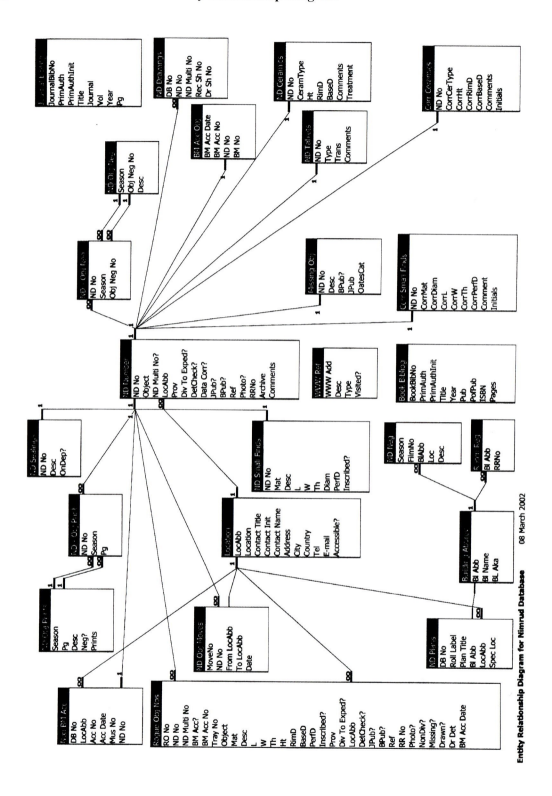

Entity Relationship Diagram for Nimrud Database   08 March 2002

Appendix II: The ND Number Form

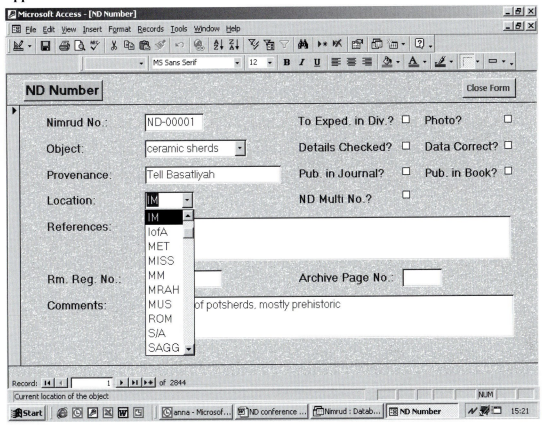

Appendix III: The Nimrud Database Switchboard

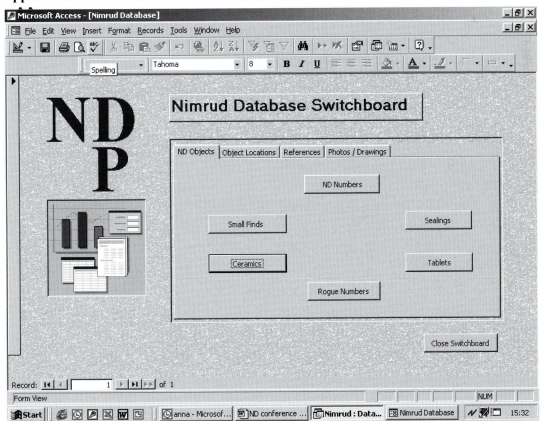

5 THE WORK OF THE IRAQ DEPARTMENT OF ANTIQUITIES AT NIMRUD

Manhal Jabr

The work of the British at Nimrud in the nineteenth and twentieth centuries was complemented and expanded by the Iraqi excavations at Nimrud. These were under the direction of Behnam Abu es-Soof from 1956 until 1959; he worked in the North-West Palace. From 1969 until the present the Iraq Department of Antiquities has been conducting both restoration and excavation work at Nimrud under a variety of directors. The first was Muyesser Said al-Iraqi from 1969 to 1970. He continued the clearing and cleaning of Rooms L and M in the North-West Palace, which had been begun some ten years earlier. In order to carry out this work, he was therefore obliged to re-excavate whole rooms. The reliefs from these rooms were transferred to the newly opened Mosul Museum in 1974 (Al-Iraqi 1982).

The second to fourth seasons (1971 –1974) were directed by Hazim Abd-el Hamid, who was also director of the Mosul Museum. He excavated Room F and the Central Courtyard in the North-West Palace. Rooms R, C, J, I, K and H were cleaned and the fallen reliefs were reinstalled. Said al-Iraqi was director for the next three seasons (1975 –1977) and cleared Rooms X, T, S, W and V. One of the most important finds during these seasons was the clearing of Well AJ to a depth of 26 m. They found there over a hundred pieces of ivory of excellent craftsmanship, some still covered with gold leaf. The ivories were published by Fuad Safar (Safar and al-Iraqi 1987) with a complete catalogue and photographs. These ivories are some of the best examples of Phoenician, Egyptianizing and Syrian art. In 1978 Abdullah Amin Agha took over the excavations, and concentrated on the Nabu Temple. This work was continued from 1985 to 1987 by Muzahim Mahmud Hussein, but from 1988 to 1991 Hussein moved to the North-West Palace (see chapter 12a by Muzahim Mahmud Hussein).

The excavations of British, Swiss and Italian teams at Nimrud are the subject of other papers in this volume by Julian Reade, Anthony Green, David Oates, Paolo Fiorina and John Curtis. Recent expeditions have been accompanied by Iraqi representatives such as Sabri Shukri and Izeddin as-Sandouq. Here too, Iraqis have made a substantial contribution: the reports they submitted after each season, accompanied by sketches of objects and architectural plans, have proved most informative.

6   RESTORATION WORK AT NIMRUD

Rabi'a al-Qaissi

In 1956 the Department of Antiquities embarked on a project of restoration works at the major archaeological sites of Ur, Babylon, Ashur, Nineveh and Nimrud, in addition to other sites such as Hatra and Samarra. This was instigated by a desire to preserve the substance of the ancient structures, and also to convey to the visitor a more vivid perception of the original plan of the buildings.

At Nimrud, Layard's excavations in the nineteenth century, and then the British archaeological expedition in the 1950s, necessitated a massive restoration work. Following consultation with Max Mallowan, the North-West Palace of king Ashurnasirpal II was considered to be top priority for preservation. Work commenced in restoring the northern façade of the throne room in 1956; this involved the re-erection of two large winged bulls, two winged genies, and the four smaller winged bulls that flank the gates to the throne room (figs 6-a–d, 10-h; Ainachi 1956).

The reconstruction of the throne room façade was the first work of its kind to be undertaken on an ancient site in Iraq (Shukri 1956). Support walls for the bulls made with stone and cement were built and concrete beams were erected to support roofings, made also from concrete to protect the sculptures from the elements (fig. 6-e). The walls and the beams were coated with cement and covered with mud-coloured paint. Missing areas of the reliefs were completed with plaster and painted the colour of the stone (Ainachi 1956).

In 1959 and 1960 further work was carried out inside the throne room. This consisted of re-excavating Layard's trenches and included parts that had not been previously planned. Fragments of reliefs were discovered and were replaced in their original positions (Abu es-Soof 1963). In the centre of the throne room, numerous fragments of painted plaster, which must have originally decorated the upper part of the walls were found. Other objects were also found in the debris of the room especially near the throne base, such as bronze nails, ivory fragments and a fragment of a stone tablet of Ashurnasirpal (Abu es-Soof 1963). The process of re-excavating Layard's trenches in many parts of the palace, revealing many surprising finds, was initiated by Mallowan and followed by the excavators from the Department of Antiquities.

In the 1973/74 season, the glazed decoration that was found in courtyard Y was reassembled and then re-erected in the its original place over the gateway from Room F (fig. 6-f).

In 1974 the Department of Antiquities went deeper down in Well AJ, which had originally been partially excavated by Mallowan, and uncovered the most remarkable and unique ivories. A catalogue of the finds was published in 1987 (Safar and al-Iraqi 1987).

Excavations and restorations continued in the rest of the palace and in 1988, while clearing the debris and tidying the brick paving of Room MM, workers stumbled on the first of the queens' tombs (Damerji 1999). This remarkable find inspired the excavators to continue digging in parts of the Harem, which had not been excavated by either Layard or Mallowan. They were rewarded in the next two seasons with two more tombs, one in Room 42 and another in Room 49, where about 1000 gold objects were found. In 1991 a fourth tomb was discovered in Room 71 (Hussein and Suleiman 2000), in which glazed pots and bronze and silver vessels were found.

The 1992 season continued with the excavation of a courtyard (80) and the rooms around it. Beneath Rooms 74 and 75, an unusual structure was discovered, a narrow vaulted passage (under room 74) leading to three small vaulted rooms. Many remarkable finds were discovered here including cylinder seals, numerous beads, glazed pottery, and an inscribed stone tablet of Shalmaneser III .

In the south-east corner of Court 80, a well was discovered. Inside it, over 400 bodies were found manacled with iron chains. There were also a number of small finds such as beads, cylinder and stamp seals, small ivory vessels etc. (see Hussein, this volume).

Excavation and restoration works came to a halt at Nimrud during most of the 1990s owing to the political situation. Work was resumed in 2001, beginning with the Ishtar temple (see Hussein article, this volume)

The other major building that was re-excavated and restored was the Nabu Temple, first excavated by Mallowan. Work began in 1976, starting at the Fish Gate, and in the following years continued throughout the temple. Many finds and tablets were unearthed after the clearing of the debris from the centre of the rooms. After clearance was completed, the walls were capped with modern baked brick to protect them from further

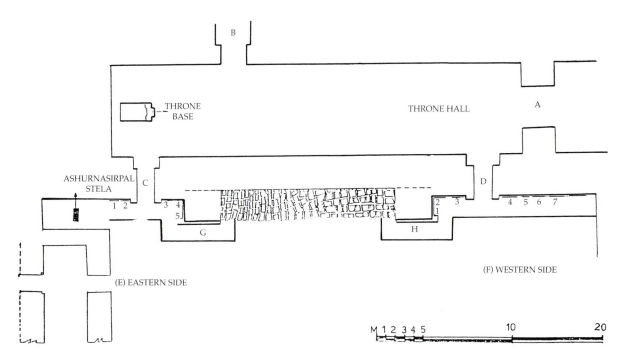

Fig. 6-a. Plan of the Throne Room façade of the North-West Palace of Ashurnasirpal II.

Fig. 6-b. Reconstructed Throne Room façade with winged bulls.

Fig. 6-c. Arched doorway with winged bulls in reconstructed façade on the left in 6-b.

Fig. 6-d. Winged bulls in situ on either side of arched gate in reconstructed façade.

Fig. 6-e. Reconstruction in progress.

Fig. 6-f.Part of the northern façade of Courtyard Y, entrance F with winged bulls. The arch is of modern construction.

deterioration following a directive from the Department of Antiquities.

Some restoration work also took place in Fort Shalmaneser, and the stone revetment of Esarhaddon was re-exposed. Work on the north side of the ziggurrat was undertaken. Clearance of the debris and earth revealed eight courses of stone blocks, and the foundation of a round tower in the north-west corner.

The Antiquities Department continues to carry out work on the major public buildings of Nimrud.

7 ITALIAN EXCAVATIONS AT NIMRUD-KALḪU CHRONOLOGICAL AND STRATIGRAPHICAL PROBLEMS

Paolo Fiorina

Excavations were carried out at Nimrud from October to the end of December in 1987, 1988 and 1989 by a team from the Centro Scavi di Torino per il Medio Oriente e l'Asia, as part of a five-year programme of targetted investigation of certain parts of the city and the determination of its layout as whole. The first step was the plotting of a traverse covering the whole of the lower city.

Nimrud occupies an area of about 3.6 km² and is surrounded by walls. Apart from the higher areas, occupied by the acropolis in the south-west corner and Fort Shalmaneser in the south-east corner, the ground is virtually flat. These higher areas comprised some forty squares and courtyards surrounded by buildings. Excavation and examination of the city's walls and the identification of its gates were among the most interesting problems concerning its urban development.

Walls and Gates

We began in 1987 with the eastern city walls at their junction with the external wall of Fort Shalmaneser. A trial trench was opened at the point where the city wall could be presumed to have joined the wall that must have encircled a large area around the Fort. The surface evidence for this wall takes the form of a straight even mound encircling a flat, almost rectangular depression around the Fort. This corner of the city, forming an angle of slightly less than 90°, was investigated during the first season. Chronologically the city wall belongs to Ashurnasirpal II (Level 1), and the external wall of the Fort belongs to Shalmaneser III (Level 2). The wall parallel to the external enceinte is later still and can probably be attributed to the son of Shalmaneser III, Adad-nirari III (Level 3) who carried out some rebuilding and renovation in the Fort itself. In the northern part of the

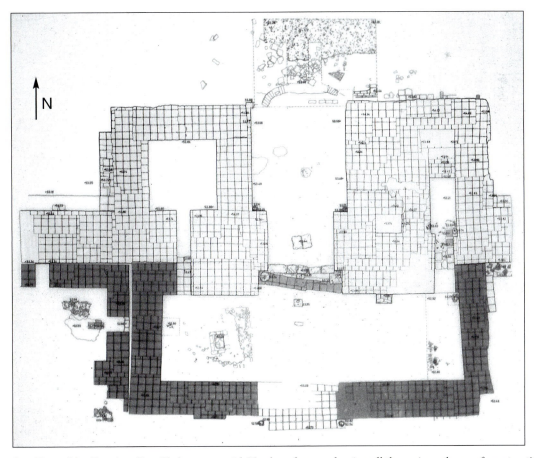

Fig. 7-a. Plan of the Gate into Fort Shalmaneser, with North at the top, showing all the various phases of construction.

Fig. 7-b. The gate: view from the east.

external wall there was only one gate from the lower city into the level area around the Fort. This gate was excavated during the 1988 campaign (fig. 7-a).

Shalmaneser phase (Level 2) (figs 7-a–b)
Those approaching the gate from the city had to pass under a semi-elliptical archway. Traces of this arch were

Fig. 7-c. Clay foundation figure.

found in the form of one radiating voussoir, collapsed on the floor. The external side of the gate was covered by a half-arch. No traces of a pavement or of an approach road were found here, but only fragments of bricks. The gateway was flanked by two towers. There was a small room within the thickness of the western tower. A doorway in its southern wall connected this room with the gate-chamber. The original floor of the tower room was laid 20 cm above the mud-brick floor of the gate-chamber. In the eastern tower there were traces of stairs along the eastern and northern walls giving access to the tower's roof. The floor of the external gateway was completely paved with mud bricks. The entrance was closed by a door: two pivot-stones were found at the corners and a rectangular stone with a central rectangular hole would have housed the long bolt closing the door.

Post-Shalmaneser phase (Level 3) (fig. 1)
A large east-west room was added to the entrance inside the earlier gateway, and the floor belonging to this phase has completely eroded as it lay just a few centimetres below the surface. Only one row of mud bricks belonging to the wall of the gate chamber came to light. This phase can probably be attributed to Adad-nirari III, but might belong to Esarhaddon as both kings carried out restoration in the Fort.

614–612 BC phase (Level 5) (figs 7-a and -c)
The gate was probably not seriously damaged during the attack of 614 BC. The paving of the external floor of the gate was repaired under Sin-shar-ishkun using complete and fragmentary baked bricks. Four foundation boxes were found under the floor. The larger was full of small bronze weapons. Also in the boxes were two unbaked clay male figures with bronze ornaments (fig. 7-c).

Squatters' phase (Level 6) (fig. 7-a)
A mud-brick wall was poorly constructed across the threshold some 15 cm above the repaving of the floor. The

Fig. 7-d. Ivory openwork plaque showing the hind quarters
of a striding winged sphinx.

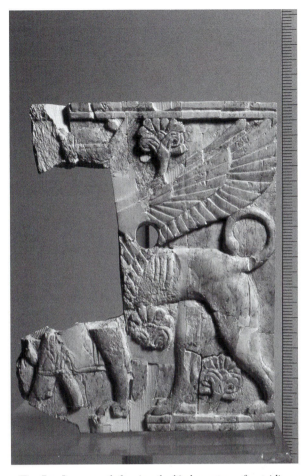

Fig. 7-e. Ivory panel showing the hind quarters of a striding
winged sphinx.

walls of the gate were still standing. The collapse of the
external arch of the gate probably belongs to this phase.

Post-Assyrian to Achaemenid phase (Level 7)
In the northern part of the gate there were three large pits
completely filled with pottery. This pottery is only slightly
different from classic Neo-Assyrian pottery. It seems that
the carinated shapes become more rounded and more
closely resembled Achaemenid pottery. The fabric is finer
and smoother than the classical Neo-Assyrian pottery.

Fort Shalmaneser

Shalmaneser phase (Level 2)
In the original phase of the south-west area of the Fort there
is a large courtyard paved with stone slabs and flanked by
two completely excavated rooms (Room A1, called SW 36
by Mallowan, and Room A2 at right-angles to A1); a small
part of three other rooms was also excavated. Near the
northern corner of the court a section of black and white
wall-painting had collapsed onto the floor.

Esarhaddon (Level 3)
During the reign of Esarhaddon, Fort Shalmaneser
became an *ekal māšarti*. The courtyard was divided into

five rooms and its stone pavement was partially repaired
with bricks. All the other rooms had mud-plastered
floors.

Sin-shar-ishkun phase (Level 5)
Some architectural differences were noted at Fort
Shalmaneser during this phase: only one door of Room
A1 (ex-SW 36) was used in this level, connecting the
room to the original south-west courtyard; the other three
doorways were completely blocked.

To this period belong all the objects found during the
excavations. Indeed in Room A2 there were four
categories of object. About 1,150 complete, almost
complete and fragmentary ivories were brought to light
(figs 7-d–e). Of these, some 90% were Phoenician in
style and the remaining 10% were Syrian. Not a single
fragment of Assyrian ivory was found here. Some 900
pieces of faience inlay (fig. 7-f) were found in the eastern
part of the entrance to Room A2, belonging to sphinx or
genii wings, wigs, lotus blossoms, sphinx bodies and
geometrical shapes. In the eastern part of the room there
were three independent groups of armour scales. They
are similar in shape but of different sizes, possibly
indicating that the scales were produced in this part of the
room, and were only subsequently connected to each

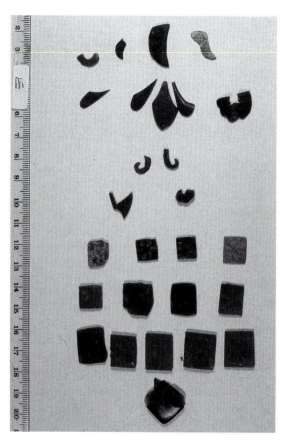

Fig. 7-f. Vitreous paste inlays.

found; the floor nearby was plastered with fragments of bricks and pebbles and the filling was very rich in sherds. The second room was only partially excavated and its floor was not cleared.

Conclusions

There are many questions that remain to be resolved. A new interpretation of the original function in Level 2 of the south-western part of the Fort seems to be suggested by its floor paved with slabs, fragments of wall-painting in the courtyard, the two doors connecting Room A1 (ex-SW 36) with the courtyard, the thresholds of these two doors in baked brick (the threshold of Room A2 was of mud plaster) and the baked bricks of the platform inside Room A1 with a stamped inscription of Shalmaneser on their upper surface. These features seem to point more to an official function than to a store. We could suppose that this area was temporarily used as a throne room at the beginning of the construction of the Fort. To test this hypothesis, it would be necessary to make a new sounding at the south-east corner of the south-west area connecting it with the throne room of the Fort.

No traces of squatter occupation were found in the Fort Shalmaneser structures excavated by the Italian Expedition. The presence of squatters is attested solely by a wall blocking the gate of the external wall of the Fort.

An important post-Assyrian settlement is attested by a large house found in the western corner of the external wall of the Fort, in two pits of Level 7 of the gate and in the kitchen with ovens found in Fort Shalmaneser. It has recently been established that the pottery found here has close parallels with the Median and Achaemenid pottery found at Tell Barri (Kahat) (P.E. Pecorella, pers. comm.).

other. In the central part of the room was a brazier made in iron and bronze, shaped to resemble a city wall with towers (Fiorina 1998; Oates and Oates 2001: colour plate 12c). In the western part of the room there were 175 shells (*xantus gravis*), one of which shows unfinished decoration with three horsemen (Fiorina 2001).

Post-Assyrian to Achaemenid phase (Level 7)
Just to the west of Room A1 (ex-SW 36) two rooms were unearthed: in one of these a row of six adjacent ovens was

8   THE BRITISH MUSEUM EXCAVATIONS AT NIMRUD IN 1989

John Curtis

I will not speak for very long because these excavations are already fully published in *Iraq* volume LV (Curtis *et al.* 1993) and there is not much to add. We will review as briefly as we can the context of the excavation and what was found. The background to this project is that between 1983 and 1986 a British Museum expedition worked at six different sites in the Eski Mosul Dam Salvage Project, three of them being Late Assyrian or post-Assyrian.[1] These were the sites of Qasrij Cliff, Khirbet Qasrij and Khirbet Khatuniyeh (Curtis 1989; Curtis and Green 1997). By 1989 we felt ready to move on to one of the major Assyrian sites and look at the problems encountered in an urban context as opposed to the rural contexts which we had been investigating up until then. The obvious choice was Nimrud in view of the longstanding association of the British Museum and the British School of Archaeology with that site, and the fact that all the Nimrud records are in the British Museum.[2] We selected for excavation Room T20 in Fort Shalmaneser. The excavation was on a small scale because we were at the same time excavating at the nearby site of Balawat. There was unfortunately only one season of excavation in autumn 1989[3] as the project was interrupted by the Gulf War in 1991 and it has not yet been possible to return.

The Nimrud excavation was focused on Room T20 in the south-east corner of Fort Shalmaneser, in the vicinity of the state apartments (fig. 8-a). This room was selected because it was believed to be previously unexcavated. It therefore represented a chance of obtaining a complete room assemblage from Fort Shalmaneser and held out the possibility of giving us an accurate stratigraphic record and perhaps more information about the sequence of occupation in Fort Shalmaneser. Also, the next door room

T10 had been completely excavated by the British School expedition under David Oates and interesting discoveries had been made. They included a large number of heavily burnt ivories and the long bones of an elephant, which of course is of particular significance for those interested in ivories, pieces of carbonized wood, bronze and iron armour scales, and fragments of shells with Neo-Hittite hieroglyphs and designs (Mallowan 1966: II, 451–52). It was hoped that finds of similar interest might be found in Room T20.

The strategy for the excavation of Room T20 was to leave a baulk across the middle of the room, partly to provide a stratigraphic check on the deposits in the room but also to retain some support for the high walls on either side. In the event this proved to be very necessary. During our season there was particularly inclement weather and a great deal of rain, so much so that the normally dry wadi to the east of Fort Shalmaneser became a raging torrent that our workmen were unable to cross (fig. 8-b). The heavy rain also affected the stability of the mudbrick walls surrounding the room, and caused the partial collapse of the wall on the north side. A large section of the surface of the wall to a thickness of about the width of a complete brick (i.e. 30–40 cm) crashed down onto the floor of the trench. Fortunately nobody was injured in this incident, but it underlined the necessity of making the walls safe which was done by removing more of the unstable brickwork that had not already fallen down. Altogether the room was found to measure approximately 18 m east–west by 4.5 m north–south, and the walls were preserved to a height of 4–5 m. We calculated on the basis of the fallen walling that they had originally been at least 8 m high. Contrary to expectations it was discovered that the British School expedition had in fact dug a 1.5 m wide trench next to the west wall of T20 (not marked on the published plan). This frustrated our hopes of obtaining a complete room assemblage, but this trench was actually not dug down to the original floor, only to a later secondary floor. Altogether, it is estimated that by the end of the British Museum excavation more than half the fill had been removed from this large room and the original floor level had been reached in about one third of the room.

We discovered that there was in fact clear evidence for two floors. The lower floor was made of beaten earth and was pale brown in colour, while about 10 cm above it was a white plaster floor. We concluded that the earlier floor dated from the foundation of the building in the time of Shalmaneser III (858–824 BC) while the floor above it

---

[1] The British Museum expedition also excavated the Hellenistic sites of Tell Deir Situn and Grai Darki (Curtis *et al.* 1987–88) and a ruined church known as Khirbet Deir Situn (Curtis 1997b).

[2] The excavation would not have been possible without the help and collaboration of our Iraqi colleagues, in particular Dr Muayyad Said Damerji, Mr Manhl Jabr, Mr Muzahim Mahmud and our representative Mr Fadhil Abbas Hamdani.

[3] The team included John Curtis, Dominique Collon, Anthony Green, Georgina Herrmann, Ann Searight (illustrator), David Tucker, Leri Davies, Diane Dollery (conservator), Peter Dollery and Simon James. During the course of the season we were privileged to receive visits from Lady Mallowan, Rachel Maxwell-Hyslop and Helen McDonald. Throughout the season we stayed at the Nineveh dig-house in Mosul which we shared with the team from the University of Turin led by Paolo Fiorina and Angelo Ghiroldi.

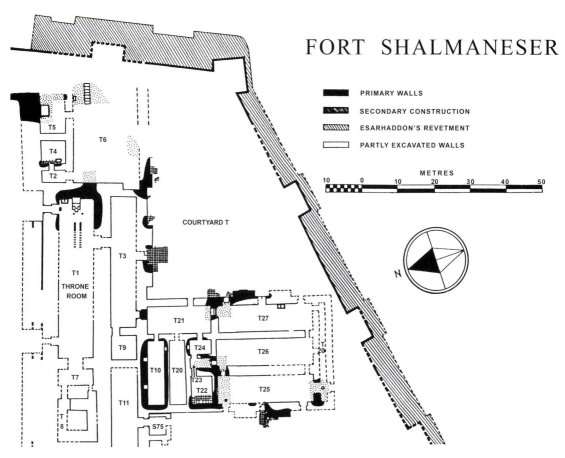

Fig. 8-a. Plan of south-east corner of Fort Shalmaneser showing location of Room T20. (From Mallowan 1966: plan VIII).

Fig. 8-b. Flood water in normally dry wadi to the east of Fort Shalmaneser in 1989.

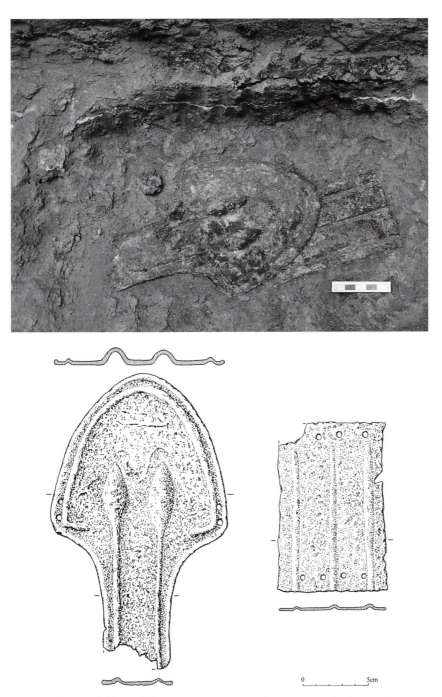

Fig. 8-c and d. Bronze blinker ornament corroded to a rectangular bronze plate.
Blinker ornament and corrugated plate. Drawings by Ann Searight.

probably dated from the time of Esarhaddon (680–669 BC), who is known from inscriptions to have done some restoration and building work in Fort Shalmaneser.[4]

If our supposition about the dating of the floors is correct, then the 10 cm deposit between the two floors should pre-date the reign of Esarhaddon. This layer, which consisted of a fine, soft pale brown deposit, contained a number of interesting objects, including items of horse harness (figs 8-c and -d). A sole-shaped blinker ornament in bronze is decorated with lotus buds and has a pair of holes on either side for attachment probably to a leather base. Such blinker ornaments are also known in ivory and stone from Nimrud (Orchard 1967: pls XIII–XIV) and they are clearly shown on Assyrian reliefs of Ashurnasirpal II (Layard 1849b: pls 26–28). Corroded to the bronze blinker ornament was a rectangular bronze plate with three horizontal ribs and holes for attachment

---

[4] See Oates 1962: 6, Mallowan 1966: II, 387, and Russell 1991:
  290, n. 10.

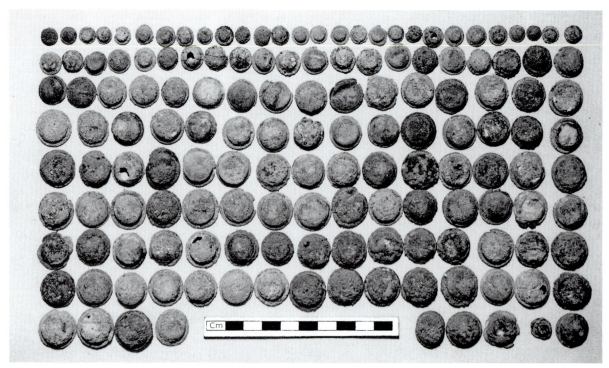

Fig. 8-e. Bronze bosses from horse harness.

at either end. The late Mrs Mary Littauer suggested in correspondence that this might have been a 'chamfrein' ('chamfron'), or horse's frontlet.[5] Around 170 small bronze bosses are also from harness. They are circular and have embossed centres with a flange around the edge (fig. 8-e). They are thought to have decorated leather bridles and were probably fixed between two sheets of leather with the embossed part sticking up proud. They can be seen on Assyrian reliefs fixed on to the leather

straps that go round the horse's neck and chest (fig. 8-f; Layard 1849b: pls 27–28). Many bronze bosses of this kind were found in other rooms in Fort Shalmaneser by the British School expedition. In addition to horse harness there were also items of military equipment scattered through this earlier deposit, notably at least 11 iron and 57 bronze armour scales of the usual types, an iron spearhead, an iron blade and an iron arrowhead (Curtis *et al*. 1993: figs 7–8,12/2–4). In addition to

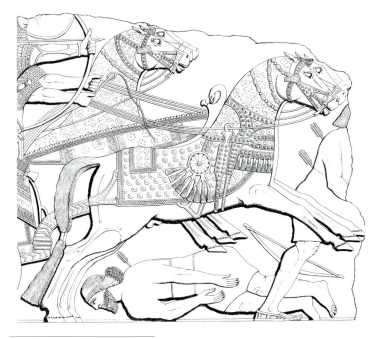

Fig. 8-f. Drawing of relief of Ashurnasirpal II showing a horse wearing blinkers and decorated harness (from Layard 1849b: pl. 38).

---

[5] Mrs Littauer was hoping to write a note on this item of horse harness, but sadly she passed away on 7th December 2005 before being able to do this.

Fig. 8-g. Blue glass plaques with rosette designs.

coming from different parts of the deposit, the armour scales did not have the appearance of originally belonging to the same suit of armour. In view of these various finds, it is tempting to think that at some time before the reign of Esarhaddon this room was used to store horse harness and military equipment.

There were also four small glass plaques of a very distinctive type (fig. 8-g). They are almost square, made of blue glass and have rosette designs recessed into the surface and filled with a different colour glass that was probably originally yellow. These plaques are to be distinguished from the smaller mosaic glass plaques that also have rosette designs but are made in a different way, with the rosettes being introduced while the glass is still viscous rather than being inlaid. I have suggested in an article in *Iraq* (Curtis 1999) that the inlaid glass plaques might have decorated ivories of a specific type, and I have pointed to ivories, possibly of Syrian origin, that show processions of bulls. Some of these ivories have recessed cavities for decorative inlays that are now missing. However, the case is far from proven and I hope that if nothing else this suggestion might inspire others to look into the interesting question of ivory inlays, for which there is extensive evidence at Nimrud. Among these inlays, there are about one hundred examples of blue glass plaques with inlaid rosettes from the British School excavations.

Above the secondary floor that is thought to date from the time of Esarhaddon there was extensive evidence for the sack of 614–612 BC, similar to that found in other rooms in Fort Shalmaneser and in many of the other buildings at Nimrud. Altogether the layer of ash, carbonized wood, burnt matting and other debris was about 2 m deep and above that were the collapsed walls. The heat must have been intense, as a 50-cm high bitumened dado around the room had partially melted and the molten bitumen had formed puddles at the foot of the walls. The plaster on the walls was also heavily burnt. In addition to a number of burnt roof beams we found a stone roof roller that must have been on the roof at the time of the sack and crashed down into the room when the roof collapsed. It may be worth remarking that the violence of these destruction levels at Assyrian sites has to be seen to be believed. In this particular case the total depth of debris was 4–5 m,

but it can sometimes be greater than this. Here would be an appropriate place to mention that in Room T20 there was definitely evidence for only one sack, and there was no evidence whatsoever for any secondary occupation or subsequent reuse of this room.[6]

From the upper level, that is from the debris above the floor that we attributed to Esarhaddon, there was a variety of objects. In the mudbrick tumble there was an iron holdfast and the broken and twisted ends of more than 25 bronze examples. These are rings with attached prongs that were apparently sunk into mudbrick walls so that the rings could be used to hang things up. As they were probably embedded in the walls, however, they could also date from the earlier occupation. More certainly associated with the later occupation were objects that included a bronze furniture sleeve decorated with embossed volutes of the type seen on the cross-bars of various types of Assyrian furniture, a collection of rectangular bone plaques pierced at either end which on analogy with comparable finds from Hasanlu might be something to do with horse harness (Curtis *et al.* 1993: 17–18), ten faience beads and an iron dagger. As always in Assyrian palaces and other buildings pottery was present but here it was comparatively scarce. Nevertheless there were some interesting forms, notably 4 large storage jars which were reconstructed from sherds and a saucer lamp. One of the large jars had stamped rosette decoration around the shoulder.

In contrast to the next door room T10 which had produced a large number of ivories, we found only one, but it was a particularly interesting example. It is a rectangular plaque decorated with three registers of figures in low relief in the Assyrian style (fig. 8-h). In the top and middle registers are figures in Assyrian dress, while in the bottom register are foreigners wearing floppy hats. Their dress suggests they come from North Syria, and parallels to the plaque point to a date in the ninth century BC. How an ivory plaque of this date could have been found in the mudbrick collapse dating from the late seventh century is unclear, but possibilities are that it was in a niche in the wall, on a shelf, or even on the roof. This ivory is unusual in being carved in low relief rather than incised as is usually the case with ivories in Assyrian style.

Also in the upper fill of this room, in the western part, were about 80 whole or fragmentary polychrome glazed bricks. More excavation is needed to establish whether these bricks were part of a complete panel, and where that panel was, or whether the bricks had been reused, but one possibility being considered is that the bricks belonged to a complete panel that had been set up above one of the

---

[6] For discussion of possible Median sacks in 614 and 612 BC and occupation post-612 BC, see Oates 1962: 2, 10ff; Mallowan 1966: II, 391; and Oates and Oates 2001: 149, 193.

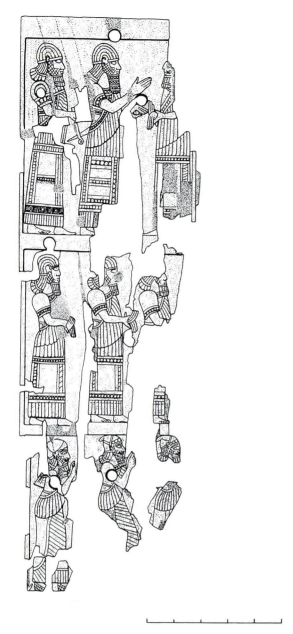

*Fig. 8-h. Assyrian style ivory plaque in low relief.
Drawing by Ann Searight.*

doorways on the northern side of Courtyard S, immediately to the west of T20. When Fort Shalmaneser was destroyed, and the building collapsed, some of the bricks from such a panel could have cascaded into Room T20. Such a suggestion would be in accord with what we know of glazed brick panels in this part of Fort Shalmaneser. A complete glazed brick panel showing Shalmaneser III beneath a winged disc had originally been above a doorway in Courtyard T giving access to Room T3. It was found in pieces by the British School expedition and painstakingly reconstructed by Julian Reade (Reade 1963). This panel was just over 4 m high and comprised 300–400 bricks. If our panel was on a similar scale we only have a small part of it, which could be a further indication that it was originally set up outside Room T20. The glazed bricks found in Room T20 are unbaked,

greyish-brown in colour and *c.* 31.5 cm–34.5 cm square and 8–9 cm thick. There are also half bricks. The glazed designs on the front edge of the bricks are in white, ochre, green, blue and possibly black. Designs include part of a winged disc, a palmette, rosettes, horizontal and vertical stripes, chevrons, and concentric circles. Significantly, the glazed decoration on some of the bricks included part of an inscription of Shalmaneser III. This inscription has been edited and restored by Christopher Walker, and is thought to read as follows :- 'Palace of Shalmaneser, great king, strong king, king of the universe, king of Assyria, son of Ashurnasirpal, king of the universe, king of Assyria, son of Tukulti-Ninurta, king of the universe, king of Assyria'.

On the upper flat, unglazed parts of the bricks there were painted signs. These signs would not have been visible when the bricks were made into panels and they are assumed to have been fitters' marks, to show the builders the order in which the bricks should be laid. There are two types of painted signs. In black paint there are Aramaic letters and groups of parallel lines and in white paint there are various sorts of pictograms and more parallel lines. Presumably the parallel lines, from two to ten in number, are indicative of particular rows. In the few cases when both black signs and white signs occur on the same brick it is clear that the white pictograms have been added later as sometimes the white paint is over the top of the black. Altogether six or seven Aramaic letters can be recognized, namely *gimel, daleth, he, lamedh, nun, resh* and possibly *taw* (fig. 8-i). (See Millard in this volume.) As we have said, on the front glazed surface of the bricks there was an inscription of Shalmaneser III, and if the black Aramaic letters were added at this time, as seems likely, then we have evidence for the use of Aramaic letters in the time of Shalmaneser III. This would be the earliest certainly attested use of Aramaic in Assyria. The white-painted pictograms include designs that resemble a plough, a mace, a human face, a door, a cross-legged table, a cauldron and a goat (fig. 8-j). There are also geometric motifs in the form of stars, a square, a circle with crossed lines, and a device of three concentric circles. The motif of the human face, which occurs twice, is particularly remarkable. It seems that the same pictograms were painted on adjoining bricks, to show where they should be laid in the panel. Thus, two bricks that are known to be contiguous because of the cuneiform inscription on the glazed part both have concentric circles close to the adjoining edges, and two bricks that have similar semicircular motifs on the glazed part both have white-painted plough and star signs. It is likely, then, that both the white-painted pictograms and the black-painted Aramaic letters

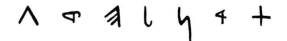

Fig. 8-i. Aramaic letters (fitters' marks) painted on top of the glazed bricks.

Fig. 8-j. Pictograms (fitters' marks) painted on top of the glazed bricks.

indicate the position of the bricks in the horizontal rows, while the parallel lines show which vertical row the bricks belong to. What is quite unclear, and actually rather baffling, is why there should have been two sets of marks. One possibility, obviously, is that at some stage the panel was dismantled and then reassembled by builders who added their own marking system. This could have happened during a refurbishment, perhaps in the time of Esarhaddon. Another possibility is that the Aramaic signs were applied by the craftsmen who made the bricks, while the pictograms were added by the builders who constructed the panel. To resolve these questions it would be helpful if we knew more about the pictograms, but at present they are enigmatic. It is unknown whether they should be associated with any particular craftsmen or ethnic group, or even whether they belong to some kind of writing system. It is very much to be hoped that in the future a proper study will be made of these intriguing signs, which will involve collecting together all the known examples.

In the meantime, it might be noted that the glazed bricks from the panel in Courtyard T in Fort Shalmaneser also had fitters' marks that are described as 'various rough combinations of squares, circles, straight lines, and squiggles' and 'occasionally a more elaborate pattern such as a pair of horns' (Reade 1963: 39). There were also groups of parallel strokes. No Aramaic letters were noted. These fitters' marks were in different colours, such as

black, white, yellow, green and blue, as well as being scratched onto the bricks. Elsewhere at Nimrud, particularly in the North-West Palace, Layard found a large number of glazed bricks, some of which bore fitters' marks. Layard remarks 'that on the back of these bricks, or on one of the sides not coloured, are rude designs, in black paint or ink, of men and animals, and marks having the appearance of numbers' (Layard 1849a: II, 13). At Khorsabad, Place observed fitters' marks on glazed bricks from Sargon's Palace (Place and Thomas 1867–70: II, 253), and panels from the temples at Khorsabad also bore fitters' marks, but 'only when the glazed design upon the surface offered an insufficient guide for assembly' (Loud 1936: 92–93; Loud and Altman 1938: 14). Further fitters' marks were noted on glazed bricks from Nineveh found during the recent excavations of David Stronach and published by John Russell (1999: 97–99, figs 7–12).

From post-Assyrian contexts, glazed bricks at Babylon carry fitters' marks (Koldewey 1914: 40, 104 ff), as do many of the bricks in glazed composition retrieved by Loftus from Achaemenid levels at Susa (Loftus 1857: 396–98). It is clear from the table of these marks published by Loftus (1857: 397 = Curtis 1993: fig. 3) that they are of three kinds, firstly scratches, secondly what appear to be Aramaic letters, and thirdly pictograms. The latter are said to have been 'rudely laid on in glaze with a brush or a stick'. Loftus observed that 'they do not belong to any known language' and 'are merely builders' marks'.

However that may be, the combination of Aramaic letters and pictograms at Susa is at present the best parallel for our fitters' marks at Nimrud.

To conclude, I think there are two things of particular interest to have come out of this excavation. The first is definite evidence for a later floor, probably dating from a reconstruction in the time of Esarhaddon. Secondly, there are the very interesting pictographic signs, which I hope will be the subject of a future study. Lastly, I would like to thank again the Iraq Department of Antiquities for their constant help and encouragement, and express the hope that at some stage we will be able to continue our work in Fort Shalmaneser.

9   MAX MALLOWAN AT NIMRUD

Henrietta McCall

Before Nimrud, Mallowan had excavated at the site of Ur, where he was initiated into the skill of excavation by Leonard Woolley, at Nineveh where he dug his deep sounding under the supervision of Reginald Campbell Thompson, and at Arpachiyah, Chagar Bazar and Tell Brak where he himself had been chief. During the War (fig. 9-a) which he spent as supplies officer in Tripolitania (north Africa), his thoughts often turned to the future. Requests for books sent to his family in England often included the biographies of archaeologists and it was probably during these years that Mallowan began to visualize his work as being in a sequence of great British archaeological endeavours. He made the decision, as he told Sidney Smith, Keeper of the Department of Western Asiatic Antiquities at the British Museum, to give prehistoric and protohistoric periods a rest. After he was repatriated, he was asked by Sir Edgar Bonham Carter about a possible joint expedition by the British School and the Iraq Museum in Baghdad, to take place somewhere in Iraq, sometime in 1947. Mallowan immediately wrote to Sidney Smith at the British Museum about where such an expedition might take place. Nimrud was one of the sites he suggested. Smith responded by telling him roundly that digging at such a site for one season was nonsense: 'Nothing much less than 10 years is any good', he wrote, something that Mallowan was perhaps to bear in mind.[1]

Fig. 9-a. Max Mallowan in RAF uniform, 1942.
(Copyright J. Mallowan).

In fact Bonham Carter's combined expedition did not take place, but early in 1947 Mallowan went out to Iraq to make a survey on his own account, 'Keeping my eye open for possible mounds to dig...it is obvious that there are hundreds of plums waiting to be pulled out of the rich Iraqi mud', as he wrote in a letter. Later that year, a combination of Sidney Smith and V. Gordon Childe the Director of the Institute of Archaeology approached Agatha Christie with a view to her funding a new chair of Western Asiatic Archaeology at the Institute. Its first incumbent was to be Max Mallowan. Christie readily agreed and on 16th October, the new professor gave his inaugural lecture entitled *The Legacy of Asia.* The terms of his new employment suited Mallowan extremely well since they made it clear that he might be absent from the Institute for five months of every year to pursue his archaeological interests in the field.

Early in February 1948 (fig. 9-b) he went once again to Iraq to contemplate mounds. But it was not until the following year, when he became the first Director of the British School (fig. 9-c) that his plans for finding and digging a major site became more concrete. He inspected Khorsabad, Nineveh and Ashur but it was at the site of Nimrud that he decided he had found the perfect mound, redolent as it was with history of the sort of archaeological endeavours he wished to emulate, and ringing with the name of archaeologists in whose tradition Mallowan was beginning to see himself: Layard, Rassam, Loftus and George Smith. On a more prosaic note, as Mallowan told Cyril Gadd, 'We have an ancient name to conjure with: it is much more difficult to raise money for an unknown site'.

Nimrud (fig. 9-d) covers an area of over 360 hectares and consists of a walled enclosure with a Citadel in its south-west corner on which were several public buildings. Fort Shalmaneser, a royal residence, arsenal and treasury which was built during the time of Shalmaneser III and restored by Esarhaddon, lay to the south-east corner.

It was not until January 1949 that the Mallowans arrived in Baghdad at the start of the decade they were to spend at Nimrud. Mallowan had been fortunate enough to have acquired the services of an old friend, R.W. Hamilton,

---

[1]   The references to quotations in this article will be found in McCall 2001.

*Fig. 9-b. Max Mallowan and Agatha Christie fly to
Iraq in 1949.*

formerly the Chief Inspector of Antiquities in Palestine. He
too had been drawn into archaeology by Leonard Woolley
and had dug at Nineveh with Campbell Thompson.
Hamilton had been offered a fellowship with the BSAI and
been appointed the Secretary/Librarian of the School in
Baghdad. On 15th February, Mallowan and Hamilton set
off for Nimrud and found a building suitable for the
excavation house, a mud-brick farm which unfortunately
soon began to melt like chocolate ice-cream in the torrential
rain. Work could not begin till 15th March. Mallowan hired
22 skilled men from a local village and they began to dig
high on the western flank of the mound where Layard had
begun over a century earlier. Max wrote somewhat theatri-
cally that, 'The pickmen had about them an air of
excitement and expectancy and, as the third generation of
skilled workers in the field, a sense of their historic
mission...The shades of Layard were in their midst; he
stood invisible like Banquo's ghost, and pointed to the last
of a long line of Assyrian kings whose realms had once
embraced the landscape...'.

It was in the footsteps or perhaps the excavations of
Layard and Loftus that Mallowan began—concentrating
his efforts on re-excavating parts of the North-West
Palace. Mallowan was familiar with the plan which
Layard had reproduced in *Nineveh and Its Remains*
published in 1849 and decided to begin his excavations
with a small rectangular room, in its south-west corner
marked Chamber V, which Layard said had yielded a
number of ivory fragments. Locating Chamber V was his

first challenge: as so often with Mallowan, luck
befriended him and despite only a vague idea of where
precisely he was in relation to Layard's plan, after a
morning and an afternoon of digging, Mallowan and his
men found mud-brick walling, with inscribed slabs of
grey gypsum soon identified by Dr Mahmud of the Iraq
Antiquities Service as belonging to Ashurnasirpal. A few
days later, Hamilton was able to confirm that they were
indeed digging Chambers V and W and in them
Mallowan, as Layard had, found ivory fragments, but in
such a state of decomposition that they could hardly be
salvaged. In the south-west corner of the room, however,
they found a small patch of undug soil which yielded a
treasure, an ivory figure of a cow with her head turned
back licking her calf (ND 362). It was a good omen.

They also began work on the so-called Governor's Palace,
the building which was the residence of the Governor of
Kalhu in the eighth century. Mallowan tells us that until
the start of his excavations there was only one clay tablet
positively identified as coming from Nimrud, and so it
was, as he said, thrilling to start finding scraps of
cuneiform as it implied that in time larger collections
would emerge—as indeed they did. In the north-west
corner of the building, right at the end of that first season,
in an almost square chamber 5 × 6 metres, paved with
baked bricks bearing the name of Shalmaneser III, the
first substantial collection of inscribed material was
found, between 17th and 25th April. The clay tablets lay

*Fig. 9-c. Agatha Christie taking tea on the balcony of the BSAI
house in Baghdad, early 1950s.*

Fig. 9-d. The site of Nimrud.

in confusion under a thin line of black ash and were in a wet and glutinous condition. Many were beyond salvation but those that were able to be rescued—numbering 76 in all—revealed important information. They had been written in the time of Adad-nirari III and were what Mallowan called business records, with a few letters, covering almost exactly one century from 808–710 BC.

To the north and south of the great open court of the building lay two large audience halls, with a row of smaller offices on either side. Some of the mud-brick walls had been carefully plastered and then painted with blue, red, black and white roundels set a little higher than eye level. In the south-west angle of these was an extremely well-preserved ceremonial bathroom similarly decorated, with a burnt brick floor overlaid with bitumen to make it waterproof. As Mallowan said, the first season at Nimrud had already shown sufficient promise to justify the planning of a series of expeditions. Indeed, sitting in the sun on almost the last day of the season, he, Robert Hamilton, Dr Mahmud and Agatha had started planning a proper expedition house (fig. 9-e), to be built opposite the Governor's Palace along the eastern wall of the mound, on a flat stretch of high ground which was not destined to be excavated. 'Our foundation platform', wrote

Mallowan, 'was worthy of Ashurnasirpal himself, for it consisted of a stump of the old acropolis wall, 45 metres of solid mud brick, an ancient Assyrian bulwark that was never likely to subside'.

From this pleasant accommodation, the team began work in the second season in 1950 both in the North-West Palace, and along the defences of the Citadel, along the west side. The third season in 1951 produced a major find: the sandstone stela of Ashurnasirpal II (fig. 9-f) with 154 lines of inscription celebrating the completion of the city in 879 BC including an inventory of its buildings and a description of the banquet held. Mallowan described how the discovery came while the team was re-examining the outside of the throne room in the North-West Palace. When they exposed the fallen winged bull outside Gate E it occurred to Mallowan that the creature must have been gazing at something. Work then commenced on the eastern side of the great paved courtyard which faced the palace and between two chambers EB and EC, they found a recess which was completely filled with fallen mud-brick from adjacent walls. At about half a metre below the surface the top of the stela began to emerge. It was not long, as Mallowan described, before they reached the inscribed burnt brick pavement on which it stood, later

Fig. 9-e. The expedition house at Nimrud, with sleeping tents in the foreground, 1950s.

*Fig. 9-f. Barbara Parker taking a photograph of the
Ashurnasirpal stela, Nimrud, 1951.*

which was released under pressure and neatly removed
any dust or dirt. This clearly inspired Gadd to adopt a
similar sand-spraying method which he later demonstrated in a film taken by Agatha Christie.

That year they concentrated on the Burnt Palace, areas of
the North-West Palace again and an administrative wing
of the palace to the south side of the ziggurat, which they
called the Ziggurat Terrace. The Burnt Palace soon began
to produce considerable quantities of carved ivory
fragments from beneath its covering of charred wood ash
and baked earth. They were mainly representations of
female heads and animal figures. In April, Mallowan
borrowed from his neighbours, the long-suffering Iraq
Petroleum Company, a great tripod and winch (fig. 03-k)
and began to empty out an Assyrian well which Layard
had started to empty but had abandoned. This was
Mallowan's third attempt to empty a well in the North-
West Palace: his two earlier attempts had been too
dangerous to complete, especially when the second
collapsed suddenly at its base. Before its collapse
however it had yielded a group of ivory and wood writing
boards which had once been covered by beeswax. Donald
Wiseman (fig. 9-g) recently described the moment those
writing boards had emerged: he was able to fit them back
together again at the hinge and to read the inscription.

raised to prevent damage by damp. In the debris
surrounding the base were two finely carved ivories—a
panel (ND1082) showing Ashurnasirpal holding a cup in
the tips of the fingers of his right hand, and an openwork
panel depicting a sphinx (ND1083).

The fourth season (1952) included Cyril Gadd as
epigraphist. He had entrusted himself to an aeroplane
which he described in a letter to Sidney Smith back at the
Museum as 'an awful type of machine...not fit for human
conveyance'. He spent three days with the American
expedition at Nippur watching their special clay tablet
cleaning process: this was a jam-jar filled with fine sand

It was the third well that produced real treasure in
quantity. Preserved in the sludge that lay at the bottom,
came the Mona Lisa (fig. 9-h), as she was instantly
christened doubtless because of her enigmatic smile. Her
Ugly Sister (fig. 9-i), as Mallowan unkindly dubbed her,
followed shortly afterwards. Doubtless among the most
beautiful ivories ever to come from ancient Mesopotamia
are the two plaques each showing a Nubian being
devoured by a lioness (fig. 9-j). The ivory had been inlaid
with gold, carnelian and lapis lazuli.

From a building at the foot of the ziggurat terrace
emerged tablets in great quantity but of great fragility. A
kiln was built in order to bake and stabilise them, another

*Fig. 9-g. Donald Wiseman, Agatha
Christie, Max Mallowan and Neville
Chittick (general field assistant) at
Nimrud, 1951.*

Fig. 9-h. Nimrud ivory: the so-called Mona Lisa.

Fig. 9-i. Nimrud ivory: the so-called Ugly Sister.

Fig. 9-j. Nimrud ivory: a lioness devouring a boy, British Museum 127412.

Fig. 9-k. Front cover of The Illustrated London News, *16th August 1952, showing the unrestored Mona Lisa ivory.*

device used by the expedition and recorded in a film made by Agatha Christie and shown in the exhibition *Agatha Christie and Archaeology — Mystery in Mesopotamia*. It looked rather lethal but seemed to have done its work. Cyril Gadd reported back to the British Museum at the end of the season how excited he had been to be present when a fresh series of ninth century sculptures on the north front of the North-West Palace was uncovered, a set, he said 'which had not been seen since Austen Henry Layard had buried them a century ago'.

The ivories created a great deal of interest; in fact the Mona Lisa made the front cover, life-size, of *The Illustrated London News* on 16th August (fig. 9-k) and in the same issue there was a full colour page reproduction of the Nubian being savaged by the lioness. A fortnight later another article published some of the smaller finds and there was a full-page illustration of the two winged colossi that flanked the gate to the second main entrance to the North-West Palace, exposed that season. There was a small Nimrud exhibition at the British Museum, which moved on to the Ashmolean in Oxford.

The fifth season had another extremely wet start. Mallowan again borrowed equipment from the Iraq Petroleum Company: two motor-driven winches with a trained operator. The plan was to investigate another 15 metre well in the North-West Palace, but first a large stone slab which covered it had to be removed. This had broken into three large pieces. They also wanted to complete the plan of the Burnt Palace, to excavate the quay wall, the ziggurat terrace, and private houses to the north-east of the mound, and to look at the outer town, north of the ziggurat where they dug five trial trenches, with disappointing results.

Mallowan did not dig at Nimrud in 1954. After five successful seasons he wanted to devote the entire year to publishing his work. By February, he reported to Donald Wiseman that he had already written 5000 words.

The sixth season (1955) had a specific object: to rediscover the great temple dedicated to Nabu and the library which it almost certainly held, somewhere in the south-west corner of the acropolis. As Mallowan wrote in *The Illustrated London News*, 'The results exceeded our most sanguine expectations'. The temple, when they located it, was buried under huge dumps of nineteenth century excavations—another problem for the Iraq Petroleum Company, who supplied an impressive bulldozer. ('Not exactly an orthodox archaeological tool', as Robert Hamilton wrote in a letter to one of his sons in England.) Once the spoil heaps were removed, the expedition team started to plan the temple, which had attached to its south side another palace building, containing a throne room with a pedestal. In this room were hundreds of ivory fragments as well as many fragmentary tablets, mainly treaties made by the king with foreign princes, one in particular being a lengthy treaty made by Esarhaddon with a prince of the Medes, some six hundred lines long and inscribed on the obverse and reverse in four columns. There was a new face on the dig this season, that of an experienced archaeologist who had been the previous year at Jebel Sinjar, David Oates.

The 1956 (his seventh) season concentrated on three main areas: the Nabu temple, the Ninurta temple, last touched by Layard in 1850, where they uncovered a colossal pair of winged lions, and a town wall above the bed of the Tigris where they found a large mud-brick construction which they thought was another palace, belonging to Ashurbanipal, the son of Esarhaddon.

Mallowan was again delayed by torrential rain at the beginning of the 1957 season, writing somewhat discon-solately to Richard Barnett at the British Museum that they were digging deep for the plan of Layard's building at the south-east end of the mound... 'but it is much plundered'. Then, an extraordinary piece of luck, described by Mallowan to his public, readers of *The Illustrated London News*: 'Whilst walking round the outer town towards the beginning of the season I was attracted to some high-lying ground which with its undulating outlines obviously contained heavy walls. As luck would have it we noticed, at a point not far from a gap which seemed to indicate a gate, an inscribed brick of Shalmaneser III...From that moment we resolved that at the first opportunity we should move half our workmen to this rich-looking cover which we named in anticipation Fort Shalmaneser....'

Fig. 9-l. Nimrud ivories: A lion's head and an openwork panel with lion, both from Fort Shalmaneser.

Fig. 9-m. Mallowan beside the stela of Ashurnasirpal II at the British Museum, British Museum 118805.

Four weeks' work revealed a ground plan showing a building some 6 hectares in area, with four courtyards, entered by a single narrow gateway. The building contained a massive collection of magnificent ivories (fig. 9-l), distributed over several rooms and embedded in heavily packed mud-brick. It was to Joan Oates that Mallowan gave great credit for their safe extraction. Fort

Shalmaneser made a spectacular end to Mallowan's decade at Nimrud. It also forced a change to his archaeological life, the very magnitude of the task ahead making him realize that his own retirement from the field was inevitable and that he should be handing over to a younger generation who would have to summon all the

Fig. 9-n. Max and Agatha in Nimrud, 1956 — Max is holding Agatha's handbag. (Copyright Palestine Exploration Fund).

energy and enthusiasm they could muster for the task ahead (fig. 9-n). He was 54. He made his plans for resignation from the field in the journal *Iraq*, volume XX. He did take part in the 1958 season but with David Oates as Director.

In his retirement, Mallowan became a Trustee of the British Museum and was photographed (fig. 9-m) beside the great stela discovered by Layard of Ashurnasirpal II. Any similarity between the two is entirely intentional. In his own remarkable way as memorable a figure as the great king, Mallowan's achievements may have been reassessed by the standards of the present day but they remain undiminished in scale. Mallowan's strengths lay in his ability to communicate ideas and enthusiasm, his energy in getting things done, the affection he inspired in most of his colleagues, his strong sense of the narrative of archaeology, his undoubted genius for picking his site, his wide-ranging historical knowledge, his lucid and readable literary style, and his unswerving loyalty and dedication to Near Eastern archaeology. The last, as he said of himself, of the Romantics.

10   AGATHA CHRISTIE AND ARCHAEOLOGY

Charlotte Trümpler

Agatha Christie and Archaeology is a wide and fascinating theme with many unexpected aspects. The first and most important aspect is the new view on the world's best-known crime novelist who much too often is equated with the fussy sock-knitting Miss Marple, who can detect human wickedness, however well concealed, and solves murders against the rural background of English villages and market towns.

Until recently only very few people knew that Agatha Christie spent several years in the Near East, together with her second husband, Max Mallowan (fig. 10-a and 10-e). She not only took part in his numerous excavations in Syria and Iraq but helped in many ways during the excavations themselves. Agatha Christie's services to archaeology are not well known, and since she was not, and never claimed to be, an archaeologist herself, this area of her life has been largely neglected. The settings of novels such as *Murder on the Orient Express*, *Murder in Mesopotamia* and *Appointment with Death* are not based on fiction but on the author's personal experiences (Morgan 1984).

The idea to create an exhibition about Agatha Christie and Archaeology (Trümpler 2001) came to me a long time ago after having read her autobiography *Come, Tell me How You Live*. The book describes in a highly amusing and lively manner her life together with Max on the digs in Syria between 1934 and 1938. This fascinating document gives an excellent view of everyday life on a dig from somebody who was not an archaeologist herself but still followed the course of the excavations from the view point of an insider.

The exhibition *Agatha Christie and Archaeology* is structured like a journey. It begins with the first voyage of Agatha Christie aboard the Orient Express to Baghdad in 1928, and it ends with her last participation in an excavation in Nimrud in 1958.

Agatha Christie decided to embark upon a trip through the Orient in 1928. She had been inspired by tales told by friends who had lived in the Orient for several years, and who had spoken enthusiastically about Baghdad. She travelled alone, which was both unconventional and courageous for the time. The journey started in London and went on to Calais where she boarded the Orient Express which took her to Istanbul. The legendary train offered a high level of comfort during the journey: at the railway stations en route the travellers were picked up by agencies of Thomas Cook and taken to the luxury hotels of the Compagnie Internationale des Wagons-Lits. The journey continued from Istanbul with the Taurus Express through Aleppo to Damascus. The last stretch of the journey to Baghdad was made in a Nairn Bus. For Agatha, this seemingly endless journey through the sandy, monotonous wasteland of the desert was at once tedious and fascinating. This bus ride moved Agatha Christie to write the short story *The Gate of Baghdad*, which appeared in the 1934 compilation of short stories titled *Parker Pyne Investigates*. In this story, Parker Pyne solves a murder on board a twelve-seater overland bus on its way from Damascus to Baghdad.

On her first tour Agatha Christie visited the ancient city of Ur of the Chaldees, the birthplace of Abraham. Then she herself became captivated by the landscape studded with ruins.

Fig. 10-a. Agatha Christie at Baron's Hotel, Aleppo, about 1930. (Copyright John Mallowan).

The lure of the past came up to grab me. To see a dagger slowly appearing, with its gold glint, through the sand was romantic. The carefulness of lifting pots and objects from the soil filled me with a longing to be an archaeologist myself. (Christie 1977: 389)

Fascinated by the Orient, the excavations and life on the dig, in 1930 Agatha Christie accepted an invitation from the Woolleys to visit Ur for a second time. During this stay she was introduced to Max Mallowan, an archaeologist who had been working as Leonard Woolley's assistant since 1925. He was 14 years younger than she was. The couple got to know one another and, after some uncertainties due to their considerable difference in age, Agatha Christie agreed to marry him in September 1930.

After her wedding, Agatha Christie found herself no longer welcome at the Ur excavation. For Katharine Woolley, the constant presence of the author was a threat to her own authority at the site.

Agatha Christie developed her impressions of Ur in the crime novel *Murder in Mesopotamia*, which appeared in 1936. Characters in the story are clearly based on some of the participants in the Ur expedition. In particular, the eccentric wife of the excavation director, Katharine Woolley, is outstandingly portrayed in the fragile and beautiful Louise Leidner whom she allows to be murdered in the book. The beautiful cover for the first edition of this book as well as those for *Death on the Nile* and *Appointment with Death* was designed by the excavation architect in Syria, Robin Macartney (fig. 10-b).

Naturally Max wanted Agatha to accompany him on his future excavations. He decided to take up an offer by Campbell Thompson and, in the winter of 1931/32 he took up a new post as his assistant at Nineveh in northern Iraq. A contract, which has been preserved in the British

Museum, stated that Agatha could participate in the excavations for one month, but that she would have to cover all her own travel costs, board and lodging and that she was not allowed to 'publish any account of things found, without reference to Dr Thompson'.

During her return from the excavations in Nineveh shortly before Christmas 1931, the Orient Express got stuck at Pythiou near the Greek-Turkish border. The two-day ordeal in the train, suffering from the cold and the lack of good food and drinking water, brought her in close contact with a variety of her fellow passengers. A letter which she wrote to Max after having arrived in London bears witness to the events. The colourful mixture of different nationalities and the recent successful kidnapping of the Lindbergh baby served her as direct material for her crime novel *Murder on the Orient Express*.

From 1933 onwards Max undertook his own explorations. First he excavated Tell Arpachiyah in northern Iraq (Mallowan and Rose 1933). The expedition was funded by the British Museum, the British School of Archaeology in Iraq and by an anonymous sponsor— Agatha Christie herself. After having successfully completed his work in Tell Arpachiyah, Max turned his attention between 1934 and 1938 to northern Syria. At that time the area was nearly unexplored. He concentrated his work on Chagar Bazar and Tell Brak (Mallowan 1936; 1937; 1947). Mallowan's goal was to explore the prehistoric periods of Mesopotamia (fig. 10-c).

During the digs which lasted 3 to 4 months Agatha Christie not only accompanied her husband, she also took part actively in them. Although she paid her own travel costs and her living expenses she worked hard with the other members of the team when required. She became an indispensable help on the dig. One of her important tasks was

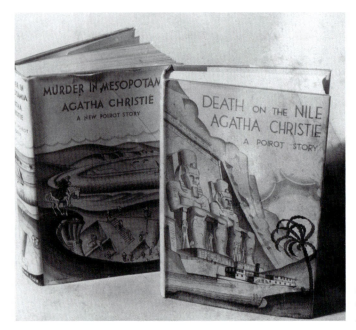

Fig. 10-b. First editions of Murder in Mesopotamia *and* Death on the Nile, *covers designed by Robin Macartney.*

Fig. 10-c. Letter from Sir George Hill, Director of the British Museum, to Max Mallowan, 14th December 1935. (Copyright Trustees of the British Museum).

to watch over the young basket carriers, who often worked too slowly.

    I have another job, too. I keep an observant eye on the basket-boys, for some of the lazier of these, when taking their baskets to the dump, do not return at once. They sit down in the sun to sort through the earth from their basket, and often spend a comfortable quarter of an hour this way! Even more reprehensible, some of them curl up comfortably on the dump and enjoy a good sleep!

    Towards the end of the week, in my role of master spy, I report my findings. (Christie 1946: 80)

One of the surviving members of the excavation team, Hamid Musli Smir, can remember her activities and describes them in the following way:

We worked carrying baskets at Tell Brak, taking earth from the pits to the heaps of spoil. Agatha Christie was a beautiful, strong woman. She supervised the workers. I remember her walking stick. She could unfold it and sit down on it. (Trümpler 2001: 300)

Apart from sorting and labelling pottery she continued to restore pottery, work which she had begun in Tell Arpachiyah. The most important of Agatha Christie's jobs at the dig, however, was taking and developing photographs of the excavations.

The first mention of her activities in developing photographs is in Max's foreword to his account of the excavations at Tell Arpachiyah in 1933, where he wrote that Agatha was responsible for developing and enlarging the photographs. He wrote in almost the same way in the introduction to the report on the Khabur valley in 1934 and the dig at Chagar Bazar in 1935.

The first mention of Agatha taking photographs on the dig herself occurs in Max's report on the 1936 season at Chagar Bazar, where he says that his wife was largely responsible for the restoration of pottery and photographs taken on the site. And in the next record of the excavations during the following seasons at Chagar Bazar and Tell Brak in 1937 and 1938 Max again wrote in his acknowledgements that Agatha had taken all the photographs of the dig.

Before the war she photographed using a Zeiss Ikon and a Leica D.R.P. III, which were equipped with various lenses. She continued to use the Leica even after the war.

With regard to her activity in developing photographs she wrote at Chagar Bazar:

> A lot of photography today, and I am introduced to my dark room. This is undoubtedly a great improvement on the 'Little Ease' at Amuda. I can stand upright, and it has a table and a chair.
>
> But as it is a recent addition, having been added a few days before my arrival, the mud-brick, is still damp. Strange fungi grow on the walls, and when one is immured in it on a hot day, one comes out partially asphyxiated! (Christie 1946: 127)

So that the heat in the small room would not become unbearable, Agatha took to developing her pictures at 6 o'clock in the morning. The early start also helped her cope with the large number of photographs that mounted up at the end of each campaign. In any case, the water became too warm later in the day and it was therefore impossible to use in the laboratory. The quality of this work, which Agatha Christie carried out under such difficult conditions, cannot be esteemed highly enough.

The evident discomfort of the darkroom was not the only challenge for Agatha Christie. She also faced the problem of maintaining the cleanliness of the water, which was necessary for developing the negatives. The fine desert sand, which penetrated everything, was also naturally present in the water, a big problem which earlier photographers of the nineteenth century had also worried about.

In 1937, Agatha Christie attended a course for advertisement photography at the Reinhard School of Commercial Photography in London. She was much inspired by the experiments which she undertook there. For example, the students applied different coloured filters while taking photographs and learned how to manipulate the appearance of objects until the resulting images had little to do with reality.

After the course, the quality of Agatha Christie's pictures showed a marked improvement. An interesting point about this new aspect is Agatha's comment that when taking the course she learned always to photograph an object several times, which was quite uncommon at that time on a dig.

The photographs of Tell Brak taken in 1938, are of better quality than those of Chagar Bazar and show different subjects. She began taking pictures of people and animals from quite close up, deliberately arranging her compositions. She assembled the domestic staff in the interior courtyard of the house or took several views of the expedition house, trying to work with perspective. Now and then she also allowed herself small experiments in taking pictures of pots which she laid down in the courtyard. A photograph shows Max sitting in the expedition car 'Queen Mary' waiting to pay the workers—as Agatha said 'looking rather like a booking-clerk at a railway station'.

Apparently it was also the course of commercial photography that inspired Agatha Christie to begin filming at the excavations. Two films made by her in 1938 in Syria and 1952 and 1957 in Nimrud give an unique insight into the countries and peoples of the Middle East. The really interesting feature is that these films do not simply record the excavations, showing the finds made and the levels uncovered, but provide an unique and humorous account of everyday life on a dig. They are treasure troves to all lovers of early amateur film. The first one consists of alternating black and white and colour sequences, given short subtitles at her suggestion. This use of colour in an amateur film is surprisingly early, and once again is evidence of Agatha's willingness to experiment. She used a Kodak camera which had a magazine for a 16 mm Kodachrome film 15 m in length. Like her autobiography, the film also illustrates Agatha's great interest in the local people, especially their daily lives.

She filmed the workmen on the dig with the affection evident in her written accounts of them, but she also makes a telling and accurate record of their varying degrees of skill. Many of the situations are amusing. Indeed the film becomes comic in almost Chaplinesque style when she shows the tedious packing of the finds in crates to be taken by lorry to the museum in Aleppo. Since the workmen had not calculated the height of the gateway of the expedition house at Tell Brak in advance, the vehicle got stuck in it and had to be reloaded.

Before and after each dig the Mallowans embarked on extended trips to other countries like Iran, Russia, Jordan and Egypt. Agatha's encounter with Egypt, which she visited in 1931 and 1933, led her to write her world-famous novel, *Death on the Nile*, which was filmed in 1978 with Sir Peter Ustinov in the role of Poirot. In the film, the Egyptian antiquities, above all the temples of

Fig. 10-d. Agatha Christie at Nimrud in 1957. (Copyright Mogens Lonborg Friis, Oslo).

the grounds of one of the gigantic palaces that had been uncovered.

In 1938 the Mallowans left Syria, and they did not return to the Middle East until 1948, when they visited Nimrud where Max started to dig in 1949. We have a wealth of black and white photographs and colour transparencies from this period in Iraq taken by Agatha Christie and also another film. Both film and the photographs record life in Iraq and on the dig (fig. 10-f).

The film which Agatha made at Nimrud in 1952 and 1957 (fig. 10-d), completely in colour, set around the expedition house, again gives a humorous and extraordinarily valuable insight into the everyday life of an archaeological excavation. Unlike the earlier film this one documents the dig itself very well. It records the finds made on the site, the workmen digging and the excavation of the well in which the ivories were found. A very long sequence records the building of a large kiln for baking clay tablets. Again as in the first film she includes humorous aspects, as for example when a workman sits in a jar explaining to somebody the results of the excavation.

The provision of food is illustrated by scenes showing women baking and making flat bread on a fire beside the

Wadi el-Sebua and Abu Simbel, formed the backdrop to Hercule Poirot's investigation.

But Agatha Christie was also impressed by ancient Egyptian culture. With the encouragement of their friend, the archaeologist Stephen Glanville, she wrote two works directly based on archaeological sources from ancient Egypt. After a prolonged period of intensive research, Agatha Christie wrote the crime novel *Death Comes as the End* and the play *Akhnaton*. Both are set in ancient Egypt and their characters are likewise historically based. An analysis of the texts clearly shows how seriously and thoroughly Agatha Christie immersed herself in her research of the archaeological sources. She integrated the available material with outstanding style, despite the fact that this posed an extremely difficult linguistic challenge.

By contrast—and perhaps understandably—the author did not use ancient Mesopotamia as the setting for one of her crime novels. Evidently she had too much respect for those cultures, which were the speciality of her husband. Max, a serious scholar, could neither imagine, nor would have wanted a fictitious murder plot set in ancient Mesopotamia. For this reason, the writer never utilized her depth of knowledge, which would almost have predestined her to write a novel on the subject—a story that could have been based on cuneiform texts and set in

Fig. 10-e. Max Mallowan at Nimrud in 1957. (Copyright Mogens Lonborg Friis, Oslo).

Fig. 10-f. Departure from Baghdad to travel to Nimrud, photograph by Agatha Christie. (Copyright John Mallowan).

house. She also filmed workers dancing and many animals such as dogs, turkeys and ducks swimming in a bath tub.

In his foreword to the report on the dig in 1949, Max mentioned the fact that Agatha alone was responsible for the laboratory work, while in the following years she only helped when necessary. He also expressly mentioned that from 1950 onwards, the epigraphist Barbara Parker took all the photographs on the site (Trümpler 2001: 245).

Agatha herself, who gave only a brief account of her time at Nimrud, wrote about the first year:

> We lived in a portion of the Sheik's house in the village between the tell and the Tigris.... I had to do the developing in the dining-room in the evenings, so Max and Robert (Hamilton) would go upstairs. Every time they walked across the room, bits of mud used to fall off the ceiling and drop into the developing dish. Before starting the next batch, I would go up and say furiously: '**Do** remember that I'm **developing** underneath you. Everytime you move something falls. Can't you just talk without moving?'
>
> They always used, in the end, to get excited, and rush off to a suitcase to take out a book and consult it, and down would fall the dried mud again. (Christie 1977: 542)

Since she was no longer responsible for the photographs of the dig she could now experiment, particularly when photographing the excavations themselves, choosing subjects which offered especially interesting scenes. She used primarily black and white photographs to capture finds and workers at the excavations, the expedition house (fig. 10-g) and visitors. She reserved colour film for ethnological subjects and landscapes, seen mainly on excursions.

The black and white photographs, especially, are of an astonishing quality and beauty. They concentrate in particular on large objects such as *lamassu* (fig. 10-h), taken from all possible angles, or stelae and inscribed bricks which were documented as the finds were conserved. Even the transport and installation of a field railway is faithfully documented. Other favourite subjects are workmen sitting, standing or resting in unconventional attitudes beside pits in the excavations. And children, either those of visitors or of workers (fig. 10-i), as well as animals, were a very popular motif.

Both film and photographs offer a glimpse into a small, self-contained world in the Middle East—a glimpse that is unique if one leaves aside scientific pre-War photographs. Agatha Christie succeeded in bringing that world to life before our eyes in both words and pictures. The title of her memoir of her time in Syria, *Come, Tell me How You Live,* suggests where her main interest lay: she wanted to show the daily life of archaeologists on a dig, but at the same time she wished to demolish prejudices and persuade people to revise their opinions. Through the distanced but nonetheless affectionate view of a traveller, who went to the Middle East for the first time in 1928, and who consequently worked and lived

Fig. 10-g. Building the expedition house at Nimrud, 1950, photograph by Agatha Christie. (Copyright John Mallowan).

Fig. 10-h. Lamassu at Nimrud, 1950, photograph by Agatha Christie. (Copyright John Mallowan).

Fig. 10-i. Children at Balawat, 1950s, photograph by Agatha Christie. (Copyright John Mallowan).

Fig. 10-j. Agatha Christie, Max Mallowan and Claude Schaeffer in France, 1972. (Copyright Odile Schaeffer, France).

there for a long period, we possess a unique view of the people, the life and the landscape of what is now partially an extinct culture.

Since she was not a professional photographer or scholar, an archaeologist or missionary, she was able to leave a more objective record than those of most western visitors to these countries. In retirement, Agatha Christie continued to support Max in his archaeological interests and they maintained links with colleagues from around the world, including Claude Schaeffer whom they met in Syria in the 1930s (fig. 10-j).

11   AN INTRODUCTION TO THE NIMRUD TOMBS

Muayyad Said Damerji

Max Mallowan may have been a hair's breadth away from the discovery of the Nimrud Tombs. These were uncovered by an Iraqi team, but although there were many indications that graves and burials were to be found on the Acropolis within the rooms of palaces and temples, nothing could have led us to expect the presence of such rich tombs. Indeed, Mallowan had found a terracotta sarcophagus under the floor of Room DD, about five feet down, and another burial at the far end of the same room (Mallowan 1966: I, 114–16), but the contents were few and, with one exception (the so-called 'Nimrud Jewel'), less spectacular.

Nabu Temple (Plan 3)

Excavations in the Nabu Temple (Ezida) were directed by Muyesser Said al-Iraqi in 1978. According to his somewhat confusing unpublished report, 'inside the western wall of one of the rooms in the Ezida Temple, at the height of one metre from the floor, we also discovered an oval terracotta sarcophagus, which is only 1 m long and 65 cm wide, with a very well preserved skeleton, painted and lying on the right side with a small brown flask or jar, with stripes around its exterior surface'. In NTS 13, beside the wall to the right of the entrance, 25 cm above (?) the floor, there was a rectangular terracotta sarcophagus 1.05 m long and 48 cm wide of reddish clay with decoration in the form of a twisted rope around the exterior, and covered with slabs of the local *helan* stone.[1] It was broken in many pieces and contained part of a skull and a metal bracelet that was completely corroded. Later, in June 1978, Abdullah Amin Agha discovered another burial facing the entrance to NTS 1, lying 3 m from the eastern corner of the entrance and 50 cm higher than the pavement of the courtyard: it measured 1.20 × 0.65 × 0.35 m, and contained a flask and a bowl, both of alabaster (not mentioned in Agha 1985–86). Behind the northern wall of NTS 12, 50 cm above (?) the platform or pavement, he discovered the skeleton of a man lying on his back, of which only the left leg and arm remained, with a bracelet on his left wrist; he found a small conical bottle 7 cm long, with a short neck, and a metal bowl (d. 14 cm; h. 5 cm), with some incised decoration, lying to the right side of the head, with the adjacent bones of the face almost complete. There were coloured beads near the left hand and also shell beads. If we add these together there are some six burials. It seems it was the custom to bury people—especially women—inside the palace area. In the temple area we may not be dealing with women, but with servants or priests, and the grave goods are much poorer than those later found inside the palace.

North-West Palace (Plan 5)

Tomb I
There were plans to restore the palace because of some problems in the domestic wing. In 1988, while clearing Room MM, which had originally been partly excavated by Mallowan, Muzahim Mahmud noticed some anomalies in the floor, which led him to dig below it. He found the corbelled vault of a brick-built chamber measuring 2.5 × 1.85 × 2 m, with some bricks naming Ashurnasirpal II (883–859 BC), possibly in a secondary context, and a sarcophagus let into the floor (1.85 × 0.65 m and 0.67 m deep). This was the first surprise, and we said, 'This is *the* discovery' and we never thought that in comparison with later finds this was going to prove very humble. The lid of the sarcophagus had been sealed with bitumen, but it was broken into many small pieces. We found a quantity of jewellery, including many beads, some of them shaped like gold pomegranates, small rock crystal objects, an extraordinary fibula, and a scarab with an inscription on its base in Egyptian hieroglyphs, 'Horus, beloved of the god of the universe' (translated by Mohammed Abdul Hatrije, Director General of the East Delta of Egypt).

Tomb II
The next year (1989), we discovered remains of the walls of new rooms that had not been excavated by the British. We rebuilt the walls of two rooms and found, below the first of these, two chambers—an antechamber and chamber reached by a shaft at one end with steps at the bottom—access may have been by means of a ladder. A small entrance had been sealed by three stone slabs, and the sarcophagus had also been sealed by slabs, similar to the burial found by Mallowan in Room DD. The antechamber was 1.40 m high × 1.20 × 1.16 m; in a niche was an inscribed slab naming Queen Yaba',[2] wife of Tiglath-pileser III (745–729 BC). The main chamber was 2.75 × 2.30 × 1.40 m, orientated on the main north-south axis, with the monolithic sarcophagus at the northern end, orientated east-west. There was a lot of pottery in the

---

[1] This seems to be a so-called 'bath-tub' coffin (eds).

[2] For details of the inscriptions referred to in the following descriptions, see Al-Rawi, this volume. For the objects, see Collon (ed.), this volume.

antechamber, and a copper/bronze 'saucer'-lamp. Stone vessels in the niches of the antechamber contained organic material, perhaps cremated body parts.

Inside the sarcophagus there were the blackened remains of linen garments and between the layers of these were the skeletons of two women of different heights. The smaller one may have been some twenty years younger, so the grave must have been reopened for the second burial. The grave was completely dry and this may have been due to the fact that any humidity was absorbed by plants whose roots hung down into the chamber like electric wires. The many inscribed objects enabled one of the bodies to be identified as Yaba'; the other was Banīti, wife of Shalmaneser V (726–722 BC) or Ataliya, wife of Sargon II (721–705 BC). This means either that the later objects were deposited after Banīti's burial, or that Ataliya had inherited Banīti's golden objects and taken them with her to the grave. This later body had been heated after death to a temperature of 150–200 degrees centigrade, perhaps in order to preserve the body of a queen who had died elsewhere and been brought back to Nimrud for burial.

For reasons of security, the tomb had to be emptied the same day. The objects were placed in plastic bags and taken to Mosul Museum were they were cleaned in a light solution of water and acid. They were in excellent condition. During the night we tried to read the cuneiform inscription. Among the jewels there were two crowns, bracelets, armlets—altogether 26 kg of gold, and numerous semiprecious stones. There were two pairs of gold anklets, the larger ones weighing 1.6 kg each; gold rosettes are similar to those still being stitched onto cloth in Mosul. A gold bowl was full of rings and beads. There were rock-crystal objects, numerous earrings, bracelets. Some fragments of the textiles were sent to Japan and others were sent to London (see Crowfoot, this volume) and both agreed that flax had been used to make the linen textiles.

Tomb III

This tomb contained the stone sarcophagus of Mullissu-mukannishat-Ninua, wife of Ashurnasirpal II (883–859 BC), mother of Shalmaneser III (858–824 BC), and

daughter of the *rab shake* (chief cup-bearer) of Ashurnasirpal, but it leaves many questions unanswered. It seems that the tomb was entered though the ceiling some time later by robbers (whether Assyrians or enemies is not known). It is not clear how the thieves knew there was a burial, and why they did not open the stone doors into the antechamber. The monolithic stone sarcophagus (2.38 × 1.32 × 1.25 m) was of Egyptianizing-type with stone knobs at the ends and on the lid to enable it to be sealed. It was so heavy that it seems to have sunk into water-logged earth at some time. The monolithic lid, bearing a long cuneiform inscription identifying the owner, had been smashed and one small piece was missing, allowing dust to drift in. We spent twelve hours clearing the sarcophagus of the mud that had accumulated inside it, but we discovered only one piece of bone and one stone bead.

In the antechamber, three bronze coffins, of a type dating to around 700 BC (see Curtis, this volume), were found at right-angles to the doors opening out of the main chamber: two side-by-side and a third placed above the eastern one. Two courses of bricks had been laid in the space between the coffins and the doors, thus sealing the doors. Beneath these bricks was the gold base of a beaker and other fragments of gold; a complete beaker with a similar base was found in one of the coffins. This would indicate that the main burial chamber was cleared in a great hurry and items from it were placed in the coffins. Whether this was as a result of a disturbance in the harem or some other event is unclear. The coffins may have contained material from the main chamber, and the famous crown and many precious objects were found there: dated objects range from the time of Shalmaneser IV (782–773 BC) to that of Sargon II (721–705 BC). Tomb III was therefore in use for some 150 years.

Tomb IV

This Tomb was discovered by Hussein towards the end of 1990. It included metalwork, glazed bottles, amber beads and some other jewellery, but is much less rich, suggesting that the occupant may have been part of the palace staff, but not an important member of the royal family.

12   RECENT EXCAVATIONS IN NIMRUD

Muzahim Mahmud Hussein
Lamia al-Gailani Werr (translation)

I. Tomb IV

Tomb IV is one of a number of burials discovered in the southern quarter of the Palace of Ashurnasirpal II. It lies at a short distance east of Tomb III (Plate 5), and was discovered during the sixteenth season of excavations in 1990, under a mass of *libn*.

When excavations began, the foundations were unearthed of two parallel walls running from north to south, narrowing probably to form an entrance and joined at the south end by another wall forming a narrow passage 1 m wide, with a drain running down towards the north (fig. 12-a).

Four courses of *libn* were lying over a mass of clay, originally wrapped in reed mats of which impressions have survived on the clay. After clearing and removing the *libn* courses, a pavement appeared, made of broken limestone slabs. It is difficult to know if the limestone slabs were broken as a result of the weight of the earth, or if they were originally broken and reused as paving stones, arranged in a haphazard way which resulted in their collapse into the space beneath, in front of the sarcophagus (fig. 12-b).

On the left side of the burial chamber is a rectangular shaft (2.48 × 0.90 cm), built of well made, plain bricks; there are no traces of bitumen, plaster or paint, as seen in the tombs found previously. The brick stairs have a landing at the top and a second at the bottom. To the east, down three further steps, is the entrance to a vaulted antechamber, 76 cm wide and narrowing at the top to 68 cm. The entrance is 1.30 m high, so that those wishing to enter this chamber have to stoop. However, it is easier to leave the chamber, as it is lower than the landing (fig. 12-a).

The burial chamber is nearly square (2.27 × 2.48 m)[1]. The corbelled vault is 1.74 m high and forms a semicircle consisting of courses of brick (figs 12-b and 12-c, left). In the eastern wall, opposite the entrance, are two niches, each of which is 30 cm wide, 70 cm high, 50 cm deep and 1.05 m above the floor. White marble [alabaster?] vessels were found in them. Two further niches were found in the western wall; inside each was a bronze lamp and a small glazed vessel. The chamber floor, which slopes a little towards the south wall, is paved with square bricks measuring 34 × 34 cm.

After examining the actual techniques used in building the chamber, it is clear that both the eastern and western walls were first built to a height of 85 cm, then the large sarcophagus was put in, and finally the north and south walls and the vault were constructed. The evidence for this is as follows: the vault cuts across the entrance to the antechamber, and the rows of bricks that form the vault are not bonded with the eastern and western walls (fig. 12-d and cf. fig. 12-b).

The sarcophagus was placed in the northern part of the chamber (fig. 12-b). Made of clean, dark brown clay, it measures 2.05 × 0.75 m, and is 0.75 m deep. It is decorated on the outside with buttresses, but is plain inside, and has a break across the body. The sarcophagus was covered with four clay slabs, each of which is 84 cm long and 40 cm wide (see the photograph in Hussein and Suleiman 2000: 190; fig. 12-c, right).

The finds from this tomb are poorer and less numerous than those from the three tombs found earlier (figs 12-e–g). Many of them were found inside the sarcophagus, and some were on the chamber floor. They vary in material and type. Some objects were made of gold, while others were made of silver, copper, bronze, semiprecious stones, white marble [alabaster?] and pottery, both glazed and plain. In addition there were fragments of white cloth, possibly part of the shroud (Hussein and Suleiman 2000:149, 152–53, figs 18–22, pics 201–22).

II. The vaulted complex beneath rooms 74 and 75

One of the most significant discoveries in Nimrud during the seventeenth season in 1992 was the unearthing of three rooms sharing one passage under the floor of rooms 74 and 75 (fig. 12-h), in the palace of Ashurnasirpal II (Hussein and Suleiman 2000: 154–56, figs 24–27).

First, room 74 (12.25 × 2.20 m)[2] (fig. 12-h) was cleared of the debris, earth and ash that filled it. This fill lacked any finds except directly on the pavement where many fine objects were found. Among the finds were a number of jumbled human bones adjacent to the south wall, together with cylinder seals and miniature glazed vessels decorated with geometric patterns. Many of these were broken. In the floor at the west end of the room a square shaft had been sunk. It was covered with undressed stone and one stone

---

[1] Note that the length of the room indicated on fig. 12-a should read 2.48 rather than 2.84 m (eds.).

[2] 10.15 × 2.5 m according to the scale on fig. 12-h (eds.).

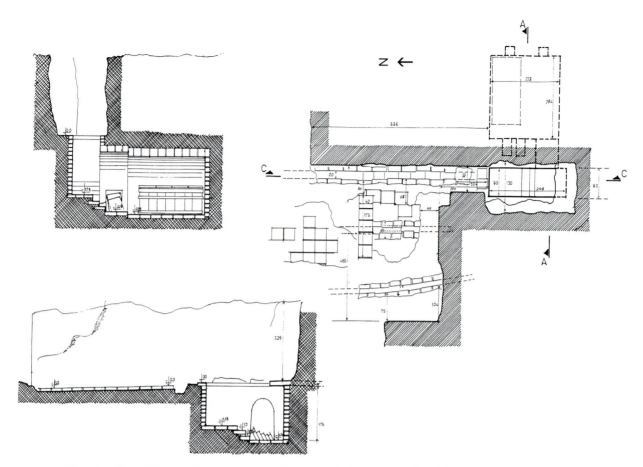

Fig. 12-a. Tomb IV. Plan of the excavations, with Section A–A (west to east) and Section C–C (north to south).

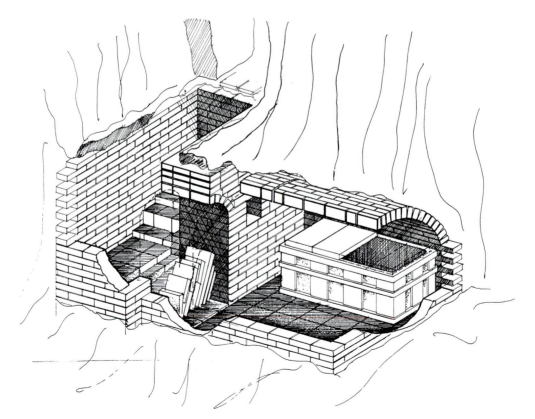

Fig. 12-b. Tomb IV. View of the shaft on the left, stairway, vaulted antechamber with fallen limestone slabs, and vaulted chamber with sarcophagus.

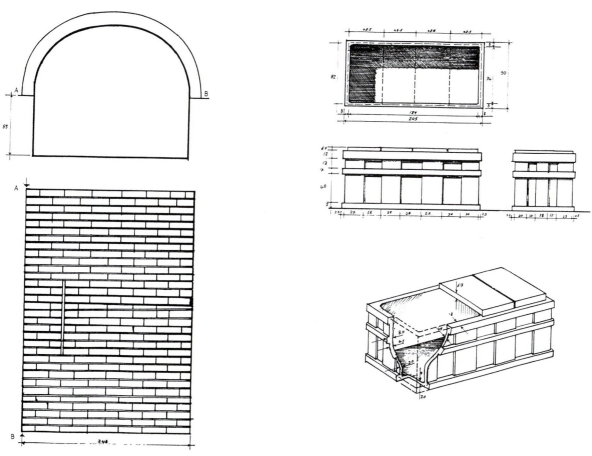

Fig. 12-c. Tomb IV. Left: north–south section through the burial chamber, and east-west view of the vault's brickwork seen from above. Right: The sarcophagus.

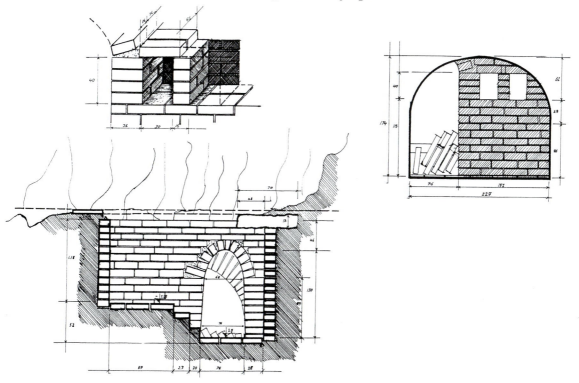

Fig. 12-d. Tomb IV. Detail of the southern niche in the west wall of the burial chamber (note the lack of bonding with the wall behind it). Section D–D shows the east wall of the shaft, the entrance to the antechamber and the vault of the burial chamber cutting across it. Section E–E shows the west wall (with niches) of the burial chamber and the springing of the antechamber vault (mostly hidden by the burial chamber vault).

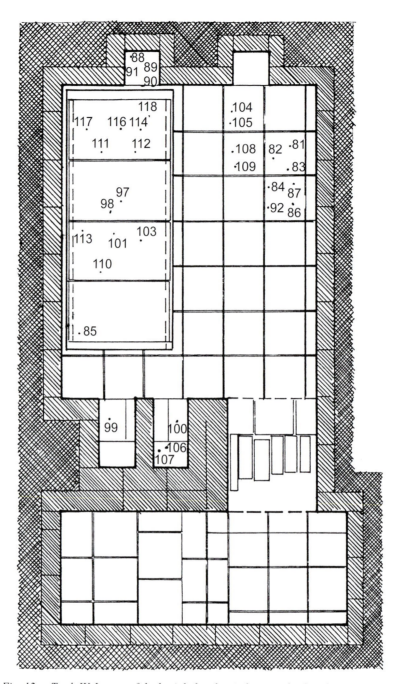

Fig. 12-e. Tomb IV. Layout of the burial chamber indicating the distribution of finds.

slab that had traces of a cuneiform inscription. The sides of the shaft were built with bricks (30 × 30 × 7 cm). At the eastern side of the room a small entrance was found leading to a passage below (fig. 12-i), parts of which had collapsed. This passage ran underneath the length of room 74. It has a fine, corbelled vault (fig. 12-j and see fig. 12-h) and was filled with earth sediment, the result of seeping rainwater.

Work on the passage was slow and difficult because it was half a metre lower than the bottom of the shaft, and from floor to ceiling it was densely packed with earth. This was difficult to remove because of the small size of the entrance and the fact that many courses of bricks had collapsed. The passage had a pointed radial vault consisting of courses of

bricks, backed by courses of *libn*, which bent inwards at an angle to form the vault (see fig. 12-j).

When the passage was cleared, a niche was found in the middle of the north wall and three entrances were revealed in the south wall, leading to three small, corbelled chambers (A, B, C) that were similar in size (fig. 12-k). Further niches had been built into the southern and eastern walls of each chamber, where lamps may have been placed. Each room is 1.5 m high (2.25 m wide by 4.0 m long according to the scale on fig. 12-k) and has a low, narrow entrance (see figs 12-j–k). At the western end of the passage is chamber A, which was filled with earth. It seems that the eastern and western sides were built first

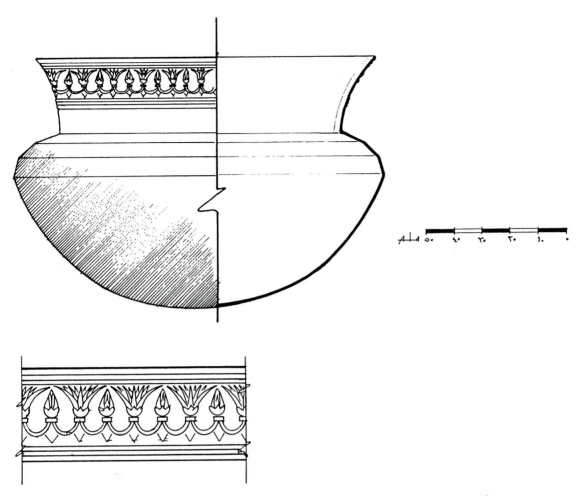

Fig. 12-f. Silver bowl (max. diam. 12.5 cm) with incised decoration from Tomb IV, MM:2130.
(Hussein and Suleiman 2000: Pic. 205).

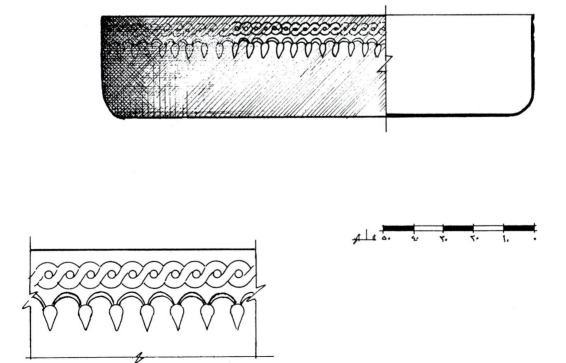

Fig. 12-g. Silver dish (diam.14.2 cm) with incised decoration from Tomb IV, MM:2128. (Hussein and Suleiman 2000: Pic. 207).

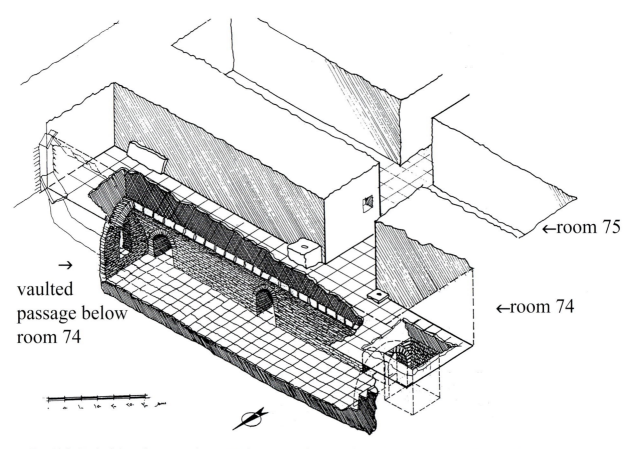

→
vaulted
passage below
room 74

←room 75

←room 74

Fig. 12-h. Vaulted Complex. View of room 74 showing its relation to the vaulted passage beneath it and the means of access from it, with room 75 behind it.

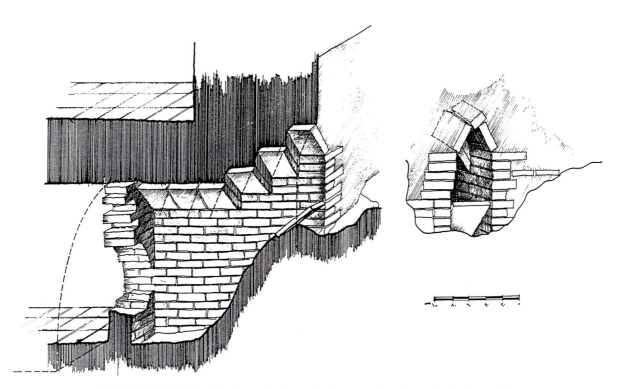

Fig. 12-i. Vaulted Complex. Access to the vaulted passage from the east end of room 74.

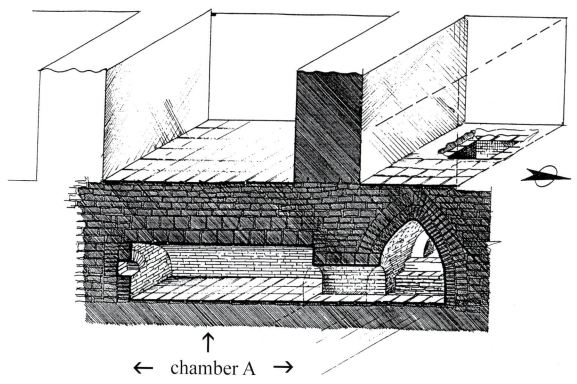

← chamber A →

Fig. 12-j. Vaulted Complex. North-south section through chamber A, the low entrance to it, the west end of the vaulted passage and the steps down from the bottom of the shaft, with the west ends of rooms 75 and 74 (with the location of the upper end of the shaft) above.

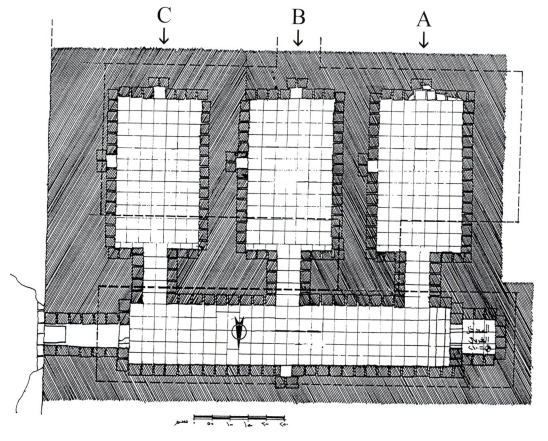

Fig. 12-k. Vaulted Complex. Plan of the complex beneath rooms 74 and 75 (broken lines show the layout of the rooms respectively above the vaulted passage, and above chambers C–A).

followed by the southern and northern ends of the vault; as a result they are not bonded into the rest of the structure. Chambers B and C are similar in plan.

A large number of objects were found in the passage and vaulted chambers underneath room 74. They include many stamp and cylinder seals, gold items, pottery bowls, small glazed vessels and cups, and decorated glazed bricks. One of the most remarkable finds is a dish with eight cups (fig. 12-l). Among the finds was an inscribed stone slab (34 × 55 cm), belonging to Ashurnasirpal II (883–859 BC). The inscription gives his ancestry, many of his titles, and lists campaigns to Nairi, Kirhi, Shubari and Nirib, and his crossing of the Tigris. However, the inscription is incomplete, as both the back and a quarter of the front are without inscription.

The following are a few thoughts on these discoveries from the 1992 season:

1 The walls and courtyards that were unearthed are a continuation of what was discovered in the previous seasons. They are part of the palace of Ashurnasirpal II, but may have been built at a later date.
2 All the small finds, the pottery, the metal objects and the seals are Neo-Assyrian in date.

3 It is difficult to identify the function of this structure in view of the paucity of information about the passage and the vaulted chambers, and the lack of any textual evidence. The slab mentioned above does not give any clue and, indeed, may originally have belonged to another part of the palace.

There are, however, two possibilities:

A The building was probably used as a temporary detention centre because this part of the palace was a fair distance from the administrative wing and the royal courts. Also, the plan of the building, the narrow passage and the difficult access, may have helped in controlling a detainee before any royal sentence.
B It is also possible that these rooms were used as burial chambers, although no coffins were found. The bodies could have been laid directly on the ground, and because of the dampness inside the chambers the deterioration of the bodies was complete. The finds could have been connected with funerary practices, as suggested by the large number of fibulae, which could have been used to fasten shrouds.

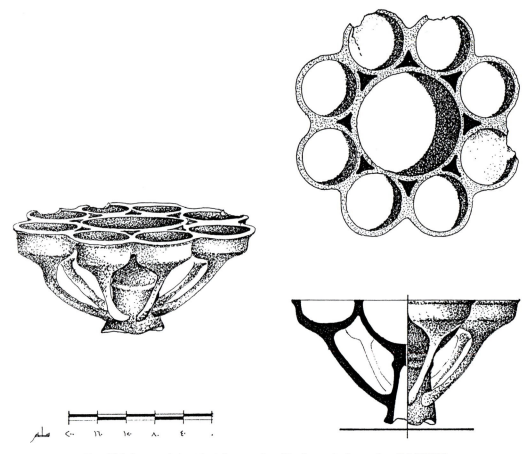

Fig. 12-l. Pottery dish with eight cups found in the vaulted complex, IM:127831.
(Hussein and Suleiman 2000: Pic. 223).

III. Well 4 in the Palace of Ashurnasirpal II

In previous excavations, three wells were discovered in the south-western part of the palace. In June 1992, a fourth well was found in the North-West Palace. It is situated in the south-eastern corner of a large courtyard in the harem quarter (no. 80 on Plan 4b); see Hussein and Suleiman 2000: 156–57).

A large mass of *libn* covered the mouth of the well, possibly built when the well was no longer in use. When the *libn* was removed, the round brick opening of the well was revealed; it was similar to the other wells at Nimrud. Beside the mouth a large, white, broken stone was found lying on the ground, one piece of which had fallen into the well. Nearby a smaller round stone was found—it was probably the lid of the well. The well was 170 cm in diameter, and the inner wall was lined with round courses of bricks. These rows of bricks narrowed at the top of the well, possibly to hold the stone lid. The lining of the well consisted of three hundred courses of bricks that varied in size, the difference in size perhaps helping to form the circular structure. The well was 25.5 m deep.

For the first 6 m, the well was filled with debris consisting of ash and broken bricks belonging to later periods. Below this layer, human bones and skeletons began to appear, probably belonging to more than 120 individuals. Some were in an extended position, some had their hands manacled with iron chains, and others had their legs in chains also. The hand manacles are smaller than the ones found by the legs; these latter were large and heavy, with a wider diameter to fit the ankles.

At a depth of 9.5 m there was an unexpected space, void of any debris; it is possible that originally the water level rose to this height. Below, at a depth of 11.80 m, more débris and skeletons appeared, with the finds and human remains packed together with large quantities of objects. Finds continued to a depth of 19.10 m, after which no more objects were found. Excavating the well took four-and-a-half months due to the difficulties encountered with water filling the well, despite the use of an electric pump operated by four workmen.

There are a number of opinions concerning the finds from the well. Originally the well was dug to provide water, but it seems it was no longer used after the sack of Nimrud in 614 BC. It is possible that it was then used to dispose of rivals or the enemy. Some individuals were still alive when thrown into the well, while others had probably been executed, although there is no evidence for this. It is also possible that the bodies were Assyrians killed during the sack of Nimrud.

The number of bodies in the well was estimated on the basis of the number of skulls. The bones were mixed together, which made it difficult to separate the individual skeletons. However, they were better preserved than the bones found in other parts of Nimrud. Possibly the water with some other element had helped in preserving the bones. The colour of the bones was mostly dark yellow, though some were dark brown. All the bodies had their teeth intact, with hardly any decay. There is no evidence of female bones and few are those of children. All the bones are now stored, and awaiting further study.

A great number of objects were found, such as large and small pottery vessels of different shapes, some glazed, among them one cauldron. There were a number of stone cups decorated with incised geometrical and floral patterns among the skeletons[3] (fig. 12-m). Wooden objects, such as combs, small cups and plates, and door knobs were retrieved. A number of items of gold jewellery and many beads were also found.

IV. First season of excavation at the Ishtar Temple

New excavations took place at the Ishtar Temple, which lies in the north-west part of the Nimrud platform to the south-east of the ziggurat (Plan 3; fig. 12-n). The location was chosen because previous expeditions had only carried out limited work in this area (see Reade 2002: 181–91).

One of the first results was the discovery of a gateway in the eastern part of the temple, flanked by two lion colossi, larger than the examples discovered in the nineteenth century (see fig. 12-o), or those still standing in the North-West Palace of Ashurnasirpal II. Because they were near the surface they have suffered extensively, and the upper parts have been completely destroyed.

The façade, on either side of the gateway, especially the north side, is decorated with engaged columns (half circles) similar to the ones on the north façade of the Nabu Temple. The south side of the façade has collapsed and very little has survived. The floor near the façade and the front of the entrance was paved with bricks, a number of which had inscriptions of Ashurnasirpal II.

Immediately behind the entrance, a long rectangular room was excavated, running from north to south. The temple has thick walls built with Assyrian-type mud bricks; the bottom of the walls was coated with bitumen to a height of 50 cm. In the centre of the south wall a niche was found, built within a recess with bricks on either side, and closed at the back with one brick. It must have been a later addition, and may have been used as an oven as evidence of burning was attested. An octagonal column was erected to support the wall above it, and two basins lined with gypsum plaster were found adjacent to the niche.

---

[3] These are to be the subject of a forthcoming article by the author and Georgina Herrmann (eds.).

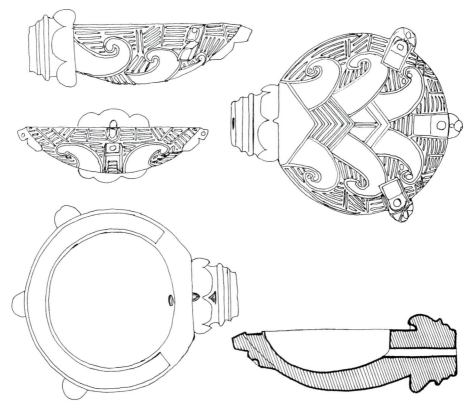

Fig. 12-m. Carved black stone cup, originally fitted on to the end of a tube, found in Well 4.

Opposite the lion gateway, in the centre of the western wall of the first room, a second entrance was discovered. It led to a large courtyard paved with inscribed bricks of Ashurnasirpal II and a few of Shalmaneser III. A wall built with large dressed limestone blocks was cleared in the south-western side, possibly a later addition by the inhabitants of Nimrud who brought the stones from another location. A number of steps were built beside the wall to provide access to the courtyard.

In 1851 Layard had discovered an entrance to the north of the courtyard. It led into a second large room and was flanked by two lions (fig. 12-o). One of the lions was transferred to the British Museum. The head of the second lion was damaged and it was left *in situ*; in 1973 it was removed to Mosul Museum. Fortunately, during this season's excavation, the missing part of the head was found in good condition. To the right of the entrance are the remains of a brick wall, but only a few bricks from the foundation on the left side were unearthed. The walls were mentioned by Layard and are visible in his illustrations of the entrance (see fig. 12-o). Part of the entrance slab is still visible, although it was damaged during the removal of the lions.

The entrance led to a large rectangular room in the centre of which, close to the pavement, was a large inscribed marble slab. The room may have served as a throne room

in the Temple of Ishtar. It was paved with bricks, although some of the bricks from the west side had been removed. The thick walls were mud-plastered, but bore no trace of coloured paint, unlike the walls in the palaces of Ashurnasirpal II and Adad-nirari III. However, as in the palaces, the lower parts of the walls were coated with bitumen. Three cube-shaped blocks of limestone were found in this room. Each has a cavity on the side. Their function is uncertain, but possibly they were used for ritual purposes, particularly since the temple was considered one of the most important in Assyria. There is a side entrance at the northern end of the east wall, leading to a side room paved with bricks. A number of stone fragments belonging to a slab were discovered in the west part of the room. The fragments are inscribed on both sides in large and clear cuneiform indicating that it is an important historical document.

Near the end of the season, work was concentrated in the central courtyard, with the aim of defining the area and identifying the surrounding wall. On the north side brick foundations and a mud-brick wall were unearthed; this wall extended west of the entrance and consists of what look like recesses built with courses of bricks and finished with mud plaster. To the south another wall was unearthed; this wall was decorated with buttresses facing the courtyard and, at its western end, it turns northwards. Future excavations may perhaps reveal further parts of the building.

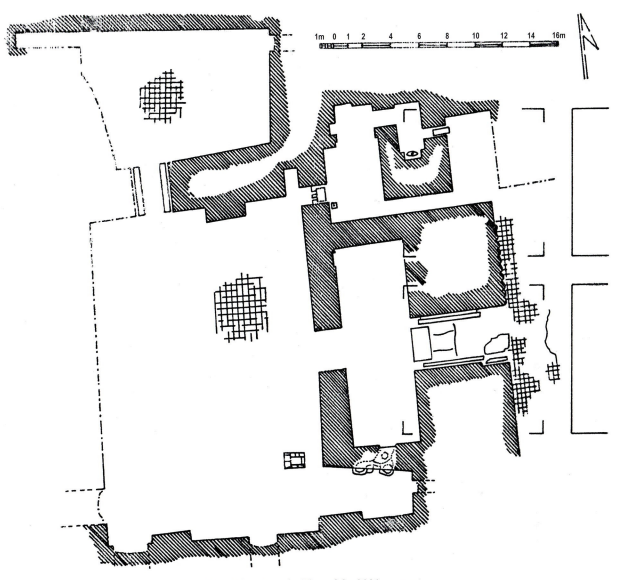

Fig. 12-n. Ishtar Temple. Plan of the 2001 excavations.

Fig. 12-o. Ishtar Temple. Illustration of the Layard lions in situ.

Fig. 12-p

*Fig. 12-p, q, r. Ishtar Temple. Fragments of glazed
bricks from the excavations.*

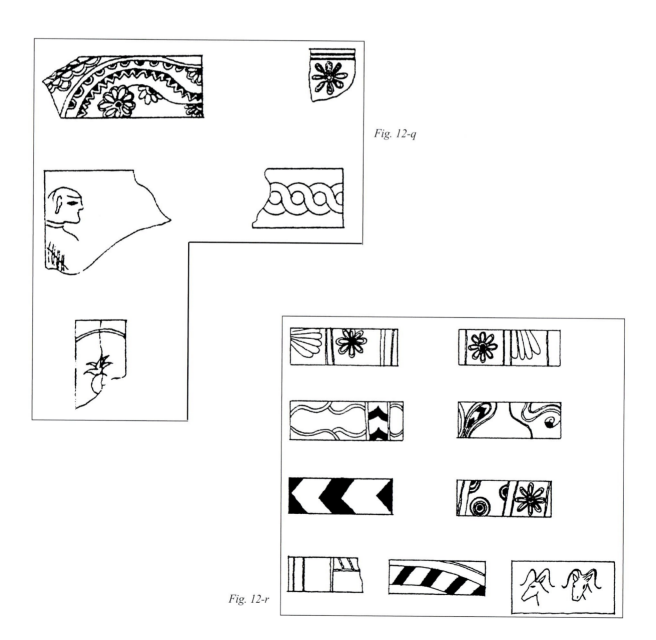

Fig. 12-q

Fig. 12-r

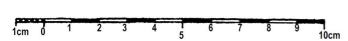

Fig. 12-s. Ishtar Temple. Fragment of glazed wall plaque from the excavations.

One of the most important discoveries from the Temple of Ishtar were fragments of an inscribed octagonal prism. Limestone incense burner stands about a metre high were found at the corners of the entrances; one of the stands was decorated with parapet motifs. Other discoveries consist of decorative and architectural elements found near the entrances or the walls, such as large quantities of glazed bricks decorated with floral and geometrical patterns, and a few with human or animal heads on the top surface. Many also have yellow and black parallel lines on the top surface (figs 12-p–r). A number of Neo-Assyrian cylinder seals were discovered, one of which has an inscription in three lines. Other finds included a fragment of glazed plaque, decorated vessels, 'Palace' ware, and a fragment of a relief plaque depicting the legs and lowered wing of a naked female figure (figs 12-s–x).

On the north side of the Temple a narrow passage was excavated. One end had been blocked with bricks which were probably reused from another location. These bricks rested on a limestone pavement. In front of the passage was a space where many potsherds and broken bricks were scattered, indicating it had been previously excavated. The passage led to a small room paved with bricks. One brick had a hole in the centre; it covered an oval pit filled with potsherds, possibly a drain. Another passage connected this building with small, narrow units where a number of tablets, fragments of a prism and cylinder seals were found.

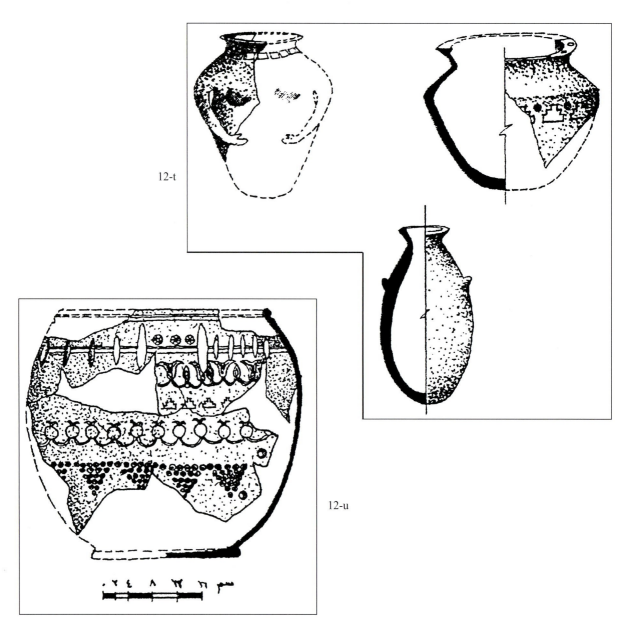

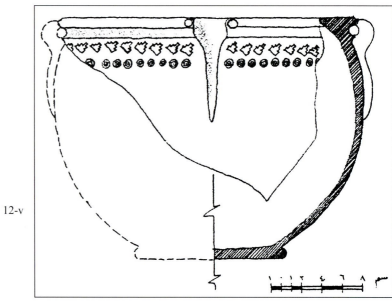

Fig. 12-t, u, v. A selection of vessels from the excavations in the Ishtar Temple.

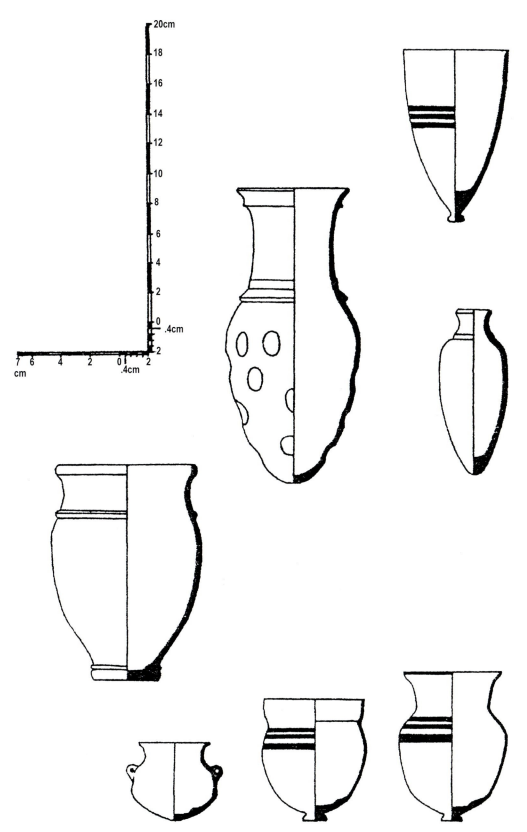

Fig. 12-w. A selection of vessels from the excavations in the Ishtar Temple.

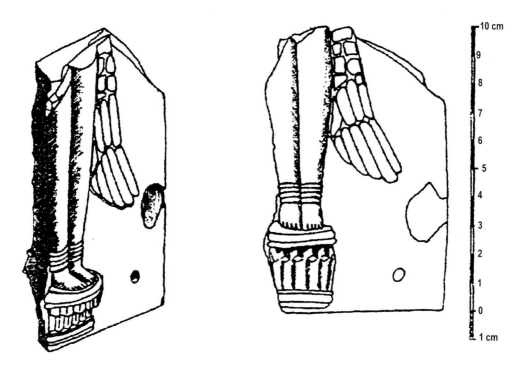

Fig. 12-x. Fragment of a plaque decorated in relief from the excavations in the Ishtar Temple.

EXCAVATION OF THE WELL IN COURT 80

Junaid al-Fakhri[1]

In 1991 work was slow due to the war and its aftermath. Torrential rain that winter led to flooding in the passage leading to the harem quarters and to Well NN, resulting in the collapse of part of the wall opposite the well. This led to the discovery of the vaulted complex [discussed above]. The clearing of the southern court, Court 80, continued, and in the south-eastern corner a new well (Well 4) was found in 1992.

The excavation of the well

The well was covered with a square limestone slab, was 1.75 m in diameter, and was lined with bricks, as had been the case with previous wells. Four metres down (equivalent to 40–45 brick courses), four skeletons were found. There were stones next to the heads and the hands and legs were shackled with iron chains. Five and six metres down, similar skeletons were found. Groups of five to six skeletons continued to be found as digging progressed. With the skeletons were personal ornaments, such as silver, copper or bronze fibulae, silver and gold rings and stamp seals, and a few beads of carnelian and turquoise. Seven metres down, one skeleton was found on its own, in a crouched position with hands on its chest. A cylinder seal was found between the finger bones of the right hand (see al-Gailani Werr fig. 19-j); around it was a string of beads of semiprecious stones, the majority of carnelian, and there were a number of rings still on the fingers. The wrists and ankles were shackled with iron chains, and around the body were several broken jars. Work continued down the well, with skeletons found according to the same pattern.

At a depth of about 12 m, I was trying to clear five skeletons that were tangled together when I came across a void. At first I thought it was the mouth of a jar, but air started coming out of it, and the noise of small falling stones. After a while, when I was sure all was safe, I enlarged the opening. I took a rope and a lamp and went down 3 m, and when I shone my torch at the area below me, I saw a most gruesome scene of skeletons tangled and 'welded' together, one on top of the other like a net, due to the drying of the mud. The bottom of this layer consisted of soft sand, which may indicate that it was originally filled with water that had dried up. I was able to remove about 24 skeletons with their belongings: fibulae, bead necklaces, earrings and a few seals. Some scattered beads were found below this group. Digging continued and at a depth of 16 m heaps of skeletons were revealed with mud between them. The finds were unusual: a first group of about thirty bodies had with them small ivory cosmetic bottles, some decorated with Assyrian motifs, a few with remains of kohl or henna. There were also ivory and wooden combs, rings, bracelets and beads. The individuals may have been hairdressers and beauticians at the palace.

After a layer of mud 20 cm thick, another heap of thirty skeletons was found. These were probably palace officials, found together with a number of seals, gold rings[2] with semiprecious stones, silver fibulae and many bead necklaces. Beneath another layer of mud 20 cm thick, and large pieces of burnt wood, there were about forty charred skeletons, evidence that after the bodies were thrown down the well, burning wood was thrown in over them. With the skeletons were a number of bottles, some made of 'crystal'[3], some coloured, and one pottery vessel with eight sides, covered with copper [?]. Other skeletons were also excavated, to a depth of 21.5 m. In the last metre, the skeletons of young gazelles, four pomegranates, date stones, remains of other fruit and much pottery were found.

The contents of the well

The pottery from the well is similar to the finds from the vaulted rooms, including a complete *kernos* with six cups, 30 cm in height; the cups have a diameter of 6 cm each.[4]

Around 400[5] skeletons were discovered, of which about 150 were buried immediately as a sign of respect (*harram*). However, each of the remaining 250 was given a coating of preservative, and placed in a plastic bag. For years no DNA tests or any other kinds of study were carried out; in fact they were not officially acknowledged.

Students from the medical school at Mosul have now studied the bones. They belong to male individuals 18–20 years of age. There was no evidence of strangulation, such

---

[1] Junaid al-Fakhri was involved in digging the well at Nimrud and sent Dr Lamia al-Gailani Werr the following report in Arabic, which she translated. This is a slightly edited version and incorporates amendments sent by M.M. Hussein who discovered the well, and had excavated it to a depth of 7m when Junaid joined the team for about a month. Note that the depths given by Junaid differ from those given in Mahmud's article, and the identifications of the bodies as beauticians etc. are conjectural.

---

[2] Mahmud states that in fact only one gold ring was found.
[3] Mahmud states that no crystal bottles were found.
[4] This may actually be the vessel found in the vaulted complex (see fig. 12-l).
[5] In fact Mahmud recorded between 125 and 140 skulls.

as broken necks. There were several types of skull, some with prominent chins, some with large and some with small eye sockets, some with flat and some with pointed noses, some with wide and some with narrow foreheads. Four or five of the skeletons had hunched backs or humps at the chest. A number showed evidence of broken bones that had healed, mostly incorrectly. Two skeletons had 1.5 cm square holes on the right side of the skull, with the cut bone replaced—evidence of surgery.

No finds appeared in the last few metres, and the bottom of the well was reached at a depth of 26 m.

The construction of the well

The well is similar to previously excavated wells. The upper edge is built of limestone. About 10 cm above the well were two large sandstone blocks. The mouth of the well was 1.75 m in diameter, and it was covered with a square limestone slab. The well was lined with about 300 courses of shaped bricks, 7 cm thick, set on sand and mud. Below this there were layers of sandstone, which were placed in circles; some of the stones protruded from the surface, and each circle was 60–70 high, followed by another layer of mud and sand. The bottom of the well was paved with a number of stones. I saw Assyrian tool marks on the sandstone, which may indicate that they deliberately placed the protruding stones, possibly to prevent and break the waves when taking water from the well, and to increase the flow of water.

A possible reconstruction of the events

This is what I think happened: the bodies that were on top were the last to be thrown into the well, the king was on his own at 7 m, and the void was the result of entangled bodies floating on the water, as the well was probably full of water, indicating that it was in the rainy season, in the spring; when summer came, the water evaporated, and the bodies were kept suspended due to the presence of mud and weeds. It should be noted that between the heaps of bodies there were gaps that were filled with layers of mud. Therefore, it seems that the victims were thrown in at intervals according to rank or profession, such as cupbearers, beauticians, cooks and guards (no weapons were found).

It is to be noted that a room (about 1.50 × 1.50 m), with no door or any opening, was discovered about 20 m west of the well. Inside it was a skeleton shackled in a similar manner to the skeletons in the well. A few pottery vessels, beads and fibulae were also found.

I think the event happened after the palace was abandoned, and was no longer inhabited by the royal family. What I noticed in the wells (and particularly, after 21.5 m, in this well), was that at the bottom the finds consisted of ordinary objects such as pottery and the remains of fruit, indicating that such objects had fallen into the well or been discarded when the palace was still occupied. This debris was similar to that in Wells NN, AJ and AB. I don't know about the well in the Burnt Palace.

AN INTERPRETATION OF THE VAULTED COMPLEX AND WELL 4 IN THE NORTH-WEST PALACE, NIMRUD

Julian Reade

Among the remarkable discoveries made by Muzahim Mahmoud and his colleagues, in the domestic quarters of the North-West Palace of Ashurnasirpal II at Nimrud, are the vaulted complex beneath Rooms 74–75, and Well 4 in Court 80. There are problems connected with them, which may be resolved by a single hypothesis, and Muzahim kindly invited me to present it together with his own paper.

Room 74 had a vaulted passage underneath it, access to which was either from the western end of Room 74, through a vertical shaft with steps at the bottom, or more conveniently through a steep tunnel leading down from the eastern end of Room 74. The passage itself acted as a single antechamber giving access to three vaulted rooms below Room 75. The passage and the vaulted rooms have arched niches in their walls. In principle, the architecture resembles that of many Neo-Assyrian tombs. Each of Tombs I–IV in the same palace (Hussein and Suleiman 2000; Oates and Oates 2001: 78–90) comprised a vertical underground shaft with steps at the bottom leading into a vaulted antechamber and burial chamber. Tombs II–IV also had wall-niches; lamps were found in two of them. Tombs I–III each had one inner chamber, closed by a stone door and containing one coffin. Tomb IV also contained one coffin, but, as there were only loose bricks in the doorway, it may have been intended for use on more than one occasion, as a communal tomb. At Ashur, in Neo-Assyrian private houses, besides burials in coffins below floors such as are also found in the North-West Palace, there were communal underground vaulted tomb-chambers, single or in groups, both with and without doors and coffins (Haller 1954). Another communal vaulted tomb was recorded near Mosul at Humaydat (Ibrahim and Agha 1983); there must be hundreds of them at Nineveh. It seems that coffins were not essential in communal tombs.

These analogies suggest that the vaulted complex below Rooms 74–75 was suitable for burials. Other tombs and graves excavated in the North-West Palace account for about twenty-six individuals, including a royal wife of the mid-ninth century in Tomb III and two royal wives of the later eighth century in Tomb II. Evidently some members of the royal household were buried in traditional style at home with their personal possessions. There may be more undiscovered graves in the palace, or in the adjoining palace of Adad-nirari III. Nonetheless the number of people active in these buildings, in the period of about 160 years during which kings from Ashurnasirpal II to Sargon often resided at Nimrud, must have far exceeded twenty-six. It would have been sensible to have communal vaults

in which to bury the hundreds of people who did not require special treatment. The complex under Rooms 74–75 could have served this purpose admirably. The unusual alternative entrance to it, through a tunnel, could have been an improvement on the original design, facilitating repeated access.

The vaulted complex produced many cylinder and stamp seals (Hussein and Abdul-Razaq 1997–98), such as one might expect to find in a communal burial place. The themes include animals, hunts, and worship. Among other objects appropriate as grave goods were a carnelian necklace and glazed polychrome jars, and there was also an elaborate glazed *kernos* vessel with multiple bowls (Oates and Oates 2001: 67–68, fig. 39). Objects found in Rooms 74–75 above the vaults, and in Room 77 nearby, included more seals of comparable types. Some of the seals had been chipped, probably because gold caps had been removed from them (as discussed in this volume by al-Gailani Werr). It is as if robbers had discovered the door into the steep tunnel at the eastern end of Room 74, entered the vaulted complex, and removed most of its contents, while missing many items in the dark.

No human bones were recorded from the vaulted complex, however: so, if this had indeed been used for burials, the bones too had been removed. There were some bones in Room 74, but hardly enough to account for all the bodies that could once have been buried in the vaults. Casual tomb-robbers would hardly have collected bones from underground; but enemy looters might well have done so, as the destruction of memorials and the desecration of tombs were widespread practices in the Ancient Near East just as they have been elsewhere. Ashurnasirpal II invoked curses on anyone who should desecrate his Nimrud palace stela by, among other options, throwing it into water, and Ashurbanipal, describing his activities in Elam in 647 BC, states that 'the sepulchres of their earlier and later kings... I destroyed, I devastated, I exposed to the sun. Their bones I carried off to Assyria. I laid restlessness upon their shades. I deprived them of food-offerings and libations of water' (Luckenbill 1926–27: I, 176; II, 310). Accordingly, the enemies who ransacked the Assyrian cities in 614–612 BC may in their turn have deliberately removed the bones of the dead from any tombs they happened to locate. This would account for the absence of bones from the vaulted complex. While there are many ways in which such bones might have been disposed of, a common procedure at the time was to throw things down wells. This is apparently what happened to the great Kultrelief in the Ashur Temple at Ashur (Reade 2000c: 106), to jewellery and equipment in the Nabu Temple at Khorsabad (Loud and Altman 1938: 60), possibly to a mace found in a well in the Nabu Temple at Nineveh (Barag 1985: 74), and to innumerable items found in Wells NN, AJ and AB in the North-West Palace at Nimrud.

The contents of Well 4 in Court 80 of the palace, now excavated by Muzahim, were exceptional. The well was

1.7 m in diameter and 25.5 m deep, with a capacity of about 58 cubic metres, and it contained, among other things, a very large number of skeletons, 'mangled together'. The work of excavation must have been extraordinarily difficult. Muzahim has given an absolute minimum of 125 bodies in the well, based on the number of skulls still preserved; earlier reports estimate the number of bodies at over 200 (al-Gailani Werr 1999: 4) and over 180 (Oates and Oates 2001: 100–3). Because the adult human body, on average, occupies about one third of a cubic metre, the well could theoretically have contained about 174 complete dead bodies if crammed solid, but this is not how the bones were distributed. In fact a large number of manacled or fettered skeletons were found in groups in the upper part of the well, and these presumably did belong to people who were thrown down the well either alive or just after they had been killed. Below a depth of 11.8 m, however, after an empty space that was 2.3 m high, the nature of the deposit in the well seems to have changed. From then on down, for a further 7.3 m towards the bottom of the well, human remains are said to have been packed tightly together with numerous objects, including seals similar to those found in and near the vaulted complex. There were also beads, kohl-pots, a mirror, glazed pottery, and even a *kernos*[1] resembling that from the vaulted complex. There could have been a great number of individuals in the lower part of the well, not as bodies but as dry bones. In other words, the lower part of Well 4 contained exactly the kinds of thing that one might expect to find in tombs. So the discoveries in the vaulted complex and the well seem to complement and explain one another, as if most of the skeletons and many of the grave-goods originally placed in the vaulted complex, and possibly in any other robbed tombs that may exist in the vicinity, were the very same as those actually recovered from the well.

If so, Muzahim has unearthed evidence for a remarkable sequence of events. The vaulted complex would be where palace attendants, perhaps divided into three categories, one in each of the three main vaults, were once laid to rest after death; most probably died before 707 BC, when the palace ceased to be a royal residence, although the harem quarters with their rich tombs must have remained under guard through the seventh century. In about 612 BC the enemies who captured the Nimrud citadel discovered the tunnel in Room 74, and entered the vaulted complex. They probably began by collecting any gold they could see, because some of the seals found inside the vaults had already lost their caps or mounts; other seals were broken in Rooms 74 and 77. Someone also decided that the remains should be desecrated more methodically. So the skeletons in the vaults, together with much of the funeral equipment, were shovelled into bags or baskets, and brought to the surface; the containers were quickly sifted for more treasure, before being taken out through Room 75 into Court 80, and unceremoniously dumped down the nearest well. Some of the work may have been done by shackled prisoners, who were finally thrown down the well themselves.

This then may be one of those remarkable occasions on which archaeology has brought the past directly and dramatically to life. If the hypothesis is sound, the bones that survive represent one group of individuals who were entitled to burial in the North-West Palace, especially during the eighth century BC, and a second group of individuals who were captured and killed around 612 BC. There are therefore many questions which might be answered by analysis of physical characteristics of the skeletal material, combined with study of DNA samples and access to all the relevant data concerning provenance: to take one obvious example, can we determine whether court eunuchs were often blood-relations, such as the superfluous sons of Assyrian kings and princes? Muzahim's discoveries, so long as they survive the latest tragedies in Iraq, may have much to tell us about who actually constituted the Assyrian court and army.

---

[1]   al-Fakhri, this volume, n. 2 (eds.).

PLATE I

(a)

(b)

(a) Gold strap work diadem from Tomb II.
(b) Gold elements of a diadem, with inlay of semi-precious stones or their imitations. From Tomb II.

PLATE II

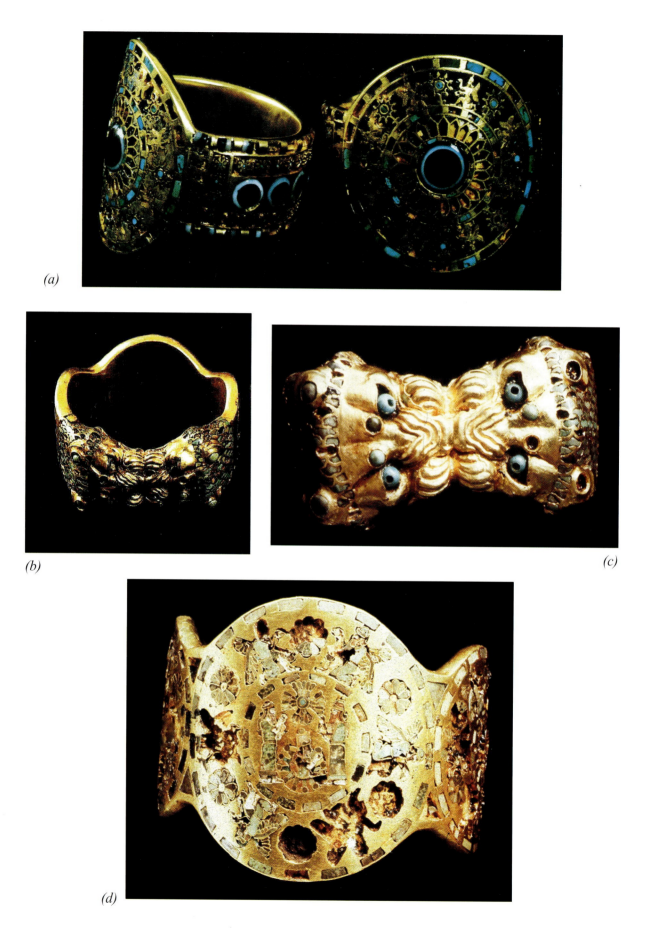

(a) Bracelet with the design in gold and the background inlaid with semi-precious stones or their imitations. From Tomb II.
(b)–(d) Three views of a gold bracelet consisting of three discs bearing the same inlaid design, and the back consisting of the heads of two lions. From Tomb II.

PLATE III

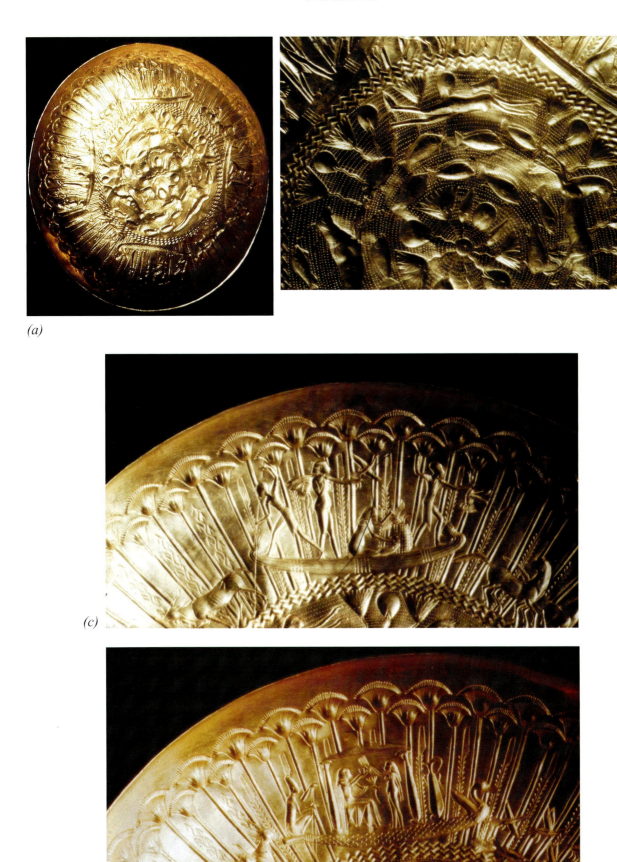

(a–d) Gold bowl and details of its Egyptianising design. From Tomb II.

PLATE IV

(a)

(b)

(c)

(d)

(a) A selection of gold bowls inscribed in cuneiform. Top left: "Atalia"; Top right: "Yaba"; Bottom left: "Banitu";
all three from Tomb II. Bottom right: "Shamshi-ilu" from Tomb III.
(b) A gold bowl in storage in Baghdad in 2003 together with gold anklets, a rock-crystal vessel inscribed "Atalia" and
necklaces (photograph courtesy of Sarah Collins).
(c) Anklets
(d) Dr Nuwala examinining the anklets in June 3003 (photograph courtesy of Sarah Collins).

PLATE V

(a)

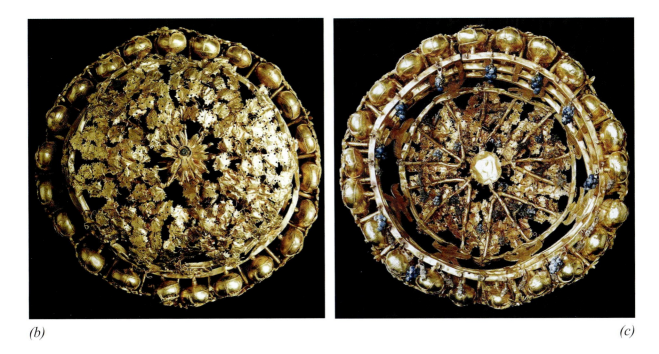

(b)

(c)

Gold crown from Tomb III.
(a) The crown with the lapis-lazuli grapes hanging down on the interior.
(b) The top of the crown.
(c) The interior of the crown.

PLATE VI

(a)

(b)

(a–b) Details of the crown shown on Plate V.

PLATE VII

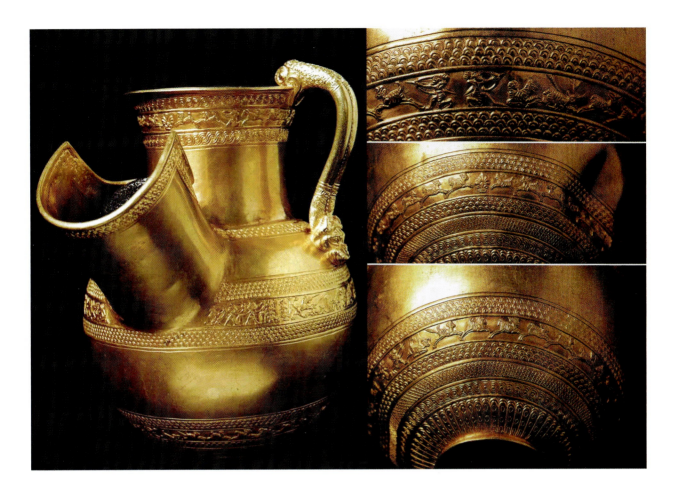

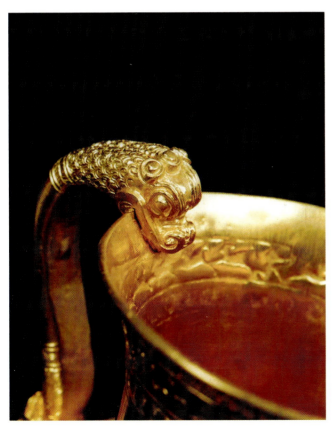

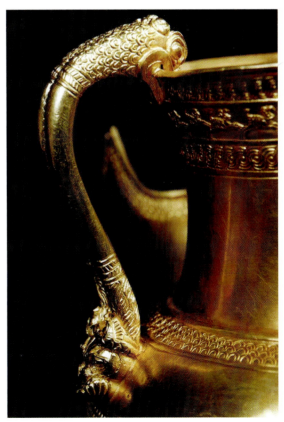

The gold jug (height 13 cm) from Tomb III.

PLATE VIII

(a)

(b)

(c)

(d)

(e)

(a-b) Some of the many necklaces made of semi-precious stones, from Tomb III.
(c) Gold necklace with eye-stone pendants, from Tomb III.
(d) Strap work dress ornament from Tomb III.
(e) Gold finger rings, inlaid with semi-precious stones, from Tomb III.

13   PRECISION CRAFTSMANSHIP OF THE NIMRUD GOLD MATERIAL

Donny George Youkhanna

In this paper we will try to answer some questions about the techniques that were used in crafting the gold material from the Royal Tombs from the city of Nimrud. But since the material is not at present available to be checked thoroughly, I believe that further questions will be raised. We will follow the techniques used by the craftsmen, and show some examples, in order to try to identify the methods by which this gold jewellery was made.

Casting

Casting gold material has a very long tradition in Mesopotamia, from the time of the Sumerian Early Dynastic Period, but we do not need to go into the history of casting here. We can find evidence for casting, for instance, in the gold pomegranates from Tomb I (fig. 13-a). It is evident that the piece was made in two halves that were joined by a very thin line of welding. The heavy bracelets and anklets, and some other pieces, were made by welding several cast pieces together to obtain the final object.

Soldering

Soldering is often used in the material we have, for example in joining the small rings to the main frame of the large crown from Tomb III (Plate VI), and also in very many other pieces from the tombs. The craftsman must have needed a very small flame, precisely controlled and at a very high temperature, in order to reach the very small areas that needed to be soldered. How did they do that? This is another question.

Hammering

Hammering is attested on many pieces, one of the best examples being the gold jug (Plate VII). We believe that first the jug was cast plain. Then it was filled with bitumen, and the friezes were hammered, using very fine chisels, as some of the friezes are less than one centimetre high. The jug has a great number of scenes all around the neck and the body, with a lot of decoration on the bottom of the piece, and of course we can see the negative of the hammering on the inside of the jug. We can still see evidence of the technique of filling the jug with bitumen and hammering. Then the jug was heated until the bitumen melted and could be poured away, as is still done in the coppersmiths' bazaars in Baghdad, Mosul and other cities in Iraq, as well as other places in the Middle East.

Weaving

Weaving with gold wire is very common in the gold material we have from Nimrud, especially in the different kinds of chains and straps (e.g. Plates I and VIIId). The first important question is how the fine gold wire was prepared. In one case we can notice that the wires were even and their section was round. Then we need to consider the style of weaving, and the regularity with which the chains were woven together: some were single and rounded, or square in section. Some were wide, as we

Fig. 13-a. Cast gold pomegranates from Tomb I.

Fig. 13-b. Drawing of woven gold wire techniques.

can see in the case of the diadem (fig. 13-b and Plate Ia). In this case the chain was six centimetres wide but not more than a few millimetres thick. In Baghdad we call such chains 'Italian chains' because the modern examples we have come from Italy. Although they are machine-made, they are almost the same as the ones we have from the Royal Tombs at Nimrud.

Encapsulation

The best example of encapsulation we have is in the crown from Tomb III, but first we need to know how this crown was built up. At first the craftsmen made a frame of square-section tubes (see Plates V and VI), then the vine leaves were added on top; most of the other decoration on the sides, such as the flowers, the winged figures and the pomegranates, was added by the encapsulation method. Did they use any kind of glue to fix the tubes together? We don't know the answer to this.

Granulation

One of the most ancient examples of granulation, we believe, comes from the site of Larsa in the Old Babylonian period; it was excavated by the French in the late 1970s (Arnaud *et al.* 1979). It was a circular gold medallion with some gold balls in the centre, and on these balls there were very small grains of gold. In our Nimrud material we have the same granulation on the petals and stamens of the flowers on the Tomb III crown (Plate VI). I believe that the same kind of granulation occurs on some Etruscan and Georgian gold.

It is not hard to understand how the small, fine grains of gold were made, but the real problem is how these fine grains were attached to a gold background. Perhaps this was achieved by different melting points for the grains and the gold surface. In February 2002, in Bochum in Germany, this idea was suggested in a discussion between Dr Charlotte Trümpler, Dr Hauptmann and myself in relation to Georgian and Etruscan granulation. However, it might be a matter of having a different kind of gold between the gold surface and the gold grains.

Inlaying

Inlaying techniques are very well known from early periods in Mesopotamia, using stone, shell, bitumen and other materials. In the Nimrud material we can find the same inlaying technique, stone inlaid with stone, gold inlaid with stone, and gold inlaid with paste. The techniques used are very fine, sometimes champ-levé and sometimes choisonné, so that either the background is cut away around the subject or the subject itself is recessed and then filled with inlay (compare the bracelets in Plate II). In all cases, inlaying in the Nimrud material is a major subject that needs further intensive study.

Gluing

In most examples of inlaying, the inlays were glued in position either with bitumen or with another material unknown to us for the time being. In the case of the grape clusters made of lapis lazuli in the large crown (Plates V and VI), the small balls and half balls made of lapis lazuli were glued together with a transparent material, which we need to analyse in the future. Until that happens, I believe this unknown material is the most long-lasting adhesive so far known!

This paper is just an introduction to a long and intensive study that still needs to be carried out on the Nimrud Treasure, once the material is available for such study. I hope in the near future, we can conduct this kind of study and others too.

14 NIMRUD TREASURES: PANEL DISCUSSION

Edited by Dominique Collon

The following discussion was centred on slides of selected objects from the tombs. There was a panel consisting of Lamia al-Gailani Werr (LG), Dominique Collon (DC), John Curtis (JC), Muayyad Said Damerji (MD), Donny George Youkhanna (DG), Georgina Herrmann (GH), Muzahim M. Hussein (MH), Rachel Maxwell-Hyslop (RMH), Roger Moorey (RM) and Jack Ogden (JO). They were asked to comment on the slides, but the discussion was open to everyone.

This summary is based on the tape recordings made at the time. Unfortunately, with a few exceptions, the questions and comments of those in the audience were not audible on the recording and can only be reconstructed now from the answers of the panellists, from notes taken at the time, and from the recollections of those concerned, sometimes supplemented with information subsequently gleaned from other sources. Some general comments on techniques, which arose as a result of the paper by Donny George (Chapter 13), have been appended there. I apologize for any errors of transcription and attribution.

General Remarks

DG drew attention to the fact that the jewellery from the Nimrud tombs showed the Assyrians in a completely different light. Whereas the Assyrians often represented themselves as cruel and blood-thirsty, the jewellery demonstrated their appreciation of beautiful things. He reiterated that it had only been possible to make a brief examination of the jewellery before it was locked away, and a further detailed study was needed when it once again became accessible. Any statements and conclusions were provisional.

Nicholas Postgate asked whether the panel thought the jewellery was native Assyrian or more western. There was some discussion, ending in general agreement with DG's view that as the Assyrian Empire encompassed so much of the Near East, and as the Assyrians imported booty, ideas and craftsmen, and harnessed them to their own needs, the jewellery could indeed be called Assyrian. RMH pointed to the similarities with jewellery from Carchemish and wondered whether Sargon could have brought back craftsmen as well as booty. Julian Reade referred to texts in which Sargon claimed to have collected objects and craftsmen, the latter enlisted in order to produce valued imperial-style objects. MD drew an analogy with modern Iraqi jewellery which, though distinctive, incorporates Indian, Pakistani, Egyptian and African influences which

are difficult to disentangle. He also pointed out that cylinder seals with inscriptions of Kurigalzu and Marduk-zakir-shumi had been found on objects in the tombs; these were probably gifts that had been stored in the royal treasury, sometimes for centuries. He noted the danger of using modern geo-political terms and cited the example of graves at Mazar in Jordan where a clay version of the bronze coffins from Tomb III, a neo-Babylonian stamp seal, and an Achaemenid stamp and cylinder seal were found alongside the local repertoire of objects (Yassine 1984: figs 2, 9, 24, 57). The question of analysis of the gold was raised, but JO pointed out that trace-element analysis would be unlikely to provide an answer since gold was constantly being melted down and recycled and such analysis had only proved useful in connection with objects from isolated early prehistoric communities. However, he noted that it would be interesting to know whether the Nimrud gold was refined, because the refining of gold was usually thought to have begun in earnest under the Persian Empire in the sixth century BC.

The objects illustrated in Hussein and Suleiman 2000, which are discussed below, are distributed between the tombs as follows:

- Tomb I: Pics 1–18 and part of Pic. 19.
- Tomb II: part of Pic. 19 and Pics 22–104, and parts of Pics 109–11 and 198–200.
- Tomb III: parts of 109–11, and Pics 112–97, and parts of Pics 198–200.
- Tomb IV: objects prefixed with MM on pp. 419 ff., Pics 201–18.
- Miscellaneous: Pics 219–23.

The descriptions of the objects are based on remarks by MD, DG and MH, supplemented by information gleaned from DG's excellent detailed photographs and the accompanying text (Damerji 1999; Hussein and Suleiman: 2000). The abbreviation IM prefixes the Iraq Museum number. Numbers in brackets without a prefix refer to the picture numbers in Hussein and Suleiman 2000.

The Crown from Tomb III, Bronze Coffin 2 (Plates V and VI)

IM 115619; Weight: 1,003.2 g; Diameter: 24 cm; Height: 16 cm.

The crown was found on the almost complete skeleton of a woman 18 to 20 years old; it was much too big for her.

Damerji 1999: Abb. 41–45; Hussein and Suleiman 2000: 373–74 (159–60); Oates and Oates 2001: pl. 4a.

The upper part of the crown is supported by an interior framework of thin round hollow tubes forming four bisected triangles and one single triangle, fanning out from the centre and attached to a circle made from a square hollow tube. At the very top, is a flower with tendrils, resembling a passion flower, but DG thought it might be associated with the canopy of vine leaves below it. He had thought there might have been a textile lining inside the crown, but in view of the fact that there were bunches of lapis lazuli grapes hanging beneath the trellis, inside the crown, he now thought this could be discounted. Below the trellis, and linking the two halves of the crown, are eight four-winged robed figures attached to the upper and lower frameworks. They have inlaid eyes and some inlay survives on the wings. The lower part of the crown is supported by an interior scaffolding or framework formed by a grid of square hollow tubes supporting lateral round tubes onto which gold pomegranates and rosettes are fitted; MD suggested these might be poppy seed-pods and flowers. Hooks along the bottom have bunches of lapis-lazuli grapes attached to them (some of the links were missing and MH replaced them with modern gold wire). There are sixty-three opium capsules in three rows, on the outer side of which are hollows for inlay surrounded by a band of granulation and by little triangles supporting very fine granulation. Alternating with the opium capsules are two rows of daisy-like rosettes, with a circle for inlay in the centre and petals alternately either edged with granulation or covered with very fine granulation.

DG stated that the black material in the gold hollows for inlay was probably bitumen used for gluing stones, now lost. This might be, he suggested, because the crown, which was made for an adult, had perhaps originally been in the stone sarcophagus in the inner chamber of the tomb, and was subsequently removed (hence the loss of some inlays etc.) and placed with the body of a young adult. The grape clusters were built up over a gold core with balls and half-balls of lapis lazuli glued to each other and to the core with a clear adhesive which had yet to be analysed, but which was probably the longest-lasting adhesive known. MD pointed out that there was evidence for the use of powdered stone to make adhesives of different colours.

JO enquired about what looked like 'beaded wire' on the pomegranates; if it was an integral part of the pomegranates, it would not be beaded wire, but if the Nimrud pomegranates really had beaded wire, this would be the earliest excavated and dated example and would be very exciting. He pointed out that beaded wire was found from Etruria eastwards all over the eastern Mediterranean, except Egypt, from the seventh century BC onwards. DG said that further examination of the pieces would establish which technique had been used.

The iconography of the four-winged figures was discussed. DC pointed out that they appeared in the second millennium but that it was unusual to find them 'prudishly' clothed. In the first millennium, they are often heroic male figures. LG said four-winged female figures occurred on cylinder and stamp seals which, she suggested, could have belonged to royal women (figs 19-a–19-d). Eric Gubel referred to their occurrence in Phoenician and Etruscan art, as caryatid figures on Syrian vessels, and at Karatepe. Michael Roaf pointed out that Assyrian treasuries contained much earlier material, and suggested that the four-winged figures might have been reused from some earlier imported piece of jewellery. MD believed the decoration should be viewed as an ecological whole with the flowers and grapes, and thought they might be bees with human heads.

RM remarked that the material was so astonishing, new and fresh that comparisons were extraordinarily difficult; it was hard to comment on it. He found this crown particularly interesting as an item of dress.

Fig. 14-a. The gold crown from Tomb II.

The Crown from Tomb II (fig. 14-a)

IM 105692; Weight: 216.70 g; Diameter: 18 cm; Height: 6 cm.

Found in the sarcophagus with the smaller of two women, both in their thirties; Damerji 1999: Abb. 26:1; Hussein and Suleiman 2000: 289 (82).

This crown is made of a band of thin and flexible gold, on the exterior of which ninety-six rosettes are attached, one above the other in three rows, by gold rivets with domed heads visible on the interior. Each rosette has eight petals edged with granulation (beaded wire?), and has a domed centre formed by the head of the rivet.

MD said he believed that this was Atalia's crown. He pointed out that earrings and anklets in this tomb had been found in two sizes. DG confirmed that it was neither solid nor strong. MD suggested that it might have been a head-band worn over a veil to hold it in position.

Diadem from Tomb II (Plate I)

IM 105696; Weight: 1.1027 kg; Width of strap: 4 cm (Damerji 1999: 7) or 6 cm (see Chapter 13); Length: 40 cm; Diameter of pomegranate pendants: 3 mm.

Damerji 1999: Abb. 25:1; Hussein and Suleiman 2000: 224 (23); and see also 231 (29), 248 (43), 261 (55), 337 (128), and below; Oates and Oates 2001: pl. 4b.

Bands of gold strap are separated by hinged elements to form a diadem with a long ribbon hanging down the back. The central element is framed by 24 round studs, each with two concentric circles of granulation, to form a long rectangle set with two almost square stones(?), each surrounded by two rows of granulation. Attached to the lower edge is a band with two rows of granulation and tiny triangles decorated with granulation from which hang loop-in-loop chains ending in tiny pomegranates. On either side and at the back of the diadem, and half-way down the ribbon are plaques, each decorated with a brown and white agate eye-stone surrounded by small triangles with granulation and by circular studs with two concentric circles of granulation. The end of the ribbon is decorated with a similar eye-stone, surrounded by two rows of granulation and by similar studs; its lower edge is formed

by a band similar to that attached to the rectangle at the front of the diadem, and with similar pendants, but it is curved. All the granulation is very fine.

JO explained the technique for making 'straps' from loop-in-loop chains. The latter, already attested in the Royal Cemetery at Ur in the third millennium BC (Woolley 1934: pl. 146), were made by the 'strip-twist' technique from a narrow strip of gold which was twisted into wire, formed into a circular link with the ends soldered together, and then pinched and folded to form a loop which could be threaded through another loop with no further soldering required. Here several loop-in-loop chains were linked together by one of two techniques to form the 'strap', either with cross-links through the middle, or woven together with a length of wire (a more debased form used in Roman times). Without a close study of the original, it was not possible to tell which technique had been used. A single necklace would need several hundred metres of gold wire. This and many other examples from the Nimrud tombs, are the earliest provenanced attestations of strap, and this particular piece is extremely complex. An example from Rhodes may date to the seventh century BC (fig. 14-b = Williams and Ogden 1994: 26).

GH inquired whether the central inlays were exceptionally dark lapis lazuli. It was suggested that they might be glass or paste, but further inspection of the original is necessary. John Russell noted the extensive use of brown and white agates and eye-stones in the jewellery from Nimrud, and enquired about the earliest attestations of eye-stones. It seems that dated examples go back to Kassite times in the fourteenth century BC (for the significance of eye-stones, see Moorey 1998: 164). DC showed a slide of a Nimrud ivory which illustrates how such diadems were worn (Mallowan 1966: I, 212, figs 148–49, and cf. Barnett 1975: pls LXIII: S146, XCIII: S334 and CXXXVI: suppl. 19).

Diadem elements from Tomb II (Plate I)

a) IM 105813; Weight: 33.40 g.
b) IM 105814; Weight: 30.35 g.
c) IM 105815; Weight: 27.50 g. (not illustrated).
Hussein and Suleiman 2000: covers and 247 (42); Oates and Oates 2001: cover.

These panels must have belonged to a diadem similar to the previous one but MH pointed out that no other

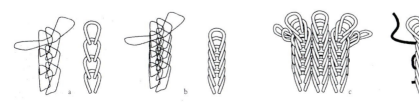

Fig. 14-b. Line drawing of strap technique.

elements were found and he suggested that they might have been attached to a band of rich cloth. The three elements are hinged so that they must have been arranged with c) on the left, b) in the centre, and a) on the right. All three consist of a gold frame. At the top is a row of balls—five each for a) and c) and four for b)—below which are two double rows of granulation. At the bottom are pendant triangles decorated with granulation and a rod on which are threaded loop-in-loop chains ending in pomegranates. The hinged sides of b) are undecorated; the sides of a) and c) adjacent to b) have double vertical rows of granulation above and below the gap for the hinge, and the other side has a gold edge with holes which would have enabled them to be stitched to the ends of a band of textile. Both a) and b) contain inlay of gold and coloured stones or glass against a background of lapis lazuli or its glass imitation; both show trees—in the centre b) an Assyrian stylized tree similar to those on reliefs from the palace of Ashurnasirpal II, on the right a), a date-palm probably standing for Babylonia; the inlay of the frame on the left c) is now missing.

Further diadem elements

There are elements similar to those at the front of the gold strap diadem, often with inlay still preserved (29, 43). Pieces fringed with gold balls on loop-in-loop chains, some with eye-stone inlay, may have come from the ends of a similar diadem (55, 128); others are attached to long gold loop-in-loop multiple chains which

may have hung down the back from a head-band (188; see also 139, 141, 191–92). There are also flexible gold head-bands (174).

9–12 Earrings (figs 14-c–14-f)

Some earrings occur only as single pairs (2 [= Damerji 1999: Abb. 12], 77, 88–89, 150), whereas others exist in numerous examples. In Tomb I, for instance, four or five lunate earrings with hanging cones were found (2 [= Damerji 1999: Abb. 11]), but in Tomb II there were 27 examples (28); indeed, there were 79 gold earrings of three different types in Tomb II (Damerji 1999: 7). In Tomb III, there were numerous examples of a type of lunate earring with clusters of ball-like pendants, sometimes in at least two tiers (114 [×24], 116 [×7], 117 [×15], 149 [×28], 161 [×41], 163 [×24]). Two outstanding pairs of lunate earrings were decorated with spherical agate beads (77, 150), and agates are also found in simpler earrings which occur in more numerous examples (76 [×6], 138 [×26]). Other types are attested (115 [×6], 123 [×12], 157 [×6 and ×15], 158 [×23], 162 [×6], 164 [×6], 165 [×12], 166 [×31], 167 [×34], 168 [×32], 177 [×8], 178 [×39], 179 [×30, each with a pendant bead], 221 (×1); of these, Pics 166, 168 and 178 are of the same type and total 102 earrings.

DG said pairs of earrings must have been personal property, whereas the earrings that occurred in large numbers may have been issued by the palace treasury, to

Fig. 14-c. Earrings.

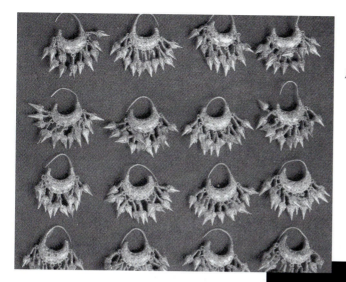

Fig. 14-d. Gold earrings from Tomb II.

Fig. 14-e. Gold earrings from Tomb I.

Fig. 14-f. Gold earrings with agate beads from Tomb III.

be worn by children, mothers, sisters etc. JC drew attention to the fact that many of the earring types appear on Assyrian reliefs.

Necklaces (Plates VIIIa–c; figs 14-g–14-i; see also fig. 13-a)

The quantity, variety and richness of the necklaces are astounding. There are gold beads of various shapes (2, 11, 21, 34, 51–52, 63–64, 70–71, 86, 90–91, 125–26, 135, 142, 153, 156, 193–200), including some decorated with granulation (e.g. 70, 72), pomegranates (10) and multiple beads (16, 26, 49, 50, 83–84, 133–34, 144). Gold beads alternate with stone beads (e.g. 19–20, 22, 24, 68), some stone beads have gold caps (69, 85, 136, 176, 204), there are necklaces made up of stone beads of different colours (e.g. 25, 108–9, 155, 193–200), stone and faience animal pendants (9, 13, 17, 175), seal pendants (4–6, 9, 12–14, 17, 127, 180–83, 189–90, [201], 202), and a very fine stele-

shaped gold pendant depicting an Assyrian goddess facing a worshipper (140 = fig. 19-g). Turquoise was apparently used for some necklaces (68, 136) but, surprisingly, lapis lazuli beads and pendants are rare (153), although it is difficult to judge because in many cases the catalogue entries refer simply to 'precious stones'. Carnelian beads are numerous (35, 193–98?, 220), and banded brown and white agate (often referred to as carnelian in Hussein and Suleiman 2000) was particularly popular (144, 198–200) and is used for eye-stone pendants on necklaces (46–47, 53–54, 66, 72, 96, 97, 100 see fig. 14-h, 129), for spherical beads (18), barrel-shaped beads (110–11) and cylinders (18, 123, 176), but rarely for cylinder seals. The agates may have been dyed to enhance the colour (see Sax in Collon 2001: 23–24). There are many necklaces made entirely of gold elements (26, 63–64, 79, 80, 101, 130, 132, 134, 144–47, 176; and 119 and 129 which look very Art Deco) (eg Pl. VIIIc and fig. 14-i). Two particularly fine necklaces from Tomb II (fig. 14-g) are very similar, with snake-heads interlocking at the back to close the necklace,

Fig. 14-g. Gold necklaces, one inlaid with banded agates, from Tomb II.

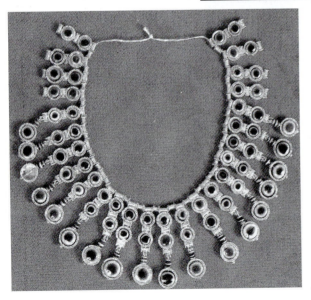

Fig. 14-h. Gold necklace with eye-stone pendants from Tomb III.

and tear-shaped pendants which are made of gold for one necklace (80), and of brown and white agate for the other (53). There are two torcs: one was decorated with eye-stones, each incised with a scorpion (73), and another was a very simple band of gold with pairs of lines round it and two movable ends that locked together (79). There are two necklaces which may have been intended to match earrings (61–62 and cf. 28 and 89). See also Damerji 1999: Abb. 8–10 from Tomb I. For comments on the stones used for Achaemenid necklaces, see Moorey 1998: 159–61.

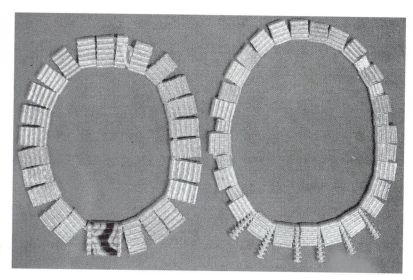

Fig. 14-i. Two gold necklaces, one with an agate bead, from Tomb III.

Bracelets (figs 14-j–14-m; Plate II)

There is a variety of different types of bracelet. The most dramatic are three pairs probably representing the type of bracelet (looking rather like a wrist-watch) worn by the king on reliefs and stelae, with a large disc bearing a radiating design. The bracelets are made of gold and the inlays are semiprecious stones or their imitations, with abundant use of the colour turquoise; the agates are brown veined with white. The bracelets are hinged at the back and secured with a pin.

1. On the curved disc of one pair (30) the design is in gold with a circle of kneeling winged genies, with cone and bucket, on either side of rosette trees on an inlaid background, between inlaid bands, with a central rosette radiating from an eye-stone. The wrist-band consists of squares of inlay set in gold and horizontal agate beads set in gold.

Fig. 14-j. Hinged armlet inlaid with semi-precious stones, from Tomb III.

2. The second pair (32) (Plate IIa) has a similar disc to the first, but the internal faces are decorated with incised lions: one on one bracelet and two on the other. The wrist-band is decorated with ten round eye-stones framed by gold stars (four at the ends and

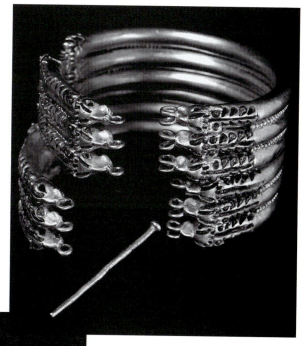

Fig. 14-k. Gold bracelets inlaid with semi-precious stones. From Tomb II.

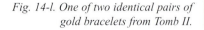

Fig. 14-l. One of two identical pairs of gold bracelets from Tomb II.

Fig. 14-m. Gold bracelets inlaid with semi-precious stones. From Tomb I.

twenty above and below), and is edged with small agates alternating with gold.

3. The third pair (31) (Plate IIb) consists of three discs, each with the same decoration which, in a reversal of the decoration on the previous pairs, consists of a gold background into which the design is inlaid. Again there is a circle of kneeling winged genies, but they frame rosettes. In the centre, the king stands on the right facing another bearded figure (the crown-prince?) with, between them, two extraordinary motifs. Above, is a cross formed by the tail elements of winged discs with a central inlaid circle. The motif below is different on each bracelet: on Pl. IIb is the upper part of a god in a nimbus, with one hand raised towards the king (Damerji 1999: Abb. 32 top), while on the other bracelet the motif is described as a 'stone bench surmounted by the winged symbol of the god Assur' (Hussein and Suleiman 2000: Pic. 31), the latter perhaps the cross already mentioned. The lower motif is certainly different, but is difficult to see on the published photograph. The wristband is formed by the heads of two lions, with turquoise-coloured beads for the eyes, on the forehead and ears, and with small turquoise-coloured chips for the mane.

In the case of Pics 30 and 32, JO said terms such as 'cloisonné' and 'champlevé' should be used with caution until a detailed study of the jewellery could establish which techniques were, in fact, adopted, and he advocated the use of 'inlaid' instead. DG said that examination under a scanning electron microscope would make it possible to ascertain which techniques were used. For comments on the colours, see Moorey 1998: 162–64.

There are numerous other bracelets:

4. A pair with three hinged sections, with two lions heads on the front ([65] = Damerji 1999: Abb. 29 top) (fig. 14-l).
5. A pair inlaid with semiprecious stones alternating with vertical gold bands ([67] = Damerji 1999: Abb. 29 bottom) (fig. 14-k), and see another pair (15) (fig. 14-m).
6. A pair with nine hinged sections inlaid with oval agates held in place by horizontal gold wire of which the edges are decorated with granulation (95).
7. Seven bracelets consisting of a horizontally-ridged gold band ending in palmettes (112).
8. A pair with five horizontal, inlaid, hinged bands, ending in snake heads ([184] top = Damerji 1999: Abb. 27–28) (fig. 14-j).
9. A pair decorated with lion's heads at the end of triple gold tubes, two plain and the central one decorated with incisions, with two triple sections with ridged decoration on the exterior and the interior smooth ([184] bottom left and see 4. above).

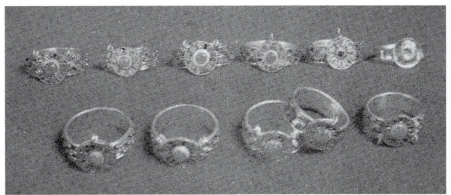

Fig. 14-n. Finger-rings.

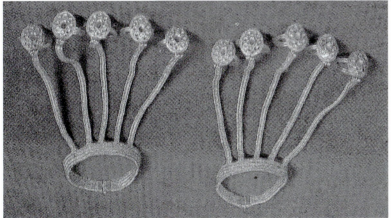

Fig. 14-o. A ring for every finger linked by loop-in-loop chains to a strap-work bracelet.

10. A pair with plain double tubes with four triple sections with ridged decoration on the exterior ([184] bottom right).
12. A final pair (possibly anklets) are coils ending in a stag's head (186).

Finger-rings (figs 14-n and 14-o)

There were many categories of finger-ring:

1. A band of gold inlaid with semiprecious stones, a plain carnelian band and two carnelian bands carved with snakes' heads (3).
2. A collection of nine four-lobed gold rings, each lobe decorated with an incised star, with the lobes linked by ridged sections (87).
3. A pair of rings formed by coils of gold wire and a pair of gold rings inset with eight tiny round agate eye-stones (102).
4. Ten gold rings with five or seven lobes decorated with rosettes with inlaid petals radiating from a small agate eye-stone, with two little rings on each side of the central disc to which a chain or ornament could be attached (103).
5. A group of 11 gold rings with inlaid bands and a central rosette with inlaid petals radiating from a small agate eye-stone, some with little rings to which a chain or ornament could be attached (104).
6. Ten assorted rings, including a plain carnelian band and two gold rings with inlaid bezels (137).

7. Five rings with vertical rows of inlaid stones (148) (Plate VIIIe).
8. A group of seventeen rings, mostly plain hoops, but one with inlay, one with lions' heads, one with a disc with granulation and some with wire wrapped around—perhaps to make them smaller (185).
9. A triple band with a disc decorated with circles of granulation (203).
10. A type, made of gold inlaid with precious stones (151), consists of a ring for every finger linked by loop-in-loop chains to a strap-work bracelet (fig. 14-o); similar items of jewellery are still used in Iraq today for children and are known as *shabbahiyyah* in the colloquial Arabic of Mosul (see also Maxwell-Hyslop 1971: pl. 181, said to have come from Ziwiyeh in western Iran).

Anklets (fig. 14-p; Plate IVb–d)

The most spectacular were two pairs from Tomb II:
IM 105710–105711; Weight: 1,613.3 and 1,593.2 g; Height: 9.7 cm; Diameter: 15 cm.
IM 105712–105713; Weight: 857.7 and 840.7 g; Height 7.3 cm; Diameter: 11.5 cm.
Damerji 1999: (Abb. 22 (*in situ*); Abb. 26 (back); Hussein and Suleiman 2000: 249–50 (44–45).

These two pairs of gold, hinged anklets are of different sizes. The hinges are fastened with a pin connecting small alternating ridged tubes at each end. The interior is

Fig. 14-p. Anklets.

smooth and the exterior is horizontally ridged, and each ridge is decorated with adjacent balls.

A further three pairs of anklets of this type were found in Tomb III; they are not in the same league as those of Tomb II, as the heaviest pair (which was decorated with grooves instead of balls) totals 1,149 g, and the other two were made up of plain tubes and were not smooth on the interior (186; Damerji 1999: Abb. 26, front). Similar bracelets, also hinged with alternating smooth and ridged tubes, were found in the tomb of the Egyptian pharaoh Psusennes I (1045–994 BC) at Tanis (Stierlin and Ziegler 1987: Ill. 33). Other types of gold anklets, or perhaps armlets, were found. The most common type consisted of a thick hoop of gold wire, sometimes plain and sometimes with ridged decoration, with the ends generally ending in an animal's head, but sometimes with three incised lines round plain ends, and sometimes with plain flaring ends (118 [×1], 121 [×9 pairs], 122 [×17 of various sizes], 143 [×8 assorted types]). Other types are also attested: an open ring with hooks at the end formed by animal-heads and with groups of gold tassels which must have tinkled when the wearer walked (118 [×1]), and a coil ending in animal's heads—perhaps a large bracelet (186 [a pair]).

Dress Decoration (fig. 14-q–14-r)

Garments seem to have had gold ornaments stitched on to them in profusion. There are innumerable rosettes and stars (some with small pendants), discs, wheels and hanging balls (33); 770 examples of one type of rosette were found (36), and 1,160 domed studs (94); seven agate eye stones set in elaborate gold frames are illustrated (29); two decorated doughnuts (102) and eight plain doughnuts (137), all of gold with suspension rings. There are also more elaborate pieces (27). Fibulae were pinned to garments (92), with seals (12 and 12a [= Damerji 1999: Abb. 14a–b], 127?) and collections of brightly-coloured stones (78) hanging from them. There are also strap bands for decorating the neck and shoulders of a robe (131) (Plate VIIId).

Fig. 14-q. Fifty gold star-shaped items for dress decoration from Tomb II.

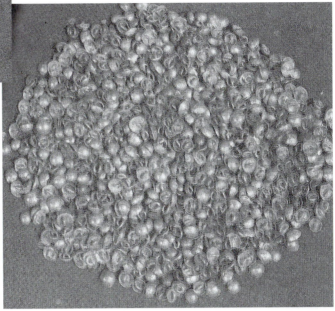

Fig. 14-r. Dress Decoration.

Egyptianizing gold bowl from Tomb II (Plate III)

IM 105697; Weight: 171.52 g; Diameter: 17.7 cm; Depth: 3 cm.

Damerji 1999: 18, Abb. 23 (left); Hussein and Suleiman 2000: 253–54 (48–49); Oates and Oates 2001: pl. 7b.

This shallow gold dish has an Egyptianizing design showing four Nile boats in which elongated figures snare birds and relax under canopies, against a background of papyrus. On the bank, between the boats, are cattle, horses and flocks of ducks. In the centre is a radiating lotus motif surrounded by water full of *bulti*-fish, lotus plants and swimming creatures: a man, a bovid, a horse and a crocodile. It is inscribed in cuneiform with the name of Yaba'.

JO drew attention to two Egyptian bowls, both made of gold, decorated in repoussé with swimming figures, set in silver, with a gold handle. One, from the Tell Basta (Bubastis) Treasure, was part of an accidental find in 1906 (Vernier 1928: 417–18, pl. CVI) which has been dated to the Nineteenth Dynasty (1291–1185 BC). The other was excavated in the tomb of the vizier of Psusennes I (1045–994

BC), which was part of Psusennes' tomb complex at Tanis (Stierlein and Ziegler 1987: Ill. 68; Tiradritti 1998: 325).

Gold jug from Tomb III, Bronze Coffin 2 (Plate VII; fig. 14-s)

IM 115618; Weight 263.3 g; Height 13 cm; Diameter of rim 5.9 cm; Diameter of spout 3.5 cm. Damerji 1999: 11, covers and Abb. 46–52; Hussein and Suleiman 2000: 366–67 (154); Oates and Oates 2001: 86, pl. IIIb.

This globular gold vessel has a convex base according to Hussein and Suleiman (but cf. Plate VIIb bottom image, where the bottom looks as though it flares out slightly and is either flat or a ring-base), a cylindrical neck flaring outwards at the top, a wide cylindrical gold spout (partly cut away at the top, and a handle at ninety degrees to the right of the spout, suitable for use by a right-handed person). There is a wooden bung in the spout, and parallels (see below) indicate that there was probably a strainer in the spout.

The vessel is decorated with bands of very finely chased repoussé design. Around the rim, between two bands of framed S-guilloche, is a band with three archers kneeling

Fig. 14-s. Drawing of the repoussé decoration on the gold jug (adapted from Hussein and Suleiman 2000: Pic 154).

on one knee, two of them back to back with rows of animals fleeing from them to right and left towards two stylised trees. On the shoulder of the vessel, just below the juncture of neck and body, there is a double-outlined band consisting of three rows of double scale pattern, probably representing mountains. Similar bands also adorn the top and opening of the spout, and frame the lower representational band (see below). Similar, but broader bands with four rows of scales frame the representational band round the middle of the vessel. In every case the rounded part of the scale is uppermost. The middle representational band consists of a series of chariots engaged in hunting and battle. The lower representational band repeats the subject of the uppermost band. Below the lower band of scale pattern is a framed band of diagonal cross-hatching enclosing impressed dots, a framed band of Z-guilloche, and a pattern of elongated, decorated petals radiating from the base. The width of the representational bands is only about 1.5 cm.

The handle consists of two S-shaped tubes side by side, with a row of granulation between them, running up the mane of the lion's head that forms the bottom of the handle. The upper end of the handle consists of the same double-scale pattern (but with the scales downwards), ending in the head of a horned serpent that holds the rim of the vessel in its jaws. The undecorated part of the handle is separated from the heads by framed horizontal herring-bone bands.

At Nimrud, in Room AB in the harem area of the Palace, Layard found a plain bronze cup on a flaring base, with a side-spout and a loop handle (Layard 1853a: 177, illustrated on p. 181). A similar vessel to that found by Layard, but with a rounded base and gadrooned decoration, was excavated at Tell Halaf (Hrouda 1962: 65, 69, pl. 48:8). The greatest number of vessels with side spouts comes from Gordion where most were found in Phrygian tumulus burials; they generally have necks, are very close in size to the present example, and all have strainers: some are made of painted or plain burnished pottery, the latter evidently imitating bronze vessels (Edgü 1983: 271, 274–75), while others are made of bronze (Edgü 1983: 279; Toker and Öztürk 1992: nos 98–100). A side-spouted gadrooned vessel, very similar to the one from Tell Halaf, is depicted on a relief from Karatepe where it is held by an attendant at a banquet (Akurgal 1962: pl. 142); from this we may deduce that side-spouted vessels were used for pouring some liquid that needed straining, but presumably one that was served in small quantities, as the vessels are all small.

Other gold and silver vessels (fig. 14-t; Plate IVa–b)

There were three gold bowls from Tomb II, inscribed with the names of three queens (Damerji 1999: 18, nos 1, 3

Fig. 14-t. Gold flask (height 13.5 cm) from Tomb II.

[NB Abb. 32, not 31], and 5, Abb. 23, 31 [top = Yaba'], 32 [top = Atalia, bottom = Banitu]; Hussein and Suleiman 2000: Pics 37 [Yaba'], 57 [Banitu], 58 [Atalia]), and a number of small, fluted gold bottles (fig. 14-t) found in Atalia's bowl (Hussein and Suleiman 2000: Pics. 56 [one with a chain] and 59 [×11]). In Tomb III there were two gold bowls: one was very similar to one from Tomb II, and bore an inscription of Shamshi-ilu (Plate IVa–b) (Damerji 1999: Abb. 31 bottom, and 40 front right; Hussein and Suleiman 2000: Pic. 152; and one omphalos bowl with gadroons forming a large rosette (Damerji 1999: Abb. 40 back left, and 46–47). A gadrooned omphalos bowl of silver (fig. 14-o) came from Tomb I (Pic. 1), and a plain silver omphalos bowl (not illustrated), with a Luwian hieroglyphic inscription below the rim (see Hawkins Chapter 16 in this volume), was found in Tomb III.

Stone vessels and objects (fig. 14-u)

Two globular pots, a decorative scoop and a pomegranate were made of rock crystal. One of the vessels was made in two pieces joined by a gold band; the other was engraved

Fig. 14-v. Small gold figure of a stag (height 5.5 cm) from Tomb III.

Fig. 14-w. Faience amulet from Tomb I.

Fig. 14-u. Rock crystal objects, the one top right inscribed with the name 'Atalia', from Tomb II.

on the rim with Atalia's name (Damerji 1999: Abb. 23, 24 (wrongly said to be Banitu on p. 46 but cf. pp. 17–18); Hussein and Suleiman 2000: Pic. 38 with an additional vessel; NB the first vessel is described as rock-crystal by Damerji, and as glass by Hussein and Suleiman, which is unlikely as clear glass is not attested until Roman times).

Other objects

A number of amulets, mostly made of faience, but some of stone, were found in the tombs, particularly in Tomb I which included a couple of pieces showing small copulating figures (fig. 14-w). A small gold stag 5.5 cm high, on a rectangular base (fig. 14-v), was found in Tomb

II (Hussein and Suleiman 2000: Pic. 113). A jug, said to be made of veined stone but probably made of combed glass, came from Tomb III (Hussein and Suleiman 2000: Pic. 187). For a discussion of further metal objects from the Tombs, see Curtis, Chapter 29.

Addendum
In a recent article R.M Boehmer has argued for an origin for the gold crown from Tomb III (Plates V and VI), discussed above, in Western Syria or east Cilicia on the basis of the iconography of the drawings of the four winged figures and the types of plants depicted (Boehmer, R.M., 2006. 'Das Herkunfstgebiet der Goldenen Krone aus Gruft III des Nordwest-Palastes zu Nimrud', *Baghdader Mitteilungen* 37: 213–19.

15   INSCRIPTIONS FROM THE TOMBS OF THE QUEENS OF ASSYRIA

Farouk N.H. Al-Rawi

The most spectacular find of treasures in Iraq during recent times was the Neo-Assyrian queens' tombs discovered at Nimrud. In 1989–90 the State Organization of Antiquities in Iraq, while reconstructing parts of the domestic wing of the North-West Palace of Ashurnasirpal II (883–859 BCE), came upon four vaulted burial chambers. In two of them, Tombs II and III, they discovered the extraordinarily rich burials of several Assyrian queens. The tombs held more than sixty kilograms of gold, bronze, silver and electron objects, hundreds of precious, semiprecious and crystallized stones, textiles and other materials (Damerji 1999; Hussein and Suleiman 2000). These objects give an idea of the splendour of Mesopotamian civilization and, in particular, Assyrian culture. Moreover, they include motifs from all over what is now the Arab world and its neighbours.

Historically speaking, the treasures range in date over a long period of time. As can be seen from the copies provided here, the inscriptions date from King Kurigalzu II (1332–1308 BC) of Babylonia to the time of King Sargon II (721–705) of Assyria. The objects represent the cultural unity not of Mesopotamia alone, but of the Arab world and its neighbours. Assyrian craftsmen and artists put these motifs together, as it were, in a ladle, melted them and produced living symbols, which allow us better to relate to them and interpret their culture.

The inscribed objects from the queens' tombs are written in pictographic, cuneiform and alphabetic scripts. They express thoughts in many languages, such as Sumerian, Akkadian, Hittite, Kassite, Phoenician, Aramaic and South Arabian. They are written upon gold, silver, bronze, stones, ivory, bricks, clay and probably other materials that have since perished. It is the purpose of this contribution to present several previously unpublished items—a set of four amulets, a duck-weight and a brick—and to complement them with my cuneiform copies of many of those inscriptions that have already been published (Fadhil 1990a; 1990b; Kamil 1999).

The writer would like to express his gratitude to Muayyad Sa'id Damerji, Muzahim Mahmoud, Ahmad Kamil, the staff members of the Iraq Museum, John Curtis, Christopher Walker and the staff members of the Middle East Department for their help and support during his work at the Iraq Museum and the British Museum.

Funerary inscriptions

Text No. 1. Figs 15-a–15-b. *Funerary tablet of Yabâ*

ND 1989/68, IM 125000. Alabaster tablet, found in a niche let into the right-hand wall of the space leading to the burial chamber of Tomb II (photograph *in situ* Damerji 1999: 51, fig. 19). The inscription is a funerary text of Yabâ, known from labels on her grave goods (Nos 18 and 19 below) as the wife of Tiglath-pileser III (744–727 BC). The text was published by several scholars in preliminary translations, such as those that appeared in the Iraqi and British media (e.g. George 1990: 29). A full edition with a translation into German was provided by Fadhil (1990a, also Damerji 1999: 52). I take the opportunity here to publish my own copy of this text. It was made according to the original shape and measurements of the tablet. For the benefit of the reader the copy is accompanied by a transliteration and a translation into English.

obv. MU ᵈUTU ᵈ*ereš-ki-gal* ᵈ*a-nun-a-ki*
DINGIR.MEŠ GAL.MEŠ *šá* KI-*ti* ᵐⁱ*ia-ba-a*
MÍ.É.GAL *ina mu-te* NAM ZI-*ti*
ik-šú-da-še-ma ur-ḫu AD.MEŠ-*šú ta-lik*
5   *man-nu* EGIR-*ú lu* MÍ.É.GAL
šá ina ᵍⁱˢGU.ZA *tu-šá-ba lu* ᵐⁱÉRIN.MEŠ É.GAL
na-ra-an-te MAN *šá ul-tú* KI.MAḪ-*ia*
*i-da-ka-in-ni lu mam-ma šá-nu-u-*ᵉ*ma*ᵉ
it-ti-ia i-šá-kan-nu ù a-na
10   *šu-ku-ti-ia qa-su ina* ḪUL-*te* LÁ-*ṣu*
šá ⁿᵃ⁴KIŠIB *šá* KI.MAḪ *šu-a-tú* BAD-*ú*
e-le-nu ina šu-ru-ru ᵈ*šam-ši*
e-té-ma-šú ina ṣu-me-e ka-ma-te
li-ir-pu-du
rev.
15   *šap-la-nu ina* KI-*tim ina na-qa me-e*
KAŠ.SAG ᵍⁱˢGEŠTIN *ú-pu-un-tu*
it-ti ᵈ*a-nun-na-ki ta-kal-li-mu*
la i-ma-ḫar ᵈ*nin-giš-zi-da*
ᵈ*bi-tu-ḫi-du-gul* DINGIR.MEŠ GAL.MEŠ
20   *šá* KI-*tim ša-lam-di zi-qi-qi*
la ṣa-la-lum li-me-du
a-na du-ri da-ri-iš

By the name of Shamash, Ereshkigal and the Anunnaki, the great gods of the earth, mortal destiny overtook Yabâ, the queen, in death, she went to the path of her ancestors. ⁵ Whoever, in the future, be it a queen who sits on the throne or a palace lady who is a concubine of the king,

Fig. 15-a. Text No.1 obverse.

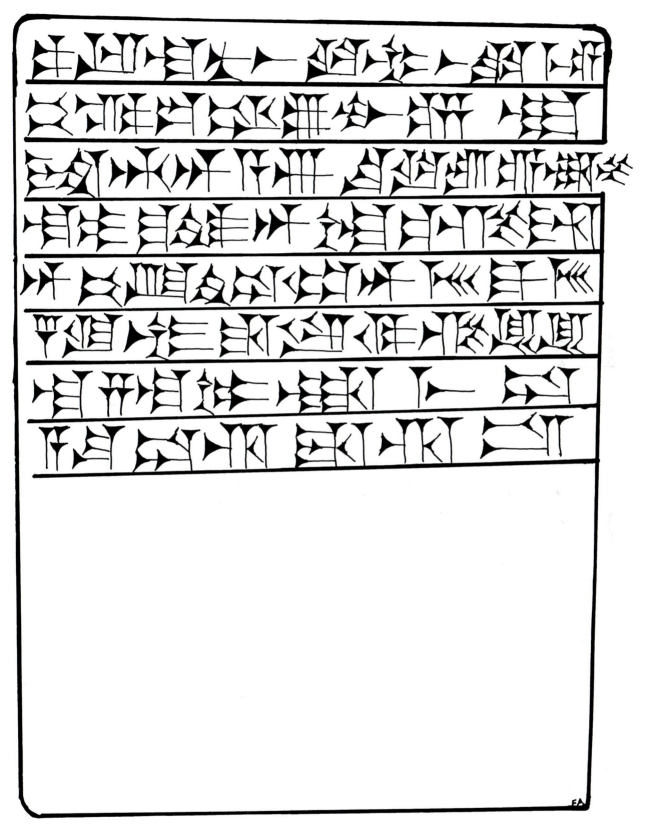

Fig. 15-b. Text No.1 reverse.

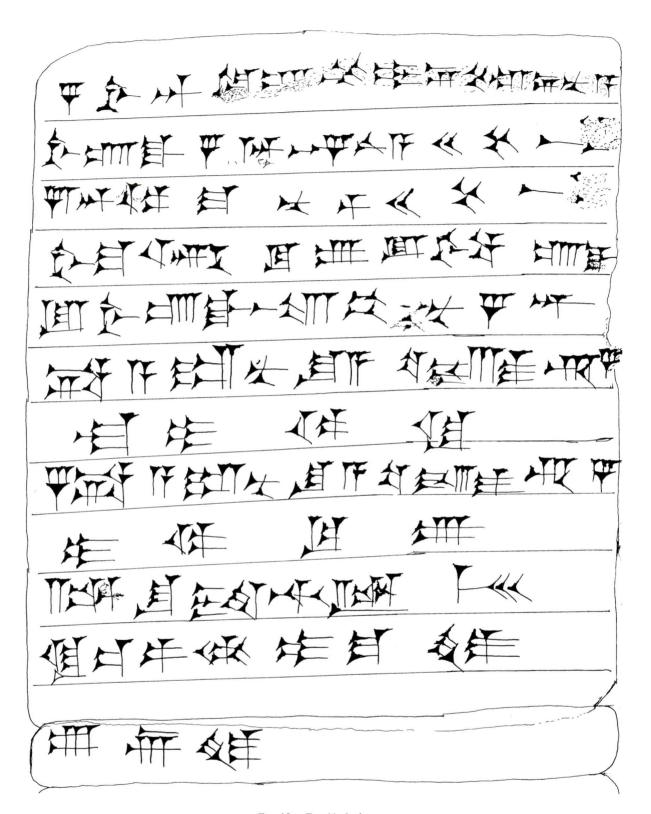

Fig. 15-c. Text No.2 obverse.

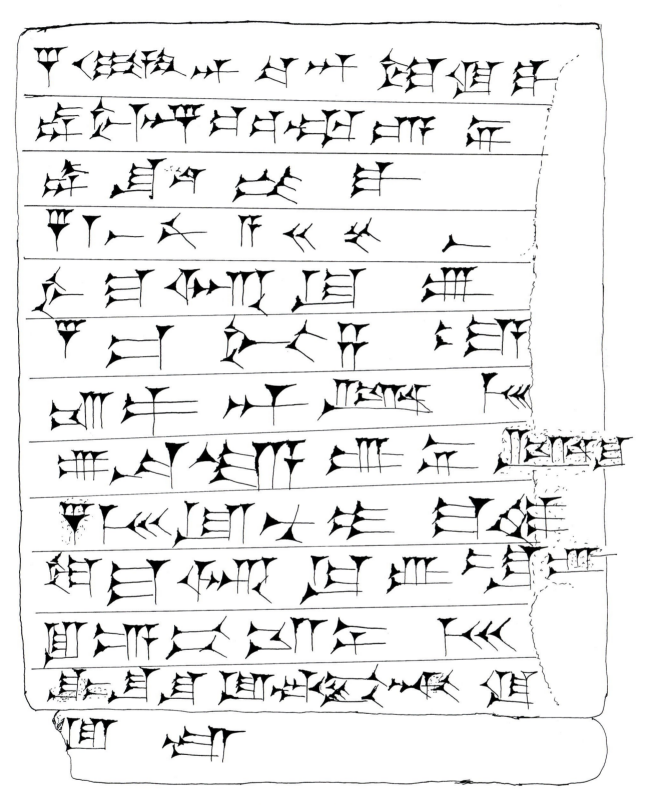

Fig. 15-d. Text No.2 reverse.

removes me from my tomb, or puts anybody else with me, and lays his hand [10] upon my jewellery with evil intent or breaks open the seal of that tomb, above (earth), under the rays of the sun, let his spirit roam outside in thirst, [15] below in the underworld, when libations of water are offered, he must not receive with the Anunnaki as a funerary offering any beer, wine or meal. May Ningishzida and the great door-keeper, Biṭu, the great gods [20] of the underworld, afflict his corpse and ghost with eternal restlessness.

Text No. 2. Figs 15-c–15d. *Funerary tablet of Mullissu-mukannishat-Ninua*

ND 1989/470, IM 124996. Marble tablet, 25.1 × 21.9 × 2.9 cm. This tablet, from Tomb III, belonged to Mullissu-mukannishat-Ninua, queen of Ashurnasirpal II (883–859 BC). The text has been edited previously by Fadhil (1990b: photographs on pls 40–41). It seems that the text was written on a tablet that had been used before, allowing us to speculate that the queen may have been buried in a hurry; however, the stone lid of the sarcophagus (text No. 3 below) seems to be well prepared. My copy of the funerary tablet was made from pencil rubbings of the original. The text runs as follows.

obv. *šá* ^{mí.dr}*nin-líl-mu-kan-ni-šat*-^{uru}*ni-nu-a*^ı
 ^{mí}E.GAL *šá* ^{md}*aš-šur*-PAB-A MAN KUR AŠ [x x]
 šá ^{md}SILIM-*ma-nu*-MAŠ MAN KUR AŠ [x x]
 mám-ma ar-ku-ú lu ^{mí}ÉRIN.É.GAL
5 *lu* MÍ.É.GAL *ina lìb-bi* NU GAR-*an*
 ^{na4}*a-ra-nu šu-a-tú* TA *áš-ri-šá*
 la i-de-ke
 šá ^{na4}*a-ra-nu šu-a-tú* TA *áš-ri-šá*
 i-de-ku-ú
10 GIDIM-*šu it-ti* GIDIM.MEŠ
 ki-is-pa ul i-ma-ḫar
 (blank space)
rev. NÍG.GIG ^dUTU ^d*ereš-ki-gal*
 DUMU.MÍ ^m*aš-šur*-^{giš}GIŠ-*ka*-KALAG-*ni*
15 ^{lú}ŠU.SÌLA.DU₈.GAL
 šá ^mAŠ-PAB-A MAN KUR AŠ
 mám-ma ar-ku-ú
 šá ^{giš}GU.ZA-*ia*
 TA *pa-an* GIDIM.MEŠ
20 *ú-na-kar-ú-ni* ⌜GIDIM-*šu*⌝
 ⌜NINDA⌝.MEŠ *lu* NU *i-ma-*⌜*ḫar*⌝
 mám-ma ar-ku-ú tap-⌜*šu-ú*⌝
 lu-lab-bi-iš Ì.MEŠ
 ⌜*lip*⌝-*šu-šu* UDU.NÍTA SISKUR BAL-*qí*

lo. e. *ú-sa-ḫar*   up. e.   DIB-*su*

Belonging to Mullissu-mukannishat-Ninua, queen of Ashurnasirpal, king of Assyria, [mother(?)] of Shalmaneser, king of Assyria, [. . .] No one later may place herein (anyone else), be it a palace lady [5] or a

queen, nor remove this sarcophagus from its place. Anybody who removes this sarcophagus from its place, [10] his spirit will not receive funerary offerings with (other) spirits: it is a taboo of Shamash and Ereshkigal!

Daughter of Ashur-nīrka-da"inni, [15] chief cup-bearer of Ashurnasirpal, king of Assyria. Anyone later who [20] removes my throne from before the shades of the dead, may his spirit receive no bread! May some one later clothe (me) with a shroud, anoint (me) with oil and sacrifice a lamb.

The missing word at the end of l. 2 could be AMA 'mother'; however, the sarcophagus inscription (No. 3) which almost duplicates this text, does not indicate such an emendation. The words inscribed on the lower and upper edges seems to be unrelated to the funerary inscription and may be inadvertently left over from a previous use of the tablet.

Text No. 3. Fig. 15-e. *Sarcophagus inscription of Mullissu-mukannishat-Ninua*

The third funerary text is that inscribed on the stone lid of the empty sarcophagus of Tomb III, previously edited by Fadhil (1990b: photographs pls 40–41; Damerji 1999: 35 fig. 36). The inscription was reported in the Iraqi media and edited by Fadhil (1990b: 471 without museum number). The copy presented here was made from the aforementioned photographs and with the aid of an unpublished drawing by Andrew George. The following is a transliteration and translation of the text.

1 *šá* ^{mí.d}*nin-líl-mu-kan-ni-šat*-^{uru}*ni-nu-a* MÍ.É.GAL
 šá ^{md}*aš-šur*-PAB-A MAN KUR AŠ
2 *šá* ^{md}SILIM-*ma-nu*-MAŠ MAN KUR AŠ *mám-ma ar-ku-ú lu* ^{mí}ÉRIN.É.GAL *lu* MÍ.É.GAL *ina lìb-bi* NU GAR-*an*
3 ^{na4}*a-ra-nu šu-a-tú* TA *áš-ri-šá la i-de-ke šá* ^{na4}*a-ra-nu šu-a-tú* TA *áš-ri-šá i-de-ku-ú*
4 GIDIM-*šu it-ti* GIDIM.MEŠ *ki-is-pa ul i-ma-ḫar* NÍG.GIG ^dUTU ^d*ereš-ki-gal*
5 DUMU.MÍ ^mAŠ-^{giš}GIŠ-*ka*-KALAG-*ni* ^{lú}ŠU.SÌLA!.DU₈.GAL *šá* ^mAŠ-PAB-A MAN KUR AŠ

Belonging to Mullissu-mukannishat-Ninua, queen of Ashurnasirpal, king of Assyria, of Shalmaneser, king of Assyria. No one later may place herein (anyone else), whether a palace lady or a queen, nor remove this sarcophagus from its place; whoever removes this sarcophagus from its place, his spirit will not receive funerary offerings with (other) spirits: it is a taboo of Shamash and Ereshkigal—daughter of Ashur-nīrka-da"inni, chief cup-bearer of Ashurnasirpal, king of Assyria.

Fig. 15-e. Text No.3

Brick inscriptions

Text No. 4. Fig. 15-f. *Brick of Shalmaneser III*

This brick was found in Tomb III. It is inscribed on two sides. The inscription was edited by Fadhil (1990b: 480, brick A (no museum number)). The text is another exemplar of a well-known inscription of Shalmaneser III (858–824 BC), catalogued by the Royal Inscriptions of Mesopotamia Project as RIMA.0.102.111 (Grayson 1996: 166–68). My copy was made from the photograph published by Fadhil (1990b: pl. 44).

Text No. 5. Fig. 15-g. *Brick of Shalmaneser III*

This brick, which was also found in Tomb III, is inscribed on the side and the face. The inscription was edited by Fadhil (1990b: 480, brick B (no museum number)). My copy was made from the photograph published by Fadhil (1990b: pl. 45). Note that the copy corrects an omission in Fadhil's reading of l. 6, which lacks *šá*. This extra sign makes the text a variant of RIMA.0.102.111.

Text No. 6. Fig. 15-h. *Brick of Shalmaneser III*

This brick was found inside one of the three tombs. Its museum number is not known. As far as I know, no one has yet published it. My copy was made from a still photograph that I extracted from the Directorate of Antiquities' film of the three tombs. The text is inscribed on the face only and is another variant of RIMA.0.102.111. The following is a transliteration and translation.

1	^{md}SILIM-*ma-nu*-MAŠ MAN GAL-*ú*
2	MAN *dan-nu* MAN ŠÚ MAN KUR AŠ
3	A ^m*aš-šur*-PAP-A MAN ŠÚ MAN KUR AŠ
4	A ^mTUKUL-MAŠ MAN ŠÚ MAN KUR AŠ-*ma*
5	*ri-ṣip-tú šá* U₆.NIR
6	*šá* URU.*kal-ḫi*

Shalmaneser, the great king, the mighty king, king of the universe, king of Assyria, son of Ashurnasirpal, king of the universe, king of Assyria, son of Tukulti-Ninurta, king of the universe, king of Assyria, (who built) the construction of the ziggurat of the city of Kalḫu.

Inscribed weights

Text No. 7. Fig. 15-i. *A bronze duck-weight of one-sixth of a mina*

ND 1989/158, IM 115432. Bronze weight cast in the form of a duck, found in Tomb II (photograph in Hussein and Suleiman 2000: 288, pl. 81 bottom row, second from left). It bears inscriptions in Assyrian cuneiform and Aramaic

letters. As far as I know, this is the first time that a bilingual text has been found on an Assyrian duck-weight. There are Neo-Assyrian duck-weights from Nimrud besides those found in the queens' tombs, e.g. in the British Museum BM 91438 (fig. 15-ji; cf. Weissbach 1907: 397, no. 14; Postgate 1976: 66; Kwasman and Parpola 1991: xxxi, fig. 6b; Powell 1989–90: 457–517; see also Zaccagnini 1999–2001: 40, fn. 5) and BM 91442 (fig. 15-jii; cf. Weissbach 1907: 391, no. 15; Postgate 1976: xxxi; Powell 1989–90: 515; also Zaccagnini 1999–2001: 40, fn. 6). There is also a duck-weight from the site of Khirbet Qasrij (Curtis 1989: 25 f.); for other Assyrian duck-weights see also Curtis and Reade 1995: 194–95; Zaccagnini 1999–2001. But none of these weights is bilingually inscribed and not all are made of bronze. The duck-weight BM 91438 bears a further similarity to our duck-weight, for it was inscribed with the same cuneiform signs, 6-*su*. There is no Aramaic inscription engraved on it; however, as can be seen from the drawing (fig. 15-ji), there are six strokes incised on it which could indicate the use of the Aramaic language. Such strokes were also made on the other duck-weight from the tombs (see text No. 8).

At the conference I estimated the weight of the smaller duck-weight from the queens' tombs as 150–180 g. It is not possible to know the exact weight for the time being, but judging from the weights of the British Museum published by T.C. Mitchell (1990), I can confidently reckon that the weight of the duck is around 170 grams, and this estimate has been confirmed to me by Dr Ahmad Kamil. We are looking forward to a time when our Iraqi colleagues can provide us with a photograph and the exact weight.

I copied the inscriptions twice, once when the object was cleaned and the second time from outside the glass case in which it was displayed at the Iraq Museum. The Aramaic label was incised on one side and the cuneiform written on the other, together with the symbol of the scorpion. My good student Dr Ahmad Kamil published the cuneiform inscription of this duck-weight (Kamil 1999: 16–17, no. 8), but did not decipher it correctly. To understand the cuneiform we need to look at it in the light of the Aramaic label and to compare them both with other inscribed weights that were not available to Kamil.

The transliteration of the incised Aramaic line in the commonly used transliteration is *štt 'rq'*, which translates as 'one-sixth (of a mina) of the land'. In their discussion of the Hebrew word *šdš*, Brown, Driver and Briggs compared it with the Arabic ست و ستة و سادس and and ignored the correct Arabic word سدس , *sudus* or *sudsun* 'one-sixth' (1907: 995b). They also ignored the exact words in Hebrew and Aramaic, as can be seen from such dictionaries as those of Michael Sokoloff (1990: 568–69) and Marcus Jastrow (1950: 1637) s.v. שׁ‎חום. However, they compared *šdš* with the Assyrian *suduš* and

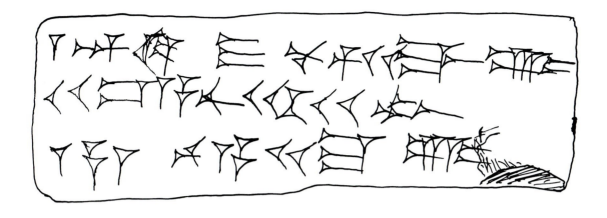

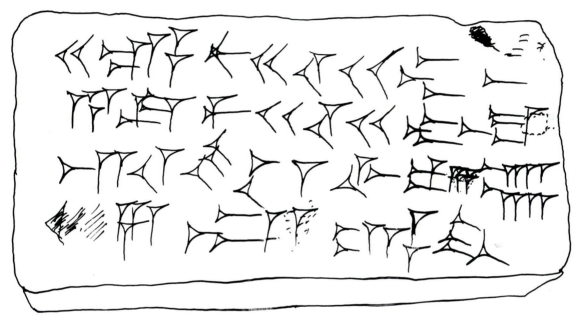

Fig. 15-f. Text No.4.

šuduš 'six-fold' or a 'group of six' as given in the modern dictionaries of Akkadian (*AHw* and *CAD* s.v.). It seems to me that the contexts cited by the latter dictionaries require the meaning 'one-sixth' of a mina rather than 'half dozen minas', since the actual given amounts were in shekels (three shekels of silver). Although this is the first time that the Aramaic fraction *štt* 'one-sixth' has appeared in such a context, other fractions appear on some weights, such as: *rb' 'rq'* 'one-fourth (of a mina) of the land' (BM 91232) and *ḥmš 'rq'* 'one-fifth (of a mina) of the land' (BM 91233). They can be compared to the Arabic fractions: ربع و خمس which we transliterate as *rub'* and *ḥums*, 'one-fourth' and 'one-fifth'.

The word *'rq'* 'land' has been comprehensively discussed by Jean and Hoftijzer (1960: 25). The word occurs in Cowley (1923: 45, ll. 13–14). It also occurs in the Old Testament, Jeremiah 10: 11. For a full discussion of the term and its implications see Fales (1995: 52–55). Although the general meaning of the term *'rq'* is

acceptable, the derivation of the word still needs to be clarified and a further analysis would be most welcome.

The transliteration of the chiselled cuneiform signs is 6-*su*; the translation is 'one-sixth (of a mina)'. Von Soden's grammar suggests that 6-*su* be read in Neo-Assyrian dialect *šadussu* (1969: 94, §70k), matching Ass. *ḥamussu* v. Bab. *ḥamuštu* 'one-fifth', etc. Oddly he did not include this form in *AHw*.

To the left of the Aramaic text there appear eight single strokes in a row, separated by a gap into a group of six and a group of two. This notation must mean the same as the other two inscriptions, the Aramaic and the Assyrian. In actual fact it should be part of the Aramaic writing to express the number one-sixth as we know it from other weight-objects. However, the fact that there are eight strokes needs to be explained. As can be seen from my drawing of the duck-weight BM 91439 (fig. 15-j*iii*), there are eight strokes on the neck of that duck too. On both the

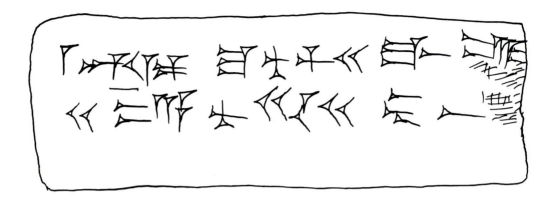

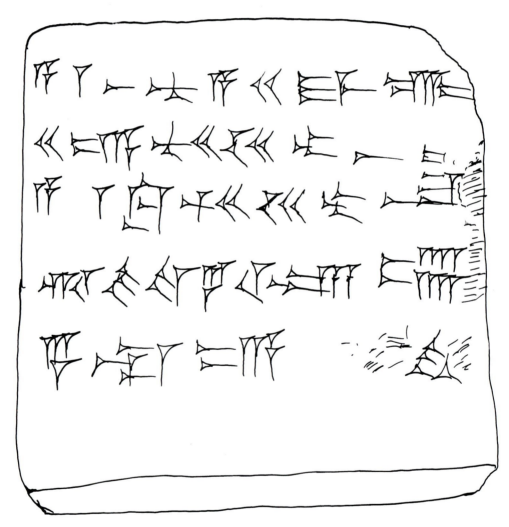

Fig. 15-g. Text No.5.

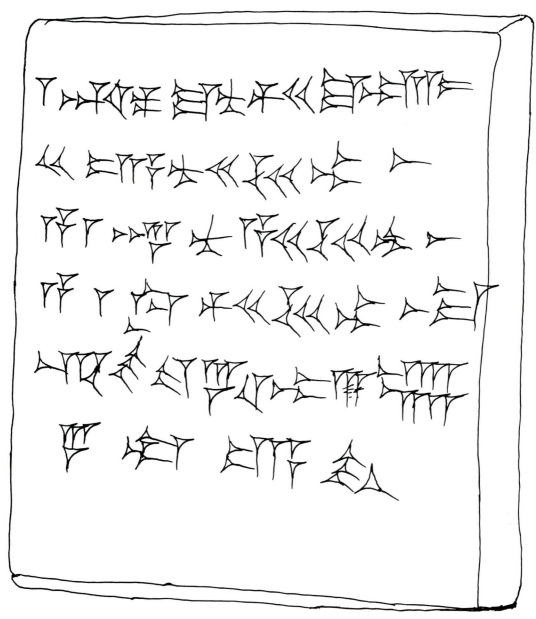

Fig. 15-h. Text No.6.

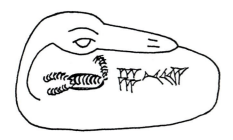

Fig. 15-i. Duck weight with text No.7.

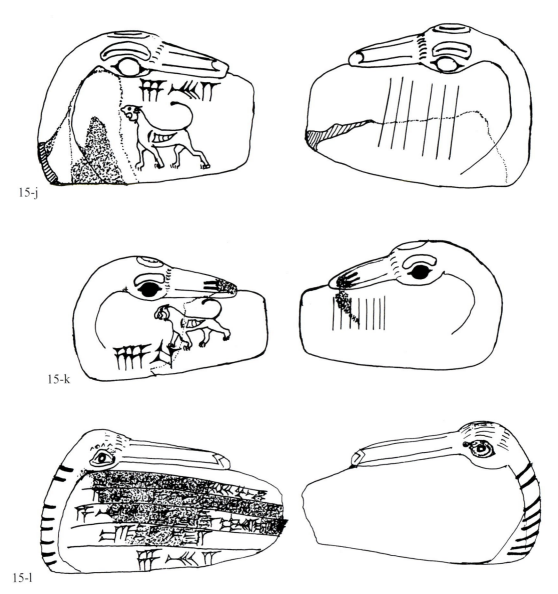

15-j

15-k

15-l

Fig. 15. Duck weights similar to No.7.
j. BM 91438
k. BM 91442
l. BM 91439

queen's duck and BM 91439 the eight strokes are divided into groups of six followed by two; moreover, the two strokes set to one side are shorter than the other six. The ancient value of BM 91439 is 6-*su* 'one-sixth of a mina'; its actual weight is 178.3 g (Curtis and Reade 1995: 194). This is 13.7 g or about two shekels less than the duck-weight BM 91438, which though also marked as a weight of 6-*su*, actually weighs 192 g. I think it likely that the extra two strokes were written to indicate a shortfall of two shekels. Thus we conclude that the notation of strokes on the queen's duck also represents a weight of one-sixth of a mina less two shekels.

Next to the cuneiform signs the scribe engraved a symbol of a scorpion. This symbol accompanies other inscribed objects belonging to Ataliyā, the queen of Sargon II (721–705 BC) (Nos 21 and 24). This fact makes it almost definite that the weight belonged to Ataliyā rather than Yabâ or Banīti, the other queens whose grave goods were found in Tomb II. Hypothetically we can suppose that it was the astrological sign of Sargon II. Symbols like lions, ostriches, gazelles, winged scarabs, winged deities, winged humans, eagles and stars were not uncommonly used on royal weights (cf. Powell 1971: 249–73). Moreover, attribution of this weight to Ataliyā rather than Yabâ would give strength to the idea put forward by F. M. Fales that the Assyrian bronze weights using the term '*rq*' '(standard weight of) the land', were products of the reign of Shalmaneser V and the Assyrian kings that succeeded him (Fales 1995: 52–55).

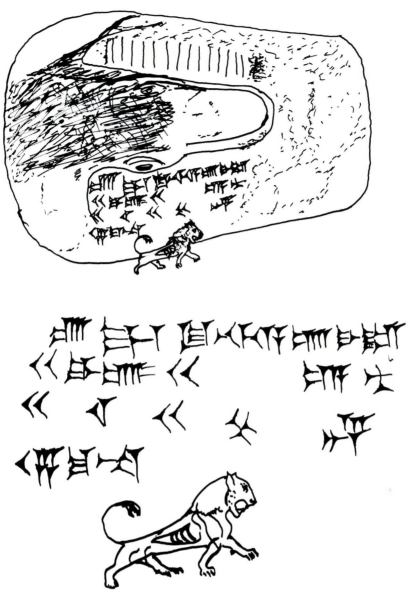

Fig. 15-m. Duck weight with text No.8.

Text No. 8. Fig. 15-m. *Duck-weight of fifteen minas*

This is a large duck-weight of fifteen minas, found in Tomb III. The text is a label of the household of Tiglath-pileser III, edited by Fadhil (1990b: 480 without museum number). According to the catalogue (Hussein and Suleiman 2000: 118–28), three duck-weights were found in Tomb III: ND 1989/267 = IM 115568 (veined carnelian), 471 = 124998 (yellow stone) and 472 = 116000 (marble). According to the photograph in Hussein and Suleiman (2000: 390, pl. 175, where the museum numbers are confused) the carnelian duck is clearly not the weight of fifteen minas, so the latter will be either IM 124998 or 116000. As noted by Fadhil, fifteen strokes are incised on the weight's right side. My copy is based on the photograph published by Fadhil (1990b: pls 42–43).

1	É.GAL ᵐTUKUL-*ti*-A-É.ŠÁR.RA
2	MAN GAL-*ú* MAN *dan-nu*
3	MAN ŠÚ MAN KUR *aš-šur*
4	15 *ma-na*

Palace of Tiglath-pileser, the great king, the mighty king, king of the universe, king of Assyria. 15 minas.

Inscribed amulets

The use of uninscribed amulets in ancient Mesopotamia can be traced back to prehistoric times (Roaf 1990: 49). During the historical periods inscribed amulets were used for protection against demons, for deliverance in the event of attack, against appalling discomfort, danger such as the hot west wind, or to protect women in childbirth and nursing mothers. For a general survey of amulet use see B.H. Goff's *Symbols of Prehistoric Mesopotamia*, especially the section on 'Cylinder seals as amulets' (Goff 1963: 195–210). It was usual for Assyrian kings, queens and men and women of rank to wear jewellery, as well as cylinder seals of semiprecious stone. Assyrian jewellery for men and women included pendants and amulets. We know from an agate bead bearing the inscription, 'neckstone belonging to Tukulti-Ninurta' (Galter 1987: 19, no. 6), and other objects with similar labels, that Assyrian kings wore such stones. A man might also wear a stone amulet hung from his neck, either in the form of a demon's head to keep away evil, or inscribed with a charm. The developed form of amulet, such as the so-called *pazuzu* and *lamashtu* amulets, bore a portrayal of the devil against whom protection was sought and a magical incantation invoking the great gods against the threatened evil. A more modest form consisted of a simple cylinder of clay or stone, bored through like a seal and inscribed with an incantation.

The four amulets of this type published here were found in Tomb II, the burial chamber of Yabâ which also contained grave goods of Ataliyā and Banīti. There is no personal label to show that the amulets were the property of a particular queen but it is possible to speculate on other evidence. In his paper 'Paleopathological investigation and scientific analysis', given at the conference, Michael Müller-Karpe observed from the skeletal remains that one of the queens of Tomb II had been boiled or treated with something, possibly to prevent their decay. Because her grave goods were discovered in the tomb of Yabâ, without a funerary tablet of her own, I think that Ataliyā the queen of Sargon II must have been buried in a hurry, perhaps because she had a contagious disease. Such circumstances might explain why the body was boiled or, in modern terms, disinfected. I suggest that if Ataliyā was ill, she was most likely the owner of the amulets. The question arises as to what kind of disease of the head occasioned the use of these amulets. Bearing in mind the limited options and the fact that our modern typology of diseases did not exist at that time, we can say, comparatively, it could be 'meningitis' or severe 'migraine' (this idea was suggested to me by my daughter, Summer Al-Rawi, a medical doctor at the General Hospital of Nottingham). An edition and discussion of these amulets and their implications follow. They are the result of a collaboration between the present writer and I.L. Finkel.

This important group of stone cylinder-amulets sheds light on the treatment of head illness in contemporary Assyria. The unique circumstances of the find make it certain that they belong and were intended to operate together, having evidently been made for one of the queens in the tomb, and thus we are entitled to interpret the inscriptions with this in mind. Two at least of these amulets, and perhaps all of them, were written against the condition called *sagkidibbû*, literally 'forehead-seizing',

possibly migraine. This condition is characterized by the authorities as an 'unidentified illness of the head' (according to *CAD* S 25, sub *sagkidabbû*), or 'migraine' (according to the late Franz Köcher, e.g. Köcher 1963: xiv sub no. 11).

Amulets of this kind are by no means common. As a rule, hard-stone cylinders are used in magic for the properties of the material itself, and while often exposed to the recitation of a spell, are not themselves used as a vehicle for an inscription, for obvious reasons. As noted above, where cylinder-amulets are to be inscribed, they are usually of clay, and various examples survive (e.g. Thompson 1940: 109–10 no. 38 and fig. 5; *PBS* 14 1088–93). A clay seal-amulet could be produced quickly and economically, and its use would probably be limited to the duration of the illness. The signs are characteristically inscribed so as to be legible on the object; they were not used for rolling, even if they were equipped with traditional end-caps of gold, as in the present case.

The incipit ÉN sag-ki mu-un-dib (text No. 9) is in fact attested in several closely related first-millennium incantations for this illness; see *AMT* 102: 29 (incipit only), *AMT* 103: 23–24, 27–29, *AMT* 104: 6–8, 11–12, 27–29, 30–31 (dup. *AMT* 13: 5 obv. 7–8), 33–34 (dup. *AMT* 13: 5 obv. 10–11), where they are part of a sequence summed up as 18 KA.INIM.MA [SAG.KI].DIB.BA.KAM (*AMT* 104: 38); see also *BAM* 485 ii 8'–10', 486 iii 1'–2', 487 iii 9', 488 ii 4'–6', 489 rev. 14'–17', 18'–20' and 21'–22'. Several of the accompanying rituals in this compilation prescribe the recitation of these spells over cylinders of various stones which are then tied on the patient, such as *AMT* 102: 28–29: [NA_4 DÙ.A.BI a]n-nu-ti e-ma SAR (for KÉŠ) *ina* SÍG.ḪÉ.ME.DA NIGIN-*mi* [ÉN sag-k]i mu-un-dib ŠID-*nu ina* SAG.KI-*šú* SAR (for KÉŠ)-*su* 'where you tie on all these stones you thread them on red wool, recite the incantation *sagki mundib* and tie them on his forehead'. But none prescribes writing out an incantation on the stone itself. Texts Nos 9 and 10 here are related to one another, and to several of these examples from *AMT*.

The lavish nature of these Nimrud amulets shows that, as might be expected, no expense or effort was spared in treating a royal affliction. The fact that the pieces were found embedded among so much wonderful jewellery probably reflects the fact that the condition of *sagkidibbû* was chronic; such high-quality pieces would scarcely be produced for one-off use, but are much more likely to reflect a lasting and recurring condition; see *AMT* 102: 1–2: *šum-ma* SAG.KI.DIB.BA ŠU.GIDIM.MA *ina* SU NA *il-ta-za-az-ma* NU DU_8 *ina* IGI *ṣi-in-di ù* ÉN NU TAR-*as* 'if *sagkidibbû* (or) Hand-of-a-Ghost persists in a man's body and cannot be removed either by compress or incantation . . .' It is probable that the queen was suffering from these symptoms at the time of her death. The cause of death was probably quite unrelated to *sagkidibbû*, but, in view of the remarks above, the likelihood is that the cause of death induced serious bodily disfigurement.

In the belief that these amulets were intended to work together, they are presented here in an order that produces coherent sense when the texts are read as a whole. From the evidence of their texts we may speculate that the four stones were strung together on a cord as part of a necklace.

Text No 9. Fig. 15-n

1	ÉN sag-ki mu-un-di[b]	Spell, it struck (my) forehead,
2	sag si-sá MIN	Ditto the healthy head,
3	[s]ag saḫar-ra MIN	Ditto the dust-(covered) head,
4	ᵈamar.utu sag-giš-ra	O Marduk smite!
5	ᵈasal-lú-ḫi MIN MIN	O Asalluḫi, ditto! ditto!
6	mu-un-dib MIN	It struck, ditto;
7	mu-un-dib-dib MIN	It struck and struck, ditto!
8	a x x ÉN	. . . Spell.

Fig. 15-n. Texts on amulets, stones and seals. No.9.

The text duplicates and restores *AMT* 104: 6–8 and *BAM* 489 rev. 14'–17' (which, however, reads sag-ki saḫar-ra as in the following spell). From the former passage it is clear that the first sign in ll. 2 and 3 here must be sag rather than KA. Compare also sag si-sá in *AMT* 103: 27, sag saḫar-ra in *AMT* 104:7, and sag si-sá mu-un-dib sag saḫar-ra mu-un-dib in *AMT* 104: 30. The meaning of sag saḫar-ra adopted here is only a guess. Headache can hardly engender physical symptoms that could be described as saḫar 'dust' (as in saḫar-šub-ba), but perhaps severe headache was sometimes traditionally treated by putting dust on the head, as with mourning? The pattern mu-un-dib mu-un-dib occurs in the related incantation *AMT* 103: 27–29. The sign (or signs) after *a* in l. 8 remains obscure.

Fig. 15-o. Texts on amulets, stones and seals. No.10.

Text No. 10. Fig. 15-o

1	MIN ÉN x	Second spell . . .
2	ᵈmes *di-ni*	O Marduk, my judgement!
3	ᵈmes *qa-šat*	O Marduk, the Bow!
4	dingir sag-ʳkiˈ	O god, it struck
5	mu-un-dib	(my) forehead.
6	[s]ag si-sá	the healthy head,
7	[s]ag iš ḫa ra	the . . . head,
8	[a]-da-pà! nun.[me]	O Adapa, sage of
9	[e]riduᵏⁱ *dan-num*	Eridu, powerful one,
10	sag-ki mu-un-[dib]	it struck the forehead,
11	sag-ki saḫar-r[a]	the dust-(covered) forehead.

1. This interpretation of MIN ÉN x is provisional, but would show that the amulets were written, and functioned, as a group.

2–3. ᵈmes is Marduk; the interpretation of *di ni* and *qa kur* is tentative, but there are other incantations on amulets written in a mixture of Sumerian and Akkadian. If *qaštu* 'bow' is correct, Marduk would be shooting at the seizing demons; cf. then the mention of gi.meš kù.meš 'pure arrows(?)' in text No. 12.

7. The other passages offer consistently sag saḫar-ra; perhaps there is contamination from the divine name Išḫara, or might the text have been derived from a tablet which had a gloss: saḫarʰᵃ-ra?

8. In view of the related incantation *AMT* 103: 27–29: a-da-pa / a-da-pà NUN.ME x [. . .] (cf. *BAM* 489 rev. 18'–20'), we may assume the first sign to be hidden under

Fig. 15-p. Texts on amulets, stones and seals. No.11.

Fig. 15-q. Texts on amulets, stones and seals. No.12.

the end-cap. Alternatively, this line could reflect the sequence zi-pà-da as found at the end of parallel incantations in *AMT* 103: 24 and *AMT* 104: 34: zi-pà-da ḫún-ga 'may the spell cause to calm down!' This would mean that the scribe, confused by his medium, has written the signs in reverse: da-pà-z[i].

9. The reading of this line is provisional and cannot be confirmed from the parallels.

Text No. 11. Fig. 15-p

1	DIB.MEŠ	Seizers!
2	KA×ŠU?-meš *šu-ni*	Twin(?) prayers;
3	NA₄ SILIM.MEŠ	Well-being stones,
4	*šá* ᵈ*ninurta*(MAŠ)	of Ninurta.

1. This dib is here taken to reflect the thematic verb in mu-un-dib of the other amulets.

2. If correct, KA×ŠU = *ikribu* 'prayer', the term would refer to the spells on the two preceding cylinders. Could *šu-ni* be related to the second-millennium dual pronoun forms *šuni*, *šunīti* (see Whiting 1977)?

4. Ninurta here, together with Marduk as in the preceding amulets, occurs often in exorcistic amulet incantations of the first millennium BC, as exemplified in the series *Ḫulbazizi* (*STT* 214–17 and duplicates). The term in l. 3 likewise is seen to refer to the preceding two cylinders.

Text No. 12. Fig. 15-q

1	na₄.gú ḫa-mu-ra-	Let (this/these) neck stone(s) be reliable for you!
2	gi *qa-a a-lap-*[*pap*]?	I twist(?) the thread;
3	BI gi.meš kù.meš	. . . pure reeds (arrows?)
4	tab [. . .]	. . . . . .

2. The sign *pap* may be obscured by the end-cap. Alternatively, the word *alappap* runs over into l. 3 (cf. ll.

1–2) and the sign BI, otherwise unexplained, is a miswritten *pap*.

3. If gi = *qanû* 'reed' means 'arrow' here, see above, no. 10. This difficult short passage sounds like the exorcist talking to his patient, i.e. the queen.

Inscribed stone

Text No. 13. *Headdress stone*. Fig. 15-r

Part of ND 1989/108, IM 105966. Rectangular stone of carnelian, found in Tomb II. The text, a label of the Babylonian king Kurigalzu, was previously published by Kamil (1999: 16–17, no. 9) where it is identified as a carnelian bead. As far as I remember, there was a bead of a grey colour bearing the name *ku-ri-gal-zu* that might have led to confusion. I traced the actual shape of this carnelian stone as seen in the copy provided here.

na₄ sag-du	Stone of the head(dress)
Ku-ri-gal-zu	of Kurigalzu
lugal	the king

The headdress stone in question could be a stone removed from the centre of the golden headdress or a

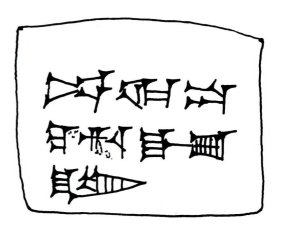

Fig. 15-r. Texts on amulets, stones and seals. No.13.

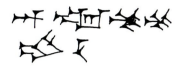

Fig. 15-s. Texts on amulets, stones and seals. No.14.

similar piece (for illustrations of jewellery inlaid with rectangular stones see Hussein and Suleiman 2000: pls 29, 42 and 43). Dr Donny George said that the 'stone' fitted in the headdress (Plate I(a)) when it was found was made out of some kind of paste. According to M. Roaf (1990: 150), 'from very early on attempts were made to manufacture artificial stones' such as 'faience, made by mixing ground-up quartz pebbles with ashes and copper ore and then heating the mixture to produce objects with a bright-blue glazed surface'. On the manufacture and use of faience, frit and Egyptian Blue see in detail Moorey (1994: 166–89). The stone-like material of the Nimrud golden headdress and other similar objects is a material of this kind. I believe that the stone edited here was the original one, and the golden headdress could have belonged to Kurigalzu himself and was later modified to suit an Assyrian queen. On the other hand it could be simply an amulet to protect Kurigalzu against headaches, i.e. it functioned like No. 9 above.

Cylinder seals

Text No. 14. *Seal of Marduk-zakir-šumi*. Fig. 15-s

Part of ND 1989/108, IM 105966. Cylinder seal found in

Tomb II. The text was previously published by Kamil (1999: 16–17, no. 10). According to Ahmad Kamil the material of this cylinder is agate.

dMES-MU-MU	Marduk-zakir-šumi
lugal šú	king of the world

The seal could alternatively have belonged to one of Marduk-zakir-šumi's governors. In that case, we would read the last line as lugal-*šú* 'his king' and translate the whole inscription as: 'For Marduk-zakir-šumi, his king', which could indicate that the seal was dedicated to the king by one of his governors or by a vassal of the king using the seal on his behalf. This practice was not uncommon in the Ur III and later periods.

Text No. 15. *Seal of a eunuch*. Fig. 15-t

ND 1989/333, IM 115643. Cylinder seal of dark blue stone with gold end-caps, length 5.3 cm, diameter 1.7 cm. Found in Tomb III (photograph in Hussein and Suleiman 2000: 396, pl. 180). The inscription on this seal was published by Abdulilah Fadhil (1990b: 481) and twice by Kazuko Watanabe (1992: 364, 4, 1, 3; 1993: 115). However, those publications were without copies of the cuneiform. The owner's name has been read as Ninurta-emūqēja-šukšid (Fadhil and Watanabe), and as Inurta-aḫīa-šukšid (Fischer 2000; I am grateful to Dr Heather Baker for drawing this reference to my attention). I think the reading of *idu* 'arm' in a dual form is more appropriate. My copy was made from a slide provided by Muzahim Mahmoud and the published photograph.

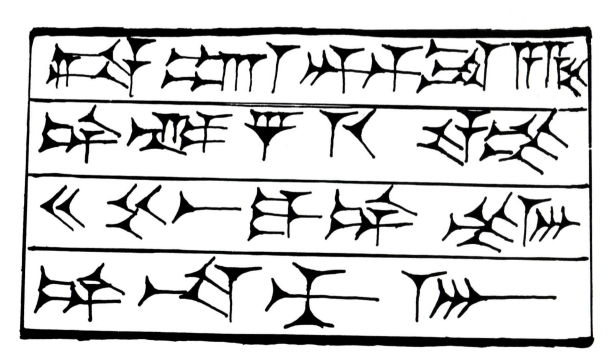

Fig. 15-t. Texts on amulets, stones and seals. No.15.

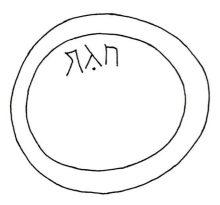

Fig. 15-u. Texts on amulets, stones and seals. No.16.

^{na4}KIŠIB ^{md}MAŠ-Á-*a-a*-KUR Seal of Ninurta-idīya-šukšid,
^{lú}SAG *šá* ^{md}10-ERIM.TAḪ the eunuch of Adad-nirari,
MAN KUR AŠ GAL king of Assyria, chief of the
^{lú}MUḪALDIM^{meš} cooks,
^{lú}NA.GADA^{meš} (and) shepherds.

Stamp seals

There were several stamp seals among the artefacts in the tombs, some of which are inscribed.

Text No. 16. *Seal of Ḥamâ.* Fig. 15-u

ND 1989/334, IM 115644. A solid gold stamp seal, height 4 cm, diameter 3.2 cm, weight 130.5 g. Found in Tomb III (photograph in Hussein and Suleiman 2000: 399, pl. 183). This seal is inscribed with one line on the rim; the length of the inscription is 9.5 cm and the width is 1.25 cm. The inscription is a label of Ḥamâ, queen of Shalmaneser IV (782–773 BC). It reads: *šá* ^{mi}*ha-ma-a* MÍ.É.GAL *šá* ^m*šul-man*-MAŠ MAN KUR AŠ *kal!-lat* ^mU-ÉRIN.DAḪ 'Belonging to Ḥamâ, queen of Shalmaneser, king of Assyria, daughter-in-law of Adad-nirari'. For Ḥamâ see Tallqvist (1905: 66 B).

Text No. 17. *Seal of carnelian.* Fig. 15-v

ND 1989/260B, IM 115554. Stamp seal of carnelian mounted in gold, weight 14.25 g. Found in Tomb III (photograph in Hussein and Suleiman 2000: 407, pl. 189). This seal bears a South Arabian or Nabatean inscription. The actual reading of the three letters are HGT, Arabic حجة, *hajah* 'pilgrimage' or *hujah* 'proof'. It could also be read as HGT, Arabic for حقة which could mean

righteous, taking into consideration that the South Arabian and Iraqi bedouin change *qaf* into *gaf*. The reading was checked from the photograph. There is a shadow line under the first letter and under the third letter. Thus the reading could be SGM or HGM. The former means 'sickened' in Arabic, and the latter means 'to bleed'. The fact that we have amulets for headaches could be taken in consideration.

Other decipherments are possible. One is to emend the text to read HM'T, i.e. the name of the queen Ḥamâ, the wife of Shalmaneser IV. However, we already have her seal (No. 16) and we do not have evidence to suggest that a person could have two different seals. On the other hand one could postulate that she might had the seal before she was married and brought it from Arabia, her native land; but we have no textual support. We might otherwise consider reading the inscription according to the ancient scripts of North Arabia. According to the table of such scripts provided by Winnett and Reed (1970: 205), the reading could be BSM, Arabic بَسَم, *basam* 'smile'. For this name in pre-Islamic Arabia see Harding (1971: 106).

Gold bowls

The treasures include four bowls made of hammered gold and inscribed with short labels of ownership.

Text No. 18. *Bowl of Yabâ.* Fig. 15-w

ND 1989/3, IM 105694. Gold bowl, diameter of rim 20 cm, height 6.5 cm, weight 985.9 g. Found in Tomb II (photographs Damerji 1999: 39, fig. 31 top; Hussein and Suleiman 2000: 242, pl. 37; inscription Kamil 1999: 14–15, no. 1). It bears the longest inscription of all the bowls, measuring about 58 cm around the bowl's neck. The text is a label of Yabâ, wife and queen of Tiglath-pileser III. My copy of it was made during the cleaning of the treasure at the Iraq Museum. The transliteration and translation are as follows: *šá* ^{mi}*ia-ba-a* MÍ.É.GAL *al-ti* ^{m.giš}TUKUL-A-É.ŠÁR.RA MAN KUR AŠ 'Belonging to Queen Yabâ, wife of Tiglath-pileser, king of Assyria'.

Text No. 19. *Another bowl of Yabâ.* Fig. 15-x

ND 1989/6, IM 105697 (Kamil 1999: 14–15, no. 2). The bowl measures 17.7 cm in diameter at the rim, and 3 cm in height on the inside. The chiselled inscription goes around the bowl's short neck, extending for a length of 37 cm and identifying the owner as Yabâ: *šá* ^{mi}*ia-ba-a* MÍ.É.GAL *šá*

Fig. 15-v. Texts on amulets, stones and seals. No.17.

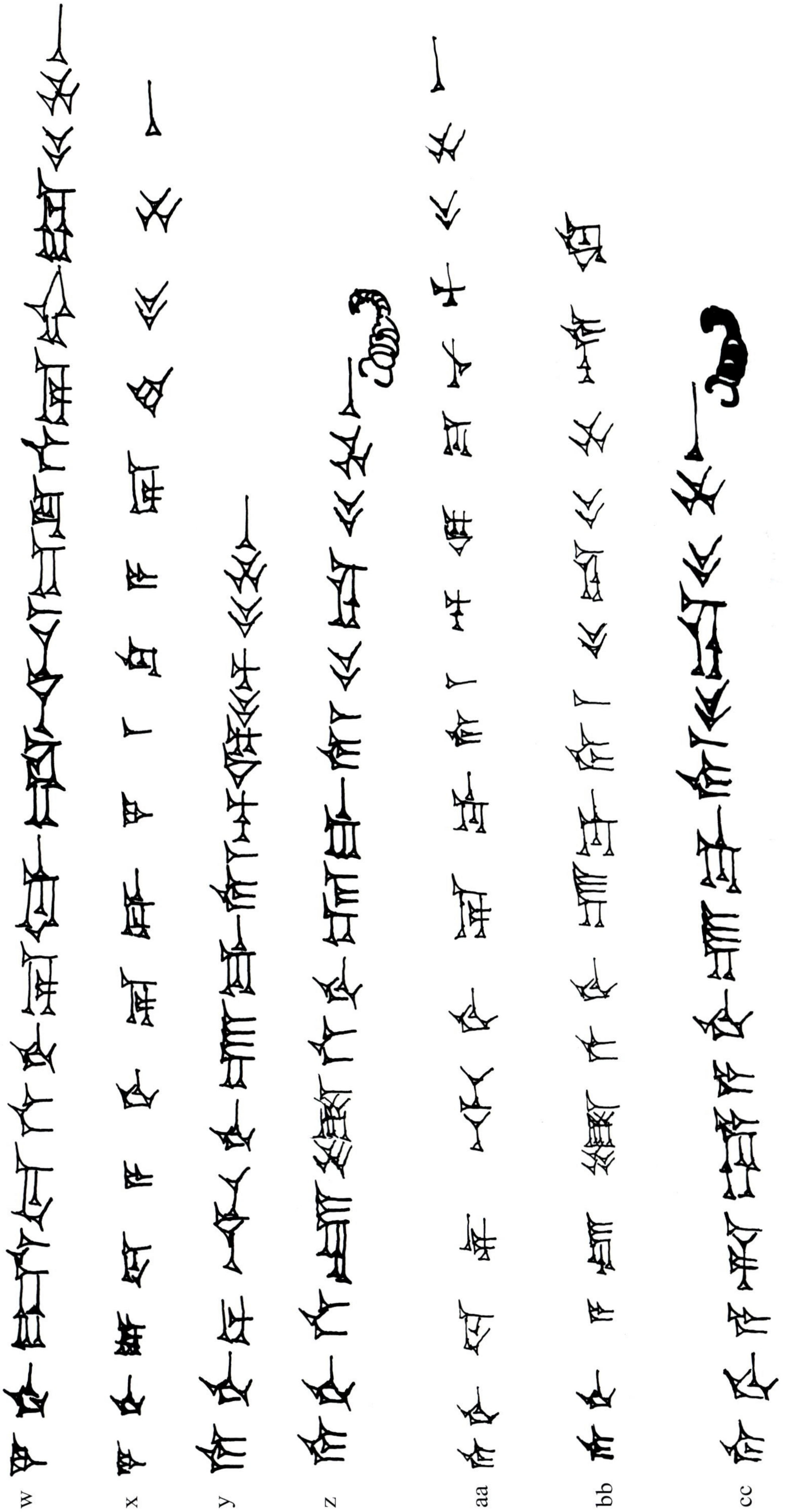

Fig. 15-w, x, y, z, aa, bb, cc. Labels on bowls, other containers and a mirror ᵐTUKUL-A-É.ŠÁR MAN KUR AŠ 'Belonging to Yabâ, queen of Tiglath-pileser, king of Assyria'.

Text No. 20. *Bowl of Banīti*. Fig. 15-y

ND 1989/7, IM 105698. Gold bowl, diameter of rim 11 cm, depth 4 cm, weight 498.53 g. Found in Tomb II (photograph Hussein and Suleiman 2000: 263, pl. 57; inscription Kamil 1999: 14–15, no. 3). It is inscribed on the upper part of the body, around the short neck, with one line 40 cm long, a label of Banīti, queen of Shalmaneser V (726–722 BC). I made my copy during the cleaning of the object at the Iraq Museum. The chiselled inscription is as follows: *šá* ᵐⁱDÙ-*ti* MÍ.É.GAL *šá* ᵐᵈSILIM-*man*-MAŠ MAN KUR AŠ 'Belonging to Banīti, queen of Shalmaneser, king of Assyria'.

Text No. 21. *Bowl of Ataliyā*. Fig. 15-z

ND 1989/4, IM 105695. Gold bowl, rim diameter 20.4 cm, height 12 cm, depth 11.7 cm, weight 980 g. Found in Tomb II (photographs Damerji 1999: 38, fig. 32 top; Hussein and Suleiman 2000: 264, pl. 58; inscription Kamil 1999: 16–17, no. 5). This, the largest bowl, belonged to Ataliyā, the queen of Sargon II. The bowl is inscribed on the upper body, around the short neck, with one line 43 cm long, a label of Ataliyā queen of Sargon II. My copy of this text was made during the cleaning of the discovered objects at the Iraq Museum. The inscription reads: *šá* ᵐⁱ*a-ta-li-a* MÍ.É.GAL *šá* ᵐMAN-GIN MAN KUR AŠ 'Belonging to Ataliyā, queen of Sargon, king of Assyria'. The inscription ends with the symbol of a scorpion.

Other vessels

Text No. 22. *Container of Banīti*. Fig. 15-aa

ND 1989/192, IM 115466. Electron cosmetics container, diameter 14.3 cm, height 2.3 cm. Found in Tomb II (photograph Hussein and Suleiman 2000: 246, pl. 41 top; inscription Kamil 1999: 14–15, no. 4). It is labelled with the following text around the rim: *šá* ᵐⁱ*ba-ni-ti* MÍ.É.GAL *šá* ᵐᵈSILIM-*ma-nu*-MAŠ MAN KUR AŠ 'Belonging to Banīti, queen of Shalmaneser, king of Assyria'.

Text No. 23. *Jar of Ataliyā*. Fig. 15-bb

ND 1989/66, IM 124999. A jar of rock crystal, diameter of rim 10 cm, depth 8 cm. Found in Tomb II (photographs Damerji 1999: 46 fig. 24 top right and Hussein and Suleiman 2000: 243 pl. 38 top left; inscription Kamil 1999: 16–17, no. 6). The label runs around the rim of the jar, the length of the inscription is 30.5 cm. It reads as follows: *šá* ᵐⁱ*a-ta-li-a* MÍ.É.GAL *šá* ᵐMAN-GIN MAN KUR *aš-šur*ᵏⁱ 'Belonging to Ataliyā, queen of Sargon, king of Assyria'.

Mirrors

In addition to the above objects from Tomb II there were several mirrors, one of them inscribed with a label.

Text No. 24. *Mirror of Ataliyā*. Fig. 15-cc

ND 1989/194, IM 115468. A mirror of electron, diameter 14 cm, length of handle 16 cm. Found in Tomb II (photograph Hussein and Suleiman 2000: 246, pl. 41 bottom; inscription Kamil 1999: 16–17, no. 7). The mirror bears the symbol of a scorpion at the end of the inscription. The chiselled writing runs as follows: *šá* ᵐⁱ*a-tal-ia-a* MÍ.É.GAL *šá* ᵐMAN-GIN MAN KUR AŠ 'Belonging to Ataliyā queen of Sargon, king of Assyria'.

16   AN INSCRIBED SILVER BOWL FROM NIMRUD

J. D. Hawkins

In August 1989 the third of the under-floor tomb vaults (Tomb III) was discovered in the North-West Palace at Nimrud, by Iraqi archaeologists under the direction of Dr Muzahim Mahmud. This was found beneath a previously unexcavated room, numbered 57 by the excavators, adjoining Room 49 where the previous tomb vault (Tomb II) had been discovered in April 1989. An entrance shaft led into a brick-built antechamber, and a tomb chamber sealed by inscribed stone doors. In the latter was a large stone sarcophagus, empty, and bearing on its lid the same inscription as on the doors, naming the queen of Ashurnasirpal II (883–859 BC), mother of Shalmaneser III (859–824 BC); the latter's name also appeared on bricks built into the chamber's vault. In the antechamber were three bronze coffins of apparently late eighth-century BC type. After the excavations, the main treasures from the antechamber were taken to Baghdad, but some of the objects requiring conservation remained in Mosul. These included a silver omphalos bowl in reasonable condition, with an estimated diameter of 18 to 20 cm (Hawkins 2000: Part 2, p. 570, XII.15. NIMRUD; Part 3, pl. 327).

From September to December 1989 a team from the British Museum was excavating at Nimrud, with Dr John Curtis as Director and Dr Dominique Collon as Field Director. On at least three occasions during her visits to the Mosul Museum, Dr Collon saw the bowl, and identified the inscription below its rim as being in Luwian hieroglyphs. She memorized the signs and later made a sketch of the bowl and wrote down the inscription from memory. I am indebted to her for the information on this inscribed object. Her sketch is reproduced here and I have accompanied it with a suggested reconstruction of what the inscription may have given (on the right) Fig. 16.a.

In reconstructing the inscription, in what appears to be a cursive form of Luwian hieroglyphs, we find that only the -ma- is problematic, in that it does not obviously conform to a known form. All the other signs were remembered in exact or easily recognisable forms. It thus seems that the name represented is pretty certainly *Santasarmas*, and is probably to be construed as genitive singular, possessive (as for instance on seals) and transliterated: *sà-ta-SARMA-ma$_x$$^?$-sa*, and translated '(of?) Santasarmas(?)'.

While the name may well be a common one, its only attested bearer is *Sandasarme* (written [1]*sa-an-da-šar-me*), king of Hilakku in Cilicia (coastal south-eastern Turkey) during the reign of Ashurbanipal, to whom he submitted in the 650s BC (Luckenbill 1926–27: II, paragraph 782). We have to consider whether this dynast could be identified as the sender of the bowl. Clearly the identification of a present from Sandasarme would be an important piece of chronological data. While the chronology and dating of the objects within Tomb III have not been worked out in detail, the other inscribed objects range in date between 810 and 727 BC. Furthermore, although Cilicia, especially Rough Cilicia, is certainly the place where hieroglyphic writing might be expected to have survived the longest, an attribution to Sandasarme of Hilakku *c.* 650 BC would make this inscription some half a century later than the latest datable hieroglyphic inscriptions, from Niğde, Ivriz and Karatepe. All in all, the identification seems possible but it makes a rather flimsy dating criterion. It could be that Sandasarme was a dynastic name and that an earlier Sandasarme of Hilakku presented the bowl to an eighth-century Assyrian king.

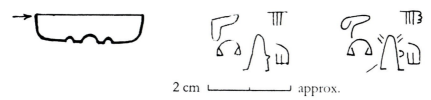

2 cm ⌐――――――⌐ approx.

Fig. 16-a. Inscription in Luwian hieroglyphs on a silver bowl from Nimrud.

17 RESULTS OF THE PALAEOPATHOLOGICAL INVESTIGATIONS ON THE ROYAL SKELETONS FROM NIMRUD

Michael Müller-Karpe*, Manfred Kunter** and Michael Schultz***

Contribution read by Michael Müller-Karpe*
Investigations carried out by Manfred Kunter** and
Michael Schultz***

In 1997, the skeletal remains of the Royal Tombs I, II and III of Nimrud were studied by Professor Michael Schultz of the University of Göttingen, Germany. Regrettably other obligations made it impossible for Professor Schultz to come to this conference himself and to talk about the intriguing results of his research. Since these will certainly be of interest to this audience, I would like to ask you to accept instead a short summary, given by an archaeologist, not competent in the field of physical anthropology and palaeopathology. But first allow me a few words about the background, the conditions under which these results were achieved.

We have just listened to the words of Queen Mullissu-mukannishat-Ninua and of Queen Yaba', cursing those who would disturb their majesties' eternal rest. When in spring of 1988 I first saw the gold objects, which had just arrived from Nimrud, still top secret, spread on a table in the Iraq Museum, like everybody else in that room I was overwhelmed and I had no presentiment about the curse that was connected with these objects, and how close a witness to its effects I would become one day.

Several years later, rumours circulated that the Assyrian queens should be honoured by a second state funeral and that this might happen very soon. At that time, I had become involved in editing a first scholarly account of the Nimrud treasures by Dr Muayad Said Basim Damerji, to be printed in our journal, the *Jahrbuch des Römisch-Germanischen Zentralmuseums Mainz*.[1] It seemed that now was the last chance for any research on the skeletons, since re-burying would certainly make this impossible for an unpredictable length of time. Therefore the idea emerged to initiate a thorough anthropological and palaeopathological study as a collaborative project. Professor Manfred Kunter of the University of Gießen, a physical anthropologist with considerable field experience in the Middle East, with whom I had

previously worked in Oman, was asked to undertake this research. Immediately he agreed: royal bones are usually not on the day-to-day agenda of a physical anthropologist. All necessary formalities (working permit, visa, bookings etc.) were arranged, when, two weeks before the scheduled departure, I received a phone call from Gießen: Professor Kunter had had a heart attack and was forced to cancel his trip. And as if a reconfirmation of this decision was necessary, a second attack followed a week later. Professor Kunter's assistant, Dr Uschi Witwer-Backofen, who also had field experience in Iraq, immediately agreed to take up his task—a welcome decision, since the order to start preparations for the funeral might have come any day. Thanks to the excellent support and co-operation of all relevant institutions, the impossible became possible in the very short time left. A working permit and visa were ready, a reservation was made on a fully booked flight. Three days before the departure, I received a phone call from Dr Witwer. Her mother, who had agreed to look after her little children, had slipped on a staircase and broken her leg. Dr Witwer had to decline too. Within minutes, and despite the mishaps of his colleagues, Professor Michael Schultz of the University of Göttingen, a leading palaeopathologist, accepted to step into the breach, although teaching obligations in America had to be cancelled within short notice. Insiders will confirm that obtaining the prerequisites for an Iraq trip within three days is totally impossible without the help of miracles. But three days later things were ready. The night of our departure, at 3 o'clock, the telephone rang. Professor Schultz was calling from a hospital in Göttingen. Very suddenly, his wife had become seriously ill and had to undergo an immediate operation. I had to travel alone, but after two weeks, when Mrs Schultz's condition had stabilized, Professor Schultz managed to come to Baghdad and immediately set to work at the table with the royal bones, which were ready, waiting for him in the Iraq Museum.

With pleasure I recall the following 18 hour working shifts in the Iraq Museum. I was sitting at my desk, piled up with third millennium metal work from the royal tombs of Ur and from time to time watching Professor Schultz on the adjacent table, studying the bones from the royal tombs of Nimrud. Every now and then he would jump up and show me an exciting new discovery he had just made under the magnifying glass: a tiny irregularity, not too impressive for the uneducated eye, but for the specialist a clear indication that her majesty had

---

* Römisch-Germanisches Zentralmuseum Mainz
** Anthropologisches Institut, Universität Gießen
*** Zentrum Anatomie, Universität Göttingen

[1] Damerji 1999.

meningitis and had survived this disease for several years. In the evenings we would discuss with our colleagues of the museum the significance of these intriguing discoveries. I cannot remember any other ten days of my life, in which I have learned more exiting things.

There is a widespread belief, even among archaeologists, that there can't be anything very spectacular about human bones, since their general shape should be known by now and that the contribution to be expected from a physical anthropologist is basically limited to a long list of measurements and to sex and age. Such an opinion can only be excused by ignorance. In the hands of Professor Schultz the ancient queens started talking, revealing a host of secrets about their lives and deaths and what happened afterwards.

The following summarizes the results obtained from Professor Schultz's ten days' stay in Baghdad and of research on samples which were taken back to Göttingen and studied there. These samples included traces of organic material of grave goods, which were mixed with the bones. This research is still ongoing. A first preliminary report by Michael Schultz and Manfred Kunter has appeared in the *Jahrbuch des Römisch-*

Germanischen Zentralmuseums Mainz.[2] Finally I will talk about samples from the contents of an alabaster jar from Yaba''s tomb, which I received from Dr Georgina Herrmann during her visit to Mainz two years ago and which are also presently being studied in Göttingen.

At this point I would like to thank all institutions and individuals, who made this unusual study come true—a study which became possible not only despite an ancient curse but also in spite of the unbearable effects of a modern curse, which has befallen this beautiful country and wonderful people and which, as we all hope, will soon come to an end. I am especially grateful to my friends and colleagues Dr Muayad Damerji, Mr Muzahim Mahmud, Mr Rabi'a al-Qaissi and last but certainly not least, Dr Donny George. Some of the slides which I will show here are borrowed from him.

The skeletal remains of 17 individuals were examined:

- One skeleton from Tomb I in room MM,
- the body from a clay coffin under the floor of a transit room, leading to room MM,
- the two skeletons from Yaba''s tomb (Tomb II) and
- the remains of 14 individuals from the bronze coffins in the antechamber of Tomb III.

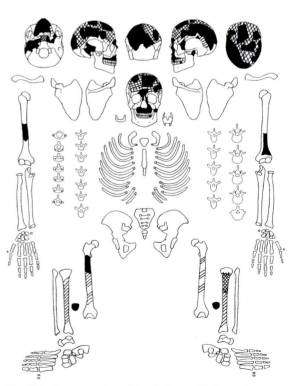

Fig. 17-a. Tomb I . The clay sarcophagus.

Fig. 17-b. Representation of the skeleton of Individual I. Black: completely preserved; cross-hatching: surface defect; hatching: preserved only in fragments.

---
[2] Schultz and Kunter 1998: 85–128.

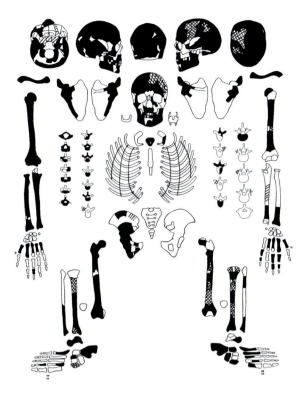

Fig. 17-c. Representation of the skeleton from the transit room, leading to Room MM. Black: completely preserved; cross-hatching: surface defect; hatching: preserved only in fragments.

Tomb I

The clay coffin of Tomb I (fig. 17-a) contained a woman with an approximate age of 50–55 years (fig. 17-b).

The body in the transit room south of room MM was also female and approximately 45–55 years old (figs 17-c and 17-d).

Tomb II

The two persons buried in the stone sarcophagus of Tomb II were identified as females, who both died at approximately the same age of 30–35 years. However, their significantly different state of preservation, i.e. the kind of fragmentation, the degree of decomposition and the patina of the bones, indicate with great certainty that the two women were not buried at the same time. Body II B (fig. 17-e) with its much more advanced stage of decomposition apparently preceded body II A (figs 17-f, 17-g and 17-h). The decomposition of the corpse buried first must already have been so advanced that it was severely damaged when the second corpse was put in the sarcophagus. Microscopic investigation showed that there were at least 20 (perhaps as much as 50) years between the two interments. The assumption of a superposition of the two bodies is also supported by the dark patina of skeleton II A. This corpse was apparently covered by a shroud or something similar, which predominantly

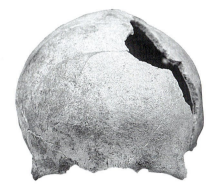

Fig. 17-d. Cranial vault from grave in the transit room, leading to Room MM.

stained the bones of this skeleton after the decomposition of the corpses.

Who were these two women? The chronological order of succession of the three names mentioned in the owner's inscriptions on the grave goods is Yaba' (wife of Tiglath-pileser III), Banitu (wife of Shalmaneser V) and Ataliya (wife of Sargon II). Therefore, individual II A, who was apparently placed in the sarcophagus last, can only be identified as Queen Ataliya. Individual II B could be Yaba' but also Banitu. All the facts mentioned before make it very probable that it was Yaba' and not Banitu. Furthermore, it was Yaba' for whom the tomb was built and it was her stone tablet with the curse, that still lay in the alcove of the antechamber.

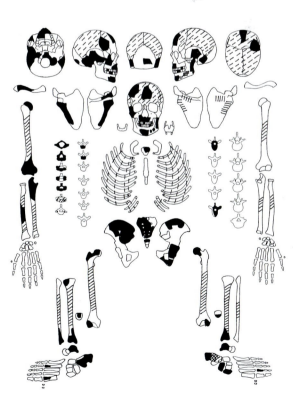

Fig. 17-e. Representation of the skeleton of Individual II B (Queen Yaba'). Black: completely preserved; cross-hatching: surface defect; hatching: preserved only in fragments.

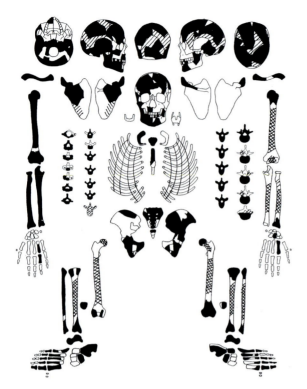

Fig. 17-f. Representation of the skeleton of Individual II A (Queen Ataliya). Black: completely preserved; cross-hatching: surface defect; hatching: preserved only in fragments.

Fig. 17-h. Individual II A (Queen Ataliya). Fragment of the right upper jawbone with first praemolar. Fistulating abscess in the socket of the canine.

still to be determined. It would be the first piece of such evidence from ancient Mesopotamia.

Tomb III

The uppermost bronze coffin in the antechamber of Tomb III (bronze coffin 1) contained bones of six individuals:

- an adult of approximately 20–29 years, possibly female (fig. 17-i),
- an 8–11 year old child, probably a boy (fig. 17-j),
- a 7–11 year old child, probably a girl (fig. 17-k),
- a fully grown foetus (8th–9th lunar month),
- a baby, 3–9 months old and
- another 7–11 year old child.

Only a few bones of each skeleton were present.

Bronze coffin 2 contained a fairly well represented skeleton of an 18–20 year old female (figs 17-l and 17-m), probably a queen, since she wore the magnificent crown on her head. With this queen were found a few fragmentary bones of a 6–12 year old child.

Fig. 17-g. Individual II A (Queen Ataliya). Cranial vault.

The microscopic investigation of samples taken from the bones of Ataliya have yielded an unexpected result. The bones were apparently heated at temperatures of about 150–250° C over several hours. This may point to some kind of desiccation, i.e. dehydration or smoking of the corpse. Whether this was part of a special mortuary practice to preserve the corpse, possibly in preparation for a long journey back home to the final resting place, has

Bronze coffin 3 contained bones of five adults, two men, 30–39 years (fig. 17-n) and 55–65 years (fig. 17-o), one individual, probably male of 35–45 years (fig. 17-p) and two adults, probably female, 35–55 years old (fig. 17-q) and the other over 55.

The interpretation of the interments of tomb III causes some trouble. In each of the three bronze coffins several individuals were found. Of course one coffin is large enough to take the corpse of a young woman and a child,

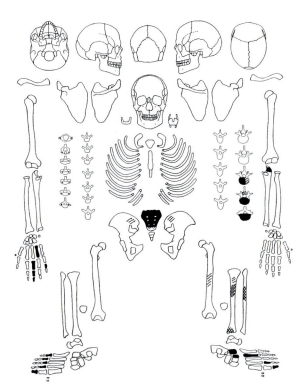

Fig. 17-i. Representation of the skeleton of Individual III 1 A. Black: completely preserved; cross-hatching: surface defect; hatching: preserved only in fragments.

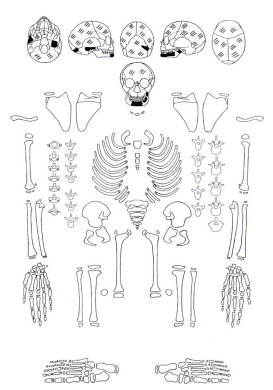

Fig. 17-k. Representation of the skeleton of Individual III 1 C. Black: completely preserved; cross-hatching: surface defect; hatching: preserved only in fragments.

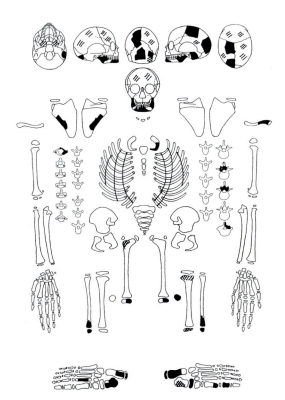

Fig. 17-j. Representation of the skeleton of Individual III 1 B. Black: completely preserved; cross-hatching: surface defect; hatching: preserved only in fragments.

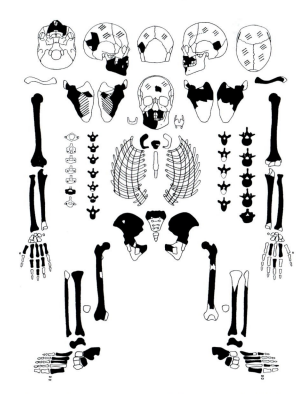

Fig. 17-l. Representation of the skeleton of Individual III 2 A. Black: completely preserved; cross-hatching: surface defect; hatching: preserved only in fragments.

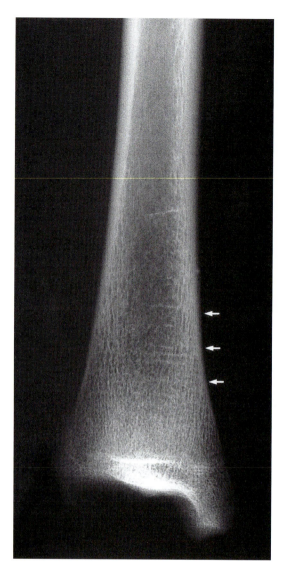

Fig. 17-m. Individual III 2 A. Radiograph of the right tibia. Harris' lines (arrows) indicate arrest of growth during childhood.

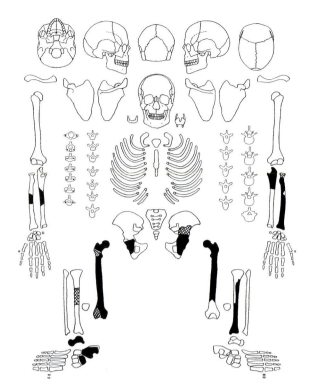

Fig. 17-n. Representation of the skeleton of Individual III 3 A. Black: completely preserved; cross-hatching: surface defect; hatching: preserved only in fragments.

but it is impossible that three adult men and two women were buried all together in one of the coffins. The idea that the corpses were placed in the coffin one after another does not seem very feasible, because the coffin is too small and the skeletons are far too incomplete. In a proper burial in a coffin the skeletons should have been almost complete.

Some skeletons show an intensive green staining caused by impregnation with copper ions from the bronze coffin, while on other skeletons this staining is hardly seen. The greener the bone is stained, the closer was its position to the bronze wall or the bronze floor of the coffin. Thus, we get some information about the position of the bones in the bronze coffins before their recovery. For instance, it could be stated that most of the long bones of the two men III 3 A and III 3 B were deposited along the coffin walls.

The morphological and particularly the microscopic investigation led to broader implications based on these

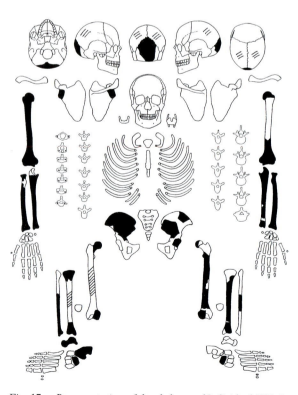

Fig. 17-o. Representation of the skeleton of Individual III 3 B. Black: completely preserved; cross-hatching: surface defect; hatching: preserved only in fragments.

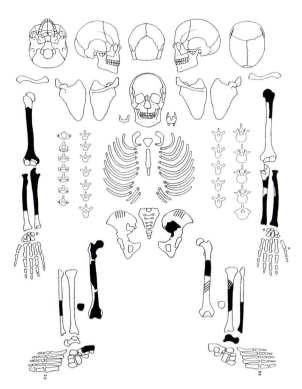

Fig. 17-p. Representation of the skeleton of Individual III 3 C. Black: completely preserved; cross-hatching: surface defect; hatching: preserved only in fragments.

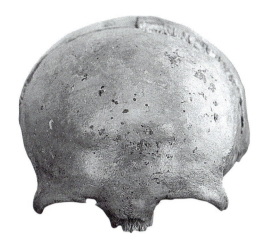

Fig. 17-q. Individual III 3 D. Cranial vault.

facts. Copper ions are bactericidal. They kill micro-organisms. Bone impregnated by copper ions right from the start is, as a rule, very well preserved at the macroscopic and microscopic level. This situation was observed on the green bones of several individuals which therefore should have been originally buried in a bronze coffin but not necessarily in the coffin in which they were found. In some other individuals whose bones also show a green staining, in several cases particularly intensive, the microscopic bone structure is only moderately, or even poorly preserved. Thus, these bones were deposited in the bronze coffins at an advanced stage of decomposition of the bone matrix and were stained secondarily. These skeletons were originally buried in a place, where they were not in contact with copper ions.

These facts led to the assumption that the bones were deposited secondarily in the bronze coffins, i.e. that they were originally buried somewhere else. Probably, these primary burials were hastily removed to prevent looting or profanation. The position of the coffins and the way in which the valuables were stored, confirm this idea.

Two inscribed grave goods might belong to persons found in bronze coffin 3 and reveal the identity of their owners: a cylinder seal belonged to Ninurta-emuqeya-šukšid, a eunuch of King Adad-nirari III, and a golden bowl was inscribed with the name of Šamši-ilu, a field-marshal. The latter served under three, or perhaps even four kings (Shalmaneser IV, Ashur-dan III, Ashur-nirari V and

possibly already under Adad-nirari III, i.e. kings who ruled from 810 until 745 BC). He must have been in active service for more than 40 years. Therefore, this man was probably more than 60 years old when he died. It is tempting to identify Individual III 3 B (fig. 17-o), who was between 55 and 65, with this general. The fact that despite his age, the man was in good physical condition when he died, supports this hypothesis.

The investigation of the diseases diagnosed in the skeletal remains led to surprising results. The high position of the individuals found in the Nimrud tombs, at the top of the social hierarchy, is reflected in the attrition and the state of health of the teeth. However, in all of the five adult individuals suitable for this examination, periodontal disease was observed. In three individuals, among them Yaba' and Ataliya, pronounced dental abscesses were diagnosed. But only one (i.e. Ataliya) suffered from dental caries. At first sight, this result seems to be unusual as the attrition of the teeth was extraordinarily slight. This is an indication of extremely soft food, as can be expected for members of the Assyrian royal court. The relatively low frequency of caries implies some oral hygiene which, however, is contradicted by the poor state of health of the periodontal apparatus.

The following results also do not fit into the picture of a noble upper class. All five adult individuals suitable for the investigation of the paranasal sinuses suffered from chronic inflammatory processes of the frontal and/or the maxillary sinuses (among these again Yaba' and Ataliya). Simple colds could have been the reason. This suggests inadequate housing conditions (e.g. damp, cold rooms) and/or an insufficient immune system of the diseased people. Such diseases are, as a rule, significantly more frequently found in individuals of the lower class than in those of the upper class.

Another important observation is that vestiges in the enamel, characteristic of deficiency or short term diseases lasting for four or five weeks in infancy and early childhood (transverse linear enamel hypoplasia), were relatively frequently observed. Five out of eight skeletons (among which were Ataliya and the young queen from bronze coffin 2 in Tomb III (fig. 17-m)) showed these lesions. This finding also does not seem to fit into a social upper class. Possibly, these people did not have such good living conditions during their childhood as should be expected at a royal court, or, more probably, they became so seriously ill in infancy or early childhood that the enamel hypoplasia could not develop in a proper way. However, because they were members of the upper class and had better food, housing conditions and medical care, they could overcome the disease. Thus, they had better chances of survival than members of the lower class.

Six out of seven adults who could be examined for the state of health of the joints of the vertebral column and the extremities, showed relatively slight changes associated with degenerative joint disease (again Yaba' and Ataliya are among them). This result, again, is not characteristic for a noble upper class population. But these changes were probably due to an untrained locomotor system rather than to excessive physical stress.

Particularly striking is the frequency of pathological changes on the internal lamina of the skull vault. Such vestiges are due to inflammatory processes of the meninges, which can be accompanied by haemorrhages. These diseases (pachymeningitis, meningitis, meningo-encephalitis, perisinuous processes) cause, even after a relatively short time period, characteristic changes which can be easily diagnosed by microscopic techniques. Out of seven individuals suitable for this investigation, six showed pathological alterations represented by newly built bone formations on the internal lamina (among them, the queen of tomb I and again queens Yaba' and Ataliya; only the young queen with the vine leaf crown did not show pathological changes on the internal lamina). Disease of this type and intensity is relatively rare nowadays.

I would like to end this paper with a few words about the contents of the alabaster jar from Yaba''s tomb. The sample which is presently being studied in Göttingen consists of a brown, decomposed organic material. According to a first examination under the scanning electron microscope and by thin ground sections viewed by polarized light the substance could not have been kidney, heart or liver. However, possibly it might be dehydrated brain, dried but apparently not burnt. Resin, as was used in Egypt for conservation is not present. Histological and further investigations are envisaged and will, I hope, give us further results.

The Assyrian queens have just begun to speak to us and we are looking forward to listening to more answers, especially to those which can be expected from DNA-analyses which are also being carried out at the Medical School of the University of Göttingen. These might even help us to understand why Ataliya was allowed to rest in Yaba''s sarcophagus, despite the curse which explicitly forbade this.

Elisabeth Crowfoot* with contributions by M. C. Whiting and Kathryn Tubb

The following report is reprinted, with permission, from *Iraq* LVII (1995), pp. 113–18.
Elisabeth Crowfoot is now deceased.

Textile fragments from the excavation of royal graves at Nimrud in 1988–89 (see *Iraq* 51 (1989): 259) may at first appear disappointing. After the magnificent array of gold jewellery, these scraps may seem of very minor interest, but though technically limited, their original fine execution can still be recognized as befitting a royal burial. The burials probably date to the second half of the eighth century BC.

The queen's body inside the bronze coffin of Tomb 2 was covered with what first appeared to be a solid layer of brittle dark brown wood, but on examination patterns of threads and weave structures could be identified in many areas. The colour varied, different layers being slightly tinged with purple and red, and careful separation by Kathryn Tubb in the Institute of Archaeology Conservation laboratory revealed different styles and qualities of woven cloth. Lines, which at first suggested to the eye the graining of fine wood, proved to be folds, in some areas probably fine pleating or goffering, and it was clear that a mass of delicate fabrics had been present, clothing and wrapping the body, or lying piled up over it (Fig. 5).

Samples from different areas were sent for examination to Professor M.C. Whiting (late Professor of Organic Chemistry, University of Bristol) and it is clear from his analysis (see below) that wood is unlikely to have been present, and this mass was formed entirely of layers of textile, deoxygenated and dehydrated. The very low percentage of nitrogen and even smaller traces of sulphur identified would exclude the presence of any quantity of animal fibres, wool or silk, while the high cellulose content indicated that the yarns in the textiles must have been made entirely of fibres of vegetable origin. This was confirmed by small fragments of well-preserved fabric including tiny areas of embroidery which had survived near to the body in Tomb 1. In these the fibres were still white and supple, and microscopic examination by Kathryn Tubb identified them as well-prepared flax. Some showed green staining from contact with the bronze of coffin or grave-goods, but in none of these, or in the varying shades of the brown layer, could Professor Whiting find any certain evidence of dyeing. Though a small content of flavone (yellow) dye could have escaped detection, it is possible that the only visible suggestion of colour, the slight tan shade distinguishable in some of the threads from tassels in Tombs 2 and 3, may perhaps suggest a clever use of the darker fibres present in some flax varieties to enhance the decoration of these ornaments. The beauty and value of the fabrics probably depended on the quality of the flax, the fineness of spinning and weaving, and the elegant variations in the simple constructions. Gold and cornelian beads, lying in the folds of one layer of the solidified textile, may have been sewn to adorn a garment rather than come from a broken necklace or bracelet; the tiny darned patterns in white threads, preserved from decoration perhaps on some area such as the border of a veil, and the beautiful construction of little tassels in Tombs 2 and 3, indicate a high grade of manual dexterity.

The spinning throughout is S, the natural direction for flax; the twist in the yarns is rather loose—fibres in flax of the quality found here can be long and strong. The weaves are variants of the simplest construction, tabby (plain weave, one-over-one, Fig. 1a). Only one selvedge is preserved here (from Tomb 1, Fig. 2b); it is simple, the edge not reinforced, like those on rather similar linen textiles from Ur. This indicates that where one thread count is higher this is likely to be the warp, a normal feature in textiles from other areas where the warp-weighted loom was in use.

Many of the brown layers have the same near-even count and slightly open weave (Fig. 5a); small bits from one slightly purplish area suggest a layer of another finer but rather similar fabric; but the 'red' layer shows a very different style of tabby-based weave, a half-basket or extended tabby in which the very fine S-spun warp completely conceals the coarser weft (Figs 1b, 5c), which, where the surface is damaged, can be seen to lie in pairs of loosely plyed yarn. This gives a ribbed appearance, a very fine and regular version of the weave later

*The author wishes to thank Dr Muayyad Said Damerji for permission to examine the samples at the Institute of   Archaeology in London and to publish this report.

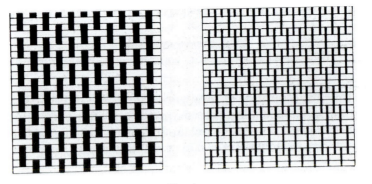

a.   *b.*

Fig. 1

commercially referred to as 'cannelé' (CIETA vocabulary). At one edge this cloth has clearly been folded or rolled round an area of the regular tabby weave.

Fragments of pattern (Figs 2*a*, 3) indicated by tiny closely darned areas can be separated from a tangle of white threads from Tomb 1. In the largest piece spots, made by as many as ten returns of soft thread, darned over three (missing) warps, are joined to each other by a single continuous thread and perhaps originally lay in a circle, like the petals of a flower; others with decreasing returns show stepped lines, or are pointed to form triangles, possibly leaves; occasional threads end in a knot. These designs could have been run in by needle, perhaps on a tabby ground to which some other areas among the loose threads may belong—a technique found in darned patterns on much later handkerchiefs—or perhaps put in while the fabric was still on the loom, on the area of bare warps sometimes found near the end of a woven piece.

Two little tassels (Fig. 4) from Tombs 2 and 3 are clearly not part of braids or fringes made with the warp ends on woven scarves or belts, but have been manufactured as separate items, and perhaps sewn to the corners of a veil or shawl. The green staining is external, and there are no interior bronze pins or tubes in their construction. The hanging threads of the tassel protrude from one end of a decorated tube, 2.3–2.5 cm long, and their loops protrude from the other, still round threads with which they were presumably fastened to the garment. A bunch of the hanging threads, broken off, survives, coarser flax, loosely plyed, of two colours, tan and white. These have been wound continuously, perhaps simply round two sticks, placed to give the length required for the whole tassel; the tube area was wrapped tightly round with flax, possibly of the darker colour in the tassels and decorated with a lattice pattern, darned up and down the tube in noticeably smooth white thread, whose returning loops make a little frill at the tassel end. This decoration also must have been put in with a needle.

The nearest comparative material to these textiles is in those preserved from Woolley's excavations at Ur, now in the British Museum (Textile fragments from PGl, Woolley 1927.5–27.310) published in 1983 by Hero Granger-Taylor (*Anatolian Studies* 33 (1983), pp. 94–95). These are sizeable pieces of fine cloth of good quality

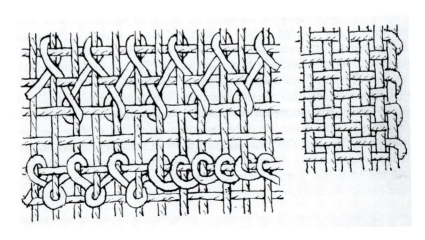

a.   *b.*

Fig. 2*a*. Patterns from Tomb 1.4; *b*. Selvedge.

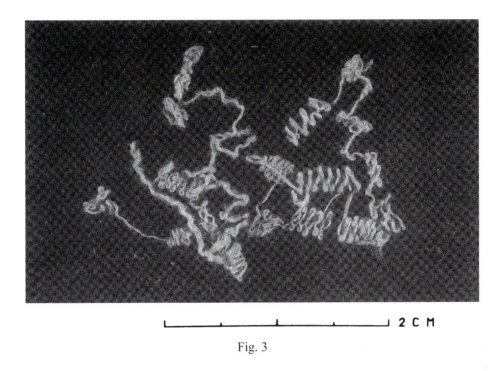

2 C M

Fig. 3

flax, undyed, the fibres still with some shine, the largest piece mounted 38 × 32 cm. The weave in all the major pieces is a fairly even tabby, the thread counts rather similar to those in the 'brown layers', finer than the preserved white scraps from Tomb 1; the variations in spinning practice are interesting, most being S, the normal spin for flax in the Middle East, but some Z, and some S, Sply, though with no indication of the 'splicing' technique familiar from Egyptian textiles. A few smaller fragments here also suggest patterning—a tiny separated

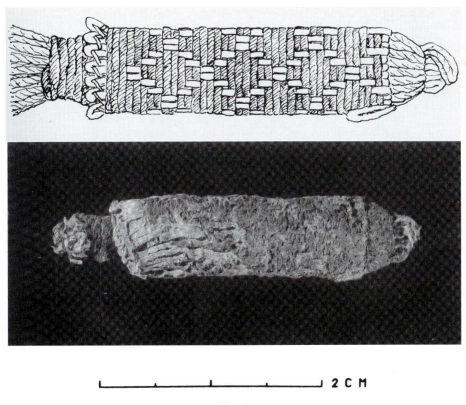

2 C M

Fig. 4

Fig. 5 "Wood" layer from Tomb 2. enlarged. Textile arrowed: *a.* Tabby weave; *b.* Fine tabby weave, deteriorated patch, under *c*; *c.* Cannelé weave (half-basket, extended tabby).

scrap shows a folded spot, as in the darned patterns of Tomb 1, and other confused areas in a lump of unseparated threads are perhaps the same linked spot patterns. In this grave traces, possibly of wool, were found, and Woolley's excavation report mentioned linen and wool cloths (C.L. Woolley, The excavations at Ur, *Antiquaries Journal* 6 (1926), pp 365–401).

Catalogue of Nimrud Textiles

Tomb 1. Fragments preserved near body, all flax, undyed. Fibre identification by Kathryn Tubb.

1. 3.4 × 1.3, edges torn. Yarns, spinning S, twist medium to close, uneven, weave tabby (plain), close, thread count 14/9–10 on 1 cm.
2. Fragments of folded strip:
    (a) length 5.0 cm, width as folded, 1.0 cm, yarns spinning S, even, medium twist, good quality, shiny surface, weave tabby, close, even, count *c.* 34 (17 on 5 mm)/14 on 1 cm. Strip folded diagonally, simple selvedge 3.3 cm preserved, turned over, ?tied round Cu alloy object, leaving heavy staining.
    (b) detached, 2.2 × 1.4, similar folding, lying across (a).
    (c) 1.3 × 1.4, similar, with mark from edge of Cu alloy ring.
3. 2.9 × 1.0, edges torn. Yarns, spinning S, twist medium, uneven, weave tabby, slightly open, thread count 14/14–15 on 1 cm.
4. Mass of detached threads, spinning S, fine, medium twist, including decoration:
    (a) two scraps, *c.* 1.5 × 1.1, 1.0 × 1.5 cm, stained Cu alloy, spinning S, one yarn fine, medium twist, ?warp, other loose twist, uneven; weave tabby, thread count 16/14–16 on 1 cm (possibly 3).
    (b) loose threads from embroidery, spin S, very light twist (Fig. 2*a*); parts can be folded back into shapes,— spots, 10 returns darned over 3 warps, joined by continuous thread; lines with stepped profile; close returns reducing to points, some with knot at end of thread—(Fig. 3) ?flower and leaf decoration.
    (c) one patch, closely folded threads, length 1.6 cm, simple returns, 16–17 on 5 mm; marks of cross-threads, 14–15 per 1 cm, showing tabby construction ?from ground weave (a)—perhaps band darned in, ?border of decoration.

Tomb 2. Brown solidified area covering body inside coffin. (Analysis, M.C. Whiting, below, dehydrated and deoxygenated textile, originally all textile, vegetable fibre, i.e. ?flax).
(a) (MCW sample 1) Upper surface, 'purple', best areas clear *c.* 14 × 7.0 cm, 13.0 × 9.0 cm; broken edges show up to 10 layers fabric, on depth *c.* 1.0–1.5 cm. Yarns fine, even, spinning S, twist loose, weave tabby, very regular, slightly open, thread count *c.* 22/22 on 1 cm. Some areas, best preserved *c.* 6.0 × 3.0 cm, show soft regular folds, ?pleats or goffers, 3 on 1.0 cm (Fig. 5*a*).
(b) below, not clear, small patches that seem to be finer tabby, spin S, count *c.* 24/48 on 1 cm (?weft count taken as 12 on 2.5 mm) (Fig. 5*h*).
(c) (MCW sample A) Underneath, 'red' area, best cleared *c.* 2.0 × 1.3, lying under (a) and *c.* 2.0 × 0.6 cm, ?wrapping round edge, yarns warp fine loose fibres, spinning S, weft (concealed) pairs, S-ply, weave ribbed, extended tabby, (half-basket weave, cannelé), thread count *c.* 60/11–12 pairs, close even ribs, 11–14 per 1 cm (Fig. 5*c*). The weft can only be seen in places where the warp surface is broken.

Tomb 2. Tassel 1 (Fig. 4).
Complete tassel preserved, apart from hanging ends, length 3.3 cm. (MCW, samples 2, 3), stained bronze. Flax, undyed, some threads tan (no dye detected, ?natural colour), threads S, Zply, loops one end round a thread (for sewing to garment); tube *c.* 2.5 cm, wound evenly round with fibrous yarn, S spun, light Zply, ?dark but no dye identified, end tucked in below loops; darned decoration length of tube, thread ?white, S, loose Zply; returns at loop end hidden under wrapping, at tassel end standing up in small loops, loops held in fringe by very fine S spun twined threads. Mass of loose threads from tassel.

Tomb 3. Tassel.
Part of similar tassel, damaged; 'tube' 2.2 cm, with remains of similar wrapping and decoration, (MCW, samples B, C); tube broken open, showing threads lying inside, S spun Zply. Mass of loose threads, longest 80 mm, lying in pairs as wound inside the tube, S spun, tight Zply, the best preserved folded in lengths *c.* 2.4 cm, some originally white, others visibly tan, but no dye present; all heavily stained with bronze, but no metal inside tube construction.

Analysis and Dye Testing (Professor M.C. Whiting)
Tomb 2 (19 March 1992).
Four samples from the brown stratified layer, and white deposit present in some areas, were analysed:

	C	H	N[1]	S[2]	Ash	O by diff. (salt)
White deposit	5.06	3.14	0.10			
Brown: (1)	60.58	6.72	1.10	0.24	10.50	
(2)	63.44	6.93	0.88	0.47	8.96	
(3)	59.52	6.73	1.13	0.38	5.55	
(4)	61.02	6.98	1.06	0.67	7.38	
Average	61.14	6.84	1.04	0.44	8.10	
Corrected for ash	66.53	7.44	1.13	—	—	24.9
Atomic ratio	5.544	7.44	0.08			1.556
	C_6	H_8				$O_{1.7}$

Cf. cellulose $C_6H_{10}O_5$ (i.e. –2 H, –3.3 O)

This indicates that the process is one of deoxygenation and dehydration, if the starting material is indeed cellulose. If it were wood, i.e. a mixture of cellulose and lignin, the analysis would be as expected, as lignin does have a high ratio of carbon to hydrogen and to oxygen. I believe that soil would give somewhat similar analyses, and the behaviour of the 'brown stuff' may be like that of the humic acids of soil.

Notes: 1. Proteins have 10–15% N.
         2. Separate analyses from the C, H, N (ash refers to C, H, N analysed).

Additional samples were sent after the separation of the layers to show the 'red' ribbed layer (extended tabby), Sample A from this layer, B and C from the tassels, B from the decoration, C from the wrapping, 30 April 1992: Professor Whiting writes that A and C are similar to the 'brown' stuff, B (of which a fibre had been identified as flax by Kathryn Tubb) is different.

Dye Testing:
Tomb 2. Loose threads from tassels (19 March 1992).
Sample (1) 'brownish' (2) 'greenish'
Both negative for indigo and madder. The green fibres (2) contained a green-blue material, completely inextractible from water, and stable in light, broad maximum *c.* 660 nm—i.e. Cupric copper, present with some sort of carbohydrate degradation product. Aqueous solutions also for material extractible into diethyl ketone (insect dyes) with no sign of their presence. The near UV spectrum of ether extracts (315–400 nm) showed no sign of a maximum, only general fall-off, typical of any degraded organic material. (2) A small content of a normal flavone or flavonol would have escaped detection, and cannot be said to have been proved absent.

Tombs 2 and 3 (30 April 1992).
Sample A. 'Red' layer.
Sample C. From wrapping thread on tassel 2.
Both these are like the 'brown' layers, negative to tests for indigo, no madder, lac or cochineal detected, and no appreciable amount could have been there. Some other yellow/orange/red/brown mordant dye may have been present, or decomposition may have given pigmented material in the large amount of general 'muck'.
Sample B. Pattern thread from tassel. (Flax, Kathryn Tubb).
Different from C, but again no indigo, mordant dyes, lac or cochineal detected.

[Ed.] The coffin in Tomb 2 was actually made of stone but contained a bronze mirror. It is possible, however, that these remains actually came from bronze Coffin 2 in Tomb 3 (see Curtis, this volume) [D. Collon, 2007].

19   NIMRUD SEALS[1]

Lamia al-Gailani Werr

Twelve stamp seals and two cylinder seals were found in the Queens' Tombs in Nimrud, five from Tomb I, five from Tomb III and two from Tomb IV; two cylinder seals were found in Tomb III (see Table; also Hussein and Suleiman 2000). Other relevant seals from the North-West Palace, excavated by the Department of Antiquities in the 1990s, particularly from the vaulted chambers below Rooms 74–75 and Well 4 (see Hussein, Sections II and III in this volume; Hussein and Abdul-Razak 1997–98) will also be mentioned in this article. The seals from the tombs are all made from semiprecious stones of which the majority are carnelian or chalcedony; one, described in the publication as dark blue stone, could be made of lapis lazuli (fig. 19-v) (Hussein and Suleiman 2000: no. 180).

The subjects depicted are limited either to one-figure representations or worship scenes. A nude winged female/goddess occurs frequently on the seals. She appears on two onyx seals that are shaped like reclining bulls (figs 19-a and 19-b). The base of the first is encased in a gold sheet that is either impressed or engraved with an elaborate winged, frontal nude female, who stands with hands stretched downwards. The decorated garment hanging behind her consists of criss-cross lines and centre dots, her head is in profile and her hair is done in Assyrian style. All the representations of the nude females show their hands held stretched downwards, with one exception where the hands are

held upwards (fig. 19-c). On one seal from Tomb IV, the nude female is not solitary but shares the seal with a horse(?) which is suckling its foal (fig. 19-d). Although the figure is usually portrayed bare headed, a cylinder seal from Well 4 shows her wearing a crown; on this seal a second winged female is also depicted, but only the lower part is visible (fig. 19-e).

A female worshipper, most probably the queen, is represented on a gold Royal Seal distinguished by a guilloche border (fig. 19-f). She is standing with raised hands in front of the enthroned goddess Gula, who is wearing a horned crown topped with a star. The stars, in the form of stylized dots, can be seen at the back of the

Fig. 19-b. Room 74, onyx stamp seal, 2.4 × 1.6.

Fig. 19-a. Tomb I, onyx stamp seal.

Fig. 19-c. Tomb I, chalcedony stamp seal, diam. 1.6 cm.

---

[1] All drawings in this article are by Lamia al-Gailani Werr.

Fig. 19-d. Tomb IV, carnelian stamp seal.

Fig. 19-e. Well 4, carnelian cylinder seal, 3.0 × 1.1 cm.

Fig. 19-f. Tomb III, gold seal, diam. 3.2 cm.

throne, which is balanced above a reclining dog. The goddess holds a curved weapon in one hand and a 'beaded' ring in the other (see Collon 2001: nos 232–34, where the weapon is interpreted as a scalpel). Behind the throne is a scorpion. The inscription round the rim of the seal gives the name of the queen (see Al-Rawi: no. 16 in this volume). Scorpions also occur incised on a gold bowl and a mirror from Tomb II (Al-Rawi: nos 21, 24 in this volume) and on a shell excavated nearby in Room HH (Mallowan 1966: I, 112, fig. 57); perhaps it was the symbol of the royal queens of the palace. Scorpions also appear on stamp seals that may have belonged to the royal household, as they also have guilloche borders (Herbordt 1992: tf 33: 1–9). The queen is probably depicted on a gold amulet from the same tomb (fig. 19-g). These two objects are the only pictorial representation of a queen from the tombs.

The female worshipper, though absent from the seals in the tombs, appears on a number of seals from the vaulted chambers beneath Room 75, and from Well 4 (see Hussein: Sections II and III in this volume). She is shown either facing the goddess Ishtar (fig. 19-e) or the goddess Gula (figs 19-h and 19-i). Gula is seen enthroned over her dog on one of the seals, where she has stars on the back of her throne; on the other she has stars on her crown and above the back of her throne (partly broken); on both seals she holds the curved weapon and the 'beaded' ring, and a female worshipper is facing her.

Gula also appears on a remarkable seal (fig. 19-j) found in the palm of a manacled skeleton, discovered separately from the rest of the skeletons in Well 4. The seal is made of a semiprecious greenish-blue stone and has gold caps with a loop for suspension. The scene shows the

Fig. 19-g. Tomb III, gold amulet, 4.1 × 2.5 cm.

enthroned goddess with her dog between her and a male worshipper; alongside is a second scene depicting a combat with a winged genie subduing two winged griffins. A horse is engraved on the base of the seal. The gold capping is identical to that on a seal discovered near Aleppo, which is also engraved on the base (Collon 1987b: no. 391). A clay lump with the impression of a seal with possibly similar caps comes from Nimrud (Collon 1987b: no. 359)

Gula's dog (fig. 19-k) appears on a broken serpentine seal found in the vaults below Room 75. It is depicted in a ritual and healing scene in two registers. This belongs to a small group of seals showing similar subjects; most are unprovenanced, with the exception of one from Tell Halaf, and all are made of the same type of stone, serpentine. This may indicate that this type of stone may have had a healing significance. One seal in the Borowsky collection could be a product of the same seal cutter as the Nimrud seal (Williams-Forte in Muscarella 1981: 129, no. 86).

In a seal from Tomb III the goddess Ishtar appears in all her regalia, wearing a feathered crown and holding the rod and ring in one hand and a scimitar in the other (fig. 19-l). There are quivers over one shoulder and arrows on the other; and she is standing on a winged lion-griffin. Ishtar is also depicted on a gold pendant (fig. 19-g), where she is also wearing a feathered crown topped with a star, and faces a female worshipper. A seal from Tomb IV (fig. 19-m), and another from Room 77 (fig. 19-n), show the goddess in a nimbus, with a star over the crown. She also appears on the cylinder seals from the vaulted chambers below Room 75, where she is standing above a lion demon, with stars on top of her crown and on the tips of the quivers, facing a female worshipper (fig 19-o). On another seal (fig. 19-e) she is in similar attire and also faces a female worshipper (upper part missing). The goddess on a cylinder seal from Tomb III (fig. 19-w) could be Ishtar, though none of her attributes is depicted.

A carnelian stamp seal from Tomb III is rather intriguing (fig. 19-p). It is pyramidal in shape and depicts a combat scene more common on cylinder seals of the Akkadian and Old Babylonian periods. Three of the faces show parts of the scene: two show nude heroes subduing two

Fig. 19-h. Room 74, onyx cylinder seal, 3.2 × 1.3 cm.

Fig. 19-i. Room 75, carnelian cylinder seal, 3.5 × 1.7 cm.

Fig. 19-j. Well 4, greenish-blue cylinder seal, 4.9 × 1.6 cm (measurement includes gold cap).

Fig. 19-k. Room 74, serpentine cylinder seal, 3.5 × 1.88 cm.

Fig. 19-l. Tomb III, carnelian stamp seal.

Fig. 19-m. Tomb IV, stamp seal.

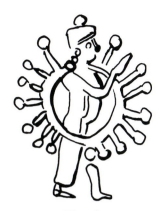

Fig. 19-n. Room 77, pink stone stamp seal.

A carnelian seal has two human-headed, winged lions on either side of a stylized tree, above are two birds, with a crescent and star in the sky (fig. 19-q). Normally on Neo-Assyrian stamp seals two bull-men are depicted on either side of a tree, with hands raised to support a winged disc. The variation here, with the winged human-headed lions, and birds perching above the tree, is unusual (cf. Herbordt 1992: tf. 13: 1–8). Another seal from Tomb I, in the shape of a bird made of chalcedony, is engraved with a solitary worshipper raising his hand towards a star in the sky (fig. 19-r).

There are three carnelian seals with West Semitic/Phoenician motifs, one from Tomb I and the other two from Tomb III (fig. 19-s, 19-t and 19-u). The first has a hieroglyphic inscription giving the name of the owner (Damerji 1999: p. 6, note 8). The second has an Aramaic or Arabic inscription (see Al-Rawi, this volume, text no. 17). All three are mounted in gold with chains for suspension. The first (fig. 19-s) has an elaborate gold border decorated with filigree work, on either side of which are pear-shaped drops, and over them, on the holder, are two reclining lions; the loop is attached to a

goats, and one face has two crossed goats with necks entwined. This seal/amulet was probably inspired by earlier seals. The fourth face is possibly a later addition, with a striding god in the Assyrian style. Multiple-faceted seals are few; most are Neo-Assyrian and Neo-Babylonian in date (Black and Green 1992: 20, fig. 14, below).

Fig. 19-o. Room 75, carnelian cylinder seal, 5.3 × 2.3 cm.

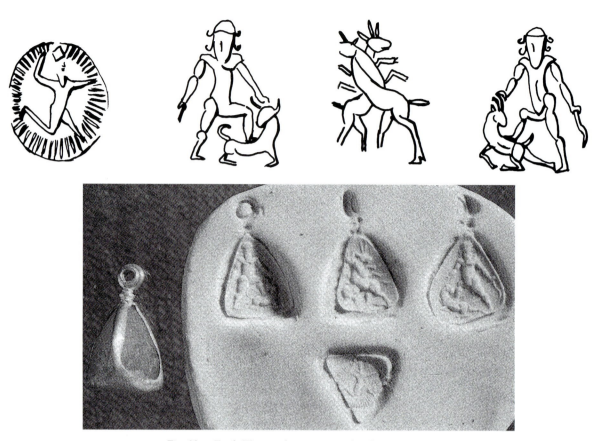

Fig. 19-p. Tomb III, carnelian stamp seal and impressions.

Fig. 19-q. Tomb I, carnelian stamp seal.

Fig. 19-r. Tomb I, chalcedony stamp seal.

Fig. 19-s. Tomb III, carnelian stamp seal.

Fig. 19-t. Tomb III, carnelian stamp seal.

Fig. 19-u. Tomb I, carnelian stamp seal.

chain which ends in a fibula decorated with a lion's head, a robed human figure, a fly and an eagle (fig. 29-t; Damerji 1999: nos 14 and 15).

As already noted, only two cylinder seals were discovered in Tomb III; one is probably made of lapis lazuli, the other of carnelian, and both are gold-capped (figs 19-v and 19-w). The first bears an inscription giving the name of an official of Adad-Nirari III (see Al-Rawi: text no. 15 in this volume). This is a distinctive seal depicting a god who holds a curved weapon and stands below a winged disc,

with the streamers coming down from the disc held on either side by the king; a worshipper stands behind one king. In the sky there are several symbols: a goddess inside a star, a lightning fork, a crown, a crescent and the sibitti dots. In the field an unidentified symbol is depicted twice, and there is a goat(?) below one streamer, between the god and the king. On the second seal (fig. 19-w) there is also a winged disc above a stylized tree; a goddess stands on one side of the tree and a king, followed by a worshipper, stands on the other side. These two seals may belong to the adult males found in Tomb III.

It is to be noted that no personal cylinder seals were found in any of the other tombs, as the frit cylinder shown in Hussein and Suleiman 2000: pic. 6 is probably an amulet similar to the group of amulets found round the neck of the queen in Tomb I, consisting of winged genie, scarabs, a Pazuzu head, and decorated cylindrical beads (*ibid.*: pic. 17. The presence of more than one stamp seal in Tombs I and III and two seals in Tomb IV, may indicate that they were used as amulets and not seals.

The seals from the vaulted chambers and Well 4, discussed here, are made of semiprecious stones; all are

Fig. 19-v. Tomb III, lapis lazuli (?) cylinder seal, 5.3 × 1.7 cm.

Fig. 19-w. Tomb III, carnelian cylinder seal, 4.1 × 1.5 cm.

either chipped or broken, with the exception of figs 19-b and 19-j. The latter, as mentioned above, was hidden in the palm of a victim's hand in Well 4. Their condition suggests that they originally had gold caps, which were torn off by the looters when Nimrud was sacked in 614 or 612 BC.

TABLE OF NIMRUD SEALS

Fig. no.	Hussein & Suleiman 2000	Hussein & Abdul-Razak 1997–1998	Material	Location
1	13		onyx	Tomb I
2		14	onyx	Room 74
3	4		chalcedony	Tomb I
4	201			Tomb IV
5		39	carnelian	Well 4
6	183		gold	Tomb III
7	140		gold	Tomb III
8		37	onyx	Room 74
9		35	carnelian	Room 75: vault a
10		36	greenish-blue stone	Well 4
11		23	serpentine	Room 74: vault b
12	127		carnelian	Tomb III
13	202			Tomb IV
14		42	pink stone	Room 77
15		38	carnelian	Room 75: vault b
16	182		carnelian	Tomb III
17	5		carnelian	Tomb I
18	14		chalcedony	Tomb I
19	12		carnelian	Tomb I
20	189		carnelian	Tomb III
21	190		carnelian	Tomb III
22	180		lapis lazuli	Tomb III
23	181		carnelian	Tomb III

John Curtis

My intention in this paper is to review the evidence for bronze coffins of the type that have been found in Tomb III at Nimrud, and to see what conclusions, if any, might be drawn about these distinctive bronze coffins. As we have heard this morning, three bronze coffins were found in Tomb III that was excavated in the summer of 1989.[1] Further details can be found in the two official publications of the tombs (Damerji 1999: 8–11, fig. 37; Hussein and Suleiman 2000: 114–28, figs 12–14). Tomb III was under the floor of Room 57 in the North-West Palace, and consisted of a main chamber with barrel-vaulted roof separated from an antechamber by an arched doorway. In the main chamber was a large stone sarcophagus with lid that was found to be empty. The inscription on the lid of this sarcophagus records that the grave is that of Mullissu-mukannishat-Ninua, queen of Ashurnasirpal (Damerji 1999: fig. 36; Al-Rawi text no. 3). The doorway between these two chambers was closed with two slabs of stone, and three bronze coffins had been placed in the antechamber, blocking access to the main chamber itself. In these coffins were bones and an extraordinary collection of gold jewellery, including the elaborate gold crown. The first coffin (1.30 m × 59.4 cm, height 51.5 cm) had been placed on top of another coffin, against the east wall with the rounded end facing to the south. The second coffin (1.40 m × 49 cm, height 57 cm) was underneath the first coffin, in the same alignment but with the rounded end facing north (fig. 20-a). The third coffin (1.47 m × 68 cm, height 57.5 cm) was on the west side of the antechamber, next to the other two, and with the rounded end facing north as coffin 2. According to Hussein and Suleiman (2000: 116) in at least one case the body was placed in the coffin with the head at the flat end. These three bronze coffins are all of the same characteristic type. They have high, straight sides, they are squared off at one end and rounded at the other, they have a ledge around the top and they have a pair of handles at either end. They are made from two sheets of bronze joined together in the middle of the long sides. The joins are covered by vertical strips of bronze applied inside and outside and held in position by rivets. The base and the overhanging ledge around the top are also attached by rivets (figs 20-bi and 20-bii).

Bronze coffins of this type are not unique in the archaeological record, and some years ago I attempted to collect together the examples known at that time (Curtis 1983).

The best known examples are two coffins from Ur in Southern Iraq. The two coffins were found during the 4th season of excavation at Ur in 1925–26 (fig. 20-c). They were in crude brick vaults which had been cut into the ruins of a building called the *giparu* which had been constructed by Kurigalzu in about 1400 BC. Now this building probably continued in use beyond the Kassite period but we do not know exactly how long for. It is possible, however, that one of the tombs was *directly under* the temenos wall built by Nebuchadnezzar (Curtis 1983: 91), in which case the burials would obviously have to predate his reign.

One of these bronze coffins is now in the British Museum (fig. 20-d), while the other is in the Birmingham Museum and Art Gallery (fig. 20-e). They are similar to the Nimrud coffins but here the vertical strips on the sides of the coffins have incised decoration showing goats standing on rosettes ((figs 20-f and 20-g); Woolley 1962: 56, 113, pls 16–18; Curtis 1983: pls XXV, XXVIIa–b). In the Late Assyrian period, the motif of goats flanking a palmette is

Fig. 20-a. Bronze coffin in Tomb III at Nimrud (from Damerji 1999: fig. 37).

Fig. 20-b(i) and b(ii). Bronze coffin from Nimrud in the Mosul Museum. (Photographs J.E. Curtis.)

well known, but this particular motif of a goat standing on a rosette is much less common. It does occur, however, on a glazed brick panel from Khorsabad dating from the reign of Sargon (Botta 1849–50: II, pl. 155). It is possible, then that the coffins were manufactured at this same period in the late eighth century BC.

Fig. 20-c. The two bronze coffins as found at Ur. (Photograph courtesy of the British Museum.)

The contents of the two Ur coffins also seem to belong to the Late Assyrian period. Inside were skeletons, said to be female, with the skulls at the flat ends of the coffins. The bodies were accompanied by a rich selection of grave-goods (Curtis 1983: figs 1–2, pls XXVIIc–XXIX) that included 3 gold earrings with elaborate pendant decoration, a crescentic gold earring, a bronze bracelet, 4 triangular bronze fibulae, 4 strings of beads, a bronze mirror, a bone comb, a gadrooned bronze bowl, 3 glazed pottery jars, 1 wooden bowl with lug handles, remains of a wooden box and a basket, and fragments of linen textile. The elaborate gold earrings can be loosely compared with earrings shown on stone sculptures of the time of Sargon (Curtis 1983: pl. XXVIIIf), the fluted bronze bowl finds parallels at Nimrud and Ashur (Curtis 1983: 92), and the glazed jars could easily belong to the eighth or seventh

Fig. 20-d. Bronze coffin from Ur. (Photograph courtesy of the British Museum.)

Fig. 20-e. Bronze coffin from Ur. (Photograph coutesy of Birmingham Museum and Art Gallery.)

century BC. I suggested previously that jars of this type should be dated to the seventh–sixth century BC rather than to the eighth–seventh century, but in view of the increasing number of Assyrian parallels (e.g. Curtis and Green 1997: no. 161 and commentary) there is no reason to suppose that they are post-Assyrian.

The Ur coffins, then, are Assyrian in style, perhaps even from the reign of Sargon, the contents of the coffins apparently date from the Assyrian period, and the stratigraphic evidence seems to suggest that the coffins were most probably buried in the Assyrian period. Penelope Weadock has made the interesting suggestion that the graves are actually those of *entu*-priestesses who lived in the *giparu* (Weadock 1975:112). Woolley suggested that the *giparu* was rebuilt by Sin-balassu-iqbi (Woolley 1965: 35–36, pl. 53) who was governor of Ur and Eridu in the time of Ashurbanipal (Walker 1981: nos 81–86).

Then, we have a single bronze coffin from Zincirli in Southern Turkey that is now in the Vorderasiatisches Museum in Berlin ((fig. 20-h); von Luschan 1943: 118–19, 171, pl. 57b–d). It has recently been the subject of a detailed technical study by Jendritzki and Martin (2001). Like the Nimrud examples it is plain, that is it lacks the incised decoration on the vertical strips on the side of the coffin. It was found in Building L in a room that was originally interpreted as a bathroom, but this seems open to doubt (Jendritzki and Martin 2001: 186). In any case, the coffin was not found in an original context but separated from the pavement of the room by a layer of earth 17–23 cm thick. It was apparently empty when found. Building L is part of a complex that is believed to have been founded by Barrakib (*c.* 733–720 BC) (Jendritzki and Martin 2001: 186). It presumably predates the violent destruction evident in many parts of the citadel that may have been the work of Esarhaddon (680–669

Fig. 20-f. Incised decoration on coffin from Ur. (Photograph courtesy of Birmingham Museum and Art Gallery.)

Fig. 20-g. Incised decoration on coffin from Ur. (Photograph courtesy of British Museum.)

BC). The coffin was therefore found in a context that should probably be dated to the late eighth or early seventh century BC.

Another coffin of this type was found in a tomb at Arjan near Behbehan in south-west Iran in 1982 ((fig. 20-i); Alizadeh 1985; Majidzadeh 1992).[2] The only observable difference from the other coffins of this type is the fact that the handles at either end have ribbed decoration. The vertical strips are apparently plain. Inside the coffin was a collection of rich grave-goods including a bronze stand, a gold bracelet, a bronze bowl and other metal vessels. The bronze stand has supporting figures at the bottom in the form of Assyrian-style figures with upraised arms that may be compared with the figures that appear as furniture components on Assyrian reliefs of the late eighth and early seventh centuries BC. The bull protomes at the base of this stand, however, are reminiscent of Achaemenid column capitals and suggest a later date. Both the gold bracelet, which has large flat terminals decorated with incised designs of winged lions, and the large bronze bowl, with incised decoration in five registers, have an Elamite inscription mentioning the name of Kidin-

Hutran, son of Kurlush. François Vallat has suggested that this Kidin-Hutran must have reigned some time in the period 646–520 BC (Vallat 1984). This would correspond with Stronach's suggested date for the tomb of the Elamite IIIb period (605–539 BC) (Stronach 2003; 2005), and this date-range would also seem to be the most appropriate for the bronze stand, the bronze bowl and the metal vessels which find parallels in a tomb at Susa.[3] However, even if the coffin was buried in the first half of the sixth century BC, it could itself date from before that time or it could have been reused.

Fragments of a similar bronze coffin were allegedly found at Ziwiye in Iran in 1946 or 1947.[4] The pieces are now distributed between the Metropolitan Museum of Art, the National Museum in Tehran,[5] and a private

---

[2] For further studies of this tomb and its contents, and further references, see Curtis 1995: 21–22; Curtis 2005: 123–25; Potts 1999: 303–6; Potts 2005: 17; Alvarez-Mon 2004; Amirkhiz and Harsini 2002.

[3] Various dates have been proposed for the Arjan tomb: Alizadeh suggested first half of the eighth century BC (Alizadeh 1985: 60), while Boehmer preferred the end of the seventh century or first half of the sixth century BC (Boehmer 1989: 142–43). See also the discussion in Curtis 1995: 21–22.

[4] The Ziwiye provenance must be viewed with caution (see Muscarella 1977) but there is no reason to doubt the authenticity of these coffin fragments.

[5] See Amirkhiz and Harsini 2002: fig. 5, pl. 6.

Fig. 20-h. Bronze coffin from Sircirli (from Wartke 2005: fig. 83).

Fig. 20-i. Bronze coffin from Arjan (from Potts 2005: fig 3).

collection or collections. The coffin apparently has vertical strips on the sides that were decorated on both the inside and the outside with designs showing goats or ibexes standing on rosettes (Barnett 1956: pl. XIV; Godard 1950: fig. 9; Ghirshman 1950: fig. 3). In this case, the flat ledge around the rim of the coffin also bears incised decoration (fig. 20-j). The best preserved piece, now in the Metropolitan Museum of Art, shows an Assyrian dignitary, attended by officials and guards, receiving a group of foreigners bearing tribute (Wilkinson 1960: pl. XXIX, figs 3–6; 1975: figs A–C). They wear floppy hats, shoes with upturned toes, and tunics with spotted decoration. On another fragment, also in the Metropolitan Museum, these same tributaries are carrying horn-shaped drinking vessels, animal-headed buckets or situlae, and models of cities or fortresses (Wilkinson 1960: fig. 2; 1975: fig. D). Animal-headed buckets are, of course, familiar from Assyrian reliefs of

the time of Sargon (Curtis 2000: 194–95). Another fragment in a private collection shows Assyrian officials and the bare legs only of other figures (Ghirshman 1950: fig. 2).

There are a number of other bronze coffins of this type, either complete or represented by fragments, that are also unprovenanced. Two coffins now in the Museum of Anatolian Civilizations in Ankara were confiscated from robbers and allegedly come from the Erzincan area. There is incised decoration on the vertical strips on the sides.[6] Another coffin, allegedly from Iran, is in a private collection in Germany; it has incised ibexes or mountain

---

[6] *Museum of Anatolian Civilizations: Museum News* no. 6 (July 1995); I am grateful to Dr D. Collon for information about the decoration.

Fig. 20-j. Drawing of incised decoration on Ziwiye coffin (from Wilkinson 1975: figs. A,D).

Fig. 20-k. Terracotta coffin from Khirbet Khatuniyeh.

goats on the side panels (Curtis 1983: pl. XXVI). Two bronze strips or panels in the Ashmolean Museum in Oxford are all that remains from another coffin; they have incised goats on the inner and outer surfaces (Moorey 1971: pl. 78, no. 494b).

So much for the bronze coffins of this type. Terracotta coffins of similar bathtub shape without handles are commonly found in Mesopotamia, particularly in Babylonia where they continue into the Achaemenid period. Examples have been collected together by Eva Strommenger (1964)[7] and Heather Baker (1995: 213–15). Terracotta coffins of this shape with a pair of handles at either end are much less common, but there

are examples from Ashur (Haller 1954: 55, figs 66–67) and Zincirli (von Luschan 1943: 139, figs 192–93). At Khirbet Khatuniyeh in the Eski Mosul Dam Salvage Project a terracotta coffin of this type was found in a Late Assyrian destruction level, evidently used for the storage of grain ((fig. 20-k); Curtis and Green 1997: 17–18, fig. 21, pls XI–XII). This morning, Dr Muayyad Damerji informed us that a coffin of this kind was in one of the half-dozen graves found in the Nabu Temple at Nimrud; he suggested that the graves might be those of priestesses belonging to the temple. In Assyria, then, terracotta coffins of this characteristic form date from the eighth–seventh centuries BC. What may be similar coffins, at least terracotta coffins with handles, are dated to the Late Babylonian period at Isin (Hrouda 1981: 41, nos 44–44a). Further afield, terracotta bathtub coffins with handles are also known in the Levant, at sites such

---

[7] See also Strommenger 1971: 584–85.

as Tell el Mazar, Tell Fara, and the Amman citadel.[8] An example was found at Tell Jezreel in 1995 (Ussishkin and Woodhead 1997: figs 31–33).

To return to the bronze coffins, it seems likely, as I suggested in 1983, that they are of Assyrian manufacture and that the decorated examples at least date from the late eighth century BC. It would not be unreasonable in fact to suggest that they are all of this date, and it is quite possible that they were manufactured in the same workshop. How would such a date work for the Nimrud examples? We have seen that the stone sarcophagus in Tomb III is of Mullissu-mukannishat-Ninua, who lived in the ninth century BC. However, there are some inscribed objects in the bronze coffins that, as Damerji has pointed out (1999: 10), are later

than this. They are a seal of Ninurta-idīya-šukšid, a eunuch of Adad-nirari III (810–783 BC),[9] a fluted gold bowl of Šamši-ilu, a *tartānu* (army commander) in the first half of the eighth century BC,[10] and a stone duck-weight of Tiglath-pileser III (744–727 BC).[11] This gives us *a terminus post quem* of Tiglath-pileser's reign for the burial of the coffins, making it entirely plausible that the coffins were made in the late eighth century BC. They may also have been buried at the same period. The relationship between the stone sarcophagus and the bronze coffins is unclear. A possible scenario is that the body and burial-goods from the stone coffin were reburied, with additional bodies and grave-goods, in the bronze coffins. Alternatively, and perhaps more likely, the stone sarcophagus and its contents may have been looted in antiquity.

---

[8] For references, see Curtis and Green 1997: 18. See also Stern 2001: 33–34.

[9] Al-Rawi, text no. 15.

[10] Fadhil 1990b: 482, pl. 39.

[11] Al-Rawi, text no. 8.

21 THE IDENTITY OF THE PRINCESSES IN TOMB II AND A NEW ANALYSIS OF EVENTS IN 701 BC[1]

Stephanie Dalley

Tomb II at Nimrud contained the inscribed objects of Yabâ the palace woman of Tiglath-pileser III, Banītu the palace woman of Shalmaneser V and Ataliyā the palace woman of Sargon. This gives us a remarkable opportunity to re-evaluate certain aspects of Assyrian history in the late eighth century. Ataliyā the consort of Sargon II has a name which is almost certainly Hebrew (although the abbreviated writing of the divine element leaves a small possibility for doubt) for which detailed arguments have recently been presented, along with a discussion of the name Yabâ (Dalley 1998; Melville 1999:14, n. 7). Since Samaria had given up its independence by the time Sargon came to the throne, it is very likely that Ataliyā came from the Judean royal family rather than from the deposed rulers of the northern Hebrews of Israel. As the consort of Sargon, one would expect that she was the mother of the Crown Prince Sennacherib. But the presence of a queen mother in a document dated 692 is probably incompatible with the age attributed to Ataliyā by forensic examination; calculations depend largely on estimated ages of breeding and age of responsibility (Frahm 2002: 1113–14). If so, Sennacherib may have been chosen as heir by Sargon from another branch of the family if Sargon had no suitable sons. For the situation of a man who changed his patronym at accession, a possibly parallel case is that of Zimri-Lim son of Hatni-[…] who changed his seal and claimed to be the son of the previous king Yahdun-Lim when he came to the throne of Mari (Charpin and Durand 1985: 336–38). Alternatively Sennacherib may have been born to an earlier wife of Sargon who did not take the position of First Lady despite being mother of the Crown Prince, gaining prominence only after her son's accession.

As Dr Damerji (1999: 8) has pointed out, the fact that the two women in the sarcophagus were buried together implies that they belonged to the same family. If so, we can give a specifically Hebrew etymology to Yabâ's name too, rather than a more general, West Semitic one. When Yabâ was queen, Damascus, allied to Israel and hostile to Judah, was at enmity with Tiglath-pileser, and when that anti-Assyrian alliance threatened Judah, Ahaz wrote to Tiglath-pileser for help. For this reason it is very unlikely that Yabâ came from the northern kingdom before the throne was usurped by the pro-Assyrian Hoshea c. 732 (Tadmor 1989: 277), by which time the Assyrian king would have had an heir in prospect. But what about Banītu, with her good

Akkadian name inscribed on a gold bowl and an electrum cosmetic container?

The suggestion I have seen so far is that Ataliyā commandeered some of her predecessor's luxury goods. This, of course, could be expected in principle; but one would expect the new queen to have the precious metal reinscribed with her own name, rather than staring at her predecessor's name when she drank or painted her face. To make such a change would not have been difficult for the goldsmiths who did such fine work as we see in the grave-goods at Nimrud.

A different possible explanation may be offered. Banītu means 'beautiful' as a female personal name in Akkadian, according to all the main dictionaries s.v. *banû* (contra Radner 1998–99: 265) and this would be an Akkadian translation of Yabâ (Yapâ) which may mean 'beautiful' in Hebrew. A good parallel for the Akkadian translation of a West Semitic name, belonging to a queen who uses both names at once, is Naqi'a also known as Zakûtu, as is well known and uncontested. An earlier example of one woman's name in two different languages with the same meaning is Ra'intu/Tattašše in two texts from Emar (Arnaud 1986: nos 23 and 24).

The suggestion that Yabâ and Banītu are one and the same person would give a fourth example of an Assyrian 'palace woman' MÍ.É.GAL who maintained her status in the reign of her deceased husband's successor, presumably her son. Tomb III at Nimrud has yielded the information that Mullissu-mukannishat-Ninua was the MÍ.É.GAL of both Ashurnasirpal II and of Shalmaneser III. Semiramis, we already know, was the daughter-in-law *kallatu* of Shalmaneser III, the MÍ.É.GAL of Šamši-Adad V, and the MÍ.É.GAL and AMA.MAN of Adad-nirari III. On the Pazarcik stela inscription she is called only the MÍ.É.GAL of Adad-nirari (Grayson 1996: A.O. 104.3). One may deduce from these examples that MÍ.É.GAL had a higher prestige than AMA.MAN as a title on formal monuments. Our third example is Naqi'a—Zakûtu, who usually calls herself MÍ.É.GAL in royal inscriptions and on dedicatory objects written during her son's reign, although she is generally addressed, or referred to, as AMA.MAN in letters. This use of titles supports the suggestion that Yabâ and Banītu, although they are the MÍ.É.GAL of two different, successive kings, are the same person.

Abdulilah Fadhil (1990b) pointed out in his careful edition of the tomb inscriptions of Mullissu-mukannishat-Ninua, that if she were the mother of Shalmaneser, one

---

[1] I would like to thank Barbara Hohmann and Yoram Cohen for help with Hittite comparisons.

would expect her to declare the honour, and this might suggest that Shalmaneser III took over his father's harem and was not actually her son. In the case of Yabâ/Banītu, as MÍ.É.GAL of Tiglath-pileser, this might mean that she was inherited by Shalmaneser V, but was not his mother. However, the comparisons mentioned suggest that the title AMA.MAN was secondary to the title MÍ.É.GAL, and was not necessarily used, since we can be sure that Semiramis and Naqi'a were each the mother of their husband's successor, yet omitted the title AMA.MAN in some inscriptions. It is nevertheless possible that Shalmaneser V was not the nominated crown prince, and that he usurped the throne, coming from another branch of the family, whereupon he took over the wife of his predecessor. In Achaemenid times we know that a new king took over his predecessor's main wife and concubines (Brosius 1996: 60).

The situation reflected in a queen maintaining her status into the reign of her son is comparable to that of the Hittite queen during the Empire period, who, if she outlived her husband, did not pass on her title to her daughter-in-law until her own death unless she was removed by judicial means (Bin-Nun 1975; Beckman 1978). It was a custom not restricted to the Hittite queen, but applied also to Hittite princesses who married vassal kings (Singer 1991). Presumably important ceremonial duties were attached to the title MÍ.É.GAL *ša* RN in Assyria, comparable in some way to the role played by the Hittite Tawananna who became high priestess of the Sun-goddess of Arinna at the death of her husband.

The two skeletons in the sarcophagus have been analysed as dying at an age between 30 and 39. Tiglath-pileser reigned for 18 years. If we suppose that Yabâ/Banītu was in her early teens when she married him at the beginning of his reign (rather than already being his wife when he came to the throne), and died soon after Shalmaneser came to the throne, we can accommodate the age. Only one inscription of Shalmaneser V is known, and he refers to himself vaguely as 'the seed of kingship' without mentioning his father.

Recent evidence has come to light to show that the chief consort of late Assyrian kings might travel on campaign with the king (Radner 2003–4:101). This may help to explain why the joints of those relatively young women in Tomb 2 were worn.[2]

A few further considerations may help the proposal that Yabâ and Banītu are the same person. The known Mesopotamian wives of kings generally have more imposing names than Banītu: Mullissu-mukannishat-Ninua takes the prize, but Sammu-ramat, Tašmetum-Šarrat, Ešarra-hammat, Libbi-ali-šarrat, and Ana-

Tašmetum-taklāk (Finkel 2000) are imposing too. Banītu's short name is unusual in such company; and would be an extraordinary coincidence as the translation of her predecessor's name.

In the context of discussing the styles of jewellery found in Tomb II, some of the items would have come to Assyria as part of royal dowries, and so reflect foreign styles popular abroad. For dowries of foreign princesses, a good precedent exists from the reign of Shalmaneser IV: Shamshi-ilu the Viceroy marched to Damascus against its king Hadianu and brought back an extensive tribute which included Hadianu's daughter 'together with her great dowry', *nudunnû* (Grayson 1996: A.O.105.1). We can be sure that such a marriage was made at a very high level, with a member of the Assyrian royal family, in the hope of improving relations with Damascus. A diplomatic marriage between king Urikki of Que (based at Adana in lowland Cilicia) perhaps accounts for Urikki's claim in a newly discovered inscription, that 'the Assyrian king and all the Assyrian house became father and mother to me' (Tecoglu and Lemaire 2000). A text from Nimrud, edited by Barbara Parker (1954: 37–39), gives some idea of a wealthy dowry: in ND 2307 a girl from a family with West Semitic names has a dowry, *nudunnû*, which includes jewellery items of gold and silver, as well as many textiles and containers. Barbara Parker suggested that the husband, Milki-ramu, was the man of that name who served as eponym official for 656 BC. He was therefore probably a member of the royal family, if evidence from the Middle Assyrian period can be applied to this time (Cancik-Kirschbaum 1999).

Two examples of Assyrian dynastic marriages can be quoted here: during the Kassite period a daughter of Ashur-uballiṭ I named Muballiṭat-Šerua married Burna-Buriaš and became the grandmother of Karaindaš, according to the Synchronistic Chronicle and Chronicle P (Grayson 1972–76: I, 50); and during the reign of Ashurnasirpal II Assyria 'conquered' and forgave Lubarna king of Unqi at Kinalua, and brought back Lubarna's brother's daughter—presumably a man of great distinction—'with her rich dowry' (Grayson 1972–76: II. 142). Almost certainly, therefore, the jewellery in the tombs is not simply native Assyrian.

If Ataliyā and Yabâ came from Judah, some implications for understanding events that took place in 701 BC, when Sennacherib invaded Palestine, are considerable, and certain new interpretations can be offered here, using in particular other material from Nimrud and Nineveh, with a view to showing how this two-generation alliance may have affected Assyrian actions against Judah, especially during the reign of Hezekiah. Even without this identification for Yabâ and Ataliyā, there is evidence from Nimrud texts and from sculpture of Sennacherib, as well as improved understanding of royal inscriptions, to suggest that Judah was more important to Assyria, more

---

[2] Cf. Müller-Karpe, this volume.

powerful and more closely allied to Assyria at that time, than is generally supposed.

Both from biblical text and from Assyrianizing stamp seals (e.g. Avigad and Sass 1997: no. 3) we know that the kings of Judah were mainly pro-Assyrian from Uzziah to Manasseh, a period of more than 180 years. Letters from Nimrud confirm this for the late eighth century: around 716 BC Judah like its neighbours Egypt, Gaza, Moab and Ammon delivered a tribute of horses to Calah (Saggs 2001: 219–21). At about the same time horses of Ashkelon and Gaza were at the disposal of an Assyrian governor in the West, Adad-hati (Postgate 1974: 387). Probably in the following year (715 according to Lanfranchi) Judeans were fighting on the side of the Assyrians against the Urartians and Manneans—far from home (Saggs 2001: 125–28). On sculptures in the passage leading from the SW palace of Sennacherib to the Ishtar temple, Judeans were acting as royal bodyguards in a procession that included the king in a palanquin, in other words in a position where loyalty was unquestionable (Barnett *et al.* 1998: pls 486–87, no. 669; Russell 1991: 168–69). This variety of information shows that the Judeans of the late eighth and early seventh centuries were loyal vassals of Assyria, before Sennacherib's campaign of 701.

At that time Judah was a prosperous trading nation, and Assyria was interested, above all, in sharing advantageously in trade with Egypt, with Arabs of western Arabia and with the eastern Mediterranean. Recently a study of Judean weights has shown that after 701 BC Judah did not give up its own system of weights and measures, but continued to flourish as an independent trading state under the Assyrian umbrella (Kletter 1998). This was a client-king relationship which enriched the client, rather than detestable vassaldom. The Assyrians ensured control by making the client king swear loyalty by his own gods, in this case Yahweh, as well as by the gods of Assyria. To break such an oath was an abomination, *ikkibu* or *anzillu*, which would inevitably bring the wrath of Judah's god down upon his own people, in addition to angering the Assyrian king and his gods (Reiner 1958: VIII.79; Watanabe1987: lines 377 and 379). This is why Ezekiel (17:12–21) stressed oaths sworn to Yahweh alongside oaths sworn to 'Babylon' when Egypt incited Judah to rebellion, echoing the situation of Isaiah 18, in which Kush was the enemy, Egypt foolish, and Assyria the agent of Yahweh.

By the late eighth century, as Grayson in particular has pointed out, Assyria presented itself in a kindlier light than had been traditional at earlier periods. One clear example of this can be seen on the Lachish relief. Whereas earlier Mesopotamian kings had shown themselves delivering the *coup de grace* in the thick of battle, firing the triumphant shot and trampling on the foe, Sennacherib sits peacefully on his throne outside the besieged town. Those who leave Lachish *en famille* in a dignified fashion with their possessions are Judeans; it is the Nubians who grovel, and the ringleaders, not ethnically distinguishable due partly to their nudity, are impaled or flayed.

Religious tolerance is a particular hallmark of Assyrian control. It is most unfortunate that early writers of Sargonid history from George Rawlinson in 1875, Olmstead in 1908 and Sidney Smith in 1929 through to Gonçalves in 1986 failed to realize this, taking their model inappropriately both from the Roman imperial cult and from fanatical, competing monotheisms of more recent times. Sargon II allowed a priest back to Bethel (II Kings 17:27) after Israel became an Assyrian province, and taxed the people of Samaria province as if they were Assyrians (Fuchs 1994: Annals l.17). Sennacherib did not interfere in the cult of Yahweh, as shown by McKay in 1973 and almost simultaneously by Cogan in 1974. It was the people of Judah themselves who discriminated periodically against the resurgence of indigenous, Canaanite polytheism and the cults of local, non-Hebrew deities.

Questions surrounding the Assyrian attack on Jerusalem have been muddied by mistranslation and the careless reading of texts. In the first place, as Arie van der Kooij (1986) has carefully shown, there was no Assyrian royal camp at Jerusalem; the account in II Kings 19:35 says the king stayed at Lachish where his camp was, and sent his officers to Jerusalem, where they negotiated from outside the city walls. This means, among other things, that we need not conjure up a missing relief in the SW Palace showing the king's camp at Jerusalem. When, many centuries later, Josephus wrote of an Assyrian camp at Jerusalem, he was referring to the camp of Nebuchadnezzar II, and suffering from the same confusion as the Book of Judith which called Nebuchadnezzar king of the Assyrians who ruled in Nineveh.

It was particularly unfortunate that A.L. Oppenheim in his translation of Sennacherib's 701 campaign account for ANET mistranslated the word URU *halṣu* as 'earthworks' which implied a full siege. He was followed very recently, unfortunately, by Cogan (*apud* Hallo 2000: 293), as well as by many writers of biblical history such as Herrmann (1981). As van der Kooij (followed by Gallagher 1999: 133) has pointed out, *halṣu* means fort or fortress, and by means of them the Assyrians blockaded Jerusalem without attempting to besiege it in an active way. A blockade required only a small force, and would not be led by the king, so there was no need to build a camp. A blockade did not require the complete encirclement of the city nor any earthworks; as Sennacherib says, he turned the exit from Hezekiah's city-gate (in the singular) into an abomination, *ikkibu*. An abomination can take the form of something nasty you tread in, consisting of water that has been used to wash a diseased person, or water which contains excrement. This would fit the context: the

Assyrians perhaps smeared or soaked the path through the city gate with contaminated water, making it impossible for the king to pass in and out. Cutting down trees around a city has now been recognized as an act signalling that the Assyrian army had given up its attempt to capture a besieged city (Tadmor 1989: 79). Sennacherib did not cut down trees outside Jerusalem, as would be expected had he hoped to capture and enter Jerusalem. The strategy of a blockade needing only a small force was reflected in Sennacherib's words: he shut Hezekiah up in Jerusalem like a bird in a cage, but expressed no intention to kill or capture him. Isaiah, too, knew that the capture of the city was not the aim, and said so in a clear prophecy (Isaiah 37:33–35).

When Sennacherib mentions Hezekiah, how mild his language is! The rebel rulers of the Philistine cities are called sinners and breakers of oaths, but no such accusations are levelled at Hezekiah, despite his treachery. This suggests that he was treated differently, for which one cause may be suggested in Sennacherib's father's marriage to the Hebrew princess Ataliyā. Moreover, Sennacherib refers rather flatteringly to Hezekiah as 'strong and mighty', *šepṣu miṭru*, as if in admiration, epithets wrongly translated as 'overbearing and proud' in ANET, but corrected recently by Gallagher (1999: 130 and 141–42) who remarks that the Assyrians 'regarded Hezekiah as a worthy opponent'.

The Assyrian evidence, both from royal inscriptions and letters dating to Sargon II's reign, indicates that for the most part the Philistine cities were subservient to Assyria, hardly surprising in view of his three campaigns to southern Palestine. Yet according to II Kings 18:8 Hezekiah 'harassed the Philistines as far as Gaza, laying their territory waste from watchtower to fortified town'. This suggests that Hezekiah was acting as an agent for Assyrian interests in the area, comparable to the role played by Arab leaders Idibilu and Siruatti, who took charge of the border area between Palestine and Egypt at the express behest of Assyrian kings. This scenario has the benefit of explaining why Hezekiah was rich and powerful, deserving the adjectives *šepṣu miṭru* when his kingdom was essentially so small.

The reconstructed relationship suggested here may also help explain the enormous number of people deported by Sennacherib at the end of the campaign of 701. De Odorico (1995) has suggested that the figure for deportees taken at the end of Sennacherib's first campaign is made up of all the various different groups of rebels encountered during the first campaign. In the third campaign Sennacherib mentions taking deportees from Ashkelon without giving a number. We may suggest that he aggregates in 701 all the deportees taken from Ashkelon, Ekron, Lachish and all the other cities which had withheld tribute from Assyria in the wake of

Sargon's ill-starred death and the Nubian invasion of the Nile Delta. This gives a figure which may be realistic, and which misleadingly appears to be connected only with the successful siege of Lachish in Sennacherib's prism text.

A significant point that can be explained from the Judean origin of Sargon's queen is the light it throws on the Hebrew language used by the *rab šaqê*, chief cup-bearer, calling up to the people of Jerusalem and advising them to abandon their rebellion. Commentators have all been at a loss to explain this use of Hebrew, and some have thought the passage which includes II Kings 18:28, likewise Isaiah 36:11, was a later insertion, for inexplicable reasons. Gallagher (1999: 75–78 and 187ff) has carefully shown that this passage is contemporary with the events it represents. If Hebrew was Sennacherib's mother-tongue, so that his close relatives at Nineveh eventually took the top military posts such as cup-bearer, it is not at all surprising that they could speak Hebrew as well as Akkadian and Aramaic.

These suggestions for interpreting the relationship between Sennacherib and Hezekiah, and Hezekiah's relationship with the Philistine cities, may also be useful for explaining in particular the release of Padi, deposed king of Ekron, to Hezekiah as the agent of Assyria in Philistia, and then to the Assyrians themselves. They also help to explain the number of 45 towns or cities and forts which were taken away from Judah and given to Ashdod, Ekron and Gaza. They were Philistine towns which had previously paid their dues to Assyria through the agency of Hezekiah, whose responsibilities were now presumably withdrawn.

A few points can be summarized in the aftermath of this interpretation. Judah was more powerful and wealthier in the late eighth century than was previously realized, benefiting from its relationship as a client-king which probably allowed it to act as the agent of Assyria in Philistine cities. For this reason Judean weights and measures were not abandoned for Assyrian ones in the seventh century (Kletter 1998). The Judean festival of Passover was harmonized with that of Assyrian Samaria (Japhet 1993: 939). Manasseh was thoroughly pro-Assyrian, demonstrating his loyalty by taking a wife from the Assyrian province of Samaria, by visiting his sisters who had been deported to Mesopotamia, and by making a big contribution to Esarhaddon's palace at Nineveh. Sennacherib had at least one magnate who spoke Hebrew because of the family background deduced from the inscriptions in Tomb II at Nimrud.

If these arguments are right, Tomb II at Nimrud had a sarcophagus which contained two queens and the personal possessions of only two queens who probably both came from Judah. An Assyrian queen who outlived her husband maintained her status until her own death. Some but not all of the queens' possessions reflect the art styles of Palestine. Sennacherib had a special interest in Judah which affected the conduct of his campaign in 701.

The excavations at Nimrud, both Iraqi and British, have uncovered most of the evidence that has allowed us to reinterpret one of the major events of Sargonid history.

Postscript

Two short papers containing further discussion of some of these issues by the same author are: 'Yabâ, Ataliyā and the Foreign Policy of Late Assyrian Kings', *State Archives of Assyria Bulletin* XII/2, 1998:83–89; and 'Recent Evidence from Assyrian Sources for Judaean History from Uzziah to Manesseh', *Journal for the Study of the Old Testament* 28, 2004:387–401.

22 THE TOMBS IN THE LIGHT OF MESOPOTAMIAN FUNERARY TRADITIONS

J.N. Postgate

The discovery of the tombs of the queens under the domestic wing of the North-West Palace was an amazing event, and an unexpected one in two ways. It was a surprise that they were there at all in the first place, and it was another surprise that so much was still there some 2,700 years later.

It was not, of course, a surprise to find tombs under the floors of a building, or even of this palace. After all Mallowan had already found the tombs of two court ladies in the north-eastern corner of the domestic wing.[1] The surprise was that queens were buried here, because as far as we knew, and still know, the kings of Assyria were buried at Ashur, and the obvious assumption, until 1988, would have been that the queens lay there too. When Parpola, discussing a Neo-Assyrian letter which he connects with the funeral rites for a queen, wrote of 'Assur, the city where the members of Assyrian royal families were traditionally buried', few would have disagreed (Parpola 1983: 190 on no. 195). Indeed, we have a fragmentary inscription from Ashur which seems to indicate that the tomb of Esarhaddon's queen Esharra-hamat was constructed at Ashur (Borger 1956: 10 §10).

Where the kings were buried

Thus it is that to place the Nimrud queens in their wider historical context it is to Ashur that we need to look first. The tombs of the kings themselves are a mystery. The German expedition to Ashur discovered 6 or 7 stone built tomb chambers beneath the south-east corner of the 'Old Palace', some still containing massive stone coffins, but very little else. Two of these certainly dated to the ninth century, bearing inscriptions identifying them as the sarcophagi of Ashurnasirpal (in Gruft V) and Shamshi-Adad V (in Gruft II), while inscribed fragments of a basalt sarcophagus from Gruft III suggest it was intended for Ashur-bel-kala, back in the eleventh century, although its place had been usurped by an uninscribed limestone sarcophagus presumably belonging to a later king (Grayson 1991: 109–10; Haller 1954: 176–77). Other brick inscriptions from the vicinity mention the mausoleum of Sennacherib, although it seems unlikely that this was one of the actual structures found.[2]

The mystery is, where are all the other kings? Most if not all of those before Ashurnasirpal must surely have been buried at Ashur, and even Ashurnasirpal himself, who re-founded Kalhu to act as his royal residence and presumably lived there more than at Ashur in his later years, returned to the ancient capital to be buried. It seems likely that one of the excavated tomb-chambers belonged to Shalmaneser III, since his successor Shamshi-Adad was also buried there. After that we can only admit our ignorance: we have six kings to account for between Shamshi-Adad and the accession of Sargon, but where were they laid to rest? Did the Old Palace site in fact extend much further than the excavations indicate, or was the burial area found to be too small, so that another new collective royal mausoleum was started at Ashur and remains to be located? Or could Adad-nirari III and his successors, who we think resided principally at Kalhu, have started a new tradition of burying the kings there?

Apparently Sennacherib seems to have intended his last resting place to be in Ashur, but this could well be a reversion to ancient practice and a deliberate avoidance of Kalhu, since we know that he preferred Nineveh to Kalhu when he decided to move the royal residence back from his father's new capital at Dur-Sharrukin. Since Sennacherib's death was violent and followed by civil war within the Assyrian heartland, arrangements for his burial may not have proceeded smoothly. But his intention at least was to be buried at Ashur. In one of his tomb bricks Sennacherib refers to the structure as a *bīt kimti* 'house of the family'. This phrase reaches back into Old Babylonian times, and it underlines the idea that one should be buried with one's ancestors, where one can receive the attentions of the living members of the family.[3] That would normally be where they themselves are living, and in Sennacherib's case there is no reason to suppose that his family did not live at Nineveh in his new royal residence, rather than at Ashur. Nevertheless, the Assyrian royal dynastic line is obviously a special case, and at present we can only conclude that there is no evidence that any of the Assyrian kings were buried outside Ashur.

This is understandable. In Assyria, unlike Egypt, royalty were only human: kings were subject to the same fate as everyone else, and were treated after death in the same way, although in a more extreme manner; but in the

---

[1] In Rooms DD and FF (Oates and Oates 2001: 79).

[2] Sennacherib's tomb inscriptions: KAH I 46 and 47; edited in Luckenbill 1924: 151 (125–26); cf. Frahm 1997: 181–82.

[3] See Frahm 1997: 182; CAD K337b for rare instances from Mari, Boğazköy and an omen text.

matter of where they were buried there was an exception. Kings may have wanted members of their family, and in particular their children and descendants, to make the funerary offerings for them, but they also had to receive such attentions in their official capacity as kings. The Assyrian royal house originates of course at Ashur, and it is at Ashur that the legitimacy of the king is affirmed and reaffirmed, at the temple of the god Ashur. This is, in one sense, the royal house. The line of kings was part of the ideology of the Assyrian state, as the king-list stretching back to the beginning of the second millennium underlines. In the early second millennium the same recognition of a royal as well as a familial succession can be seen. As part of the ceremonies for Hammurapi's ancestors, offerings were made to previous dynasties, not just to his family (Finkelstein 1966). And in the palace at Mari the *kispum* ceremony included offerings to the spirits of Sargon and Naram-Sin of Akkad, as the political predecessors at Mari of the Amorite dynasty, not as members of the biological royal family (Birot 1980). In Assyria it was intended that the same patrilinear dynasty should also stretch into the future: one letter to Esarhaddon declares that the queen's dead spirit blesses the crown prince, saying 'Let his descent and his seed govern Assyria' (Parpola 1993a: no. 188 rev. 2–8). On balance, then, one has to conclude that it is most likely that all the kings expected to be buried at Ashur, and that we just have not found all their tombs.

Where the queens were buried

Apparently, though, for members of the family not the king, things were seen differently, because as we now know Ashurnasirpal's wife was not buried with him at Ashur, but under the floor of the new palace at Kalhu. This was her residence, and her house; her family vault was here; and the same applies to the other three eighth century queens. Queens in Assyria were very closely identified with the palace. As early as the thirteenth century the polite way of referring to the king's principal wife was 'the palace' or 'the one of the palace',[4] and in the first millennium this became so much the practice that *ša ekalli* or *issi ekalli* simply became the word for 'queen' and was borrowed into other languages in the west. And it sounds from the inscription of Mullissu-mukannishat-Ninua as though once a queen had established her authority within the palace, she retained that title regardless of whether her husband was still the king.[5] What Shalmaneser's wife thought of her mother-

in-law's continuing presence on the scene we can't tell, but she was not the only dominating Assyrian queen mother, since she was followed by Samuramat the mother of Adad-nirari III and Naqi'a the mother of Esarhaddon.

Turning to the eighth century queens, Dr Dalley has underlined the generally agreed position that both Tiglath-pileser III's wife Yaba' and Sargon's wife Ataliya have West Semitic names. This is undoubted, but I believe the geographical origin of the ladies remains uncertain. We should not forget that Aramaeans were deeply embedded in the population of Assyria (see e.g. Tadmor 1982). Both Samuramat and Naqi'a also had West Semitic names. I am not sure if they too must have come from outside the borders of the directly administered lands, but if both Yaba' and Ataliya were brought to Assyria as a result of diplomatic marriages with neighbouring states then Judah is not the only candidate. Both Tiglath-pileser and Sargon would have wanted to establish friendly relations with the wealthy cities of the Phoenician sea board, especially Tyre and Sidon, which remained outside the Assyrian provincial system and thus would have retained their ruling dynasties.[6]

The funerary inscriptions

Throughout ancient Mesopotamia funerary inscriptions, and indeed all funerary monuments like stelae, are surprisingly rare if one considers their popularity in the Greek and Levantine world of the first millennium. One might therefore wonder whether they too are evidence of western influence. But on reflection I am inclined to think not. There is no reason to think that Ashurnasirpal's queen Mullissu-mukannishat-Ninua was not a native Assyrian, since her father Ashur-nirka-da''in has a good Assyrian name and was Ashurnasirpal's chief cup-bearer. Moreover, the texts of the tomb inscriptions, although unique in their way, are solidly founded in ancient Mesopotamian traditions. The underworld goddess Ereškigal, the god Ningišzida, and the Chief Porter of the Underworld, Pituh-idugal, are described as residents of the netherworld already in the early second millennium and no doubt go back earlier still. The involvement of

---

[4] See most recently Postgate 2001.

[5] She calls herself 'queen' (MÍ.É.GAL) 'of Ashurnasirpal (and) of Shalmaneser' (II.1–2). The concept of an 'official' queen seems to be expressed by the phrase 'the queen who sits on the throne' (MÍ.É.GAL *šá ina* GIŠ.GU.ZA *tu-šá-ba*) in the inscription of Yaba (Fadhil 1991a: 1.6).

[6] There are various uncertainties. The name Ataliyah in the Bible does not have a clear Hebrew etymology, and it belonged to a princess whose mother Jezebel was a Phoenician. In cuneiform the name is written both *a-ta-li-a* and *a-tal-ia,* neither of which demonstrably includes the divine name Yahweh. The name Yaba' is apparently not at present attested elsewhere, either in Hebrew or in any other West Semitic onomasticon. My sincere thanks to Dr Simon Sherwin for help with the West Semitic material.

Shamash in affairs of the netherworld is also traditional,[7] as is the reference to a chair associated with a tomb (see below).

The funeral ceremonies and grave goods

How should we imagine the funeral ceremonies for the queens, though? They probably led their life in virtual seclusion within the harem-sector of the palace, along with the other royal ladies, whose existence the tomb inscriptions explicitly mention. In the Middle Assyrian palace edicts elaborate rules were drafted to control access to the harem and also to govern practical arrangements when travelling outside the city; and the thirteenth century correspondence recently discovered at Dur-Katlimmu vividly shows that the queen and other highly placed ladies sometimes travelled like a circus with the king (see Cancik-Kirschbaum 1996: no. 10).

Assyrian letters from the seventh century refer to funerary ceremonies associated with the death of a queen or similarly highly placed lady. Some refer to the 'display' ceremony (*taklimtu*) and to associated rituals, which could include a 'burning' (*šuruptu;* Parpola 1993a: no. 233). It is not clear what was burnt: torches are mentioned, indicating that some of the ceremonies took place at night, but I suspect that the reference is to the incense burners which are also mentioned. Contemporary letters also mention the ritual display (*taklimtu*) as part of the ceremonies for the cult of Tammuz and Ishtar at Nineveh and Arbil.[8]

An intriguing text reconstructed from four fragments from Ashurbanipal's library at Nineveh seems to contain an account by an Assyrian king of the funerary ceremonies for his father, who had also been king. It is not known who they were, possibly Esarhaddon writing about Sennacherib, or Ashurbanipal about Esarhaddon. As well as a literary lament which tells how nature mourned—'the canals wailed and the ditches answered back, the faces of the trees and flowers were darkened', and so on—the text gives a matter-of-fact list of some of the grave goods, the preserved parts mainly textiles, but also including wooden items and a silver sedan chair. To introduce this list the text says: 'I laid my father nicely in the oil of royalty within that tomb, a protected place. I sealed the lid of the coffin, his resting-place, with strong copper and reinforced its sealing. I displayed before Shamash the vessels of gold and silver, all the furnishing of the tomb, and the emblems of his rulership which he loved, placed them in the tomb with my father, and presented them as presents to the underworld rulers, the Anunnaki and the gods who dwell in the earth.'[9]

What is particularly significant here is that it confirms that the 'display' applied not just (and perhaps not at all) to the corpse, but to the grave goods. Moreover, it confirms that some of the grave goods were intended as gifts to placate the underworld deities on the dead king's arrival down there. The authors of, and the listeners to, this text can hardly have been unaware of Tablet VII of Gilgamesh, in which we are told of the grave goods which accompanied Enkidu to the Underworld: they too, or some of them, were destined as gifts, *baksheesh*, to specific deities. It is interesting that this text implies that the gifts were presented by the king's son to the divine underworld recipients on his father's behalf.

What else went on at the funeral? This must have been the opportunity for everyone to pay their final respects. One of the letters about the death of a queen has an official advising the king that there are too many ladies for 'eating, drinking and pouring ointment' to fit in the space, and suggesting they are moved elsewhere (Parpola 1993a: no. 233). In the case of kings, there may well have been diplomatic delegations from other kingdoms who wished to remain on friendly terms. In the Old Babylonian period during the reign of Bilalama of Eshnunna we find the Amorite sheikhs gathering for the funeral of one of their grandees, and sending funerary gifts (Whiting 1987: no. 11) while in the burial of the unknown Assyrian king, as well as the gold and silver the list of grave offerings includes 10 horses, 30 oxen and 300 sheep which seem to be presented by the King of Urartu (KUR.URI). These cannot all have been placed in a tomb (since this is not imperial China), and I imagine that some at least of them may have gone on the menu of a funerary banquet.

Although no doubt much less than the kings themselves would have had buried with them, in the queens' tombs we meet by far and away the richest assemblage of gold and other precious artefacts to come out of any of the Assyrian palaces, whether at Ashur itself, Nineveh, or Khorsabad. The Assyrian kings boast of huge quantities of both gold and textiles in their inscriptions, whether looted or gathered in as tribute; and cuneiform tablets from the internal administration (which are less likely to have been exaggerated) also refer to plenty of gold and multicoloured

[7] For the role of Shamash as arbiter see for instance Finkel 1983–84: 11, II.12–188; emphasis may be placed on his dual responsibility for those 'above' and 'below', cf. the Epilogue to the Code of Hammurapi, Col. XXVII.34–34; King 1912: BBSt no. 2: 19–20.

[8] Parpola 1993a: nos 188 (Arbil) and 19 (Nineveh). For the hint of a surely parallel display ceremony for Adonis in third century BC Egypt, see the note of Stol (1988), who also has references to the Assyriological discussions of *taklimtu*. See also Scurlock 1991, who no doubt correctly argues that it was the grave goods which were displayed before Shamash (though this need not mean the corpse itself was not).

[9] MacGinnis 1987: 1–2, my translation accepting the identification of *šipassu* advocated by K. Deller 1987: 69–71.

textiles. Along with the gold the textiles are virtually unique among archaeological finds. In the case of the textiles it is their perishability that makes them so rare. As for the gold, it is a combination of its intrinsic value, in the currency systems of the Near East at the time, and the fact that it can be readily recycled. Its extreme value makes it the first thing anyone would save in case of fire or other disaster, and it is easily converted into currency (unlike for instance the thousands of ivories left in the arsenal at Fort Shalmaneser). Plenty of metal vessels were turned up at Nimrud having been left there during the sack of the city, but very little in the way of gold. This makes the tombs of the queens all the more unusual.

After the funeral

Brick boxes were found in the rooms on the north-east side of the palace originally excavated to the floor by Mallowan (Room DD) and over the first tomb discovered in 1988 in Room MM. We don't know what they contained, but possibly food offerings. Drink offerings, of cold water for sure but perhaps also beer and wine, would have been made, as illustrated by the libation pipe leading into the vault of Yaba', beneath the floor of Room 49 but (perhaps secondarily) covered over by brick paving.[10] It seems likely that there would have been a chair of some kind. Mullissu-mukannishat-Ninua's text says, 'If any later person shifts my chair from in front of the ghosts, may his ghost not receive its funerary offerings, may any later person drape it with a rug and anoint it with oil'. As Irene Winter has shown, the seated statues of Gudea are precisely those associated with his KI A.NAG or place for funerary offerings. In the palace at Mari in 1800 BC an elaborate *kispum* ceremony for Sargon and Naram-Sin of Akkad, took place in the 'house of chairs'. Later texts refer to the 'chair of the ghost' and I think one has to assume that these were real chairs placed perhaps in the room above the tomb.[11]

I am sure we must imagine that in these palace rooms there would have been held the funeral banquets called *kispum*. Our sources do not (as far as I am aware) mention *kispum* rituals taking place at fixed intervals after a death, along the lines of modern ceremonies of remembrance which are held after 40 days or a year. Perhaps this happened, but if we look at the Old Babylonian texts

which list several generations of departed relatives,[12] we will realize that in due course hardly a day would have gone past without someone's *kispum* having to be celebrated. Hence it is perhaps understandable that instead there may have been a collective *kispum* for the whole family.[13]

So much for the immediate aftermath of the burials, but what happened later, in the century or so during which Kalhu remained a provincial capital and occasional royal residence, before it was sacked by the Babylonian/ Median coalition? We must imagine that the palace staff knew those tombs were under the floors. The kings must surely have continued to celebrate *kispum* rites for the former queens for many years, but even if the regular celebration of *kispum* rites had ceased, there must have been some collective memory of the existence of the tombs, reinforced by awareness of some of the architectural peculiarities of the rooms above. They can hardly have been unaware of the existence and purpose of the brick boxes, and very likely also of the vertical pipe. Likely enough, therefore, funerary banquets would have been held in the relevant parts of the palace itself. I have not noted any clear mention of such ceremonies in a Neo-Assyrian or Middle Assyrian context, but one cannot help comparing the *kispum* rites described by the text edited in Birot 1980, which involved offerings to Shamash and the temple of Dagan. Sheep are sacrificed at various moments, and it is of course known that other *kispum* rituals required supplies of food and drink, no doubt offered to the dead but eaten by the living.

That the tombs escaped unplundered is a surprise. We know from curses that the idea of tomb robbery was prevalent, and when opened by the German archaeologists the Ashur tombs were cleared out of everything except the enormously heavy coffins and a stone lamp. We do not, of course, know anything precise about the circumstances of the sack of the citadel at Nimrud, but it is hard to imagine that no-one in the palace was aware of the existence of the tombs. Perhaps no one in the know survived the Median attack; or if they did perhaps they respected the curses and kept their knowledge to themselves. Whichever it was, we can be grateful that the queens were left to lie in rest, as their inscriptions plead, for more than 2000 years, to bring us this astonishing insight into the imperial splendour of the Assyrian court.

---

[10] There is plenty of textual evidence for the use of pipes for libation, see for instance CAD A/ii: 324 s.v. *arūtu*.

[11] See Winter 1992: 26–29; Birot 1980: 139–40 II. 7,10 for the *bīt kussâti* at Mari (the thrones would have been for the ghosts of the dead, not divine statues).

[12] The best example being Wilcke 1983.

[13] For the *kispum* see in general Tsukimoto 1985, and for Mari in particular Talon 1978.

23 THOUGHTS ON ROOM FUNCTION IN THE NORTH-WEST PALACE

John Malcolm Russell

My purpose in this paper is to offer an interpretation of the relationship between the decoration and function of various parts of the palace of Ashurnasirpal II, based on my reading of the layout of the relief decoration and a variety of other clues present in the architecture (see also Russell 1998). I arrived at my interpretations after scattered intuitions and bits of disconnected information led me to formulate a hypothesis that could be tested only by looking at the palace as a whole. I hypothesized that the relief decoration of the entire palace is a visual expression of Ashurnasirpal's royal ideology: military success, service to the gods, divine protection, and Assyrian prosperity. Within this overall scheme, the subjects vary from suite to suite, perhaps reflecting different primary functions for each suite. In testing this hypothesis, my approach is essentially art historical, based on close analysis of the imagery, heavy reliance on texts, and comparisons with other Assyrian palaces.

My goal here is to try to identify sculptural and architectural features in Ashurnasirpal's palace that are clues to the nature of the activities that took place therein, and by extension, to the primary function of the rooms as originally conceived. I will focus on the suites of rooms around the inner court of the palace, moving from west to east to south, from relief subjects that would have been readily understandable to a general audience, to more esoteric subjects that would probably have been fully understood only by the king and his court (fig. 23-a). The fourth suite of rooms, the throne-room suite, is the subject of Michael Roaf's paper in this volume.

West Suite

The relief decoration in the principal rooms of the west suite was poorly preserved, largely because many of its wall slabs had been removed in the seventh century BC for use in the nearby palace of Esarhaddon. If the evidence of its successor palaces is any guide, then this suite of rooms was second in importance only to the throne-room suite. Similar suites—three parallel long rooms opening onto a terrace or courtyard at both sides and projecting perpendicularly from and connected directly to the throne-room suite—occurred in each of the next three Assyrian royal palaces. In the arsenal at Nimrud, built by Ashurnasirpal's successor, Shalmaneser III, this suite was copied almost exactly. There however, the suite projects on to an open terrace with no further rooms beyond. It is probably significant that the throne-room suite and the projecting wing were the only parts copied directly from

Ashurnasirpal's palace. In other words, these two suites were the only ones essential for this building to function as a royal palace.

The same pattern of rooms occurs in both of the palaces of Sargon II at Khorsabad. In his residential palace this suite of three parallel rooms occurred twice: once in the same location as the west suite of Ashurnasirpal's palace, and again in a wing that projected northward from the main body of the palace onto an open terrace in the manner of Fort Shalmaneser. One room in this latter suite was fitted with a throne base and was clearly a subsidiary throne room, while the wall reliefs in another large room included scenes of banqueting, suggesting one possible use for this room. In Sargon's arsenal at Dur Sharrukin, the plan of the two principal reception suites follows that of Fort Shalmaneser, with the suite of three parallel rooms projecting out from the throne-room suite onto a terrace. Again, these two distinctive suites were the only ones that seemed to be considered essential.

The Assyrian designation of this suite in Ashurnasirpal's palace may be preserved in a set of threshold slabs labelled as 'from the Second House', published by Paley (1989). Although they were found in a secondary context, Paley observed that the ensemble was the right size for several of the major doorways in the west suite. If these slabs are indeed from the west suite, then the name they preserve supports the impression given by the architecture that this was the second most important suite in the palace—the 'first house' would presumably be the throne-room suite, though no such designation survives. There is possible textual evidence for one function of the 'Second House'. A group of court officials, called the 'men of the Second House', serve the king and his high officials at feasts in the palace (Müller 1937: 62, 75). If their title derives from where they work, then 'Second House' might mean 'banquet hall', which would also be consistent with the banqueting scenes in the similar suite in Sargon's palace.

The west suite is the only part of the palace besides the throne room in which two-register reliefs with military and hunting subjects were found (fig. 23-b). Because of its proximity to the edge of the mound, a number of wall slabs from this suite were removed for use in the construction of Esarhaddon's palace, and several others were found in the west suite itself (Paley and Sobolewski 1987: pl. 5). If this sample is representative of the decoration of the entire suite, then the theme in these rooms was evidently royal power: the king's

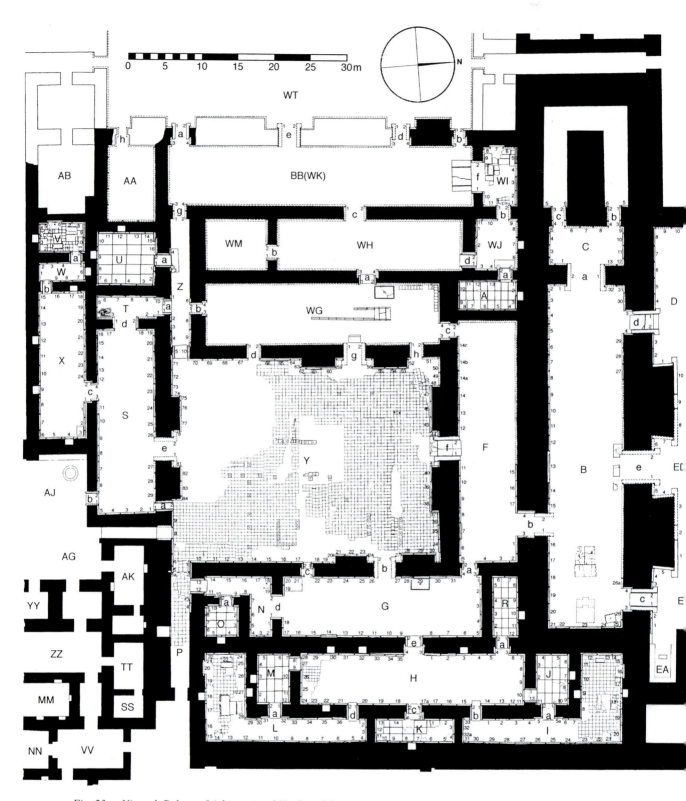

Fig. 23-a. Nimrud, Palace of Ashurnasirpal II, plan of the state apartments, drawn by R.P. Sobolewski (after Paley and Sobolewski 1987: plan 2; courtesy of R.P. Sobolewski).

ability to control Assyria's expanding territory and subdue the enemies of Assyrian order. In the case of human adversaries, these images show the king, in the words of the Standard Inscription carved on every wall slab in the palace, as 'the one who by his lordly conflict has brought under one authority ferocious (and) merciless kings from east to west' (Grayson 1991: 276). The theme of the hunts is arguably similar—by 'conquering' wild lions, which kill livestock, and wild bulls, which destroy crops, he subdues land for Assyrian economic development by destroying the enemies of husbandry and agriculture.

Fig. 23-b. West Suite, Room WG, Ashurnasirpal II passing over the mountains, W: 85cm, British Museum ME 124557. (Courtesy of the Trustees of the British Museum.)

As this was the only suite in the palace that overlooked the Tigris, and was therefore well-ventilated and scenically sited, these may have been the rooms of choice for court activities that did not require the formal setting of the main throne room, possibly being used as a secondary throne room and for such occasions as state banquets. The absence of permanent fixtures that can clearly be identified with banqueting is not in itself surprising—a text that describes the protocol for a royal banquet specifies that all of the banquet furnishings were brought into the room at the beginning of the meal, and were removed after it was over (Müller 1937). Whatever the function of the rooms, the narrative relief images on the walls of the west suite would have served their occupants both as reminders of the effectiveness of the power at the disposal of the king and as statements of the king's tireless activity as protector of Assyria from its enemies. The subjects of these reliefs would also have been much more readily understandable to visitors than the subjects of the east and south suites, which would seem to make this the suite of choice, along with the throne room, for entertaining and impressing visiting foreign dignitaries.

East Suite

The east suite was apparently a ceremonial complex devoted to liquid offerings, and may even have housed the palace shrines. The plan of this suite is distinctive. Instead of being open to the outside on both sides, as were the throne-room suite and the west suite, only the outer reception room and its southern alcove were accessible from the rest of the palace. The basic plan of the outer part of the east suite is comparable to those of the throne-room and south suites, comprising two large parallel rooms. The east suite, however, adds a third row of rooms deep inside the palace, far from the air and light of the courtyard. Two of these inner rooms are relatively large and are decorated with wall reliefs.

Architectural features may provide clues to the purpose of these deeply-recessed rooms. The floors of seven of the nine rooms in this suite are paved. Since pavement is apparently reserved for rooms that are exposed to flowing liquids, and as there was no evidence that these rooms were open to the sky, this implies intensive use of liquids

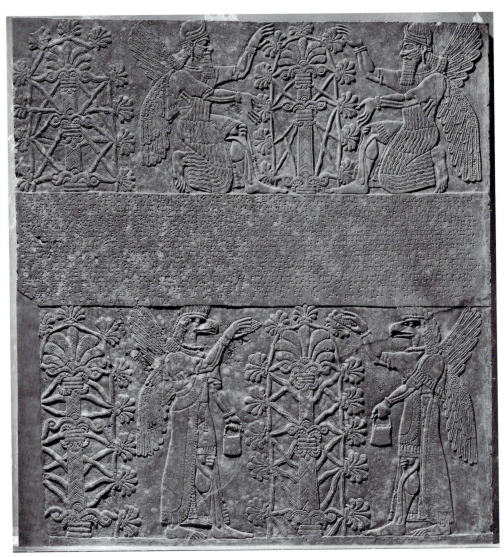

Fig. 23-c. Room I, Slab 30, apotropaic deities and palm trees, W:211cm, Metropolitan Museum 32.143.3. (Courtesy of the Metropolitan Museum of Art, Gift of John D. Rockefeller, Jr., 1932.)

in this suite. The plans of two of these rooms are unusual—'L'-shaped, with a narrow unpaved corridor opening into a broader stone and brick paved space equipped with a niche and drain. I know of no parallel for the plan of these rooms or for such a concentration of paved rooms in any other Assyrian palace. In the throne-room suites of later Assyrian palaces, however, a doorway next to the throne base opens into a paved room with niche and drain. This innovation may be a simplification of the arrangement in the North-West Palace, where an entire suite of paved rooms is located adjacent to the throne base, suggesting that the activities in the east suite may have been closely connected to those carried out in the throne room.

One other feature may provide a clue to the importance of this suite. The wall reliefs in one of the inner rooms (I) differ in format and text from those elsewhere in the palace, suggesting that this was the first sculptured room to be completed, before the standard text and relief format

for the other rooms had been finalized (fig. 23-c). As it is the closest room with a niche and drain to the throne room, the function of this room was evidently so important that it had to be finished first. All of this suggests that this suite served a critical and specialized function that involved liquids. These architectural clues are reinforced by the arrangement and subjects of the relief decoration in the east suite.

Before describing the doorways of the east suite, it will be helpful to survey the repertoire of supernatural figure types that are used. Apart from the bull and lion colossi in major doorways, there are three general types of apotropaic figures in Ashurnasirpal's palace reliefs: a winged human figure with the head of a bird, a winged human figure wearing the horned crown of divinity, and a winged human figure wearing a headband decorated with rosettes (figs 23-c and 23-j). Occasionally the wings are omitted from figures carved in narrow spaces.

The first of these figures is identified in somewhat later texts that prescribe the rituals for the production and placement of protective figurines 'to block the entry of the enemy in someone's house'. These may be figurines buried under the floors, or images 'drawn in the corners' or 'drawn in the gate' (Wiggermann 1992: 1, 90, 110, 121). The texts list an *apkallu* ('sage'), described as a 'guardian' with the face and wings of a bird, holding in its right hand a 'purifier', and in its left a bucket. This must be the bird-headed guardian figure in the doorways of Ashurnasirpal's palace, which always holds a bucket in his left hand and a pine-cone shaped object, evidently the purifier, in his right. Wiggermann (1992: 15, 48, 67, 75) has plausibly identified the action depicted here as sprinkling—the purifier is dipped in the bucket and then shaken, throwing a shower of droplets outward onto whatever is to be purified.

The human figure with horned crown may be represented in a variety of ways: holding the bucket and purifier, making a gesture of blessing or holding a stalk of pomegranates with the upraised right hand and a stalk of flowers or a mace in the lowered left hand. The human figure with headband is usually shown making the gesture of blessing with his raised right hand while holding a stalk of flowers, a mace, or a bucket in his lowered left.

The principal entrance to the east suite from the courtyard was lined with a pair of colossal human-headed winged lions whose function was evidently both to guard the door and to draw attention to it (fig. 23-d). Figures with purifier and bucket stand in all the other doors, except the one from the throne-room suite. These figures always face outward, giving the strong impression that every door except the one communicating with the throne-room suite was felt to need whatever sort of protection the purifier provided.

The decoration on the interior walls of the rooms in the east suite is more varied than might appear at first glance. The first images one would see upon entering the outer room through its central door is the pair of subjects on the east wall directly opposite. At left is the king holding a bowl in his upraised right hand and a bow in his left, standing between two courtiers. At right is the king holding a pair of arrows in his upraised right hand and a bow in his left, flanked by a pair of winged deities who hold the purifier and bucket. The same pair of subjects, with small variations, alternates along both long walls of the room (figs 23-e and 23-f).

The king with bowl is also depicted on the short north wall, but in this case he sits on a decorated chair and footstool, weaponless, a bowl in his raised right hand, one courtier in front and two behind, all bracketed by a pair of winged deities with purifier and bucket. The equivalent wall in the throne room is where the throne base is located. In this room, therefore, this image of the enthroned king marks his place, and when the king was present, the image would have reinforced the impact of his enthroned person.

What is the king doing in these images in which he holds a bowl? To our eyes, the visual evidence is ambiguous, as the bowl is neither held near the lips as for drinking, nor tipped away as for pouring libations. The prominence of weapons in these scenes would seem to argue against drinking, as does their alternation with scenes of the armed king with deities. There is, by contrast, considerable textual and visual evidence that the king is shown here pouring a wine libation. One such scene in the outer room is placed above an actual ablution/libation slab set into the floor. In a text that describes the building of Nimrud, Ashurnasirpal states: 'I pressed wine and gave the best to Assur my lord, and the temples of my land' (Grayson 1991: 252). This statement finds support in the somewhat later Nimrud Wine Lists, a series of wine ration texts found in the Nimrud arsenal. The first entry on all the lists is a substantial wine ration for 'the regular offering' for the gods and for ceremonial purposes, and additional amounts are listed 'for libations' (lit. 'for the ground'; Kinnier-Wilson 1972: 112–13).

In the throne room, two relief images of the king with bowl leave little doubt that he is shown in the act of pouring libations. Both depict the aftermath of a hunt, with the slain bull and lion at the king's feet. He stands in exactly the pose of the reliefs in the east suite. While he is neither shown drinking nor pouring, a comparable image from the palace of the seventh-century king Ashurbanipal at Nineveh actually shows the libation being poured over the dead lions. Because the pose of the king in the hunt scenes is identical to that in the other images that show him holding a bowl, it seems plausible that pouring libations is depicted in all of these images.

And what of the image of the king with bow and arrows? The king's personal identification with this image is even stressed by its use as decoration on garments that he wears on the reliefs in this room (Canby 1971: pls 16b, 19a). Here the king and his weapons, the supreme manifestation of earthly royal might, are purified by protective deities. This serves as a reminder that the king's weapons are very special. In the Standard Inscription, Ashurnasirpal gives the source of his weapons: 'Assur, the lord who called me by name (and) made my sovereignty supreme, placed his merciless weapon in my lordly arms' (Grayson 1991: 275).

What are we to make of the alternation of images of the king with bowl and king with bow in the reliefs in this room? Brandes (1970: 151–54) noted that the king here appears in the roles of priest and military leader, and that in both roles the focus of activity is on his weapons. He suggested that the ceremonies represented recorded ceremonies actually held here involving invocations for

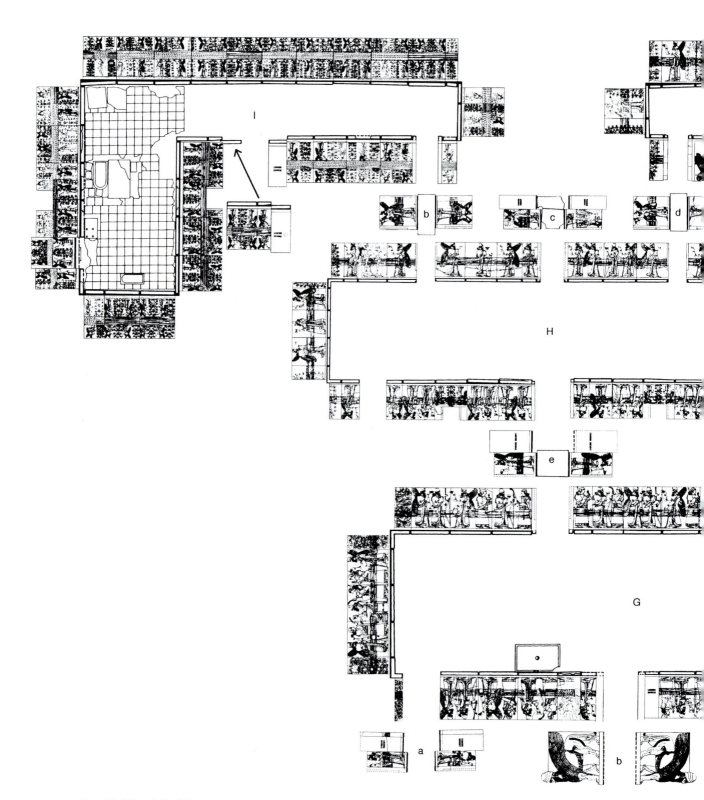

Fig. 23-d(i) and 23-d(ii). East suite, layout of the decoration, assembled by the author after Meuszyński 1981, and Paley and Sobolewski 1987. (Courtesy of R.P. Sobolewski.)

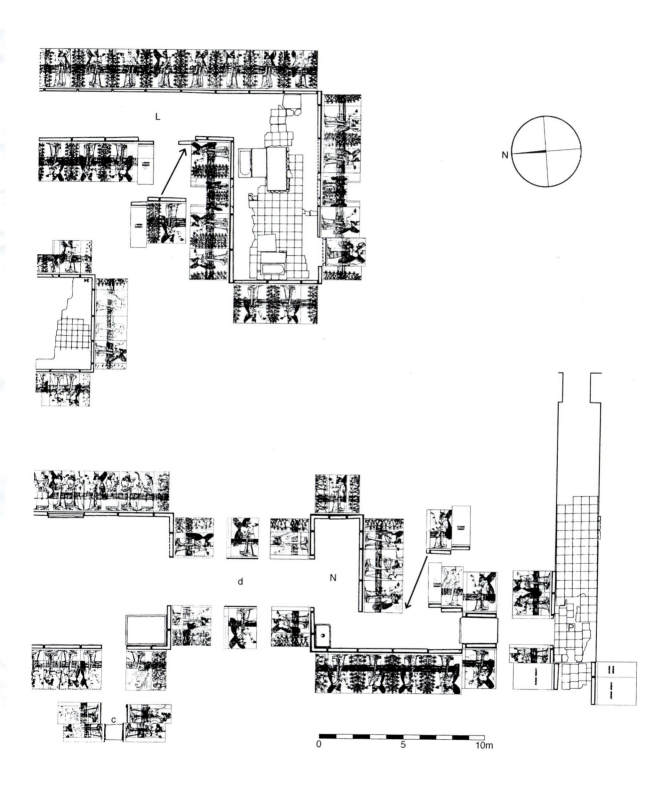

Fig. 23-e. Room G, Slabs7-8, Ashurnasirpal II making a wine offering, W:465cm, Metropolitan Museum 32.143.4 and 32.143.6. (Courtesy Metropolitan Museum of Art, Gift of John D. Rockefeller, Jr., 1932.)

Fig. 23-f. Room G, Slabs 22-24, bird-headed figure with cone and bucket, purification of the king's weapons, W: 567. (Copyright of the author.)

divine favour and purifying lustration. Furthermore, he noted the curious fact that the king as priest is shown in human company, while the military leader is accompanied by divinities. Both of these groupings stress the king's role as a link between humans and gods—the human high priest who transcends his fellows by reaching out to the gods, and the human commander-in-chief whom the gods have singled out from his fellows to receive their favour. These two aspects of kingship are explicitly linked in the text on the Nimrud Monolith, a large stone stele that commemorates the foundation of the North-West Palace: '(Ashurnasirpal), provider of offerings for the great gods, legitimate prince, to whom is perpetually entrusted the proper administration of the rites of the temples of his land, whose deeds and offerings the great gods of heaven and underworld love so that they (therefore) established forever his priesthood in the temples, granted to his dominion their fierce weapons, (and) made him more marvellous than (any of) the kings of the four quarters with respect to the splendour of his weapons (and) the radiance of his dominion' (Grayson 1991: 239).

There is one further subject on the walls of the outer room, a subject that occurs in nearly every sculptured room in the palace. This is a stylized palm tree, carved on each of the four monolithic corner slabs in the room. There are apparently no references to such a tree in Assyrian texts, and there is no consensus either on the meaning of the motif for the Assyrians, nor on its function in the decorative programs of Assyrian palaces. It is most often interpreted as a symbol, variously equated with the Assyrian pantheon, the king, agricultural abundance, fertility, or prosperity (Parpola 1993b: 165–69; Porter 1993: 129–39; Albenda 1994: 124, 132–33; Richardson 1999–2001: 156–66). The deities that sometimes flank the tree contribute to its symbolism, either by fertilizing it with a male pollen cluster, or by cleansing it with a purifier. While it is not possible to disprove these interpretations, it should be noted that there is no compelling evidence in their favour either. Indeed, on the basis of the available visual, textual, and contextual evidence, the stylized palm tree in Ashurnasirpal's palace serves a basic function that is quite different from the usual interpretations.

Most interpreters follow the common practice of reproducing images of the tree flanked by winged figures, without considering the fact that the majority of trees in the palace are depicted without attendant winged figures. In Room H, and in most of the other sculptured rooms in the palace, the stylized tree is carved on the slabs in the corners of the room. They may be accompanied by winged figures with purifier and bucket, but usually they are not. Apparently the stylized tree does not require winged attendants in order to perform its function. The consistent use of the tree in corners suggests that it served a specific purpose. The figurine texts mentioned above describe where each type of figure is to be placed in the building, and one such location is corners. The stylized palm trees in the corners of the rooms should therefore be performing an apotropaic function. As we will see, images of the tree and deity with purifier are concentrated in particularly sensitive rooms in the palace—in what are probably bathing rooms and the king's private apartment—further suggesting an apotropaic rather than purely symbolic function.

The most radical interpretation of the tree was offered by Parker (1983: 38–39; 1986), who suggested that the image of the stylized palm tree is to be read as a stylized palm tree. She has been the only scholar to introduce textual evidence for her interpretation, observing that palm fronds and offshoots occur in Assyrian texts as apotropaic instruments for exorcism. Indeed, in Assyrian texts virtually all of the references to palms are in apotropaic and exorcism contexts. For these purposes both the palm frond and the palm offshoot are prescribed to repel evil, and thereby to purify or protect whatever is in its vicinity (Wiggermann 1992: 68–69, 84–85). The Babylonian origin of these exorcism texts is clear from their liberal utilization of the palm frond and offshoot, which are common waste products of date culture and easily available there. In Assyria where palms do not flourish, by contrast, palm by-products would have been harder to come by, which may have made them more desirable. Interestingly, Wiggermann (1992: 67, 84) observes that the pine cone, a plentiful by-product of pine trees that was readily available in Assyria, can have the same function in exorcism texts. This suggests that the purifier that looks like a pine cone is in fact a pine cone.

Based on these textually attested uses of the date palm and pine cone, it appears that Ashurnasirpal's tree is to be identified with the palm offshoot or frond, and that the primary function of both the tree and cone is apotropaic, defending vulnerable spots such as doors and corners from evil intrusions, protecting the image and person of the king, and through multiple repetition, creating highly secure spaces within the palace. Indeed, in Ashurnasirpal's palace, the stylized tree looks very much like a palm tree surmounted by its characteristic plume of fronds, surrounded by an arc of smaller offshoots, the palmettes (Dowson 1982: 79–91). Since both the fronds and offshoots are apotropaic, this combination should provide powerful protection indeed.

This hypothesis receives further support in the relief decoration of the middle room, H. Here the sole occurrences of the stylized tree are in the corners and beneath the four air shaft openings, where they are depicted flanked by a pair of bird-headed *apkallu* holding the purifier and bucket. Although this is the supposedly standard grouping, in this context it appears that the relationship between the figures and the tree is not one of mutual dependence, but rather functional similarity. The tree and *apkallu* are actually both performing the same function, namely warding off evil. The true explanation for these figures beneath the air shafts in this room, therefore, is not that this potential entrance for demonic intruders was decorated with an emblem of agricultural abundance, but rather that the tree protects the centre of this vulnerable space, while the two *apkallu* face inward toward the opening from either side, performing the same function. The apparent interaction between the figures and the tree, as Parker (1986: 145) observed, is due only to the artistic decision to crowd these independent apotropaic elements together in order to fill the available space.

Elsewhere in Room H a single subject predominates: the king holding the bow in his left hand and a cup in his upraised right hand. He is flanked by a pair of winged human figures with headbands, each of which holds the bucket in his left hand and makes the gesture of blessing towards the king with his right. In this inside room, therefore, the emphasis in the reliefs is entirely on libations, and these offerings are now made before divine or semi-divine figures that show divine sanction for his offerings.

The two L-shaped inner rooms of the east suite, I and L, are decorated almost entirely with the stylized tree alternating with winged figures (fig. 23-c). Whether these paved rooms served for ablutions or offerings or both, their occupants would have been mightily protected against evil and impurity. In both rooms an unusual figure—a beardless human, possibly female—was depicted in the niche behind the drain (fig 23-g). This is most likely to be a special type of apotropaic figure whose specific function is to guard against demonic intrusions through the drain, although the possibility that she herself is the recipient of offerings poured there cannot be ruled out.

Overall, the theme of the relief decoration in the east suite seems to be divine legitimization of Ashurnasirpal's royal authority. In the outer room, G, the king is shown making offerings to the gods and receiving divine purification of his person and his weapons. In the middle room, H, these two subjects are conflated, as the offerings of the king are

rewarded directly with divine blessing. The inner rooms, I and L, are entirely lined with apotropaic figures, which ensure that the occupants and activities therein will be immune from evil influences. This would be a very secure location, for example, for rituals such as those depicted in the two outer rooms. It would also be an ideal venue for bathing, ritual or otherwise, during which time the king, possibly weaponless and disrobed, would be particularly vulnerable to both demonic and physical threats.

South Suite

The south suite has the smallest rooms of the four suites grouped around the inner court. Its plan is also simpler than those of the west and east suites, and is comparable to that of the throne-room suite, though on a much smaller scale: a large outer room (S) that opens from the court, with an alcove at its west end, and a large inner room (X), with a pair of small rooms also at its west end, including a

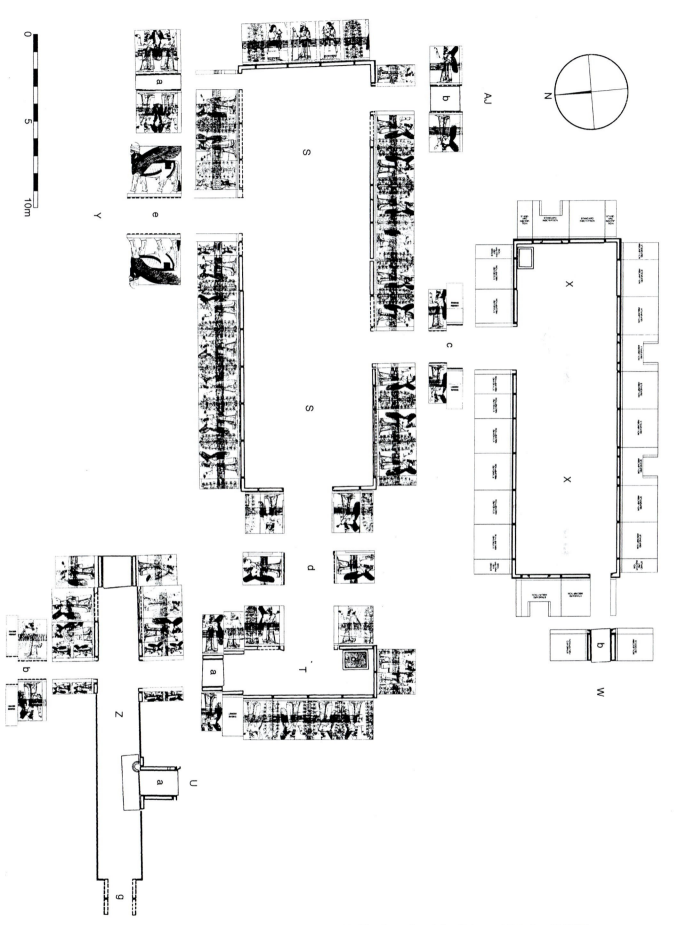

Fig. 23-h. South suite, layout of the decoration, assembled by the author (after Paley and Sobolewski 1987). (Courtesy of R.P. Sobolewski.)

Fig. 23-i. Room S, Slabs 20–22, apotropaic deities and palm trees, W: 646cm. (Copyright of the author.)

paved room with niche and drain. Turner (1970: 194–99) has shown that this plan is the most frequently occurring type of suite in Assyrian palaces. This plan should therefore exemplify the standard Assyrian residential suite, and more complex suites presumably represent modifications of the standard plan for specialized functions. Reade (1980: 84) proposed that the south suite was the king's own 'residential suite', and I believe that the architectural and decorative features support this.

Architecturally, the south suite displays several suggestive features. The principal outside entrances face north, so that in the summer it would have been cooler than the large reception rooms in the east and west suites. It is the innermost and least accessible of the decorated reception suites. It is also the only suite with direct access to the private wing of the palace, through a back door into court AJ. These small undecorated inner rooms were for the palace domestic services, as suggested by the presence of wells. In addition, vaulted tombs, at least two of which contained the rich burials of Assyrian queens, were found beneath the floors of several rooms in the area directly behind this suite, suggesting that this area was the residence of Ashurnasirpal's queen and palace women.

This architectural evidence indicates that the south suite was the most private and comfortable of the decorated suites, and it is indeed tempting to see this as the king's private suite, which would also be consistent with its

Fig. 23-j. Room T, Door a, Slab 1, apotropaic figure holding a scapegoat, W: 124 cm, British Museum ME 124561. (Courtesy of the Trustees of the British Museum.)

direct access to the proposed women's quarters. This hypothesis seems to be supported by the relief decoration in the south suite, which consists almost entirely of apotropaic imagery (figs 23-h and 23-i). On the walls of the outer room, S, the stylized palm tree alternates with the winged deity with purifier and bucket. This overwhelming emphasis on the apotropaic suggests that this was meant to be a very secure room.

This heightened security is evidenced in an unusual way in the doorway that connected the west and south suites. Here each jamb is decorated with a winged human figure with a headband, facing outward toward the corridor (fig. 23-j). In one hand he holds a small goat against his side, and in the other what appears to be a palm frond. Following Barnett (1970: 12), Parker (1983: 37) identified the goat here as a 'scapegoat', used in Assyrian rituals to avert evil, presumably by serving as a host for wandering demons that might otherwise possess the human inhabitants of the palace (Wiggermann 1992: 77). Mallowan (1966: I, 120) found the skeleton of a similar small quadruped, tentatively identified as a gazelle, under the pavement of the floor in a nearby corridor—this animal may also have served as a scapegoat. Such figures appear in only one other place in the palace, in the public entrance to the throne room, suggesting that they may be a particularly powerful type.

All of these features seem to support the identification of the south suite as Ashurnasirpal's private residential suite. The overall emphasis on apotropaic imagery in the outer room and the particularly potent protective figures in the outer doors are readily understandable if this suite was the location in which the king conducted his private affairs: receiving high court officials, entertaining palace women, eating, bathing and, especially, sleeping. While the king was engaged in these pursuits, the protective images carved all around the walls of the outer rooms would have provided a measure of magical protection, and at the same time would have reminded those closest to the king (and therefore potentially the most dangerous to him) that the king rules by the will of the gods and enjoys their protection.

The walls of the large back room, X, were panelled with unsculptured stone slabs, each of which was carved only with the 'Standard Inscription'. This was by far the largest room in the palace to remain unsculptured, and this absence seems particularly surprising since X is clearly one of the two major rooms in the south suite. This may be understandable, however, if this room was in fact the king's private retiring room, as it would then presumably have been inaccessible to all but his most trusted servants. Whatever else the function of carved figures may have been, they seem to have been used only where there was the potential for a human audience to be impressed by the raw power that the production of huge carved slabs represents. Such a message in an inaccessible location would have been largely wasted, and magical protection could have been afforded through less costly means.

We now see that Ashurnasirpal stood on the brink of the greatest empire the world had ever seen, but Ashurnasirpal himself could see only the past: how precarious Assyria's position had been during the previous two centuries, characterized by Aramean incursions and Assyrian contractions and retrenchments. Assyria's claim to greatness may have been a given, but the implementation of that greatness lay solely in Ashurnasirpal's hands. The relief program of his palace lays out a recipe for Assyrian security and prosperity, displaying each of the ingredients in the location where it would have the greatest effect on the groups who could assure his success. This program communicated with its audiences at two levels: the overt level of meaning expressed through images associated with architectural contexts, and the more covert message of power expressed through costly display, embodied in the profusion of sculpture within a monumental architectural setting. That these sculptures were confined to the more accessible rooms suggests that, whatever magical power the images may have been thought to possess, the choice to depict such images through the expensive medium of sculpture reflects an intention to influence human, as well as divine and demonic, occupants of the palace.

24   CREATING A VIRTUAL REALITY MODEL OF THE NORTH-WEST PALACE

Samuel M. Paley

The University at Buffalo's Virtual Reality Laboratory of the Department of Mechanical and Aerospace Engineering and Learning Sites Inc. in Williamstown, Massachusetts are preparing interactive, Virtual Reality models of the North-West Palace of Ashurnasirpal II with a portfolio of 3D images that can be used for publication and education. The models are being built in two technologies: an Onyx2 model for supercomputers that can be used for distance learning between institutions with Immersadesk™ and CAVE™ technology and a PC version, for individual and classroom use.[1]

Previous work on the theoretical reconstruction of the Palace and its decoration was limited to the identification, using two-dimensional drawings, of all known surviving examples of its bas-relief as well as hypothesizing about what was missing. Teaching the palace as part of a general ancient art or even a Mesopotamian art and/or archaeology course meant using dozens of slides over many hours, without really gaining an understanding of more than the iconography of the decorative motifs and the floor plan, a tedious exercise, resulting in an incomplete understanding. Theoretical considerations of the meaning and use of the individual rooms have been based on iconography and the study of excavation reports. Actually, since the nineteenth-century excavations, few scholars have taken the opportunity to study the palace as a whole, with all its decoration, in its environs, as originally designed. Owing to the enormity of the task of spreading out and explaining the whole data set to a class, we hypothesized that digital technologies with their three-dimensional aspects, textual and oral interfaces, could now begin to address seriously the problem of teaching the North-West Palace. Technology can combine extant artifacts, narrative and textual information with ongoing theoretical research about the architecture and the symbolic meaning of the visual iconographic elements. For younger people we can create scenarios that might help them visualize the use of the rooms of the palace and spur their imaginations and curiosities to investigate life in this ancient Mesopotamian world. We hope that this comprehensive 'picture' will illustrate what has not been previously possible, resulting in a near first-hand experience, in one 'digital place', along with the newest interpretations, so that students in the Humanities, Social Sciences and other disciplines can study Assyria from the perspective of one of its greatest monuments. We feel that an interactive environment will make the learning experience more accessible as well as more exciting and meaningful. We plan to publish this research on DVD and over the World Wide Web. This paper is an introduction to our methods and some of the categories of information from this emerging publication. There are still many elements missing and many corrections to be made.

Over the course of Layard's excavations at Nimrud and then later during those of his assistant Hormuzd Rassam, and seemingly with Ottoman approval, and the approval, support and assistance of Henry Rawlinson, the British government's representative in the area, the stone bas-relief decorations that once decorated the walls of the North-West Palace were distributed to friends, acquaintances, family, the Ottoman Sultan and the British Museum (Lloyd 1980; Larsen 1996; Curtis and Reade 1995: 9–16, 210–21). The site continued to be visited and stripped of more of its decoration even into the twentieth century, and recent robberies of its storerooms have resulted in more loss. Today, we find bas-relief decoration from the North-West Palace at Nimrud in sixty-seven museums and private collections across the world, and this count does not include the museums of Iraq, the site museum at Nimrud itself, or stolen pieces.

Many of the examples we know are fragmentary, either conveniently broken pieces that were spirited away or, having been cut up into smaller pieces, loaded on camels, donkeys and boats so that they could be more easily transported over land or on the Tigris to be loaded on

[1] There are several colleagues involved in this project under my direction: Dr Donald Sanders, an architect-archaeologist, President of Learning Sites, Inc.; Richard Sobolewski, architect and 'Second Director' of the Polish excavations at Nimrud from 1974–76; Professor Thenkurussi Kesavadas, Director of the University at Buffalo Virtual Reality Lab and his graduate assistant, Mr Youngseok Kim; Professor Alison Snyder, Department of Architecture, University of Oregon; Professor Stuart Shapiro, Department of Computer Engineering, University at Buffalo, a specialist in natural language interface; Dr Julian Reade, British Museum (ret.) for the painted decorations that accompanied the bas-relief; and Dr Elizabeth Hendrix, Materials Research Laboratory at the Massachusetts Institute of Technology, a specialist on paint and painted stone. We hope that we can add to the list of contributors as funding grows. One of my students in our Honors College program, Ms Colleen Snyder, is preparing a workbook for school children based on our model; and Nathanael Shelley, a major in my Department, is preparing an interactive database of jewellery and garment decorations, his senior research project for the Bachelor's degree. Attendance at and participation in the Nimrud Conference was made possible by a travel grant from the American Friends of the British Museum. This project is supported by grants from the University at Buffalo, Learning Sites, Inc. and private donors.

ships bound for Europe or America. A letter from the records of Williams College in Williamstown, Massachusetts, dated 29th November 1882, from Dwight Whitney Marsh to Professor A.L. Perry, recalls one occurrence of this practice:

> …. All slabs sent by Layard to Europe had gone down the Tigris & by Persia and India to England. That was an entire water route but requiring too many transshipments to get to America. I concluded to take an entirely new course to reduce the thickness of the slabs by sawing from about a foot to about four inches, & then to make each slab into three, making in all six pieces, which were boxed with their planks & made into three camel loads. These were loaded and unloaded night and morning the long journey of about four hundred miles to the Mediterranean & so eventually from Beirut in an American woolship to America. …. (Stearns 1961: 2, note 8 for the correspondence about the bas-relief and this letter discussed on page 7; and, recently, on Layard's activities in this regard in Larsen 1996: 125 ff.)

Examples can be found in nearly every collection. For example, the Art Institute of Chicago owns the head of a genius figure, room S, slab 10 (Paley and Sobolewski 1987: 40–41, pl. 2.9); and, there is a head of a royal attendant from the throne room, room B, slab 12, which was sold in London several years ago at Sotheby's (sale on 8th December 1994, lot 68). Tracing the buying and selling of these slabs over the last 150 years has become a daunting task for those interested (Unger; Merrill; Gadd; Weidner; Stearns, *et al.*, see Stearns 1961) in understanding the palace as a whole, or at least as close as possible to the way Layard found it.

Janusz Meuszyński and Richard Sobolewski, then Richard Sobolewski and I, prepared theoretical reconstructions, which were rendered in line drawings, of each room's wall relief from which we can now understand the layout of the decoration and begin to see the relationships between the iconography of one room and another, perhaps understanding how the decoration flowed from one space to another and the uses of the various spaces in the palace. This was the subject of a recent article by John Russell, reusing these theoretical reconstructions (Russell 1999; see also Winter 1983; and briefly, earlier, 'generalizing', Reade 1979: 335–39).

But, in over a century and a half since its excavation, there have been virtually no attempts to revisualize the remains of the North-West Palace as a whole building (fig. 24-a). Most textbooks and professional publications still reproduce Layard's commissioned watercolour in which an audience hall, usually called the throne room, is envisioned from the vantage point of somewhere near of the middle of the hall, and looking west toward room C. That visualization has a distinctly Victorian aesthetic, which we have become used to: ceiling, light well, pastel shades of colour and all. The rendering is more appropriate to the Crystal Palace exposition. When I was a student, I was told that it was made as a rendering by the architect to show what such a room at the exposition would look like. I rather like calling it Layard's Victorian palace. It has had a profound effect on our conception of the palace and its decoration. Another view of the palace area is less well known, but influenced movies, like *Intolerance*, D.W. Griffith's famous 1916 spectacular (Solomon 2001: 225–41; Layard 1853b: pl. I; and Curtis and Reade 1995: 217, fig. 244).

Our critical study of Layard's interpretation was the beginning of our 're-envisioning' the palace's throne room original appearance and, extrapolating from there, what the other rooms of the palace might have looked like. Among the problems we saw in the Layard reconstruction were: 1) the major beams cantilevered from the walls to support the light well would have collapsed, given that the opening seems to stretch across a consider-

Fig. 24-a. Reconstruction of an Assyrian throne-room (Layard 1849b: pl. II).

Fig. 24-b. Photograph of the opening of the Assyrian Galleries at the Metropolitan Museum of Art. Photography courtesy of Geoff Emberling.

able part of the length of the throne room as we see it in the rendition; 2) the light well, covering so much of the room, would seem to have let in too much weather, dust and blinding sunlight, damaging to the bas-reliefs, the people in the room, and the mud brick floor—there is no drainage in the room; 3) the people depicted are either too small or the bas-reliefs are too big (fig. 24-b). This also indicates that in the Layard drawing the room's proportions are incorrectly shown—if the width were correct, then the bas-reliefs are too large and the ceiling too low. If the height of the bas-reliefs were correct, then the width of the room is somehow wrong. If it were really the North-West Palace throne room, a doorway to the outer court is missing on the right, the scenes on the bas-reliefs represent the topics of the imagery not the reality of the finds even from the little that we know, and the size of room C, beyond the throne room, is represented as being much too large. Reade and Curtis have also

commented on the problems with this Layard watercolour (for example, Reade 1983: caption to fig. 22; Curtis and Reade 1995: 216, caption to fig. 243).

When Richard Sobolewski made his plans *in situ*, wherever there was real evidence, he took care to measure the precise size of each surviving architectural feature and bas-relief that still remained in place or could be attributed to a specific place along the palace walls (Meuszyński 1981: plans 3–7.) We set up a proportional system based on Sobolewski's plan, ancient precedents and modern architectural analysis to determine how high the walls might be, the nature of the ceiling, and the height and shape of doorways. At this writing we have not reviewed and considered Layard's words on the subject of architecture as recorded in an *Athenaeum* article of 1848 (Larsen 1996: 149, n. 82). Also, identifying the location and type of the decorative elements in brick or painted plaster that accompanied the bas-relief, as much as is still possible, has not as yet been accomplished.

To create 3D images is rather straightforward. Using a software program called 3DStudioMax, the plan of the palace is aligned to an angle of view that is appropriate for the next step, which is to build a wire frame on the plan that outlines the widths and heights of the walls. Then the wire frame is covered with 'wall-paper' upon which are drawn the textures and colours that give the 3D image its effect of depth and reality (see: http://www.learningsites.com/Nimrud/Nimrud_home.ht ml 'Northwest Palace of Ashur-nasir-pal II; How We Build a Rendered 3D Model').

In previous work, we had arrived at the decisions to raise the walls to certain heights; we had chosen how the

Fig. 24-c. Façade of the throne room suite, view towards the south-west corner of the Great Northern Courtyard. (Image copyright 2007 and reprinted courtesy of Learning Sites, Inc.)

ceiling appeared, the shapes of the arches and the configurations of the doorways. That research was now passed on to the computer modellers, who then prepared the real-time VR model. Models of still and moving figures (we will call them intelligent agents and avatars) were constructed and the preliminary decisions regarding painted decoration were adapted to the Virtual Reality models.

We arrived at the heights of the walls and associated architectural elements in the following manner (after Snyder and Paley 2001):

1. Given the height differential between the interior and exterior bas-relief, we first surmised that the height of the throne room and perhaps the whole northern wing of the North-West Palace (the principal throne-room suite) were probably governed by the exterior façade of the throne room (fig. 24-c). The exterior façade is comprised of what Layard called courtyards D and E and into which Sobolewski and I reconstructed a complete central doorway from extant remains found in the excavations: the thresholds for the door, the seats for the door posts, and fragments of the *lamassu* door figures. Here we were following Julian Reade's suggestion of many years ago (Paley and Sobolewski 1992: pl. 4, for example; Reade 1965: plan).

2. After examining the extant evidence of flat and arched doorways of various periods of Assyrian history on the Nimrud citadel (Rassam 1897: opposite p. 226; Mallowan 1966: I, fig. 7), at Fort Shalmaneser (Mallowan 1966: II, figs 349, 365, 375, 379, 380), at Khorsabad (Sobolewski 1981: 243–44, fig. 6 and Curtis and Reade 1995: 64), on the doorways sculpted on bas-relief decoration (Room B-4 lower: BM 124554; B-17 upper: BM 124538; B-18 upper: BM 124536; B-28 lower: Meuszyński 1981: 24, pl. 3,2) and elsewhere (Damerji 1999: passim), we also used as reference one of the arch shapes drawn upon a painted and glazed brick panel fallen from above a doorway and discovered at Fort Shalmaneser and dated to Shalmaneser III, Ashurnasirpal's successor (after Reade in Mallowan 1966: II, fig. 373).

Julian Reade's reconstruction (fig. 24-e) of the Fort Shalmaneser brick panel allowed us to formulate a proportional system of bas-relief to arched opening. Then from the larger size of the bas-relief flanking the central section of the throne room's outer façade, we surmised that the central doorway was tallest, with a parabola-shaped arch springing from the area of the *lamassu* heads. Richard Sobolewski had made drawings of arched doorways some years ago, but

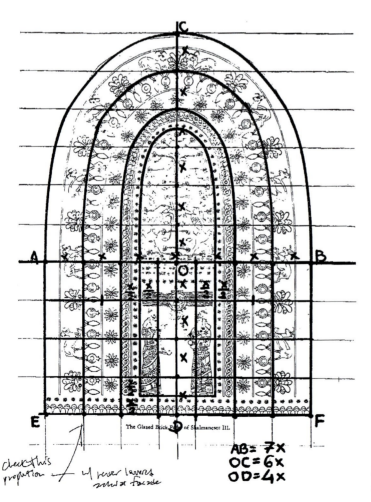

Fig. 24-e. Brick panel marked up by Richard Sobolewski, with apologies to Julian Reade.

Fig. 24-f. Barrel arch reconstructions by
Richard Sobolewski.

these, in the end, did not satisfy our aesthetic. Somehow these parabola-shaped arches did (fig. 24-f).

3. Once we set the height and shape of the central doorway at *c.* 8 m and the side doorways at *c.* 6 m, we set the height of the top of the throne room façade so as to include room for the interior roof structure of the throne room (fig. 24-c). On the exterior we surmised a parapet with canted crenellations at the top of the wall giving us a height of 12 m for the façade from the paving surface of the façade courtyard to the top of the crenellations.

Passing through the western archway of the façade from the courtyard, the archway was modified and became a higher, flat ceiling on part of the interior passage measuring 6.4 m in height (fig. 24-d). Our reasoning for this was predicated on the remnants of rectilinear door elements found at Balawat and the hypothesis that there could have been a brick panel above the inside of the door.

Also, bringing the tall exterior arch to a flat arch allowed for a height transition that works well with the smaller interior bas-reliefs. It also gave a nice rectangular pocket into which the doors closed.

The proportions of the throne room itself, measuring approximately 10 m wide and 48 m long, seen in conjunction with our layout of the exterior courtyard façade, led us to hypothesize an interior throne room approximately 10 m high. Inclusive in the room are wood beams spanning this width and set every 3 m along the length of the room. Beams of this length are not considered a problem (as explained to me by Professor Peter Kunniholm. See also the possible kinds of wood in the written sources that would have been available in Postgate 1992: chart one, s.v. *erēnu* and *miḫru*).

To begin to suggest the grandeur of the throne room, we selected a series of decorative motifs and placed them along the tops of the bas-relief. The idea for the layout of

Fig. 24-d. Section drawing through the
throne room façade, from the Great Northern
Courtyard into the throne room. (Image
copyright 2002 and reprinted courtesy of
Learning Sites, Inc.)

this decoration comes from the throne room at Fort Shalmaneser, repainted in the time of Esarhaddon (Mallowan 1966: II, figs 307–8). We also studied painted wall plaques, round and shield-shaped, and decorative elements from fragments of painted wall plaster and brick found by Layard and during the British and Iraqi work in the palace (Curtis and Reade 1995: 102–3, figs 50–52; Mallowan 1966: I, fig. 7) and by Campbell Thompson in Ashurnasirpal's palace at Nineveh (Campbell Thompson and Hutchinson 1931: pls XXVI.4–XXXII; Russell 1999). This promised to become so complicated that, short of replicating Layard's brave attempt at decoration in his Victorian throne room, we decided, at this stage of our work, to use simple geometric decoration, which could be easily replaced, so that we could at least consider what decoration might look like on the walls of our model. Figural decoration is for the future, as is painting the plinths of the slabs, restoring painted brick to the arches, painting the bas-reliefs and so forth. The idea for the painted rafters with rosettes and centre dotted circles came from the remains of the throne room decoration in King Sargon's palace at Khorsabad (Loud 1936b: 68–71, pls II–III). Layard's colour drawing also surmised rafters, but only across the entrance from the throne room to the room behind and across the latter room's ceiling. Corbels in the shape of hands support the rafters (following Curtis and Reade 1995: 104, figs 53–55, after an idea of Walter Andrae; and also Frame 1991).

The throne room itself is not well preserved (fig. 24-g). The actual bas-reliefs, most of which are in the British Museum, and the published drawings allow us to study the decoration individually or as part of a decorative scheme (fig. 24-h). Our model will have all the evidence we can muster and present it in a virtual environment that will be easily visited and studied. There are several kinds of software programs that can be used to teach the student the extent of *in situ* preservation, the theoretical recon-

struction on paper and a final fully rendered model. The parts that are rendered in this view of the throne room can be shown in different, interactive ways. Learning Sites had developed software that can 'move' a student from excavation views compared to a virtual reconstruction (fig. 24-i). Bas-relief slabs, objects found in the excavation and even reconstructed furniture can be studied with a digital caliper (fig. 24-j).

In the course of the virtual reconstruction, the measurements of which have to be as precise as possible, we discovered some anomalies in Richard Sobolewski's floor plan and Halina Lewakowa's drawings. These are not major, but we had to make adjustments to help us make a correction in perspective. An example of one of these adjustments is the back wall in room C that faces room B—the wall that faces the throne, a wall that the king would have been able to see in the distance when he was sitting on his throne (Meuszyński 1981: pl. 4, 2–3). We were working on the drawings of the western wall of room C in the Meuszyński volume to see if the imagery integrated into the layout of the iconography of the throne room. We thought it did because the western wall was visible from the throne room through the very wide doorway that connected the two rooms. When Julian Reade and John Russell discovered the upper part of one of the missing bas-reliefs from this wall, the sizes of the various slabs attributed to the back wall of room C had to be modified in the reconstruction drawing. Alison Snyder's re-rendering of that wall in the *MIHO South Wing Catalogue* (70; see also Paley 1999: 18, fig. 2) makes this small but telling correction. The scene, which was somehow a little off centre when rendering this wall in VR based upon the version published in the Meuszyński volume, could now be realigned (fig. 24-k). This is one of the advantages of rendering in VR. The drawing is precise and one can view the results easily from many angles. By correcting the widths of the slabs

Fig. 24-g. The throne room at Nimrud. (Photograph courtesy of M. Weigl and F. Schipper.)

Fig. 24-h. Throne room reconstruction showing the various kinds
of source material that can be used for teaching its
reconstruction. (Image copyright 1999 and re-printed
courtesy of Learning Sites, Inc.)

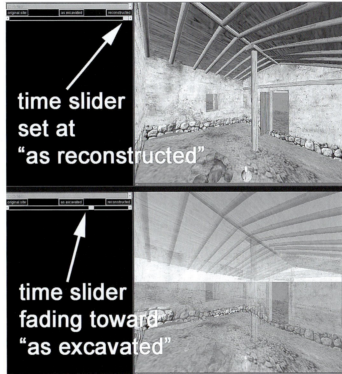

Fig. 24-i. "Time Slider" programme. (Image
copyright 2002 and reprinted courtesy of Learning
Sites, Inc.)

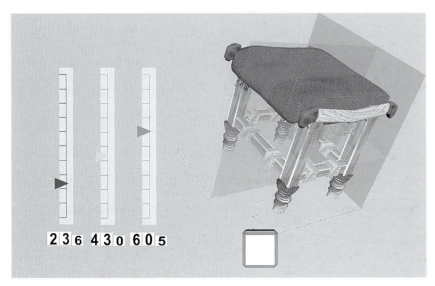

Fig. 24-j. Digital calliper. (Image
copyright 2002 and reprinted
courtesy of Learning Sites, Inc.)

Fig. 24-k. View from the throne room into Room C vestibule. (Image copyright 2002 and reprinted courtesy of Learning Sites, Inc.)

on the western wall and thus making the wall a bit shorter than on the floor plan, the representation of geniuses and attendants flanking the king were more centred in the view through the doorway. Thus an idea that the western wall of room C could be considered as part of the overall iconographical decorations of the throne room is more probable.

As a teaching tool, especially for young people, we have decided to people the rooms of the palace and add some furniture. This again was done for the purpose of enlivening the empty spaces. We were not trying yet to make any statements about court protocol, for example, whether the furniture was brought in for certain occasions or which figure belonged in which space, when and why. We are considering this for the future, with avatars (fig. 24-j). We began by building a throne for the throne room using the seat and footstool from the scene of the seated king carved on the north wall of room G, and extruding that seat from the bas-relief. The technology used here is the same that is used for building buildings. As a check we also referred to the furniture fittings found in room AB in the palace and trench P near the center of the acropolis. This suggested to us the kinds of materials out of which the throne and its footstool could be made: wood, bronze, copper and perhaps stone (Curtis and Reade 1995: nos 83, 85, 86–88). The fabrics of the cushions were coloured using the palate we knew from clothing material in the Til Barsip paintings (Parrot 1961: frontispiece, and figs 109–20, 336–40, 342–47). The wood is new cedar.

Human figures were a different problem. We started with billboards, that is, a flat rendition of the attendants we saw associated with the king in the presentation scenes. The first figure we chose was the usher/herald. But to make a 3D figure was an entirely different story, and one that

moved even more complicated. Mr Youngseok Kim, a graduate student in Mechanical Engineering succeeded by building the model using Maya software, and then learned how to make the figure inside the clothing move without poking through the garments (remember this is not real but digital) so that the garments move naturally. And the figure had to be made so that eventually it will be able to move in real time. For this he had to experiment with the number of polygon models and Non-uniform Rational B-splines (NURBS) (Kim 2001: 22ff., figs 3–15 to 17(sic!)). After he had created the various parts of the king's body, he used the figurine of Ashurnasirpal II from the Ninurta temple to model his head and face with more or less realistic features. Then he worked on body proportions by rotoscoping from the statuette of Ashurnasirpal in the British Museum (Kim 2001: 38, fig 3–20). The next step was to develop sets of joint positions and develop sets of motion data so that the figure moved properly (Kim 2001: 26ff., fig. 3–4 to 24). Then Mr Kim had to map several dozen points in order to fit the garment and let it move over the body (Kim 2001: 42ff, figs 3–25 to 36). The result is Ashurnasirpal walking across his throne room for the first time in 2870 years. Learning Sites adapted this model of Ashurnasirpal for the PC and has him climbing on to his throne base (fig. 24-l). The PC version can be viewed on the North-West Palace web page at http://www.learningsites.com/NWP_ThRm_renders.html, and the Onyx 2 model on the UB Virtual Site Museum web page (see below).

Eventually we will program the king and his attendants (these kinds of figures are called intelligent agents) to answer questions in conversation with the program users in order to teach certain ideas about this palace, its history, architecture and decoration and thus the history of Assyria. We have been testing an avatar, which is a figure that represents the user of the model, that is, one of us

Fig. 24-l. Throne room, showing the king mounting his throne. (Image copyright 2002 and reprinted courtesy of Learning Sites, Inc.)

visiting the palace (http://www.classics.buffalo.edu/htm/ UBVirtualSiteMuseum/samplesMain.htm).

Linking text, image databases and natural language interfaces to the architecture via an avatar and intelligent agents and in text-only modes will allow users to move freely and communicate 'with' the virtual palace environment. Users will be able to access oral information in conversation with the intelligent agents or study background informational text and images. The intelligent agents will be programmed with longer and shorter pieces describing and analysing the bas-reliefs, the palace, the excavation, Assyria and its empire in Ashurnasirpal's time and other objects within the virtual world. The intelligent agents will have the ability to answer a series of typical questions usually asked by students, teachers and scholars, based on the text materials, and following a script that will introduce students to Assyrian court protocol. We are working cross-platform, so that individuals can use our project in a university super-computer setting or on their own PCs. If successful, it would be a good model for other similar projects in digital archaeology around the world.

Much of what we have done with the painting is in its preliminary stages. There are two aspects of this part of our study. First we must consider all the examples of the painted plaster and brick and try to reconstruct the nature of the decorations that accompany the carvings as best we can, and second the paint residues on the carved bas-relief must be analysed. For example, some of the problems we have considered but have not solved are the decorations

Fig. 24-m. View towards B-13. (Image copyright 2002 and reprinted courtesy of Learning Sites, Inc.)

above the figures of the king and the sacred tree behind the throne ((fig. 24-m); B-23) and across from the central doorway ((fig. 24-n); B-13). Richard Sobolewski suggested once, in his paper for the Charles Wilkinson conference at the Metropolitan Museum, that the arched niche decoration finished in the painting of a brick arch above both these scenes and that the scene was visible through the central doorway from the great northern courtyard, a theme which we have discussed elsewhere (Sobolewski 1981a: 253; Paley and Sobolewski 1997: 332–33). What kind of decoration could there have been in the space within the arch above the relief? Perhaps it was the king in a war chariot with his attendants? I hypothesize this because in Donald Wiseman's Nimrud field notebook of 1951—a xerox of which Julian Reade sent me some time ago—is mentioned a piece of brick with a chariot wheel and human figure painted on it; it was discovered at the foot of B-23.

Concerning the painting of the relief work itself, Elizabeth Hendrix has been collecting paint residue samples from Ashurnasirpal II bas-reliefs in US collections. On the basis of her preliminary results, and comparison with the paintings from Til Barsip, we have begun the process of colouring the bas-reliefs. One test was made for a recent Williams College exhibition (fig. 24-o). It begins to help us understand how colourful the palace may have been in antiquity. Colouring the bas-relief also helps us see the whole relief much more clearly. We think that this is an important exercise as it is likely that Layard's observation that 'the sculptured reliefs were merely subservient to the colour laid upon them' (Larsen 1996: 104–5) is correct, and that colouring them will perhaps provide us with a more real sense of what these rooms looked like to the Assyrians as finished products. Hopefully soon we will be able to update the images to

reflect more of Dr Hendrix's findings and, if possible, collect other tests to expand the results of her sampling. We are using her test results as a guide. Colour is very difficult to reproduce. The tables from Dr Hendrix's report (consolidated into one table here, Table I) identify hematite as red pigment on a sandal, bone or charcoal as the black on tassels, and on a belt and armband of a human-headed genius in Williams College. Red ochre on a vertical line at the edge of the slab, and perhaps black on a feather, but certainly on the sandal strap, are the colour remains on the bird-headed genius in the same collection. Hematite and charcoal for red and black, raw sienna for brown, cinnabar for red and cobalt for blue have been identified on bas-reliefs in the Metropolitan Museum and bone and cinnabar for black and red have been found on the bas-reliefs at Yale Art Gallery. What is interesting and as yet unexplained is the presence of barium and zinc in addition to calcium and sulphur in the white pigment, which may identify the nineteenth century pigment 'lithopone'. This study is really just beginning. It has also to be reconciled with other tests that have been made in other museums of the paint residues and other records (Curtis and Reade 1995: 217, 219, figs 245, 248; Russell 1999; Tomabechi 1986).

In conclusion, we continue to question and investigate aspects of the building structure, bas-relief attachment and light, natural light and manufactured lighting—a big problem and one we hope new lighting software will help us test. So far we can only go back to the fourteenth century AD for the position of sunlight at Nimrud. We also have to take into account drains in the floors, roof drains, and brick sizes and interior and exterior surface material. Because of the possibilities that digital technology brings, we are now in the process of adding a database with digital images of all the decorations on the

Northwest Palace, Nimrud
Entry ED, view into Throne Room
© 2002 Learning Sites, Inc.

Fig. 24-n. View through centre doorway of the throne room façade. (Image copyright 2002 and reprinted courtesy of Learning Sites, Inc.)

Fig. 24-o. Room F, partially painted. (Image copyright 2000 and reprinted courtesy of Learning Sites, Inc.)

garments of the figures in the palace. If we can manage it, this will be the largest database of the images etched on garments that we will have. The technology will allow us to study these images together or separately, by place where they are found—sleeve, hem, chest, on bucket and so forth—and by type of image, to compare and contrast them and perhaps to arrive at theories about why certain images appear in certain places on the garments of these figures.

In the end we hope that the visitor to the VR space will be able to experience the whole palace as one building and learn more about it than we could possibly teach in an exhibit or normal book layout.

Table I: ANP II NW Palace pigment distribution

Location	human-headed genius	bird-headed genius	eunuch
Room F, black on sandal		**bone** or charcoal (W)	
black on feather	bone?		
Room G, red on sandal	hematite (W)		
black on tassel	bone or **charcoal** (W)		
black on belt	bone + charcoal (W)		
black on tassel	bone (W)		
black armband	bone (W)		
red on sandal			cinnabar (M)
black on sandal			bone + charcoal (M)
red on sandal			hematite (M)
blue on feather	cobalt-modern (M)		
red/brn on thumb		cinnabar (Y)	
ground for tree		calcium carbonate (Y)	
Room L, red on sandal	hematite (M)		
black on sandal	bone or **charcoal** (M)		
Room S, red on sandal	hematite (M)		
red on sandal	cinn. or hematite (Y)		
red on sandal	cinnabar (Y)		
black on sandal		charcoal (M)	
black on sandal	bone or charcoal (Y)		
black on sandal	bone or charcoal (Y)		
white eyeball	*calcium sulfate (Y)		
white eyeball	*calcium sulfate (Y)		
Room T, brown on leg	raw sienna (M)		
red on sandal	cinnabar (M)		
black on sandal	**bone** or charcoal (M)		

n.b. The calcium sulfate may derive from the gypsum substrate rather than an applied pigment.

(W, M, Y = current collection, respectively Williams College Museum of Art, The Metropolitan Museum of Art, Yale University Art Gallery)

Notes for Table I

*Sample Collection:
The surface of each relief was examined with focused illumination and low (x4) magnification for evidence of pigments. Observations of colors that appeared distinct from the substrate stone and sufficiently distant from areas of restoration to avoid confusion with modern materials, were noted on photocopies of black-and-white 8×10 photographs of each relief. A few particles of color were removed from design elements on which pigments were relatively well-preserved. A scalpel fitted with a No.15 blade was used to scrape the particles from the surface onto a leaf of glassine, a procedure carried out under low magnification to ensure that as little substrate as possible was removed with the sample. These samples were placed in appropriately-labeled glass vials and the sample location noted on the photocopy.

Sample Preparation:
This phase of the project was carried out in the Sherman Fairchild Center for Objects Conservation at The Metropolitan Museum of Art, and at the Center for Materials Research in Archaeology and Ethnology at the Massachusetts Institute of Technology.

In the conservation laboratories each sample was tapped out onto a glass microscope slide. Another slide was placed on top and gently pressed down in order to crush the sample and separate individual pigment particles. Under the low-power magnification of a binocular microscope ($\times$10–$\times$40) a scalpel with No.11 blade was used to coax representative pigment particles onto a clean glass slide labeled with the accession number of the relief and the sample number. The macroscopically-observed color was also written on the slide label, with a space below it for microscopic optical identification. A coverslip prepared with a solidified droplet of mounting medium (Aroclor, refractive index 1.662, in the case of the Williams and Metropolitan Museum samples, Cargille, refractive index 1.662, in the case of the Yale samples) was placed on top of the pigment particles in order to seal them and provide an environment with known refractive index with which to contrast the particles.

Sample Identification:
With the high magnification ($\times$100–$\times$400) of a polarizing light microscope it is possible to observe the morphology and optical properties of mineral pigments, often with enough certainty to make a positive identification. Size, shape, aspect ratio (long vs. short axis), color in plane-polarized light, color with polarizing filters crossed, refractive index relative to the mounting medium, and presence of associated minerals, are the variables that combine to form a characteristic "package" of properties for each pigment. This procedure is known as polarizing light microscopy (PLM).

In the case of the project at hand, a table was made with rows for each of these variables and a column was established for each sample. This prompted me to treat each sample in the same way, and enabled me to make comparisons between particular samples more readily.

In addition to PLM, two samples from The Metropolitan Museum reliefs were analyzed by Mark Wypyski in the Sherman Fairchild Center of Objects Conservation at the Museum. The technique he used was SEM/EDS (scanning electron microscope [SEM] equipped with an energy dispersive X-ray spectrometer [EDS]. See Hendrix 2001, pp. 55–56 for a description of the techniques of PLM and SEM/EDS).

His analysis confirmed the presence of the element cobalt in the blue sample from MMA 32.143.6. According to Wypyski (personal communication 5 September 2001), the high percent of iron in the red pigment from the same relief suggests it is hematite rather than red ochre.

25   THE DECOR OF THE THRONE ROOM OF THE PALACE OF ASHURNASIRPAL*

Michael Roaf

The talk that I gave at the Nimrud conference was not intended for publication: at the request of the organizers I have submitted the following text, but the reader should be aware that further research may invalidate the suggestions outlined here. My thanks are due to the organizers of the conference and the editors of the proceedings. I am also grateful to the many scholars who have offered useful comments and especially to Sam Paley who also provided reconstructed illustrations of the Throne Room which I showed at the meeting.

One of the most remarkable features of the North-West Palace constructed early in his reign by Ashurnasirpal II on the citadel of Kalhu is the extensive relief sculpture on the walls. The most frequently illustrated of these reliefs show small scale narrative scenes of hunting or warfare, that were in the Throne Room and in one or two rooms in the West Wing (Curtis and Reade 1995: 44–55). The vast majority of the reliefs found in the palace, however, show large scale scenes of supernatural beings such as winged genies, sacred trees and colossi with animal bodies.

Julian Reade (1979: 28–29) classified the subjects of Assyrian wall decoration in five categories: narrative, formal, apotropaic, ornamental and hieroglyphic. Formal scenes (large scale scenes) may also have narrative content, as for example in the procession of tributaries on the outer wall of the Throne Room (D and E). All the rooms of the palace have some 'apotropaic' imagery, in which supernatural beings not only ward off evil (apotropaic *sensu stricto*) but also encourage good to enter: several contain exclusively apotropaic content while the other rooms also include occasional depictions of the king and his courtiers or servants. This is in contrast to later Assyrian palaces where such supernatural images are confined to the façades, to the jambs of doorways, and to the occasional corner.

Of all the many supernatural images available to the Assyrian designers only a limited range were used in the North-West Palace. Six-curled heroes (*lahmu*), lion demons, scorpion men, etc., were not chosen, while the winged genies and sacred trees typical of the North-West Palace (fig. 23-c) appear in diminishing numbers in Sargon's Palace at Khorsabad and Sennacherib's South-West Palace in Nineveh and are completely absent in the motifs found on the walls of the latest Assyrian palaces.

There are a number of different versions of winged genies on the walls of the palace: some have human heads either with a diadem or a horned cap and some have bird heads (see figs 23-e–g, i–j). These can be identified as the divine sages known as *apkallu*, and figurines of these sages were buried in the doorways and in the corners of rooms to keep out evil and to allow good to enter the building (Curtis and Reade 1995: 57–60, 112–15; cf. fig. 7-c). Texts describe these figures as having bird, fish, or human heads and as carrying a variety of objects, most commonly a *mullilu*, 'cleaner, or purifier' and a *banduddû*, 'a bucket': these can be identified with the pine cone-like object and bucket carried by many of the winged genies.

In Mesopotamian religious belief, the *apkallu* were responsible for transmitting divine wisdom to mankind and for 'ensuring the correct plans of heaven and earth' (Parpola 1993a: XX). The most famous of these divine sages was the proverbially wise Adapa. Their successors were the *ummiānu* or scholars at the king's court as is shown by a Hellenistic text from Uruk, which listed kings from before the flood with their sages (*apkallu*) and later kings with their scholars (*ummiānu*). These scholars were not only scribes but also experts in a number of disciplines including astrology, divination, exorcism, and medicine (Parpola 1993a). The *ummiānu* were responsible for overseeing the relationship of the king with the gods and in particular for the determining rituals needed to protect the person of the king. The presence of the divine sages on the walls of the palace was perhaps a reflection of the important role that the human sages played within the walls of the palace.

Another rather remarkable feature of the North-West Palace is the fact that on almost every stone slab an inscription was carved: on blank slabs, between the registers on two register reliefs, and even across the middle of the full-size reliefs. This is the so-called Standard Inscription, which begins with the name and titles of the king, continues with a summary of his military successes followed by another list of titles, and ends with an account of the building activities of the king. Irene Winter, in two influential articles, proposed that there was a detailed parallelism between the Standard Inscription and the decoration of the Throne Room of the North-West Palace. In the first of these (1981) she equated the sections of the Standard Inscription with the decoration of the Throne Room.

	Standard Inscription	Throne Room
1	(Palace of) Ashurnasirpal	King on throne
2	Vice-regent of the god Ashur	King flanking tree and Ashur (B-23)
3	Titulary I. attributes (action: consequence)	Hunts and battles: generic attributes (action: consequence) (B-20 to B-17)
4	Annalistic account of specific campaigns	Individual battle sequences (B-11 to B-3)
5	Titulary II. more attributes including 'praiseworthy king'	King seated on throne or standing (Room C-7)
6	Description of building of palace plus tribute received (founding of capital; centre of empire)	Throne Room as a whole, including tribute scenes on Court D and E façade

Parallelism between the Standard Inscription and the decoration of the Throne room according to Winter 1981

Although this scheme has been widely praised and accepted, it is not very convincing. The inscription, it is true, begins with the name of the king and the title *iššakki Aššur*, which is sometimes translated 'vice regent of Ashur' but is perhaps better understood as 'representative or high priest of Ashur'. There is no particular reason, however, to separate the name and the title and to equate one of them with the king on his throne and the other with a repeated image of the king either side of a sacred tree. The remainder of Titulary I consists of epithets stressing the support of the gods, the standard royal titles, the names of the king's father and grandfather, both with the standard royal titles, and a series of epithets describing various qualities of the king. Titulary I is thus not concerned with hunts and includes qualities other than military success. There is no reason to think that the reliefs showing war scenes should be divided into two groups, with B-18 to B-17 illustrating generic attributes and B-11 to B-3 illustrating individual battle sequences. Nor is it clear why Titulary II should be distinguished from Titulary I or why this should refer either to the king on his throne or the relief of the king in Room C, while the four images of the king on the south wall (B-14 to B-12) are ignored. Nor is it clear why the description of Ashurnasirpal's building activities should refer to the Throne Room alone rather than the whole city of Kalhu including the canal system.

> The palace of Ashurnasirpal, vice regent (i.e. chief priest) of Ashur, chosen by the gods Enlil and Ninurta, beloved of the gods Anu and Dagan, destructive weapon of the great gods, strong king, king of the universe, the king of Assyria; son of Tukulti-Ninurta, great king, strong king, king of the universe, the king of Assyria; son of Adad-nirari, also great king, strong king, king of the universe, the king of Assyria; valiant man who acts with the support of Ashur, his lord, and has no rival

among the princes of the four quarters; marvellous shepherd, fearless in battle, mighty flood-tide, which has no opponent; the king, who subdues those insubordinate to him, he who rules all peoples, strong male who treads upon the necks of his foes, trampler of all enemies, he who breaks up the forces of the rebellious, the king who acts with the support of the great gods, his lords, and has conquered all lands, gained dominion over all the highlands and received their tribute; capturer of hostages, he who is victorious over all countries.

The name and first set of titles and epithets of King Ashurnasirpal at the beginning of the Standard Inscription carved on the orthostats of the Throne Room of the North-West Palace (Grayson 1991: A.O. 101.23 lines 1–5a).

For those readers who found her first interpretation unsatisfactory Irene Winter in a second article (1983) proposed more specifically that the reliefs in the Throne Room illustrate the first titles in Titulary II in the Standard Inscription.

	Standard Inscription	Throne Room
1	[I am] Ashurnasirpal,	King on throne
2	attentive prince, worshipper of the great gods,	King in attendance upon the sacred tree and the god Ashur (B-23 and B-13)
3	ferocious dragon,	King as heroic hunter of wild bulls and lions (B-20 and B-19)
4	The conqueror of cities	King as victorious in battle, conqueror of enemy citadels (B-18, B-17 B-11 to B-3, B-27, B-28, etc.)

Parallelism between the beginning of Titulary II in the Standard Inscription and the decoration of the Throne room according to Winter 1983

> [I am] Ashurnasirpal, attentive prince, worshipper of the great gods, ferocious dragon, the conqueror of cities and entire highlands, king of lords, encircler of the obstinate, crowned with splendour, fearless in battle, merciless hero, he who stirs up strife, praiseworthy king, shepherd, protection of the (four) quarters, the king whose command disintegrates mountains and seas, the one who by his lordly conflict has brought under one authority ferocious (and) merciless kings from east to west .

The name and second set of titles and epithets of King Ashurnasirpal in the Standard Inscription carved on the orthostats of the Throne Room of the North-West Palace (Grayson 1991: A.)O. 101.23 lines 12b–14a).

This, too, does not work: the association of the title 'ferocious dragon' (*u-šúm-gal-lu ek-du*) with hunting is not attested. In fact the Concise Dictionary of Akkadian translates *u-šúm-gal-lu* not only as 'great dragon, snake' but also as 'monarch, sole ruler' noting that it is the epithet of deities and kings. Furthermore there is no reason why the reliefs should be equated with the first three-and-a-half of the 15 epithets or titles in the second group listed in the Standard Inscription between the account of Ashurnasirpal's military campaigns and his building activities. Surely the first group was more significant. Why should two different titles ('attentive prince', 'worshipper of the great gods') refer to a single image, while only the first half of the title 'conqueror of cities and entire highlands' be considered significant? Why are the remaining titles and epithets ignored? Furthermore not all the subjects of the reliefs are included in either of these schemes. The supernatural figures by the doors, the trees in the corners, and most of the scenes in Room C have been left out.

Nevertheless, even if there is no exact correspondence between the Standard Inscription and the subjects of the reliefs, there is a general similarity of content, which may be explained by the fact that the scholars not only composed the texts but also contributed to the visual decoration of the Throne Room.

The Standard Inscription contributed more materially to the decoration of the Throne Room in another way. It is carved on all the orthostats. The carving of the Standard Inscription over the reliefs is rather like the way that cylinder seals were rolled over tablets conferring authority to them, giving as one might say the 'seal of approval'. The inscription was often carved straight over—or more exactly into—the relief, showing that the presence of the inscription was more important than the visibility of the relief. Sometimes, but not always, the inscription avoided some parts of the figures, such as fringes of the robes, rosettes on bracelets, fingernails, decorated chapes of the king's sword sheath, or palmettes and tendrils of the sacred tree. In exceptional cases the inscription avoided also the incised designs on the figures, such as the winged disc on a genie's bucket. When the Standard Inscription was carved on detailed bits of carving such as the feathers on the wings of the genies, the result is that both the relief and the inscription are difficult to decipher. Similarly when partially obliterated by the Standard Inscription, the incised designs are almost impossible to reconstruct. What seems to have been important was not that the texts or the images could be easily read or understood by later observers, but that they had been made and were present in the palace.

Larger scale images of the king were placed on the axes of the Throne Room as they were in the other rooms of the palace. Elsewhere in the palace the king was shown flanked by members of his court or by winged genies, but in the Throne Room there are two reliefs showing the king either side of a sacred tree, one opposite the central entrance and the other in the middle of the south wall behind the king's throne (here flanked by the king and his weapon bearer). A further standing figure of the king was carved on the main axis in Room C at the far end of the Throne Room.

Even though placed on the axes, reconstructions by Sam Paley and Donald Sanders show that the reliefs would not have been easy to recognize. The scenes showing the king would not have made much impression on a visitor coming from the bright sunlight of the courtyard into the dark interior of the Throne Room. Even had the reliefs been painted in bright colours (perhaps with the garments of the king a distinct colour such as purple), the relatively small size of the figures in relation to the height of the room and the gloom that must have ruled in the room would have made the reliefs extremely difficult to appreciate even with the aid of clerestory lighting or oil lamps. Looking from the throne westwards towards the axial image of the king in Room C, the size of the room and the winged bulls flanking the entry from Room B into Room C would have been much more dominant than the more distant image of the king. In this case too it seems that the important point was that the representation of the king was in a significant location and not that it made a stunning visual impression on the observer.

Slabs B-13, the central panel on the south wall of the Throne Room, and B-23, the corresponding scene on the east wall behind the throne dais, are emphasized not only by their central position but also by being carved within stepped niches raised above the floor. The distinction between the central scene and figures on the adjacent blocks was also marked by the way that the surface of the stone outside the niche is left roughly hewn. One unsatisfactory effect of placing the scene in a niche is that those of the less important kings, which were carved to the full height of slabs B-14 and B-12 to the left and right, are larger than those on slab B-13. Had it been intended to make the central figures of the king dominant, a taller stone orthostat could have been used so that the scenes of the tree, the god in a winged disc, the kings and the genies would have been more impressive.

One of the most curious features of these scenes is that the Assyrian king is shown twice even though there was only one Assyrian king. Such a repetition is not common in earlier Mesopotamian art and when it occurred as on the wall plaque of Ur-Nanshe from Tello or the stele of Ur-Namma from Ur, the king was involved in different activities. A closer parallel is the symbol socle of Tukulti-Ninurta I from the Ishtar Temple in Ashur, where the two images of the king standing and kneeling are normally interpreted as indicating motion.

Repetition was clearly thought of as effective in the art of the Ancient Near East and is frequently found from the

Uruk period onwards. Also important in Assyrian art was the desire for symmetrical compositions (Albenda 1998). Symmetrical compositions are common both on Middle and Late Assyrian seals; and indeed repeated images on a seal impression can create an apparently symmetrical arrangement.

Symmetry is also evident in the figures protecting doorways which we know, from royal inscriptions, were also used in the Middle Assyrian period. In these cases the figures are shown from both sides through a combination of reversal (seeing the figures from the other side) and reflection (substituting left for right as in a mirror) (Roaf 1983: 60). A possible reason for such repetition might have been so that both sides were visible and nothing was left in the dangerous darkness of the wall.

A different explanation for the two kings was proposed by Burchard Brentjes (1994). He suggested that they are not two images of Ashurnasirpal, but instead represent his father and his grandfather and that differences between the two, such as the position of the mace, the left arm, and the ends of the diadems, which on the left king end in tassels and on the right in a straight fringe, indicate that they were different individuals. Similarly the incised rosettes on the hems of the left hand king's tunic have 8 petals and of the right hand 16 radiating lines. There are other discrepancies not recorded by Brentjes, for example, the ties hanging down from the tunic neck have different forms, the strands of the necklaces in one case are close together and in the other separated and have double not single spacer beads, and the numbers of incised lines above the beard and hair curls vary. There are other variations in the headdress, the armlets, and bracelets. Furthermore the right king points upwards while the left king points straight ahead.

Such small differences are not confined to the kings, but are also present on the genies as well as on the tree in the middle. For example, the positions of the arms and cones and the lengths of the wings of the genies are not identical. The surface of the left hand bucket, unlike the right hand one, was covered with a mat design with a symmetrical handle, and the bracelets also differ. Similarly the carving of the two sides of the tree show marked differences in the palmettes and spirals.

Most of these differences clearly result from different craftsmen working on the left and right sides of the relief, and cannot be used as evidence that the kings on the left and on the right represented different individuals.

The interpretation of these central scenes has exercised the imaginations of many scholars, but there is no general consensus. The winged genies are *apkallu* warding off evil and letting good come in. The kings wear the long shawl wound round their bodies indicating that they are involved in religious activity and may be carrying out

their role as *iššakku* or high priest (vice-regent) of the god Ashur. The interpretation of the sacred tree, however, is not so simple and there is probably no single explanation which explains all the occurrences of the tree in the North-West Palace.

Sacred trees were shown flanked by kings in the Throne Room and by various supernatural genies in other rooms; they were placed in the corners of the rooms and below the niches or air vents in the palace and, as John Russell (1998) has stressed, in such positions the trees have an apotropaic function. The location of the Assyrian trees and their association with supernatural beings justify the use of the term 'sacred tree' rather than the less loaded term 'stylized tree': the term 'tree of life', however, with its rich connotations in biblical literature and in other cultures is not applicable to the Assyrian sacred trees.

Scenes with sacred trees flanked by genies or by the king were also incised on the reliefs of the North-West Palace on garments of the king and of other figures, as well as on various objects such as buckets, sheaths and quivers. Outside the North-West Palace sacred trees are less common. One appears in a glazed brick panel from Fort Shalmaneser together with kings and god as in the Throne Room reliefs. There are a few on the reliefs in Sargon's palace at Khorsabad, normally in the corners of rooms. Sacred trees were also depicted on the garments of later kings and their close attendants. Furthermore sacred trees were often shown on Assyrian cylinder seals, some similar in form to those in the North-West Palace and others very differently stylized (Parpola 1993b). The essential central part of the sacred tree is a palmette on a stalk: the place of the sacred tree on the Black Stone of Lord Aberdeen is taken by a palmette on prisms of Esarhaddon (Roaf and Zgoll 2001), and on incised drawings in the North-West Palace the sacred tree is often replaced by a palmette on a stalk.

Some scholars have suggested that the tree was essentially a symbol of fertility or fecundity or prosperity, but such an interpretation ignores its evident apotropaic function (Porter 1993; Albenda 1994). A recent ingenious suggestion by Seth Richardson (1999–2001) that the trees in the North-West Palace can be identified with deceased rulers in the Assyrian king list arranged in two series and with different 'dynasties' in different rooms, is not convincing and does not explain the presence of the tree between two kings or genies or the location of the trees in the corners.

Simo Parpola's theory (1993b) that the tree embodies the secret wisdom of the Assyrian theologians has not found much favour amongst scholars, but nevertheless a religious interpretation is likely. In a study of the symbols on the Black Stone of Esarhaddon, Annette Zgoll and I developed the proposal of Irving Finkel and Julian Reade (1996) that the symbols called hieroglyphic by Reade and astroglyphic by Roaf and Zgoll (2001), correspond to the cuneiform signs used to write the name and titles of the king, with the top line being interpreted as 'Esarhaddon, king' and the bottom line as 'of the land of Assyria, king of the four quarters'. In this interpretation the first three signs are used to write the name of Esarhaddon, *Aššur-ahu-iddina*, meaning 'the god Ashur has given a brother', with the divine headdress on a pedestal corresponding to Ashur, the king shown as the high priest of Ashur corresponding to the sign *PAB* used to write the word *ahu* 'brother' and the sacred tree corresponding to the sign *AŠ* for the verb *nadānu*, 'to give'. The tree appears twice on this monument, once as an individual symbol and once on the pedestal on which the horned headdress rests. Since the horned headdress is an emblem for Ashur in Assyria and, since the god's name may also be written with the sign *AŠ*, there is a double connection of the sacred tree with Ashur, the chief god of Assyria.

In scenes with a sacred tree the god in the winged disc is sometimes replaced with a plain winged disc. The winged disc was normally a symbol for Shamash, the god of justice and the sun god, but it is possible that it may also stand for Ashur, who is described as having the attributes of different Assyrian gods. Since the finger of one king points to the god in the disc and the other to the tree, it is possible that they are both the objects of worship of the king and that, as on the Black Stone, the king is shown in his most important role as high priest under the protection of the chief god of Assyria. In such an interpretation it is difficult to decide whether the tree should be taken as a substitute for Ashur or just as a suitable emblem for the god.

Such a scene with images of the gods flanked by images of the king may be compared with the reliefs at Malthai or Bavian, where the Assyrian king Sennacherib is depicted twice, once in front facing the anthropomorphic divine images and once behind them. If the Throne Room reliefs are also to be interpreted as the king flanking images of

the gods, one may ask why avian and arborial representations of the gods were used instead of the normal anthropomorphic deities, as for example in the wall painting in the audience hall of Residence K at Khorsabad. A possible answer might be the position of the relief behind the king's throne. In this position the king, when he was sitting on his throne, visually occupied the central part of the scene, obscuring and replacing the tree and the god in the winged disc. In Rooms F, G, H and N, too, the king is placed between winged genies in the position normally occupied by the stylized tree.

Such variations suggest a parallelism between the sacred tree and the king, and it may be no coincidence that in the astroglyphic inscriptions of Esarhaddon the palm tree stands for the word king in the title 'king of the four quarters', and that one of the pair of beautiful pendants found in Tomb II at Nimrud has a sacred tree and the other has a palm tree. Such relationships between sacred trees, palmettes, and palm trees make it difficult to distinguish the various interpretations whether royal or divine or to assign a unique meaning to these symbols. One should perhaps not expect this religious imagery to correspond in a one-to-one way with concepts known from textual sources, but rather one should accept that the interpretation of the symbols varied according to the contexts in which they were used.

In the specific interpretation proposed in the paper presented to the Nimrud conference, the central scene of the Throne Room illustrates the king's primary role as representative of the god Ashur. At the same time directly behind the king are the divine sages, who through their intervention protect the king from evil. These sages were also responsible for conveying the wisdom of the gods to mankind through the scholars who served the king and thus these reliefs may also indicate the important role of esoteric wisdom in the design of the palace of Ashurnasirpal.

ADDENDUM MARCH 2008

U. Seidl and W. Sallberger, 'Der "Heilige Baum" ', *Archiv für Orientforschung* 51 (2005–6), pp. 54–74.

M. Giovino, *The Assyrian sacred tree: a history of interpretations* (Orbis biblicus et orientalis 230, Fribourg 2007).

A. Shafer, 'Assyrian royal monuments on the periphery: ritual and the making of imperial space', in J. Cheng and M.H. Feldman (eds.), *Ancient Near Eastern Art in Context. Studies in Honor of Irene J. Winter by Her Students* (Culture and History of the Ancient Near East 26, Leiden and Boston), pp.133–59.

26 NIMRUD IN THE CONTEXT OF NEO-ASSYRIAN POTTERY STUDIES*

Arnulf Hausleiter

The Neo-Assyrian site and its pottery

The question from which vessels the 69,574 guests drank when the newly erected North-West Palace of king Ashurnasirpal II was inaugurated at Kalhu in the seventies of the ninth century BC, or whether only the 47,074 'men (and) women who were invited from every part of my land' were drinking from pottery vessels has not been investigated so far, though it might turn out to be interesting.[1] However, pottery studies, even in sites with such an array of monumental remains as Nimrud, have proven extremely important, well beyond simple comparison with textual evidence. On the following pages we shall deal with the Neo-Assyrian[2] pottery corpus from the site which was excavated by the British School of Archaeology in Iraq between 1949 and 1963. A certain part of it is today exhibited or stored in the British Museum. The latter also conducted a season of excavation at Nimrud in 1989 producing a set of pottery vessels. Therefore, seen from the viewpoint of pottery studies, it is most appropriate that both institutions are the organizers of the present conference.

As in the past, Neo-Assyrian pottery from Nimrud is also nowadays mainly considered as relevant for the chronology of the Neo-Assyrian ceramics as part of the material culture in general. One can still say without exaggeration that Nimrud in this respect is used as a chrono-typological backbone for Assyria and partly beyond. More interesting questions, such as distribution patterns within the site and its buildings or how to trace the relationship between the political development of the Neo-Assyrian empire and the ceramic production at Nimrud have not been posed at all.

This article offers a brief review of the discovery and context of the Neo-Assyrian pottery from Nimrud and its potential for the discussion for Iron Age ceramics. In the second part, we discuss the role of those finer fabrics from Nimrud, which are labelled 'Palace Ware'.

History of pottery studies at Nimrud

As a result of the research aims in the early and pioneering days of the mid-nineteenth century when excavations in Assyria started, pottery was at that time not recorded at all.[3] This situation affects the pottery record from the Assyrian capitals and those sites of lesser rank in Northern Mesopotamia which were excavated at that time.

Looking at the long history of exploration of Nimrud,[4] at the earliest a little more than 100 years after the first general excavations in 1845, an interest in pottery can be attested for the first time. Preliminary excavation reports started to contain detailed information about single items of pottery. Still today these reports serve as an indispensable source of information about location, findspot and, sometimes, context of most of the vessels discovered. Additionally, a number of articles about pottery were published as early as 1954, such as the contribution of P.S. Rawson on 'Palace Wares' and the two articles by Joan Oates on pottery from the private houses in TW53 and from Fort Shalmaneser (the latter published in 1959).[5] Mallowan's publication from 1966 offered an eclectic summary of the information on pottery already given in the preliminary reports. He focussed on the so-called 'Palace Ware', mainly from the Governor's and North-West Palaces,[6] and the ram-headed rhyton.[7] However, he clearly recognized and underlined the value of the Nimrud pottery corpus for the dating of any pottery from

---

* I would like to thank the organizers of the Nimrud conference for the invitation to this remarkable event, in particular Dr John Curtis. I am grateful to Dr Anthony Green for correcting my English and for further suggestions.

[1] Information from the 'banquet stela' of king Ashurnasirpal II which was discovered by Mallowan in room EA of the North-West Palace; cf. Grayson 1991: 293 (A.0.101.30, lines 141ff).

[2] The chronological term 'Neo-Assyrian' covers the period between the rise of the Neo-Assyrian empire until its fall, i.e. a period of about 400 years from the tenth century BC until the end of the seventh century BC. This term is based on knowledge of historical events. 'Late Assyrian' is used alternatively, but often (as in the case of 'spätassyrisch') refers to the 'Sargonid' period, this is basically the seventh century BC; cf. Hausleiter 1997: 271, n. 2; 1999b: 132, fig. 2; cf. Miglus et al. 2000: 51, Anhang A. Although there is an ongoing discussion of the internal division of the chronological entity 'Iron Age', there are three phases which can be identified; cf. Lebeau 1983: 21–26; Bernbeck 1993: 120; Parker 2002: 376, note 1; for a slightly different view, cf. Jamieson 2000: 264, Tab. 1.

[3] Cf. the statement of M.T. Larsen quoted by Jamieson 2000: 259.

[4] For a detailed overview, cf. still Postgate and Reade 1980; see also Larsen 1996: 70–78, 206–14. Now Oates and Oates 2001: 1–11. Cf. Reade, Green, J. Oates, this volume.

[5] Rawson 1954; Lines 1954; Oates 1959.

[6] Mallowan 1966: 50–51, figs 13–17; 178–80, figs 110–14.

[7] Mallowan 1966: 190–93, fig. 124; cf. Curtis 2000: 195–96; see also Curtis and Green 1997: 16–18.

other Neo-Assyrian sites.[8] After an interruption of 27 years, newly excavated pottery was published following the British Museum's excavations in room T20 of Fort Shalmaneser in 1989.[9] The first colour photographs of Neo-Assyrian pottery from Mallowan's and the Oates' excavations at Nimrud appeared in 1995, some of them presenting previously unpublished material.[10] Some years later, I gave a summary of the Neo-Assyrian pottery recorded from Nimrud including the pottery from the Polish excavations in the 'Central Building' on the main mound.[11] At about the same time some photographs with jars from royal tomb II in the North-West palace were published,[12] as well as two small glazed jars from tomb IV[13] and a vessel composed of nine bowls from the vaulted area in the North-West Palace.[14] Finally, a chapter in Joan and David Oates' book on Nimrud is dedicated to the pottery record from the site;[15] single findspots of pottery, however, are discussed within the relevant architectural context.

The bulk of the ceramics which have been published with descriptive details on fabric and typical morphological comparisons were discovered in the TW53 houses and in Fort Shalmaneser. The vessels are mainly made of a common ware fabric but some 'Palace Ware' objects were present as well. Curiously, the much praised assemblage from Room S in the Governor's Palace[16] was never published in a similar way. As to the context, the 'Private Houses' belonged to wealthy merchants of the seventh century BC, one of them named Šamaš-šarru-uṣur. By far the greatest quantity of pottery came from Fort Shalmaneser, the *ekal mašarti* of the Assyrian capital. Apparently, the circumstances of the excavations, the size of the vessels and possibly also the format of the journal *Iraq* prevented the depiction of section-drawings of large storage jars from the magazine-rooms in the North-West Palace and the temple of Ninurta, some of them bearing inscriptions indicating the quantity of the content.[17] The same is valid for the containers in the so-called 'wine cellar' of Fort Shalmaneser, Room SW6.[18] Many of them,

however, can be recognized in photos and plans.[19] Overwhelmingly, the published plates show rather handsome bowls, jars, beakers, goblets, etc. Large 'torpedo-shaped' jars were published in 1954 and 1989.

In addition to the ceramics from the above-mentioned findspots, pottery from the Burnt Palace, the Temple of Nabû and the 1950 building on the main mound and the area of the Town Wall Palace east of it were also mentioned.[20] However, a number of findspots apparently cannot be located precisely any more.[21] The unbalanced relationship between published Neo-Assyrian pottery from Nimrud and the comparatively large number of findspots is illustrated here by two plans indicating the rooms or areas where pottery has been recorded and published (figs 26-a and 26-b).

The remaining sherds and vessels from the British excavations are still under study and not yet published. An increase in available material may be expected from the publication of a completed pottery catalogue. In recent years the open access policy of the British Museum, the present holder of most of the Nimrud pottery outside Iraq[22], has allowed study of the material by interested scholars.

The significance of the site of Nimrud for Neo-Assyrian pottery studies

As a result of the increasing number of archaeological activities, such as surface surveys and excavations, in the area of the Assyrian provinces or beyond, where Iron Age or Neo-Assyrian sites and material have been discovered,[23] a renewed interest in the Neo-Assyrian ceramics from Nimrud can be observed. Meanwhile, additional material from previous excavations at other sites in Assyria proper, such as Tell al Rimah,[24] or excavations in the Assyrian capitals which were carried out in the late 80s of the twentieth century and at the beginning of the third millennium AD,[25] have been published as well. If we compare the pottery from Nimrud

[8] Mallowan 1966: 178; see, however, Oates and Oates 2001: 250–51.

[9] Curtis *et al.* 1993: 28–29; fig. 27.

[10] McDonald 1995.

[11] Hausleiter 1999a.

[12] Damerji 1999: 50 (Arabic pagination: *33), fig. 20.3; 51 (*32), fig. 19.2

[13] Hussein and Suleiman 2000: *431, fig. 213; *432, fig. 214. Further pottery is recorded from tomb no. 1 (*ibid.*: 100), tomb no. II (.: 111), tomb no. III (*ibid.*: 126–28) and tomb IV (*ibid.*: 133).

[14] Hussein and Suleiman 2000: *441, fig. 223.

[15] Oates and Oates 2001: 250–53.

[16] Cf., e.g., Mallowan 1950: 170.

[17] Mallowan 1952: 10; Mallowan 1966: 91.

[18] Mallowan 1958: 107–8.

[19] Cf. Oates and Oates 2001: 108, fig. 65; 110, fig. 66 (temple of Ninurta).

[20] Discussed in Hausleiter 1999a: 19–25.

[21] Such as the spots DE.M. or O.10; cf. McDonald 1995: 153; 159.

[22] Cf. Hausleiter 1999a: 18, n. 11.

[23] Cf. Wilkinson's (2000) map (223, fig. 1) and table (224, table 1); for the excavations at Qal'at 'Ana on the Middle Euphrates cf. Killick 1988: 56–57; for the area of the Upper Tigris cf. Matney et al. 2002.

[24] Cf. Postgate *et al.* 1997: 57.

[25] Green 1999, Lumsden 1999, and other contributions in Hausleiter and Reiche 1999. For Neo-Assyrian pottery from recent excavations at Ashur cf. Miglus *et al.* 2000: 49–50, figs 29–30.

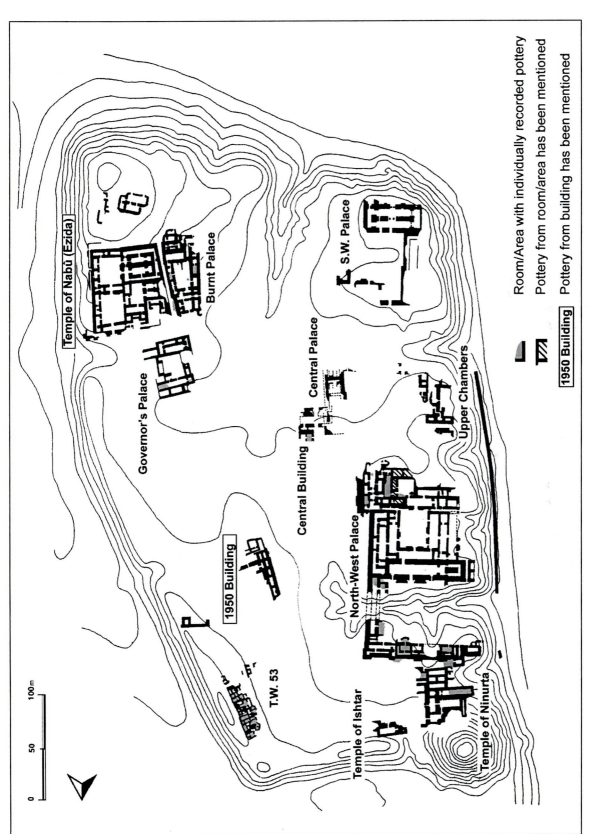

Fig. 26-α. The main mound at Nimrud (after Matthiae 1999: 35) indicating areas from which Neo-Assyrian pottery has been recorded.

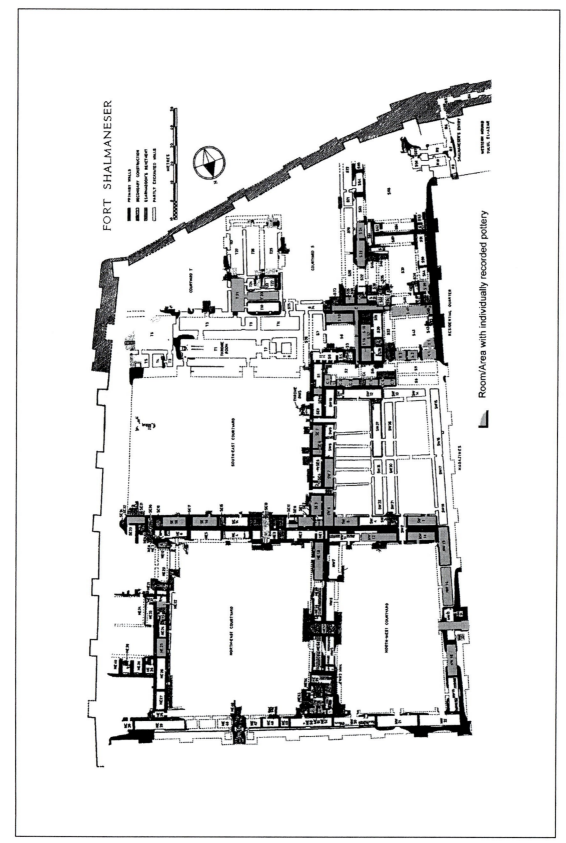

Fig. 26-b. Plan of Fort Shalmaneser (after Mallowan 1966: Plate VIII) indicating areas from which Neo-Assyrian pottery has been recorded.

with ceramics of other Neo-Assyrian sites in terms of quantity, it becomes clear that assemblages from other sites offer a larger corpus (see fig. 26-c). One of the basic problems in compiling data for the table given in fig. 26-c lies in the fact that the most recent publications depict individual vessels whereas earlier works show morphological 'types'. At several sites it remains difficult or it is impossible to establish the exact quantity of the vessels. This is the case with Nimrud. However, from the explanatory information we can get at least approximate information about common or rare vessel types. Finally, fig. 26-c underlines the fact that some of the small rural and sometimes remote sites offer a better potential in terms of quantity.

Apart from the quantitative aspect alone, the role of the site of Nimrud for the study of Neo-Assyrian ceramics can be characterized by the following main points:

Context: So far, the pottery comes exclusively from a context of the residences of the Assyrian elite—though for the most part from a time when the capital had already been transferred to another place. The choice of the term 'Palace Ware'—though one should be more careful with this term nowadays—certainly reflects this association. A probable exception to this context is the so-called 'squatter occupation' in Fort Shalmaneser, if it is not just reused material.

Pottery from the lower town was collected by the Italian expedition by means of surface survey. Similar to other Neo-Assyrian lower town areas (such as at Nineveh or Til Barsip), a mixture of affluent residential buildings and more modest dwelling quarters could be expected at Nimrud, the latter theoretically ascribable to parts of the population of a different social rank. Whether these differences are represented in the pottery record will have to be answered at a later stage. The same goes for the numerous Neo-Assyrian vessels and jars found in graves (either as grave goods, gifts for the gods or remains of the *kispum* ritual).[26]

Production process: No pottery workshop was uncovered at Nimrud by the British excavations, and as to the fabric types represented, there is a general summary based on observations in the 1950s.[27] A detailed fabric analysis of the available material including the application of scientific methods and statistics remains a task for future excavations on the site. Pottery kilns from the Neo-Assyrian period are known from British Museum excavations at Khirbet Qasrij in the Eski-Mosul area and from a pre-Shalmaneser III-context at Ashur.[28] As

Muzahim Mahmud Hussein has informed me, Iraqi archaeologists recently excavated three kilns in the north-eastern part of the citadel of Nimrud. Possibly, a potter's or craftman's quarter can be expected somewhere in the NW of the site, similar to Neo-Assyrian Nineveh, where a high concentration of wasters ('pottery and metal ware') seems to support this hypothesis, suggesting by this a regular serial or mass production.[29] The location of an artisans' quarter in a similar topographical area of a city may be evoked by the term 'Tabira'-gate for the NW part of the site of Ashur, though this term is not linked to the production of pottery.[30] Finally, the term 'Palace Ware', though firstly discovered and identified as 'Assyrian' by Petrie at the site of Tell el-Jemmeh,[31] has been associated at Nimrud with an excellent fine fabric class of beakers and bowls—including finely made rhyta—as well as some other fabric types.[32]

Shapes: As an aim and result of the production process, there are numerous morphological repetitions, so-called 'types',[33] which are significant for the repertoire of Neo-Assyrian pottery at Nimrud. In the seventh century BC, morphological uniformity of Neo-Assyrian pottery is clearly visible at all types of settlement—from small hamlets to Assyrian capitals. It may still be too early for a comparison, but results from Ashur seem to suggest that, apart from these common standards, each of the capitals developed its own pottery 'tradition'. Whereas in Ashur a visible tradition in the pottery from the Middle to the Neo-Assyrian period should be expected, the situation at Nimrud would have to be interpreted as more innovative. But there remains a caveat since this impression may just be due to the deposits reached by excavation. Since the context consists mainly of public buildings it was difficult to establish a stratified and extended pottery sequence where change and continuity of shapes could easily be observed (a deep sounding, similar to the trench at Nineveh, has not been excavated at Nimrud). This is to be considered as one of the key problems of this site. In addition to the assumption that Kalhu was probably a Middle Assyrian provincial capital,[34] and the mention of a Middle Assyrian king Shalmaneser in the texts of Ashurnasirpal II as founder of Kalhu,[35] archaeological remains from the Middle Assyrian period were discovered

---

[26] As for the graves of Ashur cf. Hausleiter 1999b: 141–47.

[27] Lines 1954: 165–67 and Oates 1959: 135–38.

[28] Curtis 1989: 21–22; figs 15, 19b, 20; pls Va; IX; Andrae 1913: 141, fig. 252 and pl. LX,2.

[29] Stronach and Lumsden 1992: 228.

[30] AHw: 1298, s.v. tabiru/a 'Kupferschmied'.

[31] Petrie 1928: 7; 23–24; cf. Mallowan 1950: 170, n. 1.

[32] For the term 'Palace Ware' at Nimrud cf. Rawson 1954 and Oates 1959: 135–36. The term was also used elsewhere, such as for finer fabrics from the palace of Kapara at Tell Halaf: cf. H.F. Schmidt in Oppenheim 1931: 260–61 with Fig. 4 discussing '*Palastware im engeren Sinne*', however without a clear description of the term.

[33] For a critical evaluation of the discussion of 'types' cf. Rice 1987: 274–77; 283–85; 484 (definition); see also Sinopoli 1991: 49–56 and Orton *et al.* 1993: 152–53.

[34] Postgate and Reade 1980: 320.

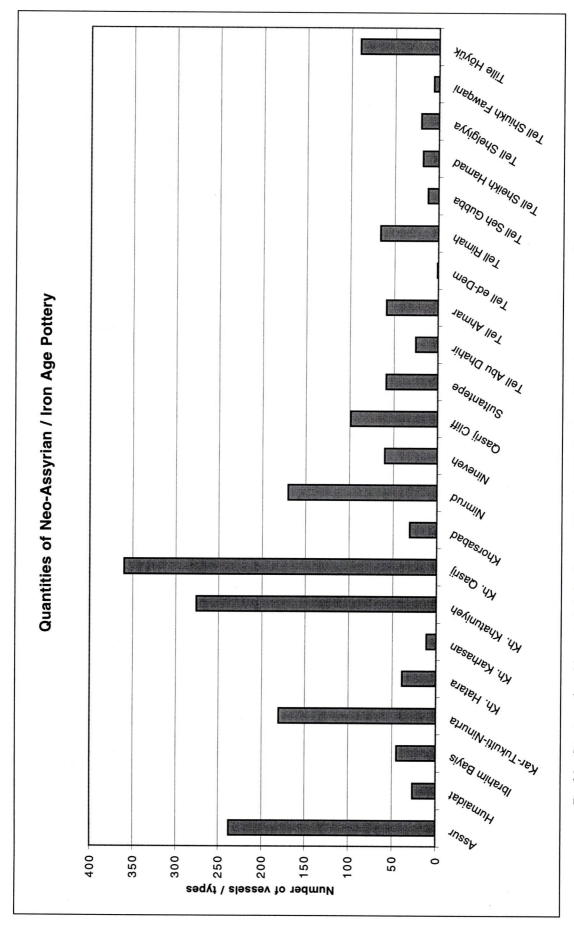

Fig. 26-c. Sites in northern Mesopotamia indicating quantities of published excavated Neo-Assyrian pottery (from Hausleiter in preparation).

in TW53, Room 18[36] in Trench A.49 between TW53 and the 1950 building[37] and in the street between the Temple of Nabû and the Burnt Palace.[38] However, they were not further excavated.

Chronology: The excavated Neo-Assyrian pottery from the site could in theory range from the ninth century down to the end of the seventh/beginning of the sixth century BC, thus covering the rise, peak, fall and aftermath of the Assyrian empire. The situation for the ninth and eighth centuries is hardly clear, since no stratified deposits from these centuries have been analysed together with the pottery record. However, it would not at all be surprising, if the amount of eighth or even ninth century material should later increase at a site which was at its peak in these earlier centuries of Neo-Assyrian rule.[39] This, however, would not be in the palaces or public buildings, not even in private houses, but in streets, pits and wells. So far, the majority of the published pottery from Nimrud can be dated to the late seventh and early sixth centuries BC (fig. 26-e).

On the other hand, for the transition from the Neo-Assyrian to the 'Post-Assyrian' period, Nimrud offers most relevant information: In Fort Shalmaneser, evidence for two post-destruction levels was identified. These 'destruction levels' were ascribed to post-614 and post-612 BC dates. They are associated with the so-called squatter occupation, which is thought to have lasted until *c.* 550 BC, thus covering what is termed the 'Post-Assyrian' period. Even though some contexts would not exclude a pre-seventh century BC date at Nimrud, Joan and David Oates have recently warned us not to expect too much from these contexts.[40] Before, in 1979, it was John Curtis who stated for the chronological analysis of the metal objects, that 'for most of the material from Nimrud we have only a *terminus ante quem* of 614 BC. Although much of it probably is of seventh century date, some of these objects clearly derive from the ninth or eighth centuries. It is unfortunate, then, that we cannot find confirmation of this in the archaeological record'.[41]

Recently, the term 'Post-Assyrian' as applied to remains of the material culture from the period immediately after the fall of the Assyrian empire has been questioned by

Anthony Green.[42] Furthermore, he has convincingly argued against a generally valid differentiation between Neo-Assyrian and Post-Assyrian pottery by means of shapes and/or fabrics. As far as the shapes are concerned, the evidence at Nimrud does not at all point to a visible break. Therefore, we would have to differentiate between 'Neo-Assyrian' as a strictly historical term (ending in 612/610 BC) and 'Neo-Assyrian' as a term for those parts of the material culture which remained unaffected by historical events. Even though one could still label these periods as 'Imperial' and 'Post-Imperial Neo-Assyrian', it seems that the application of the term 'Iron Age' is more appropriate for pottery as an element of the material culture being—in this case—independent from political events.[43]

The Assyrian empire and the distribution of 'Palace Ware'

One result of the Assyrian empire was the rise of a certain widespread unity within Assyrian material culture, even outside the core area. In the arts and elsewhere this tendency reflected not only a clear code of communication but also thought of a cultural identity. As could be shown for the Western provinces, there was a mutual exchange of cultural features between the subdued areas and the Assyrian heartland.[44] Whereas at some provincial sites there are typically 'Assyrian' features at other places the artefacts are described as 'Assyrianizing', or else as imitations or as produced in a provincial style.[45] Recent excavations and surveys in the area north of the heartland at the northern frontier of the Assyrian empire provide additional information in this respect.[46]

As far as pottery is concerned, the 'sherds of the empire'—adapting the title of an article by Reinhard Bernbeck[47]—seem to extend from the heartland to the Euphrates in the West and to the Upper Tigris region in the North.[48] The situation at the southern end seems to be less clear. Sites with an eminent significance within the provincial administration of the Neo-Assyrian empire, such as Tell Sheikh Hamad, Sultantepe or Tell Ahmar/Til Barsip show a typically Assyrian-style pottery

---

[35] Grayson 1991: 222 (A.0.101.1: iii 132b ff.); see also Postgate and Reade 1980: 320.

[36] Cf. Postgate and Reade 1980: 316–17.

[37] Cf. Postgate and Reade 1980: 320.

[38] Postgate and Reade 1980: 320.

[39] Cf. McDonald 1995: 158, with an eighth century BC date for a jar (ND 4023) from the Burnt Palace; for 8th and possibly ninth century BC material from recent excavations and survey at Nineveh cf. the note of Lumdsen 1999: 3.

[40] Oates and Oates 2001: 250–51.

[41] Curtis 1979: 19.

[42] Green 1999: 94, n. 18.

[43] Cf., e.g., Fleming 1989: 176 recognizing an uninterrupted pottery tradition in mid-first millennium Southern Mesopotamia 'in spite' of the rise and establishment of the Achaemenid domination.

[44] Winter 1987; cf. the conclusions of Howes Smith 1986 for a unidirectional distribution of Iron Age metal bowls; cf. Pedde 2000 for the fibulae.

[45] Cf. Green and Hausleiter 2001: 150–51 with note 36.

[46] Green 1999; Matney *et al.* 2002; Parker 2002.

[47] Bernbeck 1999.

[48] Lehmann 1998: 28, fig. 14; on the use of the term 'ceramic provinces' cf. Bernbeck 1999: 159.

Site name	Glazed Fabrics	'Palace Ware'	Ivories	Reliefs/ Sculpture	Palace/ Residence	Temple/s	NA Texts
Central Assyria							
Ashur	X	Xd	X	(X)	X	X	X
Nimrud	X	Xd	X	X	X	X	X
Khorsabad	X	Xd	(X)	X	X	X	X
Nineveh	(X)	Xd	(X)	X	X	X	X
Balawat		Xd			X	X	
Ibrahim Bayis		Xd				X?	
Kar-Tukulti-Ninurta		Xd					X
Kh. Khatuniyeh	X	Xd					
Kh. Qasrij	X	Xd					
Kh. Shireena		Xd					
N-Jazira No. 113		Xd					
Rownak		X					
Tell Abu Dhahir		Xd					
Tell Baqaq2					X		X
Tell ed-Dem		Xd					
Tell el-Hawa		X				X?	X
Tell Rimah		Xd		X		X	X
Tell Shelgiyya		Xd					
Tell Taya	X	Xd					
Khabur Valley							
Girnavaz		X					X
Tell el-Hamidiya	X		X		(X)		
Tell Abu Hafur E		X					
Tell Rad Shaqrah		Xd					
Tell Fakhariyah		Xd		X			X
Tell Halaf	(X)	Xd					
Tell Boueid		Xd			X		
Tell Ajaja		(X)		X	X		
Tell Sheikh Hamad	X	Xd	X	X	(X)		X
Upper Euphrates							
Sultantepe	X	(X)			(X)		X
Tille Höyük	X	Xd			(X)		
Tell Ahmar	X	Xd	X	X	X	X	X
Tell Shiukh Fawqani	X	X					X
Middle Euphrates							
Yimniyeh		(X)			(X)		
Bijan		(X)					
Ju'ana		(X)					

X = recorded   (X) = reported   d = dimpled   ? = questionable

Fig. 26-d. The occurrence of 'Palace Ware' and of features of the material culture of the Assyrian elite (after Hausleiter in preparation).

repertoire.[49] It seems evident that the entire area between the heartland of Assyria and the bordering regions shows corresponding elements within the pottery record. Furthermore, there are several sites in Palestine, such as, for example, Tell el-Jemmeh and Tel Dor where 'Assyrian' pottery types occur, and these are not only 'Palace Ware'.[50] Parallel to this tendency, the material culture and thus the pottery shows the existence of local trends.[51]

It is, of course, interesting to address the question of whether there is a direct relationship between the political expansion of the Neo-Assyrian empire and the pottery itself. For Middle Assyrian pottery production a division between 'official' and 'domestic' pottery was proposed by Peter Pfälzner,[52] a division which has not been accepted unanimously.[53] His conclusions were based on the observation of the following four main criteria: 1. Carelessness in the shaping process; 2. Standardization in shape and fabric; 3. Standardized vessel sizes; 4. Ability of the bowls (*Knickwandschalen*) to be stacked.[54] Furthermore, the occurrence of vessels corresponding to these criteria pertained to sites with 1. Representative buildings of the Middle Assyrian period; 2. The office of administration or a governor; or 3. The capitals of the Middle Assyrian empire.

Applied to the Neo-Assyrian period, the picture seems to be different,[55] even though some of the characteristic features selected correspond to the criteria indicated above. A high degree of distribution of information and the exchange of goods, connected with a moving population (forced or not) within the area can be considered as some of the factors and mechanisms which may have influenced the production of pottery.

In this context, a look at the occurrence of 'Palace Ware' within Northern Mesopotamia is interesting. Even though without a proper definition of the term itself, at Nimrud 'Palace Wares' originally pertained to visible[56] technolog-

ical characteristics of several different clays: 'The commonest clay body (...) of which the Palace Ware is made, is of a drab buff-grey greenish colour, and is of extraordinarily fine and homogenous texture'.[57] The term 'Palace Ware' at that time (1954) referred also to a coarser clay of pink colour of vessels with a fairly thick body; to vessels with haematite ring-burnished pattern and, finally, even somehow to grey wares, which admittedly 'lie outside the ordinary run of the Palace Wares'.[58] Five years later, in 1959, Joan Oates suggested 'to follow the customary practice at Nimrud and reserve this term for the extraordinarily fine hard ware, generally grey or greenish-buff, which Rawson referred to as the commonest Palace Ware'.[59] Already before, the term had been used in this sense.[60] The suggested differentiation between 'Palace Ware' and a 'true Palace Ware'[61] seems to take up this definition as well. Nowadays there is the impression that 'Palace Ware' is generally used for finer fabrics of Neo-Assyrian pottery, sometimes combined with beakers or bowls with a dimpled surface.[62] The context, i.e., the presence of a palatial building, does not seem to play an important role. In spite of this rather arbitrary application, a combination of a specific fine fabric combined with morphological features, such as carinated shapes of goblets, bowls and sometimes jars, altogether similar to metal vessels, should be considered as the constituents of the term 'Palace Ware'.[63]

There is a wide distribution of pottery made of this 'Palace Ware' within the Assyrian empire and beyond (fig. 26-d). If we discuss the significance of this 'ware' for the interpretation of material remains of the Neo-Assyrian empire, it becomes clear that only the combination of several elements of the élite culture, such as glazed pottery, reliefs/sculptures, public buildings or texts, help us to define sites as centres of colonial power.[64] Therefore, I think that 'Palace Ware' as circumscribed above, at least in the later part of the seventh century, is an imitation of the precious vessels of the royal élite[65] and is not automatically a relevant indicator

---

[49] Cf. for the pottery from the 'Rotes Haus' at Tell Sheikh Hamad, Kreppner 2006 (not included in fig. 26-c).

[50] Cf., e.g., Gilboa 1996 and, for a general overview on bowls, Schneider 1999.

[51] For local imitations of Assyrian 'Palace Ware' in Palestine (against the apparent opinion of Ohtsu 1991: 141) cf. Engstrom 2004; see also Na'aman and Thareani-Sussely 2006.

[52] Cf. the conclusions of Pfälzner 1995; 1997.

[53] Cf. Duistermaat (1999: 442) who states, that the conclusion 'that there exists a Middle Assyrian 'official' and a 'domestic' kind of ceramics that can be separated from each other in ware and shape cannot be maintained simply on the basis of the material from Area L in Sheikh Hamad'; cf. ibid. 443.

[54] Pfälzner 1997: 337.

[55] Cf. Bernbeck 1999: 152 who recognizes a 'high degree of regional ceramic variability for some types in Assyria'.

[56] I.e., without microscopical or scientific analysis. Cf. the warning by Rawson 1954: 169, n. 1 that 'it has not yet proved possible to carry out kiln tests and chemical analyses of the wares, so that much of the following discussion is speculative'.

[57] Rawson 1954: 169.

[58] Rawson 1954: 171.

[59] Oates 1959: 136, n. 1.

[60] Mallowan 1950: 170; Lines 1954: passim.

[61] Green 1999: 109.

[62] Cf. Green 1999: 108–9; for the Wadi Ajij area cf. Bernbeck 1993: 98 (*Ware* E8); his *Ware* E10 is different in colour and decoration.

[63] Achaemenid 'eggshell-ware' can clearly be distinguished from Neo-Assyrian 'Palace Ware' as pointed out by Fleming 1989: 169–70.

[64] Hausleiter 1999c: 275.

[65] Cf. Fleming 1989: 169; see before Hamilton 1966: 3–7.

Phase A	
Earlier than 8th to 7th century BC	North West Palace Central Area
	Burnt Palace Well
Phase B1	
8th to 7th century BC	Governor's Palace
	Burnt Palace
	Temple of Ninurta installed jars
	PD. 5 Adadnirari III building bathroom
2nd half of 8th to 7th century BC	North West Palace EB/EC and Z.T. 30/31 (installed jars)
	North West Palace Z.T. area
	Temple of Nabû
	PD. 1–4
	PD. 5 Adadnirari III building
Phase B2	
Mid-7th century BC	T.W. 53, level IV
7th century BC	Fort Shalmaneser installed jars
	Fort Shalmaneser T 20
	Central Building
2nd half of 7th century BC	T.W. 53, level III
Phase C	
1st half of 6th century BC	Fort Shalmaneser squatter occupation

Fig. 26-e. Chronological range of excavated Neo-Assyrian pottery from Nimrud
(cf. Hausleiter in preparation).

for the presence of Assyrian administration[66] (in this sense, the presence of 'Palace Ware' can be recognized, in a wider sense, as a concept rather than a technological feature alone). The precious drinking vessels were made of metal, such as silver and gold, or of other rare materials like glass, faience and stone.[67] It is mainly these vessels which can be identified in the texts and which are most often depicted on the reliefs.[68] However, vessels of these luxury materials are rarely to be found in palace buildings. Only undisturbed and sealed contexts, such as some of the royal graves recently discovered at Nimrud, illustrate the wealth and richness of the Assyrian court.[69]

This is also, why there is less hope for archaeological evidence for the inauguration banquet for the North-West Palace at Nimrud.

Final remarks

Ceramics from Nimrud in the context of Late Assyrian pottery studies remains an important factor, though a long time has passed since their excavation. Future publication of the material from the British excavations at the site— either as a printed book or as a digital publication—may provide us with some addition to the existing corpus of Neo-Assyrian pottery. Since there is growing evidence and knowledge of Neo-Assyrian pottery from the rural areas in the heartland and many sites within the provinces, it seems consequent but also ironic to underline the importance of pottery studies in central sites and especially the capitals of Assyria, where 150 years ago the archaeological exploration of Assyria started. From the ceramicist's point of view, future work should not necessarily start in temples and palaces but at different places with different approaches—taking into consideration also the area outside the site itself.

---

[66] Against Ohtsu 1991: 141 who (however) warns of 'hasty conclusions' in this matter.

[67] Cf. material from different contexts at Nimrud discussed in Curtis and Reade 1995 and Hussein and Suleiman 2000.

[68] Cf., e.g., Stronach 1995: 176, fig. 12.1; 178, fig. 12.2; 181, fig. 12.3; 191, fig. 12.8; see ibid.: 187–88.

[69] Cf. Damerji 1999; Hussein and Suleiman 2000. However, how far this cultural model was followed, is illustrated by the distribution of bronze bowls in Neo-Assyrian graves from Ashur: cf. the preliminary results of Hausleiter 1999b: 145; 146, fig. 14.

27   THE IVORIES FROM NIMRUD

Georgina Herrmann

More ivories—literally thousands—have been found at the great Assyrian city of Kalhu/Nimrud than anywhere else. They have been found both in the palaces of the citadel and in Fort Shalmaneser, the military arsenal in the south-east of the Lower Town (Barnett 1975; Mallowan 1966). Some were made locally and were carved in the distinctive Assyrian style (fig. 27-a: Mallowan and Davies 1970), well-known from the Assyrian reliefs. However, the majority of the ivories were imported—as 'gifts', tribute or booty, mostly from the city-states in Syria and the Levant. The political situation there during the early first millennium was complex and fluid: this was the time when 'a great number of Levantine territorial states and urban polities developed their own visual language with peculiar regional vocabularies' (Uehlinger 2000: xviii). This suggests one explanation for the relatively limited range of subjects represented in a multiplicity of styles on these imported ivories—that they represented the official arts of these independent states. If this hypothesis is correct, the ivories should enable us to understand the arts of the area at that time, especially if we can identify where they came from. However, unfortunately, they lack any convenient 'Made in Birmingham' labels on their backs, although we do sometimes get a few Aramaic letters. Trying to make sense of this extraordinary assemblage is a challenge, but one well worth while, particularly if we can establish where they came from and see what the different outputs of the varying states of the time were.

Who Found Them

The first ivories were, of course, discovered by Austen Henry Layard in the mid-nineteenth century in the North-West Palace (Barnett 1975: 15–18, 169–90, pls I–XIII). He found the ivories in Room V adhering 'so firmly to the soil, and ... in so forward a state of decomposition, that I had the greatest difficulty in extracting them, even in fragments. I spent hours lying on the ground, separating them with a penknife from the rubbish by which they were surrounded' (Layard 1849a: II, 8).

This problem of recovering ivories from their encompassing mudbrick was one with which members of the British School of Archaeology in Iraq's expedition to Nimrud from 1949–63 were well familiar. Some practitioners preferred to separate the ivories from their mudbrick matrix when they were still damp but very soft, while others preferred to clean them when they had dried out

and were stronger, but the mudbrick had hardened. Cleaning them was an art described by Agatha Christie (1977: 456–57):

> 'I had my own favourite tools, just as any professional would; an orange stick, possibly a very fine knitting needle ... and a jar of cosmetic face-cream, which I found more useful than anything else for gently coaxing the dirt out of the crevices without harming the friable ivory. In fact there was such a run on my face cream that there was nothing left for my poor old face after a couple of weeks!'

Fig. 27-a. A furniture panel showing Assyrian courtiers, IM 79537, ht. 13.3 cm., found in Well AJ of the North-West Palace.

Fig. 27-b. The 'Mona Lisa of Nimrud' from Well NN of the North-West Palace, ND 2550 (Iraq Museum). One of the largest ivory heads, 16 × 13.2 cm.

Although further discoveries were made in the nineteenth century by other archaeologists, particularly William Kennet Loftus, the majority of the ivories were found by the BSAI. From 1949 to 1956 the expedition, directed by Max Mallowan, worked in the palaces and temples of the acropolis. Mallowan's finest ivories were found in Well NN of the North-West Palace (Mallowan 1966: I, 122–47), of which the great head known as the 'Mona Lisa' (fig. 27-b) is the most famous (Mallowan 1966: I, pl. II and fig. 71). Agatha gave a vivid description of its discovery (1977: 457):

> '… And the most exciting day of all—one of the most exciting days of my life—[was] when the workmen came rushing into the house from their work clearing out an Assyrian well, and cried: 'We have found a woman in the well! There is a woman in the well!' And they brought in, on a piece of sacking, a great mass of mud.
>
> I had the pleasure of gently washing the mud off in a large wash-basin. Little by little the head emerged, preserved by the sludge for about 2,500 years. There it was, the biggest ivory head ever found: a soft, pale brownish colour, the hair black, the faintly coloured lips with the enigmatic smile of one of the maidens of the Akropolis. The Lady of the Well—the Mona Lisa, as the Iraqi Director of Antiquities insisted on calling her— one of the most exciting things ever to be found .'

In 1958 the excavations, directed by David Oates, moved to the great military arsenal, known as Fort Shalmaneser,

where literally thousands of ivories were found, especially in the storerooms of the South-West Quadrant. More recently, in 1989, a few ivories were recovered by an Italian mission from Turin, led by Paolo Fiorina.

However, without doubt, the finest examples of first millennium ivory work were recovered by our Iraqi colleagues in 1975, when they were able to complete the excavation of Well AJ of the North-West Palace. This was first investigated by Mallowan in 1952, who abandoned work there because the walls near the bottom were seriously undercut and liable to collapse (Mallowan 1966: I, 149–51). Nearly a hundred pieces, many complete and some with remains of their gold overlays and inlays still in position, were recovered by the Iraqis and published with exemplary speed (Safar and al-Iraqi 1987). These include superb examples of pyxides, lion bowls and bridle harness, as well as parts of a remarkable chryselephantine statue and many other superb pieces. And in the 1990s Muzahim Mahmud Hussein, Director of Excavations at Nimrud, found yet another cache of ivory and bone tubes from a well in the corner of Court 80 (Oates and Oates 2001: 65 and 100). We can be sure that many more await discovery in the soil.

Ivory was obviously available in large quantities in the palaces of the great Assyrian capital city, Kalhu/Nimrud. However, interestingly and perhaps significantly, almost no ivories were found in the Royal Tombs, *the* outstanding discovery at Nimrud, despite a wealth of material in gold, silver, bronze, stone, textile and ceramics. Only a few ivory lids are listed in the publication of the contents of the tombs by Muzahim and Suleiman (Hussein and Suleiman 2000). Since these tombs were found undisturbed, this must reflect deliberate choice. Together with the relative paucity of ivory in ceremonial areas of the palaces, this must raise question marks about the Assyrian liking for the material. Apart from those in Assyrian style, the majority of the ivories found at Nimrud were found stripped of their gold overlays and stored in the magazines of Fort Shalmaneser (Mallowan 1966, II).

Found in this way, smashed and out of any meaningful context, they present a challenging puzzle, both as to their place of manufacture and their date. Fortunately many ivories were used in sets of similar panels, and the first task is to assemble like with like, as in the furniture panels from the storeroom SW12, showing a familiar scene of Pharaoh figures holding ram-headed sceptres and jugs saluting stylized trees, below winged discs with rows of *uraei* or cobra above (figs 27-ci and -cii). Next, sets need to be formed into larger groups or style-groups representing the possible production of a workshop or centre. The ultimate aim is to suggest where these centres may have been located.

The easiest group to recognize and locate is, of course, those carved in Assyrian style, as in the modelled version

27-c(i) and c(ii). A set of furniture panels from Room SW12, Fort Shalmaneser, each showing a pair of Pharaoh figures flanking a stylised tree beneath a winged disc and a row of uraei or cobras. (Left, ND 11035, Metropolitan Museum of Art, New York; right, ND 11032, Iraq Museum, Baghdad.)

of Assyrian courtiers from Well AJ in the North-West Palace (fig. 27-a). Official Assyrian style ivories have usually been found in or near throne rooms, which suggests that this type of ivory may have been used to decorate the royal thrones and to amplify the messages already illustrated on the walls in sculptures and paintings (Herrmann 1997).

Traditions and Style-groups

Most Nimrud ivories were, of course, imported from the West and belong to three main regional groups, long known as the North Syrian and Phoenician traditions, with a transitional group between the two, the Intermediate tradition. The term 'tradition' is simply a convenient way of grouping half a dozen or more style-groups, themselves possibly the products of cities, into larger, related regional groups. The Phoenician tradition consists of ivories with a clear debt to the art of Egypt, as in an elegant kneeling Pharaoh figure (fig. 27-d), the North Syrian is more allied to the bas reliefs found in sites such as Zinjirli, Carchemish and Tell Halaf, as in a squat and powerful sphinx (fig. 27-e), and shows little debt to Egypt, while Intermediate ivories are—not surprisingly—between the two: one sphinx for instance is wearing the Egyptian double crown but the crown is barely recognizable as such (fig. 27-f).

Fig. 27-d. A kneeling Pharoah figure of the Phoenician Ornate Group, ND 7589, from Room SE3, Fort Shalmaneser, ht. 10 cm.

Fig. 27-e. A winged, human-headed sphinx, ND 10342, from Room SW37, Fort Shalmaneser, of the 'Roundcheeked and Ringletted' group of the North-West Syrian Tradition, w. 10.5 cm.

Here, perhaps, it would be useful to consider the political situation in Syria in the first quarter of the first millennium BC, the probable time of production of most of the ivories found at Nimrud and the centres from which they originated. Recent archaeological work in Syria and analyses by Bunnens, Mazzoni, Sader and others (see Bunnens 2000) are beginning to clarify the previously little known phases of the Iron Age and the emergence of the first millennium city-states. Our first references to the new Aramaean cities come in the final decade of the tenth and the early ninth centuries (Hawkins 1982: 381), and it is reasonable to assume that these states took shape during the tenth century. The principal Aramaean states stretched from Bit Bahiani and Bit Adini in the Jazira, to Hamath and Damascus. Most were new foundations and consisted of a number of cities (Sader in Bunnens 2000: 73), strongly fortified but relatively small, *c.* 20–50 hectares. To the north were, of course, a series of Neo-Hittite states, of which Carchemish was the principal power: it had survived as a major centre throughout the disturbances of

the late eleventh–early tenth centuries with an unbroken line of kings. Along the Mediterranean coast were the Phoenician city-states, Tyre, Sidon, Beirut, Byblos and Arvad, and to the south the emerging powers of Israel, with its capital at Samaria, and Judah. Each of these, and many more, probably developed a distinctive state art of their own, following the long-established Neo-Hittite tradition illustrated at Carchemish, Ain Dara and Zinjirli (fig. 27-g).

Each state had a different political history, as alliances formed and broke, and territories expanded or contracted. The cities of Bit Bahiani and Bit Adini in eastern Syria were, for instance, absorbed into the Assyrian empire by Shalmaneser III in the mid-ninth century (Hawkins 1982: 391), while Hamath and Lu'ash further west remained independent, being united by Zakkur at the end of the ninth century (Hawkins 1982: 402–3). This pattern of political flux and change, with numerous centres united by a common heritage but developing state arts differing in style rather than in content, fits the emerging pattern of ivory style-groups and traditions. The style-groups of the 'Phoenician' tradition with their closer connection to the canons of Egyptian art can probably be considered to be the state arts of the Phoenician city-states along the Levant coast and possibly in Cyprus. Those of the Intermediate tradition may belong to states from Unqi to Israel, while the North Syrian tradition can be divided in two, with a North-West Syrian group, defined by Wicke, centred around Samal (Wicke 2005: 67–110) of which a magnificent bowl is an example (fig. 27-h), and a North-East Syrian group, the principal style-group of which is the 'flame and frond' group (Herrmann 1989). A superb pyxis or box (fig. 27-i) is a fine example of the latter group: both pieces were found by the Iraqis in Well AJ.

Looked at from an ivory perspective, our current task, then, is to form coherent style-groups. As can be demon-

Fig. 27-f. An openwork furniture panel showing a human-headed sphinx of the Intermediate 'Crown and Scale' group, ND 12132.

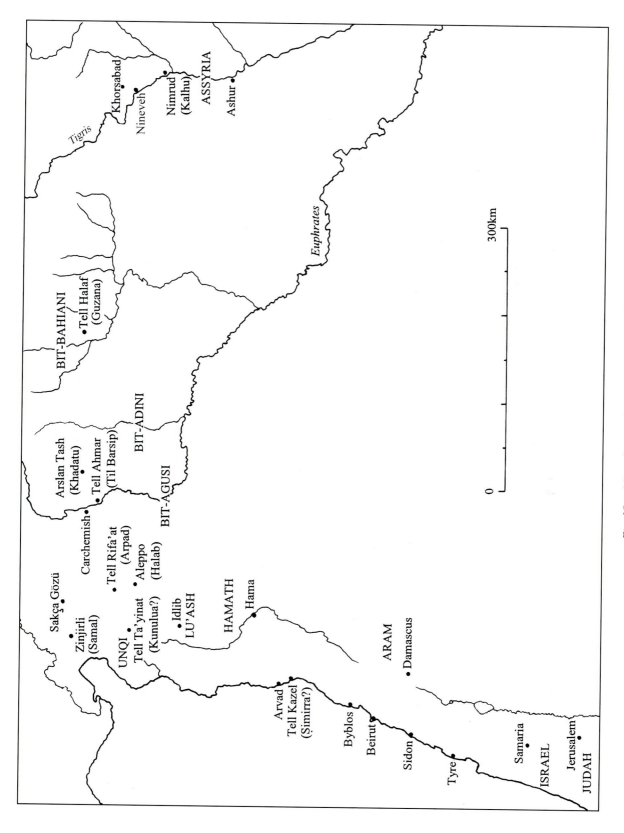

Fig. 27-g. Map of areas where ivories were found.

Fig. 27-h. A remarkable 'cosmetic palette' of the 'Roundcheeked and Ringletted' group of the North-West Syrian tradition. IM 79501/s, l.24.0 cm., found in Well AJ of the North-West Palace.

Fig. 27-i. A pyxis showing a banqueting scene belonging to the 'Flame and Frond' school of the North-East Syrian tradition, IM 79513, found in Well AJ of the North-West Palace.

Fig. 27-j. The banquet scene on the sarcophagus of Ahiram, Byblos.

strated by two very different style-groups, the 'flame and frond' of the North-East Syrian tradition and the Phoenician 'Ornate Group' (Herrmann 2002), each with a strong stylistic and technical signature, the output of a centre was rich and varied, both in the type of objects made and the techniques employed. For instance, the 'flame and frond' group included parts of furniture, as well as a range of small objects, including an extraordinary carved tusk, a lion bowl and numerous pyxides, all from Well AJ (fig. 27-i), as well as fan handles. Techniques were equally varied, with modelling and incision, silhouettes, statuettes, gold overlays and coloured inlays. And we can match the style both to the carved reliefs of Tell Halaf, and to a bronze bowl from the superb collection found by Layard in Room AB of the North-West Palace (Curtis and Reade 1995: 138, no. 101).

What I find of particular fascination about this group is that the design on one of the Well AJ pyxides (fig. 27-i) shows an enthroned king feasting: a scene which can be paralleled on the well-known tenth century, massive stone sarcophagus found at Byblos and belonging to King Ahiram (fig. 27-j). The scene is essentially identical: however, the function, the material, the scale and the style are entirely different. This remarkable parallelism suggests that there must have been a pattern book of designs circulating through the area, with each state applying its distinctive style or signature to the various designs: a common language with numerous dialects.

While many of the images may have travelled throughout the area, I personally think that different centres or areas concentrated on making different types of object, as they still do today. For instance, our flame and frond workshop made pyxides, and caryatid fan handles, examples of which were also carved in other North Syrian style-groups, but I have not found similar pieces in the Intermediate or Phoenician traditions (for examples, see Barnett 1975: pls XVI–XXI, LXX–LXXXIX). The latter traditions seem to specialize in plaques that form little stands, wider at the bottom than the top, perhaps a stand for a cup or goblet, such as the griffins of fig. 27-k, or pieces of bridle harness, great ivory blinkers and frontlets, among much else. All traditions carved furniture panels of varying sizes and belonging to different forms of chairs and beds.

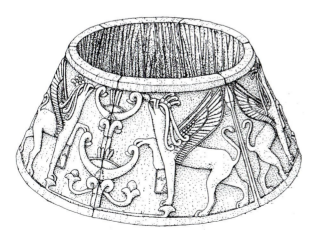

Fig. 27-k. A reconstruction of a circular stand for goblets based on Herrmann 1986: 153–155.

A number of factors help in grouping sets of ivories into style-groups. Obviously, style and technique are the primary factors. For instance, in flame and frond it was both the characteristic physiognomy and method of depicting the musculature as well as technical factors such as the method of inlay, the carving of panels on the back, and a characteristic dowel hole, that made it possible to form such a large group. The Ornate Group of ivories is very different: it employs a limited range of motifs originating in Egypt, an unusual method of forming the wigs with raised pegs holding glass cylinders, and the frequent use of a double rather than a single frame. Ornate Group ivories include furniture panels, small plaques and statuettes of Pharaoh figures. Further study should make it possible to expand this group to include other ivories, such as bridle harness. However, it is better to expand groups slowly and add to them as sufficient evidence can be garnered, rather than to make loose groupings that have later to be broken down. It is a balancing act between, on the one hand realizing that our ultimate aim is to form a limited number of larger groups and then attribute them to the various political centres of the time, and on the other not to misattribute groups, for once written up in the literature, even in a tentative way, an incorrect assemblage may get accepted and become difficult to change.

Another important factor in reassembling style-groups is provenance. Obviously Kalhu was sacked more than once, and there was massive looting and disruption. For instance, Joan Oates has recently pointed out that a fragment belonging to a beautiful Phoenician alabaster amphora from the ZT area of the North-West Palace was found 150 m away in the Town Wall Houses (Oates and Oates 2001: 41). Two halves of the same ivory blinker were found in Well NN and Well AJ of the North-West Palace: it had been broken and thrown down different wells. The primary interest of the looters would, of course, have been in any remaining gold overlays on the ivories rather than the bulky and heavy ivories themselves. Thus, having ripped off the gold, the ivories would have been dropped, not necessarily far from their original site. Their provenance, therefore, is another valuable factor in establishing style-groups and providing information. For instance, Assyrian style ivories are not found in store rooms, while ivories with Assyrian narrative scenes, rather than naturalistic or geometric motifs, are concentrated in areas of ceremonial importance, such as throne rooms or near daises. Equally, the ivories from the Fort Shalmaneser store rooms were all imported: all fragments of gold overlay had been carefully removed before storage. They were presumably stored as booty or a source of raw material.

Where we are now with ivory studies

The majority of the ivories from Nimrud have already been published. The first major publication in 1957 was

Dr R.D. Barnett's magisterial catalogue of ivories in the British Museum, which principally covered the nineteenth century Layard and Loftus collections, but also those donated to the British Museum by the BSAI. Sir Max Mallowan's account of work at Nimrud, *Nimrud & Its Remains* (1966), was written in the spirit of Layard, and combined a lively account of work at the site with an overall view of the principal discoveries. It set the ivories in context. The School itself has published five of a total of eight or nine catalogues, and our Iraqi colleagues have published the ivories they found in Well AJ (Safar and al-Iraqi 1987). One of the BSAI catalogues currently in preparation covers the ivories from the North-West Palace: this will include the ivories found in both the nineteenth and twentieth centuries and will be arranged by context—and here the School would like to thank our Iraqi colleagues warmly for giving us permission to republish the magnificent Well AJ ivories, and particularly to Sd. Muzahim Mahmud Hussein for agreeing to the first publication of his new ivories in this catalogue.

Two other catalogues will, it is hoped, cover the ivories from the Burnt Palace and the Nabu Temple, again uniting nineteenth and twentieth century ivories, and the large number of ivories found in Room SW12, the last of the store rooms in the SW Quadrant of Fort Shalmaneser excavated by the BSAI. This will make available a huge corpus of ivories for the next stage of research, which will involve detailed analytical study—the ivories form a major and unique record of the art of Mesopotamia and the Levant in the early first millennium BC. This will take many years and the efforts of numerous scholars, each of whom will have a refreshing and different contribution to make.

Dominique Collon

Seals from Nimrud can be divided into three main groups: those excavated and acquired by Austen Henry Layard in the middle of the nineteenth century, those excavated by Sir Max Mallowan in the 1950s, and those excavated by Iraqi archaeologists from the 1980s onwards. I shall concentrate here on the first two groups; the seals from the Iraqi excavations are discussed by Lamia al-Gailani Werr elsewhere in this volume (see also Oates and Oates 2001: 225, fig. 138).

The Layard Seals

There are only five Layard cylinder seals in the British Museum, registered in July and November 1848, for which a Nimrud provenance is assured. All are Neo-Assyrian. Two depicting chariot scenes, and one with a stylized tree approached by a winged quadruped, were excavated by Layard 'in tombs over the Central Palace'; these tombs are Parthian and the seals were therefore in a secondary context (Layard 1849a: II, 17–19; Collon 2001: nos 93–94, 198; figs 28-a–c). One seal depicts a stylized tree flanked by goats and birds (Collon 2001: no. 188), and one is a faience seal with an archer and winged bull (Collon 2001: no. 29; fig. 28-d).

However, Layard found a large number of cylinder seals in his excavations and others he acquired through purchase. Of these, some 122 cylinder seals and 81 stamp seals are registered in the British Museum in a long undated list with the prefix C (for cylinder) or N (which could stand for Nimrud or Nineveh!). Fifty-three of these seals are Neo-Assyrian cylinder seals, although there is no way of knowing how many of them are from Layard's excavations at Nimrud. In 1853, Layard published a number of seals and bullae on plate 69 in the second volume of his *Monuments of Nineveh*; unfortunately the caption indicates only that they came 'from Assyrian ruins' (see Collon 1987a: 206–9 and n. 7 for details). The same year he also published a number of seals in *Nineveh and Babylon* (see Collon 1987a: 206–9 and n. 8 for details). A further 33 seals from Layard's personal collection in Venice were catalogued by Borowski (1952) and Van Buren (1954) in the journal *Orientalia*; at the time they were in the hands of a collector in Rome (Borowski, pers. comm.).

In 1912, Layard's widow bequeathed to the British Museum a set of jewellery consisting of a necklace, bracelet and earrings made up of ancient Near Eastern seals (14 cylinder seals and 4 stamp seals) in Victorian Assyrianizing gold settings made by the jewellers Phillips; the jewellery was presented by Layard as a wedding present to his fiancée in 1869, and it is now in the Department of the Middle East (Barnett 1978; Rudoe 1987; fig. 28-e). Lady Layard is shown wearing this jewellery in a fine portrait painted by Vicente Palmaroli y Gonzales of Madrid in 1870 (Rudoe 1987: 214–15; fig. 28-f) which is also now in the Department of the Middle

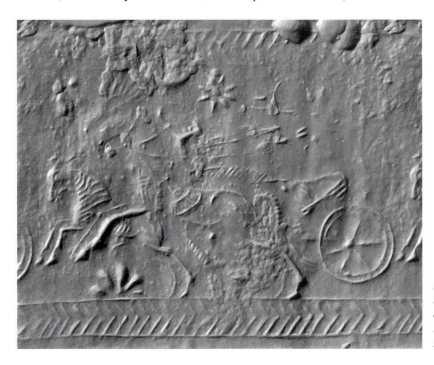

Fig. 28-a. BM ME 89799. Grey limestone, h. 4.3 cm. Bull hunt from a chariot. Neo-Assyrian, but found by Layard in Parthian tombs over the North-West Palace.

Fig. 28-b. BM ME 89829. Dark red soapstone, h.2.75 cm. Bull (?) hunt from a chariot. Neo-Assyrian, but found by Layard in Parthian tombs over the North-West Palace.

Fig. 28-c. BM ME 89830. Milky quartz, h.1.9 cm. Neo-Assyrian, but found by Layard in Parthian tombs over the North-West Palace.

Fig. 28-d. BM ME 89419. Faience, h. 3.5 cm. Neo-Assyrian, from Layard's excavations.

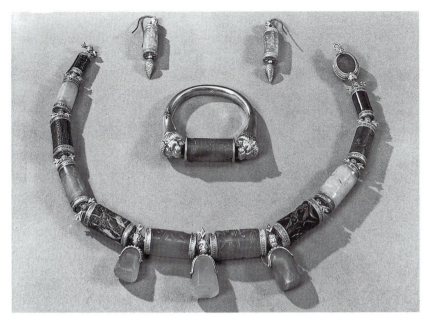

Fig. 28-e. Lady Layard's "Assyrian" jewellery.

East. Lady Layard wore her 'Nineveh necklace' when invited to dine at Osborne House in the Isle of Wight by Queen Victoria in 1873, and recorded in her diary that it was 'much admired' and that the bracelet was 'passed around for inspection'. She maintained that the large carnelian cylinder which adorned the bracelet had been the seal of Esarhaddon (680–669 BC) and came from Nineveh (fig. 28-g); the seal is uninscribed, and Barnett believed that it was 'evidently found in the Palace of Esarhaddon at Nimrud' (Barnett 1978: no. 7, pp. 177–78;

see Appendix). Whether or not it was found in a seventh-century Assyrian context, on stylistic grounds this seal should probably be dated to around 800 BC and, I believe, originated in a workshop which produced high-quality seals combining Babylonian, Assyrian and Iranian iconography which 'may have been located in a town on a main trade route linking these areas, or even in the Median capital, Hamadan' (Collon 2001: no. 153, pp. 89–90). The cylinders making up the necklace and earrings date from the later third millennium (one Akkadian, recut), the second millennium (three Old Babylonian seals, one Elamite and one Mitannian), and the late eighth and seventh centuries BC (seven Neo-Assyrian, some strongly influenced by Babylonia; Collon 2001: nos 135, 146, 154, 228, 270, 275, 361); two of the stamp seals are Neo-Babylonian, and the other two are Achaemenid and Greco-Persian. For the analysis of the seal materials, see the Appendix on p. 242.

The Mallowan Seals

Here, finally, we find seals which can not only be identified as coming from Nimrud, but for which, in many cases, we have detailed provenances. Some 124 cylinder seals and about 70 stamp seals are listed in the Nimrud records and their numbers are prefixed by the letters ND. Many of the seals and the seal impressions on tablets, dockets and bullae were published in two excellent articles by Barbara Parker in 1955 and 1962; selections were also published by Mallowan in his final report in 1966 and the seals have been further discussed by Joan and David Oates (2001: esp. 220–25). Many of them are now in Baghdad, but 39 cylinder seals are in the British Museum, of which 14 date from the late second millennium and the remaining 25 belong to the Neo-Assyrian period (for the latter, see Collon 2001: nos 7, 31, 39, 40, 42–44, 46, 72–74, 77, 81, 102, 127, 183, 186, 189,

Fig. 28-f. Portrait of Lady Layard by Vincente Palmaroli y Gonzalez, 1870.

Fig. 28-g. Black and white image of impression. BM ME 105111. Carnelian, h.3.6 cm. Lady Layard's Neo-Assyrian bracelet (see fig. 28-e).

220, 221, 265, 308, 385, 396, 399). There are also some 26 stamp seals in the British Museum and numerous impressions on tablets, dockets and bullae. The Ashmolean Museum in Oxford has 6 cylinder seals (Buchanan 1966: nos 574, 587, 606, 618, 658, 927), 5 stamp seals, and 6 impressions on a tablet, a docket and bullae (Buchanan and Moorey 1988: nos 57–68). In the space available, it is impossible to do more than present a few of the most remarkable glyptic finds from the Mallowan excavations at Nimrud.

Fig. 28-h. One of the Vassal Treaties of Esarhaddon (ND 4327) sealed with seals figs 28-i–28-k. Clay, h. 45.8 cm. Neo-Assyrian, c. 700 BC.

From the historical point of view, it is the seal impressions and sealings which are the most important. The Vassal Treaties of Esarhaddon, inscribed in cuneiform on several huge tablets which were found smashed in the private throne-room in the north-west wing of the Temple of Nabu, bore the impressions of three heirloom cylinder seals (figs 28-h, 28-i, 28-j and 28-k). The actual seals have not survived, but they were probably made of semi-precious stones and were fitted with metal caps, most likely of gold, of which the impressions are clearly visible; two were exceptionally large (7.0 cm). They were probably all seals of the national god Ashur, and two had presumably been kept in the treasury at Ashur over the centuries and were taken to Nimrud when the administration of the empire moved there in the ninth century BC. The oldest and smallest can be dated to the nineteenth century BC (Middle Chronology). It was probably made of haematite, or possibly lapis lazuli, and shows a suppliant goddess and a king in ceremonial robes, cut in the local Old Assyrian style; the inscription states that this is the 'Seal of the god Ashur of the City Hall', indicating that it was the seal of the city administration at the time when Ashur was engaged in trade with Anatolia. The second seal dates to the thirteenth century BC, in the Middle Assyrian period, and depicted a kneeling king being introduced by a minor deity to a god who is probably Ashur while the storm god Adad looks on. It bore a long cuneiform inscription, written horizontally around the seal, but unfortunately this is largely illegible. Wiseman (1958: 21) and Porada (1979: 7–8) suggested that this might have been the seal of the Kassite king Shagarakti-Shuriash (1245–1233 BC) which was captured and recut by Tukulti-Ninurta I of Assyria (1243–1207 BC), but Watanabe (1985: 387) has argued convincingly against this interpretation. The third seal shows Esarhaddon's father Sennacherib (704–681 BC) between the god Ashur and his consort, the goddess Mullissu. The long inscription reads:

'The Seal of Destinies, with (which) Ashur, king of the gods, seals the destinies of the Igigi and Anunnaki of

Fig. 28-i. Ancient impression of the "(Seal) of Ashur, of the City Hall" (see 28-h), h. 3.4 cm. Old Assyrian, 19th century BC.

Fig. 28-j. Ancient impression (h.7.0 cm, see 28-h) showing a kneeling king being introduced to various gods. The long inscription is not shown. Middle Assyrian, 13th century BC.

heaven and the underworld, and of mankind. Whatever he seals he will not alter. Whoever would alter it, may Ashur, king of the gods, and Mullissu, together with their children, slay him with their terrible weapons! I am Sennacherib, king of (Assyria), the prince who reveres you—whoever erases my inscribed name or discards this, your Seal of Destinies, erase from the land his name and seed!'

There are also a number of impressions on bullae and tablets (Parker 1955:110–25, pls XX–XXIX; Parker 1962: 29–31, 36–40, pls X:3, XII:4; XIX–XXII). Among them are several of sealings of city governors, especially of Kalah (Nimrud) (Watanabe 1993: 5.1–4, 7). The stamp seal of Adad-nirari III (810–733) was impressed on a docket (Parker 1955: 38–39, ND 7104; fig. 28-l), and there are multiple impressions of the stamp-cylinder of Esarhaddon's palace on a jar sealing (Parker 1955: 38, ND 7080; fig. 28-m). This latter was a cylinder seal mounted in a gold setting which transformed it into a stamp-cylinder; an actual example of such a seal survives (Collon 1987b: no. 391, and see also Parker 1962: pl. XII:4 for an impression of the stamp-cylinder of a governor of Kalah). These two royal seal impressions demonstrate the transition from cylinder seals to stamp seals, which was dictated by the increasing use of the Aramaic alphabet, written on materials other than clay and sealed on small bullae which provided a much reduced area for sealing. In another case, on a seventh-century docket (Parker 1962: 37, ND 7070; fig. 28-n), a

Fig. 28-k. Ancient impression (see 28-h). King Sennacherib stands between the god Ashur and Ashur's consort. The long inscription has not been drawn. Neo-Assyrian, c. 700 BC.

cylinder seal was impressed as if it were a stamp seal, so that only the central winged genie is visible, and not the creatures (probably sphinxes) he held. The seal was in a distinctive drilled style that was very popular and of which there are several actual examples in the British Museum collection (Collon 2001: esp. nos 364–66). Another example of the impression of such a seal was

Fig. 28-l. The ancient impression of the stamp-seal of Adad-nirari III.

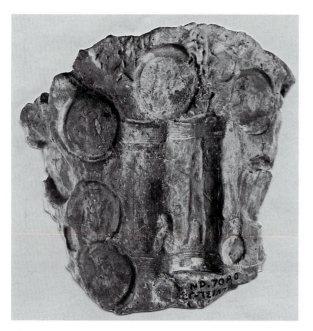

Fig. 28-m(i). Ancient impressions of the side and base of the stamp-cylinder of Esarhaddon on clay.

found on a tablet from Sheikh Hamad, again with just the central figure impressed (Kühne 1993: 82–83, 102, 107, figs 24 and 36).

Some interesting facts emerge from the study of the types of seals from the excavations. To give one instance: many black serpentinite cylinder seals depict the Assyrian king, seated holding a cup, or standing holding a cup and a bow, facing an attendant with a fan, with a stand or a cauldron between them; this is one of the most common types of Assyrian cylinder seal and is believed to date predominantly to the ninth century because similar scenes appear on the reliefs in Ashurnasirpal's palace at Nimrud. However, very few of these seals have actually been found at Nimrud (Parker 1955: pl. XIV:1; Parker 1962: pls IX:3, 5, XVII:9—see below, (fig. 28-s); Collon 2001: no. 127?), and the scene seems to have been more popular in Syria (Collon 2001: nos 103, 105–6, 110, 116, 118, 122, 128) and at Ashur (Moortgat 1940: nos 654–55, 657–61, 665, 668–73). It is regrettable that the many

Fig. 28-m(ii). Drawing of the design of the cylinder showing the king fighting a lion.

Layard seals with this subject are unprovenanced (Collon 2001: nos 108–9, 112–13, 115, 121, 123–26, 129–30, 133.

Two—perhaps three—extraordinary seals must have been manufactured in royal workshops at Nimrud before the capital moved to Nineveh. They were, I believe, made by, or under the influence of, craftsmen who had been brought from Babylonia by Tiglath-pileser III after his capture of Babylon in 729 BC, or by Sargon II after his defeat in 710 BC of Marduk-apla-idinna II (known in the Bible as Merodach-Baladan). The Babylonians, with their greater expertise in cutting hard stones, and with

Fig. 28-n. Cylinder used as a stamp on a docket.

Fig. 28-o. Modern impression of a cylinder seal (present whereabouts unknown) belonging to a Nimrud priest. Neo-Assyrian, c. 700 BC.

finer tools and abrasives at their disposal, revitalized seal-cutting in the metropolitan centres of Assyria. The first seal is, unfortunately, known only from a modern impression published by Ursula Moortgat-Correns in 1988 (fig. 28-o). It must have been cut in a hard stone such as chalcedony or carnelian, and depicts Ashur-shumu-iddina, priest of Nergal and Adad at Kalhu. The standards of Nergal and Adad flank Ninurta, who stands on his scorpion-tailed dragon, and behind the priest stands the warlike goddess Ishtar.

The second seal (Collon 2001: no. 207; Oates and Oates 2001: 223–24; fig. 28-p) is made from an unusual mauve

chalcedony which was available locally. Its workmanship is technically superb but there are many unusual features. It is evident that the top and bottom of the seal were ground down, since the cock and god in the winged disc are incomplete and the standing figure lacks feet. Unusual 'helmets' or 'pots' at the top are probably re-cut chips. The seal may have been badly damaged when gold caps were wrenched off it during the sack of the city in 612 BC. It was, indeed, found in Room B adjoining the bathroom in the Governor's Palace (ND 305), in ashy fill used to raise the floor level in the course of repairs 'probably shortly after 612 BC' (Mallowan 1966: I, 49), but in the interval someone had ground down the ends to hide the damage. This exceptionally beautifully executed seal was probably made for the high official (either a young man or a eunuch) who is depicted as a worshipper on it. The composition is unusually crowded, to the extent that there was insufficient room for some of the details. The undulating ground line, which would have been even more marked when the worshipper's feet were present, recalls seals from Syria, particularly a seal with Egyptianizing motifs and an

Fig. 28-p. BM ME 130865. Mauve chalcedony, h.3.05 cm. Found during Mallowan's excavations.

Fig. 28-q. BM ME 134764. Grey chalcedony, h. 3.5 cm. Ex Spencer Churchill Collection. Said to be from Nimrud.

Aramaic inscription (Collon 1987b: no. 398). The latter seal is worked with comparable skill and, although the feather pattern of the lion-griffins is different, the heads are similar and the hexagonal patterning of the genie's dress resembles that of the worshipper on the present seal. The offering table before the worshipper is, as far as I know, unparalleled and does not seem very practical; it may be an abbreviated table with only one leg shown, though tables normally have lions' feet; the traces of recutting around the table do not make sense. Although the stance of the worshipper is Assyrian, the small drill-holes on the cheek of the Atlantid figure recall Babylonian usage, as does the very fine patterning of the bodies executed with the cutting-wheel, while the hair of the Atlantid figure and the worshipper and the patterning of the latter's dress are paralleled by a seal, probably by the same seal-cutter, in the Iraq Museum (Collon 1987b: no. 369). It may be no coincidence, therefore, that this latter was a votive seal dedicated by Merodach Baladan II. The Nimrud seal would have been cut at Nimrud by a

deportee Babylonian craftsman shortly after 710, used damaged less than a century later, and re-cut before ending up in destruction debris reused as fill.

To these two seals can perhaps be added a further cylinder (fig. 28-q), which is said to have come from Nimrud although the reason for this attribution is not known. It was acquired by the British Museum in 1966 from the Spencer-Churchill Collection (Collon 2001: no. 331). It is a high-quality Babylonian version of a subject which became popular in Assyria in the final decades of the eighth century BC, with a winged genie holding up two bulls by their hind-legs.

Finally, there are two very interesting collections of seals. The first was a votive deposit found in a cache at the back of the sanctuary of the Ninurta Temple (Parker 1962: 31–33, pls XIII–XVI:2, and cf. pl. XII for seals and a sealing found elsewhere in the Ninurta Temple; Collon 2001: nos 7, 77, 81; Oates and Oates 2001:

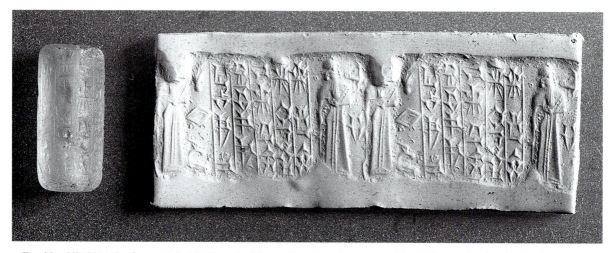

Fig. 28-r. ND 5374. Rock crystal, h. 2.7. From the Ninurta Temple cache excavated by Mallowan (Parker 1962: Plate XIII.1). Kassite c.1350 BC. Baghdad.

Fig. 28-s. ND 6083. Black stone, probably serpentinite, h. 3.0 cm. Neo-Assyrian, 9th–8th century BC. Excavated by Mallowan in Hellenistic Grave PG 21. (Parker 1962: Plate XVII.9).

107–10). The earliest seal is a worn Old Babylonian one, the finest is an Early Kassite rock crystal cylinder (fig. 28-r); there are also Late Kassite and other faience examples (Parker 1962: pl. XV, all in the British Museum) and several seals of the early first millennium BC, some of which may have originated in Iran. The quality of the seals is generally poor and several are broken; they are not the type one would normally associate with a votive deposit. The other group was deposited in Hellenistic grave PG 21 (Parker 1962: 34–35, pls XVI: 6; XVII; Oates and Oates 2001: 224) which had been dug down into Neo-Assyrian levels in Area AB. As, with one exception, all the seals are of ninth–eighth century date, they could have been found while the grave was being dug. One of them is a rare example of the type discussed above: a serpentinite seal

Fig. 28-t. BM ME 140393. Amethyst, h. 2.35 cm. Neo-Assyrian, c. 700–650 BC. Excavated by Mallowan in Hellenistic Grave PG 21.

Fig. 28-u. ND 6098. Black stone, probably serpentinite, h.2.5 cm. Akkadian, c. 2250 BC. Excavated by Mallowan in Hellenistic Grave PG 21. (Parker 1962: Plate XVII.1).

showing the king, an attendant and pots on a stand (fig. 28-s). Another was a fine amethyst seal of the late eighth century or early seventh, but the lower part is missing, again perhaps broken when a gold setting was wrenched off during the sack of the city in 612 BC (fig. 28-t). However, the exceptional item in the grave-group, an Akkadian contest scene of about 2250 BC, is one of the earliest objects to have been found at Nimrud (fig. 28-u).

Appendix

The materials of the seals from Lady Layard's jewellery were analysed by Margaret Sax of the British Museum Research laboratory in 1993 as follows:

1. Cylinder seal (bracelet)	Neo-Assyrian 105111	Quartz, carnelian (flawed)	Red-brown with black inclusions
2. Cylinder seal (earring)	Neo-Assyrian 105112	Quartz, chalcedony	Blue-grey
3. Cylinder seal (earring)	Neo-Assyrian 105113	Quartz, chalcedony	Blue-grey
4. Cylinder seal (necklace)	Mitannian 105114	Hematite	Dark brown
5. Cylinder seal (necklace)	Neo-Assyrian 105115	Quartz, chalcedony	White-grey
6. Cylinder seal (necklace)	Old Babylonian 105116	Hematite	Black
7. Cylinder seal (necklace)	Neo-Assyrian 105117	Quartz, chalcedony	White-grey
8. Cylinder seal (necklace)	Old Babylonian 105118	Quartz, brecciated jasper	Dark red and white
9. Cylinder seal (necklace)	Neo-Assyrian 105119	Quartz, chalcedony	Blue
10. Cylinder seal (necklace)	Neo-Assyrian 105120	Quartz, chalcedony	Grey-brown
11. Cylinder seal (necklace)	Akkadian 105121	Serpentinite	Black and dark green
12. Cylinder seal (necklace)	Neo-Assyrian 105122	Quartz, agate	White and cream
13. Cylinder seal (necklace)	Elamite 105123	Hematite	Black
14. Cylinder seal (necklace)	Old Babylonian 105124	Goethite	Black and brown
15. Ovoid stamp seal (necklace)	Achaemenid 105125	Quartz, chalcedony	Grey-brown
16. Eight-sided conoid (necklace)	Achaemenid 105126	Quartz, chalcedony	Light grey
17. Eight-sided conoid (necklace)	Achaemenid 105127	Quartz, chalcedony	Blue
18. Eight-sided conoid (necklace)	Neo-Babylonian 105126	Quartz, agate	Grey and white

29   OBSERVATIONS ON SELECTED METAL OBJECTS FROM THE NIMRUD TOMBS

John Curtis

Introduction

The title of this lecture as delivered at the conference was 'The Nimrud bronzes: local products or imports'. However, I have now changed the title to reflect more accurately the content of my lecture and also of this paper. My intention is to compare some of the metal objects found in the royal tombs at Nimrud with metal objects found in other excavations at Nimrud and also in other Assyrian contexts. This will give us an indication of the frequency of particular forms in Assyria, and perhaps throw some light on whether those forms are local products or imports from outside Assyria. For information about the metal objects from the royal tombs I have relied on the publications by Dr Muayyad Damerji (1999) and Muzahim Hussein and Amer Suleiman (2000). Other metal objects found at Nimrud derive mainly from the excavations of A.H. Layard between 1845 and 1851 and the British School of Archaeology in Iraq between 1949 and 1963, although other excavations at the site have also produced metal objects (Curtis 1988; Curtis *et al.* 1993).

Many of the metal objects found by Layard were actually from the so-called 'Room of the Bronzes', which is Room AB in the North-West Palace. Here, Layard found 12 bronze cauldrons, some of them apparently originally standing on tripods. In the cauldrons were objects including bronze bells, horse harness and maceheads. Some of the maceheads and the tripods had West Semitic alphabetic inscriptions (Barnett 1967). Near the cauldrons was a pile of bronze bowls. About 120 can now be accounted for. Some of them are plain and some are represented only by fragments, but many are decorated with scenes and designs in what have been identified as Phoenician and Syrian styles (Layard 1853b: pls 57–68; Barnett 1974). Some of these have been analysed in the British Museum and they, like other bronzes found at Nimrud, are standard tin bronzes with about 10% tin and no zinc (Curtis, Lang, Hughes and Leese 1986). There were also in Room AB items of furniture including a throne and a footstool (Curtis 1996). Elsewhere in the North-West Palace, metalwork found by Layard included a set of bronze lion-weights from the Throne Room (Mitchell 1990). These discoveries have been supplemented by finds made by Mallowan and Oates in the various buildings they excavated at Nimrud, particularly Fort Shalmaneser. Coming on now to the bronzes from the tombs, I have already discussed at this conference bronze coffins and I have attempted to show they were probably Assyrian in inspiration and manufacture. I propose now to look at selected items from the tombs that can be paralleled by objects from other excavations at Nimrud or from other Assyrian contexts.

Saucer lamps

At least four bronze saucer lamps have been found in the tombs. These lamps have a lower straight-sided bowl in the centre of which is a tube or pillar supporting an upper carinated bowl with a pinched spout. There is a handle mounted on the rims of the two bowls. Presumably the upper bowl was filled with oil and contained the wick, the end of which would have rested on the spout. Perhaps the purpose of the lower bowl was to catch any overflowing oil or pieces of burnt wick. Two examples of these bronze saucer lamps were found in Tomb II and two in Tomb IV (figs 29-a, 29-b and 29-c).[1] These lamps were in niches in the walls of the tombs (Hussein and Suleiman 2000: 103, 131), except for one of the lamps in Tomb II which had fallen onto the ground (Damerji 1999: fig. 19). There may also have been one example in Tomb III.[2]

Fig. 29-a. Bronze saucer lamp from Tomb II.

---

[1]   Hussein and Suleiman 2000: pls 75, 215–16; Damerji 1999: fig. 19; Oates and Oates 2001: fig. 48 on p. 88.

[2]   Cf. Hussein and Suleiman 2000: 127, ND 486/IM 126274.

Fig. 29-b. Bronze saucer lamp from Tomb IV.

Fig. 29-c. Bronze saucer lamp from Tomb IV.

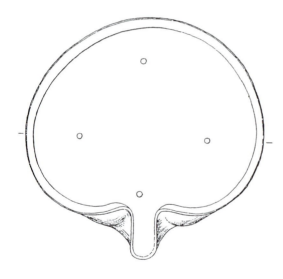

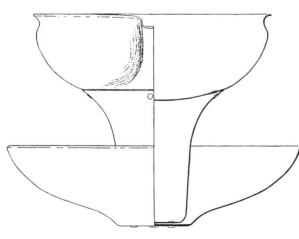

Fig. 29-d. Bronze saucer lamp found by A.H. Layard at Nimrud, British Museum N 125. Drawing by A. Searight. Ht. 20.0 cm.

Layard found a comparable saucer lamp, but lacking a handle, apparently in one of the cauldrons in Room AB in the North-West Palace:-

• British Museum N 125 (fig. 29-d)—overall ht. *c.* 20.0 cm, diam. of upper bowl *c.* 24.0 cm, diam. of lower bowl *c.* 29.5 cm. Upper part only of lamp published in Layard 1853a: 181.

There is also a bronze saucer lamp from Tomb 30 at Ashur (Haller 1954: pl. 22b), the same tomb that contained a bronze bowl with an inscription of Ashurtaklak, who may have been eponym in 805 BC.

Similar saucer lamps in pottery are also attested in Assyria, with examples from Nimrud (Oates 1959: pl. XXXIX/104–6; Curtis and Reade 1995: no. 152; Curtis *et al.* 1993: fig. 27/10), Ashur (Haller 1954: pl. 5/ak, al) and Tell Billa (Speiser 1932: 6; Bache 1933: 14).

The saucer lamp form, therefore, both in bronze and pottery, is well-known in Assyria. Bronze saucer lamps also occur outside Assyria, for example at Baba Jan in Iran (Goff 1969: 126, fig. 7/2), and the pottery examples are widely distributed in the Ancient Near East and even further afield. However, there is no reason to suppose that the bronze lamps from the tombs are not Assyrian products.

Carinated bowls

From the tombs there are a number of carinated bowls, that is bowls with a sharply defined shoulder, a waisted neck and a flared rim. Several of these bowls have embossed flutes or gadroons. The finest examples are in gold (fig. 29-e) and include three bowls from Tomb II inscribed with the names of Yaba', Banīti and

Fig. 29-e. Inscribed gold bowls from Tomb II (top, bottom left) and Tomb III (bottom right).

Ataliya.[3] Another inscribed example in gold comes from Tomb III,[4] as does a carinated gold bowl in the form of an embossed lotus flower (Hussein and Suleiman 2000: pl. 155a). There is also a fluted silver bowl from Tomb I (Hussein and Suleiman 2000: pl. 1). From Tomb IV come carinated bowls in silver and bronze respectively (Hussein and Suleiman 2000: pls 205–6). The bronze example seems to be plain, but the silver bowl has a frieze of lotus-and-bud decoration around the outside of the rim.

Amongst the bowls found by Layard at Nimrud and now in the British Museum are five bronze bowls of carinated shape. Three are plain but for groups of incised lines around the outside just beneath the rim, one has a crudely incised winged disc in the centre and the fifth is decorated with a central rosette. The following are examples of plain and decorated bowls:-

• British Museum 91297/N 94 (fig. 29-f)—carinated bronze bowl, plain but for groups of incised lines around outside just beneath rim, diam. 13.2 cm, ht. 5.4 cm. Published Curtis and Reade 1995: no. 105.
• British Museum N 46 (fig. 29-g)—carinated bronze bowl with group of incised lines around outside just beneath rim and incised rosette in the centre surrounded by three concentric circles, diam. 12.2 cm, ht. 4.9 cm.

Carinated bowls of bronze and silver were also found by Mallowan at Nimrud (Mallowan 1966: I, fig. 59, II, fig. 357), and the large number of bronze bowls found in the graves and tombs at Ashur (more than 70) included many carinated examples (Haller 1954: *passim*). It has long been recognized that the carinated bowl is a typical Assyrian form (Luschey 1939), and there are numerous examples in pottery and glass as well as in metal. Bowls of this form are also shown on Assyrian reliefs. Therefore, there is no reason to believe that any of the carinated bowls found in the Nimrud tombs are of foreign manufacture, even though it is true that in the ninth–seventh centuries BC the form became popular over much of the Ancient Near East reflecting the spread of Assyrian influence across the region.

Straight-sided bowls

Two containers from the tombs are in the form of dishes with low, straight sides. The example from Tomb II (fig. 29-h) with a diameter of 14.3 cm and a height of 2.3 cm is plain but for a cuneiform inscription around the outside just beneath the rim (Hussein and Suleiman 2000: pl. 41). This reads 'belonging to Banīti, queen of Shalmaneser, King of Assyria' (Al-Rawi, text no. 22). The object is described by Hussein and Suleiman as 'a large tin dish' and by Al-Rawi as an 'electron cosmetics container'. To judge from the photograph the dish may be of bronze, but in an exceptionally good state of preservation. The second dish comes from Tomb IV (fig. 29-i), and is said to be of silver (Hussein and Suleiman 2000: pl. 207). All around the outside, just beneath the rim, it has an incised

---

[3] Hussein and Suleiman 2000: pls 37, 57–58; Damerji 1999: figs 31–32; Oates and Oates 2001: pl. 8b.

[4] Hussein and Suleiman 2000: pl. 152; Damerji 1999: fig. 31, bottom; Oates and Oates 2001: pl. 8b, bottom right.

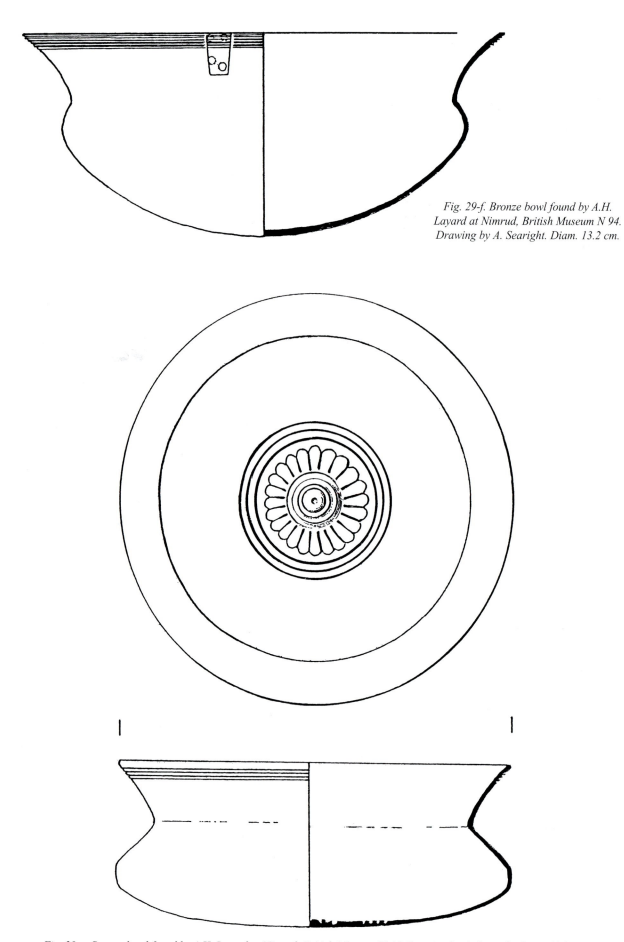

Fig. 29-f. Bronze bowl found by A.H. Layard at Nimrud, British Museum N 94. Drawing by A. Searight. Diam. 13.2 cm.

Fig. 29-g. Bronze bowl found by A.H. Layard at Nimrud, British Museum N 46. Drawing by A. Searight. Diam 12.2 cm.

Fig. 29-h. Bronze (?) bowl from Tomb II with a cuneiform inscription recording it as the property of Banīti.

Fig. 29-i. Silver (?) bowl from Tomb IV.

Fig. 29-j. Bronze bowl found by A. H. Layard at Nimrud, British Museum N 41.

design consisting of a cable pattern beneath which is a frieze of inverted lotus buds.

Amongst the Nimrud bowls, there are two dishes with low, straight sides. They are:-

- British Museum N 41 (fig. 29-j)—bowl with cast and incised decoration showing a central rosette surrounded by two registers of lotus flower design, diam. 13.3 cm, ht. 3.2 cm. Published in Layard 1853b: pl. 57D.
- British Museum N 47 (fig. 29-k)—bowl with incised decoration showing three or four registers of lotus flower design around which is a single band of cable pattern design, diam. 16.51 cm, ht. 3.17 cm.

The crude and degenerate lotus flower patterns on these and other bronze bowls, hardly recognisable as linked lotus flowers, were dubbed by Barnett 'marsh pattern' as they reminded him of the symbol for marshes on British Ordnance Survey maps (Barnett 1967: 3–4; 1974: 21–22). The design occurs on a number of bowls from Nimrud, some with elaborate figural decoration, and on other Syro-Phoenician bowls, for example from the Idaean Cave in Crete (Barnett 1967: fig. 2, pls II–III, V, VI; 1974: fig. 2, pls II, IX–XIV). The lotus flower pattern occurs together with designs that have been identified as both Syrian and Phoenician. It is interesting that the lotus flower pattern appears on both of the straight-sided bowls from the Layard collection, while on one of the bowls from the

tombs there is a frieze of lotus buds. These are much more carefully executed than the 'marsh pattern' design on the Layard bowls, and they should probably not be associated with each other. It is possible, then, that the two bowls from the tombs (including the example with the cuneiform inscription) were made in Assyria, while the two bowls in the Layard collection were made in the area to the west of Assyria, in a Syrian or Phoenician centre.

Strainer bowls

From the tombs come two bronze strainer vessels. The first is in the shape of a carinated bowl with a funnel-shaped base (fig. 29-l; Hussein and Suleiman 2000: pl. 212). A similar strainer, with a ring of embossed petals or leaves at the top of the conical funnel, was found by Layard in one of the cauldrons in Room AB of the North-West Palace:-

- British Museum 124601/N 611 (fig. 29-m)—ht. *c.* 13.2 cm, maximum diam. *c.* 11.1 cm. Published Layard 1853a: fig. on p.181, Moorey 1980: fig. 5 on p.193.

Another strainer of this type, but with a 'curved snake-head handle' was found in a Late Assyrian grave at Tell Billa (Speiser 1930: 12, 14), and there is a further example from the 'Assyrian' cemetery at Mari (Parrot 1952: 188, pl. XVII/I).

Fig. 29-k. Bronze bowl found by A.H. Layard at Nimrud, British Museum N 47.

Fig. 29-l. Bronze strainer bowl from Tomb IV.

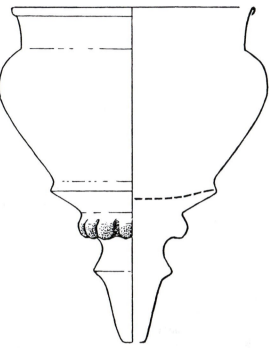

A more elaborate strainer vessel was found in Tomb II (fig. 29-n).[5] This consists of a beaker-shaped container with an upright handle on the rim. This handle turns over at the top and ends in a goat's head. At the bottom of the vessel is a pipe-shaped funnel.

Two very similar strainer vessels, both unprovenanced, have been illustrated and discussed by Roger Moorey in his article on metal wine sets in the Ancient Near East (Moorey 1980: pl. IV a–b). He also refers to an example found by Louis Vanden Berghe in a tomb at Chamahzi Mumah in Luristan (Haerinck and Overlaet 1998: ill.11/14, fig. 49, pl. 65, col.pl. G). It may also be worth noting that a strainer jug in the British Museum, in the form of a bowl with a long open-topped spout, has a similar handle ending in a goat's head (fig. 29-o; Moorey 1980: figs 2–4, pl. IIIb).[6] Although this vessel, collected by Sir William Temple in the nineteenth century, allegedly comes from Ruvo in Italy, it has incised decoration in unmistakeable Assyrian style and its Assyrian connections are undeniable.[7]

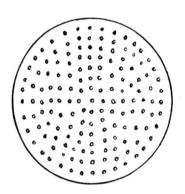

Fig. 29-m. Bronze strainer bowl found by A.H. Layard at Nimrud, British Museum N 611. Drawing by A. Searight. Ht. 13.2 cm.

Cylindrical terminals

From Tomb II come various "copper pipes" that are closed off at one end (fig. 29-p; Hussein and Suleiman 2000: pl. 170). They are cylindrical in shape, and are slightly flared at the bottom (closed) end. Five examples are illustrated in the catalogue by Hussein and Suleiman, apparently in two different sizes. They may be compared with some bronze fittings found by Layard at Nimrud:-

• British Museum 91265–91268/N 751–4 (fig. 29-q)— four hollow bronze terminals with slightly concave sides, convex bases, and narrow lip at rim, hts 14.25 cm–16.6 cm, maximum diam. 7.3 cm–7.8 cm.

The exact findspot of the Layard examples, or their function, are unknown, but some years ago I speculated that they might have been feet from a piece of (wooden)

---

[5] This strainer is not illustrated in either Hussein and Suleiman 2000 or in Damerji 1999. It was, however, photographed by G. Herrmann and was seen by J.E. Curtis on exhibition in the Late Assyrian gallery in the Iraq Museum in 2002. It has the number 197 in Arabic. The inventory for Tomb II has under no. 197 a 'copper container' (IM 115471) (Hussein and Suleiman 2000: 111).

[6] BM 124591.

[7] Strainers with handles ending in animal heads are also found in Achaemenid metalwork (eg Curtis and Tallis 2005: nos 132–33), but here the strainers are small bowls with horizontal handles.

Fig. 29-n. Bronze strainer vessel from Tomb II.

furniture (Curtis 1979: I, 312, II, 90, pl. LXXXIII). The new discovery adds support to the theory that they might have been furniture sheathings. A photograph in Damerji (1999 (fig. 29-r)) shows what are apparently the same pieces in the south-west corner of the main chamber in Tomb II; they are scattered on the floor of the chamber together with some large bronze vessels. It seems very likely that they could have belonged to a table or stand that supported the bronze vessels that would have collapsed when the wood decayed. Assuming this hypothesis to be correct, whether the bronze sheathings belonged to the feet or some other part of the furniture is unclear.

Triple arm fitting

From Tomb II (Hussein and Suleiman 2000: pl. 171) is an enigmatic object with three arms (fig. 29-s). It is described by Hussein and Suleiman as 'a piece of oxidized copper, which may have been a base for a candlestick or a large container with three arms meeting in the middle'.

A similar object is amongst the bronzes found by Layard at Nimrud, the only difference being that a ring is mounted on the central part:-

- British Museum N 545 (fig. 29-s)—11.5 cm × 12.1 cm × 12.4 cm, maximum ht. 3.35 cm.

Both objects have studs or buttons at the ends of the arms, and although the example from Tomb II now lacks a ring, one may originally have been present. It seems likely that the object was suspended by means of the ring, and that further items were fixed to or suspended from the ends of

Fig. 29-o. Bronze strainer jug formerly in the collection of Sir William Temple, British Museum ME 124591.

Fig. 29-p. Bronze furniture sheathings (?) from Tomb II.

Fig. 29-q. Bronze furniture sheathings (?) found by A.H. Layard at Nimrud, British Museum N 751-4.

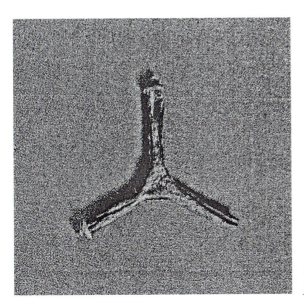

Fig. 29-r. Bronze triple arm fitting from Tomb II.

Fig. 29-s. Bronze triple arm fitting found by A.H. Layard at Nimrud, British Museum N 545.

Fig. 29-t. Gold fibula from Tomb I, attached by a double chain of plaited gold wire to a stamp seal in red stone.

the arms. One possibility is that these 3-armed objects were from balances, and that pans were suspended by 3 strings from the arms, but it is hard to see why a balance, or part of a balance, should have been buried in the tomb. For the time being, therefore, the purpose of these objects remains obscure.

Fibula with figural decoration

The last item that I would like to consider is the magnificent gold fibula from Tomb I (Damerji 1999: fig. 14; Hussein and Suleiman 2000: pl. 12). It is attached by a double chain of plaited gold wire to a stamp seal in red stone set in a gold swivel mount with recumbent lions on top. The fibula itself has a Pazuzu head and the bust of a woman on one side of the bow, and a bird of prey on the other (fig. 29-t). This object belongs to a comparatively rare class of fibula with figural decoration on the bow. Generally this figural decoration is in the form of Pazuzu

heads and birds of prey (Curtis 1994; Pedde 2000: pl. 73). The only other example of a fibula with figural decoration in the form of a female bust comes from Tell Deir Situn in the Eski Mosul Dam Salvage Project (fig. 29-u). This was unfortunately a surface find, and the identified remains at Tell Deir Situn belong to the Hellenistic period (Curtis *et al.* 1987–88), but nevertheless the site is on the edge of the Assyrian heartland and the presence there of such a fibula added support to the theory that they were of Assyrian origin. This is now confirmed by the discovery in Tomb I of the gold fibula, which is almost certainly the product of an Assyrian goldsmith.

Conclusion

It emerges that good parallels can be found for some of the bronze objects in the tombs from amongst the existing Assyrian repertoire, which encourages us to believe that such objects may be of Assyrian manufacture. However,

Fig. 29-u. Part of bronze fibula found at Tell Deir Situn in the Eski Mosul Dam Salvage Project, Northern Iraq.

even if an Assyrian pedigree can be established for many of the objects from the tombs, there are clearly some objects that are likely to have been manufactured elsewhere. For example, the gold bowl from Tomb II, showing boats and lotus flowers around the edge and various animals including a crocodile in the centre

(Hussein and Suleiman 2000: pl. 48; Oates and Oates 2001: pl. 76), is probably of Phoenician origin. Then, the elaborate gold jug, also from Tomb II (Hussein and Suleiman 2000: pl. 154), may be compared with the 'side-spouted sieve jugs' that have been found in Anatolia and particularly at Gordion, where vessels of this shape in pottery or bronze have been found in all four of the major early tumuli (G.K. Sams in Young 1981: 251–54, pls 19–20, 59, 88, 92–93; Toker and Öztürk 1992: nos 98–100). It seems likely, then, that many of the objects in the tombs are of local Assyrian origin, but with the addition of a smaller number of imported foreign pieces. Perhaps the same applies to some if not most of the wonderful gold jewellery from the tombs. I know that a number of you at this conference have suggested that the jewellery was made by foreign craftsmen who were brought to Assyria by various kings and put to work perhaps in the royal workshops. However, the fact that we do not have parallels in the Assyrian repertoire for much of this material should not surprise us too much because the Assyrian archaeological record is clearly very incomplete. Also, I was struck by Dr Herrmann's suggestion that the absence of ivories in the tombs is another possible indication that on the whole what we have here are things of Assyrian origin and manufacture, the sorts of things that would have been in daily use in the Assyrian court.

In conclusion, I think the starting point when looking at the objects in the tombs should be that they are Assyrian unless proven otherwise, and the onus should be put on those who want to demonstrate that they are foreign or imported to do so.

Christopher Walker

My involvement with the Nimrud texts has been absolutely miniscule, at the beginning and more or less at the end of my career. I am the sole surviving Assyriologist who began to learn Assyrian under Peter Hulin, the intrepid and extremely determined Assyriologist to whom David Oates made reference—the man who insisted on getting underneath the throne-base of Shalmaneser as it was being lifted into the air. From my experience of him it is amazing that they got any further before he had completed copying the inscription. I was certainly taken through that inscription line by line, and there was a time when I could have told you everything you would need to know about the number of times Shalmaneser crossed the Euphrates and the exact chronology of his campaigns. The better part of 35 years later, after Jeremy Black had published the Nabu Temple texts, I realized that one of them held the clue to a puzzle which I had been working on for about 35 years (ever since I did my B.Phil under Oliver Gurney on the ritual that the Babylonians used for inducting their statues into the temple): what was the title of this ritual? One of the two alternative titles was written there in the colophon of one of the Nabu Temple texts previously misunderstood. So I had reason to be grateful to Jeremy for his edition of the Nabu Temple texts.

Between that I have acted simply as the custodian of the British School's share. I may or may not have had reason to collate the tablets for anybody. I never had reason to read them, because we had more than enough else to deal with. If I say anything at all, therefore, it is because during the last few years I have made some contribution to the business of pulling together a Nimrud database, and in particular trying to piece together what has been done with the tablets. I speak, therefore, in the role of the auditor.

Let me begin then by remarking on the extraordinary working relationship that existed at Nimrud between the archaeologists and the epigraphists, something that I think it would be hard to emulate anywhere else. One has the impression, and it has been remarked to me more or less in this way from time to time, that the tablets coming out of the excavation were the equivalent of a newspaper. They didn't have an English language newspaper at Nimrud, so at breakfast time or lunchtime or whenever it might have been the cry would go up, 'Well, Donald, what have we got today?' And that was today's news. The interest permeated everything that then followed. Every report that Max wrote on Nimrud contained as much information as he had managed to squeeze out of the epigraphists at the time of writing, the tablets he was

finding in each room, what they were all about, who they concerned. That carried on into his magisterial two volumes, *Nimrud and its Remains*. The story of excavating the tablets and their content is repeated over and over again. And the same tradition, I have to say, continues with David and Joan Oates's book on Nimrud. There is a chapter on the written evidence, and again it permeates every chapter in the book. It was a marvellous tradition. It was not one that you found elsewhere. The Oateses took it on to Rimah and Brak. But I have memories of working with the Germans at Isin. The first season that I was there our epigraphist was von Soden, while I was on the mound enjoying digging up the tablets. We only discovered what we had dug up at the end of the season when he deigned to tell us at the time of registration. And I remember Hrouda telling me that this was absolutely par for the course on a German excavation. His memory was of digging at Uruk.

What would happen at Uruk was that you would dig up the tablets and hand them over to the epigraphist, who would work on them for a few days and then write a letter to his Assyriological colleagues whether in Münster, Berlin, Munich, or elsewhere—and the epigraphist in Münster, Berlin or Munich would then cross the street or go to the pub with his friends from the archaeological institute, and say, 'By the way, do you know what they have been finding at Uruk?' And the archaeologist would then write to his colleagues at Uruk, saying, 'Congratulations. I hear you have dug up such-and-such.' And by this roundabout route a month later the archaeologist would find out what the Assyriologist sitting next to him had been reading a month ago. Thank goodness the same did not apply at Nimrud.

The second thing I would comment on is that Nimrud was interesting from another point of view. It was the first time that British excavations had had to deal on a major scale with unbaked tablets, and consider the problems of how they were to be restored, cleaned and conserved. Previous British excavations at places like Nineveh had largely been dealing with baked tablets, whether purposely baked in antiquity or baked by the fires of destruction. So there was relatively little experience of handling unbaked tablets. One of the solutions used was to set up their own baking kiln on the site. This was in some respects more experimental 50 years ago than it may now sound. At that time the British Museum had only very recently started the business of baking its own tablets. Henrietta (see McCall this volume) has talked of Gadd going down to Nippur and being shown what sound like rather exotic methods of dealing with tablets. Anyway at Nimrud the tablets were baked, and I have heard people like Harry Saggs telling me of their wild and wonderful experiences with the sand-blaster used to clean the tablets. What I would say is that during that time they must have built up a considerable amount of experience of dealing with unbaked clay tablets in the field, and it strikes me as somewhat regrettable that no one has managed to take all this experience and distil it into something to be read by future generations. In the Museum, despite the fact that we supposedly pioneered the business of baking tablets, our conservators are becoming increasingly reluctant to undertake any conservation that is not absolutely vital.

I say it is regrettable that nothing has been put on record, but you will see some remarks in David and Joan Oates' book about the problems of dealing with unbaked tablets (Oates and Oates 2001:195). There are some remarks in Harry Saggs's edition of the Nimrud Letters (Saggs 1955) on what he picked up from looking at them. And there are a perceptive couple of sentences in Julian Reade's 1982 account of Nimrud in *Fifty Years of Mesopotamian Discovery*. Those who have actually worked with him over the years know that behind a couple of sentences from Julian hides a wealth of experience and a lot more that he might have said. I have to say I am aware that wasn't the end of it, because he and Nanina did in fact write an account of what they understood to be the principles underlying treating tablets in the field. Unfortunately they sent it to the *Journal of Cuneiform Studies*, whose editor had never, so far as I know, worked on an excavation nor even been to Mesopotamia, and I understand that he rejected it because he did not believe that Assyriologists could be trusted to carry out the procedures as advocated without serious risk to the tablets. So Julian's article remains unpublished. I hope that at some point he will bring it out of the archives again. It does seem to me that otherwise we will have lost a wealth of experience that we need to preserve.

Having said that, the other thing, which I in my capacity of auditor look forward to, is probably a single A4 sheet of paper entitled 'Nimrud for dummies'. Every excavator builds up his own jargon. It goes into the notebooks. The people who work on the excavation are entirely familiar with it, but a generation or two later you puzzle over what's going on. We have that puzzle with Leonard Woolley at Ur—Terence Mitchell can give you a good guide to Ur, but most of the rest of us look through the notebooks and wonder what some of the abbreviations mean. I hope that future people working on the records will not do as I did and spend half an hour puzzling over the curious fact that at Nimrud house no. 53 on the Town Wall seemed to have more rooms than everywhere else put together. That of course is rubbish. It merely meant the house was dug up in 1953. Anybody who worked at Nimrud would have laughed at me. But the fact remains that in 50 years' time there is a risk of other people going

through the same process. It may not be obvious to somebody reading the records in 50 years' time that SEB is a corner of the Nabu Temple. I noticed once or twice looking through the records that there was some suspicion that rooms excavated had been renumbered. Julian Reade told me last week that he had come to the same conclusion, and had not been able fully to disentangle it. Well if Julian can't disentangle it you know there's a minor problem, which I hope will be addressed before those who can address it have left us.

That said, what then did we dig up at Nimrud? A grand total, according to the database, of about 1700 tablets, split in the proportion of about 55% in Baghdad and 45% sitting here in the Museum. That of course includes tablets ranging from the large Vassal Treaties of Esarhaddon down to pieces that might be the size of my thumbnail. They come from more or less every part of the excavations.

I will start with Fort Shalmaneser, and I am not going to go into any great detail on this. Most of it is published. In Fort Shalmaneser something like 180 tablets were found, including the wine lists—and David Oates has already shown you the wine jars *in situ* with tablets scattered among them—and including the archives of the Arsenal, military affairs, dealing with equipment and the like, and also affairs of the queen's household and officials called the *rab ekalli*. That archive covers most of the eighth century and part of the seventh century. Most of the material comes from the time of Sargon and his predecessors, but after that the building continues in use. The archives of Fort Shalmaneser have now been fully published by Dalley and Postgate (1984). You can read all about it. I don't need to tell you any more. That one's well done.

We then come to the Governor's Palace (Postgate 1973), excavated in the first seasons of excavations at Nimrud/Kalhu, the palace of the local governor dealing with the province of Nimrud. Here the archives begin in the reign of Adad-nirari III (810–783 BC). There are but two earlier tablets. You have two rooms, which appear to have been his chancery, his filing cabinet as it were—the principal governors appearing in the archive as Bel-tarsi-iluma and Bel-dan. You have his own administrative and economic records for the period down to the reign of Sargon II (721–705 BC), when the capital moved to Khorsabad, and after that they peter out. One of the sad things about Nimrud is the fact that, as I have said, there are only two tablets there earlier than the reign of Adad-nirari. The administration of Nimrud/Kalhu and its area in the first 50 years after the city was re-founded by Ashurnasirpal have disappeared virtually without trace.

We move then briefly to the Burnt Palace, which produced a relatively small number of tablets, about 25, but including a number of letters to King Sargon. These have already been fully dealt with for the most part by Postgate in CTN 2 (Postgate 1973).

The Nabu Temple was one of the most prolific sites for tablets. There, as David Oates has told you, they found the Vassal Treaties of Esarhaddon, in rather more than 200 fragments, which have been edited twice by now, the last time in Japan by Dr Watanabe (Wiseman 1958; Watanabe 1987). It also produced the Library, which has now been fully published for us by Jeremy Black and Donald Wiseman in CTN 4 (Wiseman and Black 1996). Jeremy will tell us more about it. It also produced a small archive, about 40 tablets, from the administration of the temple, and Barbara Parker, in publishing these, remarked that this was the first Assyrian temple archive so far discovered—actually very small, little beyond a few heart shaped tags with the string still in them, probably to be tied to sacks of grain—dealing with loans, probably made by the temple to small farmers (Parker 1957). The tablets from that area mostly cover the reign of Ashurbanipal and his successors. That material remains to be re-edited in a forthcoming volume of CTN.

Then the Town Wall houses produced a number of private archives, the largest of them from a eunuch by name of Shamash-sharra-uṣur. Again the material from this site is exclusively from the reigns of Esarhaddon, Ashurbanipal and their successors—nothing earlier (i.e. between 680 and 612 BC).

The most intriguing site has always been what Max started by calling the Ziggurat Terrace, the northern wing of the North-West Palace, the wing built by Shalmaneser III (858–824 BC). Here were found the letters, which Harry Saggs has finally published after devoted attention of almost 50 years (Saggs 2001). It must be one of the longest time spans over which anybody has worked on an archive, but finally he's made it, and he has to be congratulated on a magnificent volume. If you want to know what life was really like in the late eighth century BC read that book. It all comes out. My teacher Professor Kraus in Leiden spent half his career working on letters, and taught us all that the great problem in dealing with letters is they don't deal with facts, they deal with feelings and nuances. You have to work and work at a letter to find out what's really going on. Anyway finally the Nimrud letters are published.

The northern wing of the palace also produced two archives of economic texts, one in the west half of the northern wing and one in the eastern half. The archive from the western half belongs to the reign of Sargon and his predecessors and deals with administrative, political and all the other affairs of the empire. Most of the tablets were found in the intriguing room 4, and a few in room 5. They deal, as I say, with affairs of the empire during the time of Tiglath-pileser III and Sargon (745–705 BC). In the eastern half the archives were again administrative and economic, and they cover much of the time-span from Adad-nirari through to the end of the Assyrian empire. Barbara Parker published some of this material

many years ago, but there is more that remains to be published (Parker 1954; 1961).

My impression is that there remain something like 500 tablets to be re-edited in what may be two more volumes of CTN. But I have the impression that all the preliminary reports that we have had have given an extremely good idea of what was dug up in those areas. I don't believe there are any significant surprises coming.

With that I might conclude. The School has done extraordinarily well in terms of publishing its results, and one might hope that within the present decade the whole job will have been finished off. And then the next generation will be able to tell us by means of computer analysis, digital photography, and goodness knows what else, that they can do a whole lot better, and a third generation of publishing will begin.

I do, however, have just a few other remarks to make, partly again about what's missing. What has not been discovered at Nimrud is any of its early history. Max apparently identified a small group of sherds from nineteenth century work at Nimrud as belonging to the Ninevite 5 period, proving that there was already a settlement at Nimrud by the third millennium BC. Was anybody literate at that period? There is one, and only one, tantalizing piece of evidence, and I apologize to my colleague Irving Finkel for stealing his thunder, for he is the one who is the expert in this. There is a fragment of a tablet found in the Nabu Temple that actually belongs to the same tablet as a fragment dug up by Layard. It has always been taken as Assyrians fooling around with early writing. It is a list of sign forms. The left hand sign is a speculative picture of what an early sign might have looked like, and the right hand sign is how we nowadays write it in Assyrian (fig. 30-a). My colleague Irving has looked at this for many years and come to the conclusion that perhaps we were being a little unfair to the Assyrians. Just possibly this is not quite as wild and speculative an exercise as it looks. Just possibly this represents a variant form of early writing other than the form known from Uruk. Wait and see. But it just opens up the possibility that Ashurnasirpal's agents or architects fossicking around in the remains of the earlier village over which they built found something earlier, something perhaps which would take an enormous effort to find today, but maybe in a century or two someone will come up with the evidence that in fact this kind of writing was attested at Nimrud.

Secondly, I have already remarked on the fact that even when Ashurnasirpal II (883–859 BC) arrived the first fifty years of Nimrud/Kalhu are virtually unknown in terms of the written record. What was going on? We have the Banquet Stele and then the better part of fifty years is silent.

One of the other curiously missing things is the fact that although Max dug up something like 90 prisms or

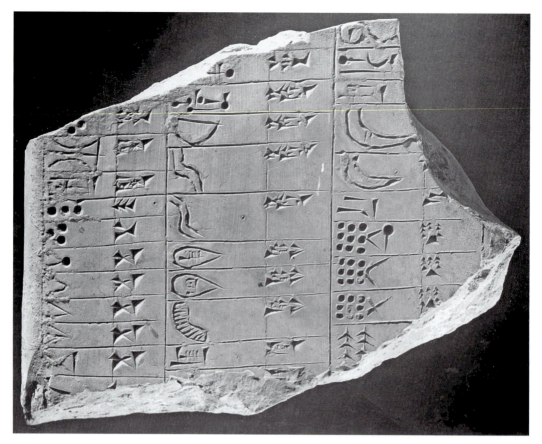

Fig. 30-a. Fragment of reverse side of lexical text from Ezida inscribed in four columns, ND 4311, Iraq Museum.

cylinders on the site, so far as I am aware none of these has been found *in situ*. The assumption has always been that these items were made to be buried in the foundations of buildings, but we have yet to find them there. If you go to Babylonia, Woolley dug up cylinders in the corners of the ziggurat at Ur. Mac Gibson did the same at Nippur. We have them from Sippar, dug up and reburied by Nabonidus. We have yet to find an Assyrian prism buried in the foundations of any building at either Nineveh or Nimrud—and I have to say that we probably never will, because the times have moved on. We are no longer in the business of looting, we are in the business of careful excavation and restoration, and I don't believe now we would easily persuade our Iraqi colleagues to demolish Nimrud simply in the hope of finding another prism.

Finally I made the mistake of titling this lecture, 'Archives'. I admit that Nicholas also called the texts from the Governor's Palace an archive. I have the feeling, however, that we are probably misusing that term. I do not get the impression that what survives at Nimrud can now properly be called archives—they are the leftovers. We know what archives look like. They are the tens of thousands of tablets that were dug up in Sumer, at Umma, Drehem and Tello, dug up clandestinely, ripped from their context, and the only things to give you an indication of how they might have been stored are the clay labels attached to the reed baskets. We know that at Sippar,

Rassam found the temple archives of Ebabbar in one or two storerooms, but there is precious little record of how they might have been found. At Babylon in around 1870 the archives of the Egibi family are recorded as having been found in clay jars. Budge reports the same of all the tablets that he purchased from illicit excavations at Tell ed-Der. So we have the impression of tablets being found in jars or stored in reed baskets. We know nothing, or next to nothing, about how archives might have been stored at Nimrud/Kalhu, about why it is that we are left with what we have, whether what's left over or what was thrown in the bin, or trampled into the floor, or to what extent what survives represents any kind of considered archive keeping.

There is only one more tantalizing piece of evidence at Nimrud, which has been illustrated and alluded to from time to time—David Oates alluded to it in his comments—and that is the archive room in the north-west wing of the palace of Ashurnasirpal. The tablets in this room were found, according to Max Mallowan, in a great heap three or four feet deep, but having evidently been disturbed and thrown back in. But in the bottom of that room was this curious structure, on the left a bench and in the middle two rows of boxes of clay bricks, and Mallowan speculated that this was indeed the chancery, the chamber where tablets were brought in and sorted, where they were written, where they were recorded, and

Fig. 30-b. Archive room ZT4 in the north wing of the North-West Palace. About 350 tablets were found in the rubbish debris which filled this chamber.

maybe those boxes represent a filing system. Unfortunately, as I say, his perception was that the tablets found there had been thrown back in. On other sites where such constructions have been found in an area of scribal activity the assumption has generally been made that either these are the recycling bins—you chuck the clay back in and reuse it—or they are the bins where you store the clay or the sand ready for making tablets. The idea that this had been used as a filing system had not, so far as I know, previously been suggested prior to Max finding this structure at Nimrud. We wait to see whether anyone finds such structures elsewhere. I wait to see whether, when our colleagues complete the publication of Nimrud with the discussion of the archives in this area, what comment they have to make on what strikes me as a somewhat unusual filing system, if such it be; but one treats a suggestion made by the likes of Max with very considerable respect.

With that tantalizing picture I leave you.

31 THE LIBRARIES OF KALHU

Jeremy Black

Introduction

Literacy at Nimrud was present in several different languages and more than one writing system, since we can be sure that alphabetic writing for Aramaic was widely employed in addition to cuneiform. Local Assyrian dialect was used for documents and letters, and the Mesopotamian cultural standard which we call Standard Babylonian was used for literary works. Sumerian was the language of some magical and religious works; usually these were provided with an Akkadian translation.

Standard Babylonian was also used for royal inscriptions and annalistic accounts. Of course there are plenty of stamped bricks all over the site, as well as annalistic inscriptions *in situ* on various wall slabs, door slabs and, for example, the throne dais from Fort Shalmaneser. Clay hands, *sikkātu* (decorative wall bosses) and inscribed objects (such as figurines and bowls) are also common.

So where are we to look for the libraries of Kalhu, and what should we expect to find in them? The neat distinction has been made that 'archives' are collections of documents, whereas 'libraries' are collections of 'literary' or copied writings of the 'stream of tradition' (Black and Tait 1995; Pedersén 1998), and the evidence of other Assyrian cities and towns suggests that libraries are typically located in private houses or in temples.

The principal library to be discussed here is that of E-zida, the temple of the god Nabû.[1] But there were other temples in the city—Ashurnasirpal II claims to have (re)built nine temples, including new temples of Enlil and Ninurta. Some of these have been located, viz. the temple of Ninurta, and two temples of aspects of the goddess Ishtar: Ishtar *bēlet Kidmūri* (a building which perhaps dated back to Middle Assyrian times) and Ishtar *šarrat niphi*. Any of these might have had libraries. So might the several palaces on the acropolis. In principle, however, other collections of tablets that have been found are 'archives', for example, those from the North-West Palace, the Governor's Palace and from the house of the eunuch Šamaš-šarru-usur, TW53.

Literary tablets in other locations

Of course literary tablets have been found in locations other than libraries. One must bear in mind the disruption at Kalhu after the city's destruction. After perhaps repeated ransacking of the city in 614 and/or 612, and abortive attempts to salvage and tidy up in between, it is not unexpected that modern archaeologists should have problems in assigning objects to their original locations.[2] It is known too that rooms in some of the city's public buildings were reoccupied later for different purposes. Consequently we should not place too much reliance on the association of stray objects with any particular location. Quite a few finds were made on or near the surface as well.

In the Governor's Palace, amongst the archives of the governors of Kalhu, an extispicy prayer, a perfume recipe and a lexical work were found.[3] And in the vicinity of the Burnt Palace, but on the surface, a report prepared in 714 BC for Sargon II on some ceremonies performed at Ashur was found (ND 1120; Wiseman 1952: 65ff., and CTN II: 246; CTN IV: 28). But I am currently inclined to doubt that any of these should necessarily be considered as originating in the library of the temple of Nabû (CTN IV: 7).

In the North-West Palace, which (as we now know) was in continuous use from its foundation in the 870s BC until the fall of Kalhu (Oates and Oates 2001: 202), there was a chancery office (ZT 4), where pigeonhole boxes on the floor represented a storage system for tablets.[4] It was filled with letters and documents from the reigns of Tiglath-pileser III, Shalmaneser V and Sargon II. And in the same office were a fragment of a Sumerian hymn with Akkadian translation, and a nine-sided barrel cylinder with annals of Sargon II.[5] In another room in that section

---

[1] The reader is referred throughout to the introduction to Wiseman and Black 1996, and to Oates and Oates 2001.

[2] As pointed out in Reade 1982: 110.

[3] CTN IV: 7, n. 83. ND 279: GP, room H: unidentified lexical, CTN II: no. 216; CTN IV: 33; ND 411: GP, room S; *Šamaš bēl dīni* extispicy; CTN II: 214; CTN IV: 15; ND 460: GP, room S: perfume recipe, CTN II: 215; CTN IV: 28.

[4] See Veenhof 1986: 13 (referring to Mallowan 1966: I, 172, with photo, 'chancery' for letters and documents from TP III, Shalmaneser V, and Sargon [up to his move to Khorsabad]).

[5] In the chancery locus ZTW 4 were: ND 3474 bilingual, perhaps a hymn, Wiseman 1953: 147; CTN IV: 27; ND3411, 9-sided barrel cylinder of Sargon II written in Babylonian script, 'ZTW 4 in fill against S. wall of room' (Wiseman 1953: 138ff; copy by Gadd 1954: 198).

of the palace, there was a copy of tablet VI of *Enūma eliš* (room 25 on the *Nimrud and Its Remains* plan),[6] smashed fragments of an octagonal prism of Sargon II (in a corridor),[7] and, in a room in the south-east corner of the private part of the palace, a copy of the Ashur version of the so-called 'Marduk ordeal', a couple of tablets of incantations, two lexical tablets and a stone tablet with the text of Ashurnasirpal's first campaign.[8]

At the *ekal māšarti* or arsenal ('Fort Shalmaneser'), several prisms and cylinders of Esarhaddon were found. These had been stored on an upper floor, but may originally have been *in situ* foundation deposits in the building, so they form a slightly different category of document (Millard 1961; Oates and Oates 2001: 212, 216).

I think it is fair to assume that none of the above-mentioned finds of Standard Babylonian literary and historical tablets is evidence of a library. Either they are the results of the general disruption of the major buildings of Kalhu, or for some reason they were in use or stored in various buildings within the citadel on the elevated acropolis or at the arsenal. It is too uncertain, and probably implausible, to assume that they had been borrowed by readers of the Temple of Nabû library who had forgotten to return them and incurred thereby the ultimate maximum fine. In fact there is no evidence for library collections as such anywhere else in the excavated part of the city. So in general terms it seems that the vast majority of the 'literary' tablets we have from Kalhu are from the library of the temple of Nabû, and that other collections of tablets are from documentary archives in various places.

The Temple of Nabû

The temple of the god Nabû, the god of scribes, was a substantial and important building. 'This building', writes Julian Reade, 'with its two sets of twin shrines, had probably developed by the late 7th century into the principal religious building of Kalhu' (Reade 1982: 111). The majority of the building was excavated during the

6th–8th seasons (1955–57), although it had been explored by earlier excavators.

Located on the south-east corner of the acropolis, the temple was set back from the street leading up from the lower town, its entrance flanked by two gilded mermen (CTN III: 95). The refoundation of it (*ana eššūte…addi*) is claimed by Ashurnasirpal II, but it was substantially rebuilt by Adad-nīrārī III, probably including the rooms ringing the south-east courtyard. This happened most likely around 798 BC, the year in which Bēl-tarsi-ilūma, the governor of Kalhu, held office as *limmu*. Later restoration work in the shrines of Nabû and Tašmētu was carried out by Esarhaddon, in whose reign it was used for a *hašādu* (divine marriage) festival of the god and goddess. Further restoration was effected by Ashurbanipal and later by Ashur-etel-ilāni. At the sack of Kalhu, the two major shrines were stripped and destroyed by fire; other chambers were also plundered but not structurally demolished.

It is clear that the *gerginakku* (library) was located in NT 12, a room with a wide west-facing door to admit light, directly opposite the entrance to the shrine of Nabû.[9] (The wide doorway is reminiscent of the library in the *āšipū* family's house at Ashur.) In the north-east corner of the room was a narrow well, providing a water source convenient for work on tablets. (Mallowan's field notes refer to 'a big stone' which had covered the well.) No archaeological evidence survived of any other installations such as tablet boxes or a pigeonhole storage system.

When the ruined buildings were reoccupied in the post-Assyrian phase G, the new inhabitants left their own debris in the library. Subsequently an attempt was made to rebuild parts of the temple for accommodation (phase H), and from the level associated with that later phase a deep pit was dug down into NT 12, damaging the doorway and cutting away part of the western wall. The chambers were seriously disturbed by these activities, and the tablets encountered (which were of no interest to the builders of this post-cuneiform phase) were carelessly shovelled out and later refilled back into various pits, along with some bits of gypsum plaster and bitumen, thereby damaging them further in the process. Some had been shifted again by nineteenth-century excavators. During Iraqi SOAH excavations in 1985–86, a few more tablets were recovered (some of which join fragments from the earlier

---

[6] Locus ZTE 25 (25 on plan in Mallowan 1966); ND 3416 *Enūma eliš VI*, Wiseman 1953: 139; CTN IV: 29.

[7] ND 3400+, octagonal prism of Sargon II 'scattered on pavement ZTE corridor' (marked on *Nimrud and Its Remains* plan). See Wiseman 1953: 138ff.

[8] Room FF (south-east corner of private part of palace): ND 812A: Ashur version of 'Marduk ordeal', CTN II: 268; CTN IV: 31; ND 812B: incantation or ritual, CTN II: 269; CTN IV: 34; ND 821A: incantation and ritual, CTN II: 270; CTN IV: 21; ND 821B: unident, lexical, CTN II: 271; CTN IV: 34; ND 821C: unident, lexical, CTN II: 272; CTN IV: 34, along with a stone tablet of Anp. 1st campaign (see Wiseman and Kinnier-Wilson 1951: 104–5).

[9] Only four literary fragments were recovered from the adjoining room NT 13 (although some pieces from the 1987 SOAH season may have come from there). Oates and Oates 2001: 15 note that these perhaps came from backfill (the soil was taken from nineteenth-century dumps). Oates and 2001: 207 state that 'rooms NTS 9 and 10 may also have been scribal offices' (also p. 115). The library tablets were published by Wiseman and Black 1966.

excavations).[10] Almost certainly further tablets remain to be found at the bottom of the well, but so far it has proved too narrow and airless to investigate.

The library originally contained getting on for 300 tablets. All the literary tablets are in Standard Babylonian (or Sumerian with Akkadian translation). If, as we believe, this range of rooms was the work of Adad-nīrārī III (810–783 BC), then at least two tablets are older than the building itself: a hemerology written by an official of Ashurnasirpal II, and an incantation possibly dated in 814.[11] These may have come from an earlier library somewhere. The only other dated colophons are from 787 and 676 BC.

Although of modest size compared with other Assyrian libraries, the library was well stocked, including some already known works as well as some hitherto unknown (the numbers are those of tablets or fragments):

30   celestial omens (mostly *enūma Anu Ellil*)
5   teratological omens (*šumma izbu*)
16   terrestrial omens (*šumma ālu*)
11   hemerologies and menologies
3   extispicy texts
10   prognostic and physiognomic omens
75   magical and medical
20   prayers and hymns
16   ritual texts
6   works of reference (uru-an-na, *šammu šikinšu*)
38   lexical

The narrowly 'literary' works are few in number: just one tablet each of the popular Sumerian poems *Lugale* (IX) and *Angin* (I), tablet I of *Gilgameš*, tablet II of *Enūma eliš*, one tablet of *Ludlul* (I), two tablets of proverbs, and an *aluzinnu* composition.

Very roughly the proportions work out as
     30% divination
     30% magic
     15% prayers, hymns, rituals
     20% reference and education.

There are no indications of school work as such (like the schoolboy tablets from the library at Huzirina (Sultantepe)). But there is a limited collection of lexical lists which indicate that scribal training at some level did take place: several copies of Hh II, and an almost complete set of *malku-šarru* (tablets II, II, III, IV and V). It is comparable to the balance of the *āšipū*'s library at Ashur, but that was considerably larger, with *c.* 800 tablets.

Palaeography

The range of hands represented is quite considerable. Some are genuinely calligraphic, while others are frankly coarse. Many have distinctive sign-forms peculiar to this library. So far as one can tell, the typical Kalhu *ductus* found in a large number of the tablets was perhaps more conservative than that of Nineveh. A large proportion are written in a standardized format with two columns per side. Some tablets (about nine) are in Babylonian script; these are not all by the same scribe, and one is written by a real novice. We know that writing in Babylonian script was an accomplishment of some Assyrian library scribes, so it need not be assumed that these tablets were imported (Saggs 2001:2). Within the set of *malku-šarru*, tablet V and one copy of tablet II were in Babylonian script; I, II, IV and another copy of II were in Assyrian. This suggests that someone had tried to collect gradually a complete set of the work.

Scribes

About seven or eight different scribes are known from colophons. Two tablets (one copied from an original from Babylon) belonged to the *āšipū* Banūni. One may have been written for the son of the well-known *kalamāhu* Urad-Ea.

It is possible that one highly-placed scribal 'family' represented here has as its youngest member a royal scribe and scholar of Adad-nīrārī III, with his great-grandfather Issarān-mudammiq, an official of Ashurnasirpal II (about a century earlier, so perfectly plausible). This family is known to have had Babylonian ancestors.

Up to four tablets are the (possibly early) work or property of Adad-šuma-issur, later known as the eminent *āšipū* and adviser of Esarhaddon and Ashurbanipal (Luppert-Barnard 1998), and a descendant of Gabbi-ilāni-ēriš, a scholar of Ashurnasirpal II and Tukultī-Ninurta II.

Another tablet in the library may possibly be the work of his brother Nabû-zēra-līšir. Both were sons of the illustrious Nabû-zuqup-kēna, who is well-known for his editorial work from tablets dated in the reigns of Sargon and Sennacherib from Nineveh (the Kouyunjik collection).[12] Some of these tablets of Nabû-zuqup-kēna are explicitly said to have been written at Kalhu,[13] suggesting that the family may have worked at Kalhu before moving (being promoted, perhaps) to Nineveh. It

---

[10] With the kind collaboration of Muzahim Mahmud, I was able to publish these in *Sumer* (Hussein and Black 1985–86).
[11] Hemerology (no. 58): scribe (or owner?) is a *šangamahhu* of Ashurnasirpal (883–859), and incantations (no. 133) dated to *limmu* Bēlu-balāt, 814.

[12] I am grateful to Dr Heather Baker for providing me with information from the *Prosopography of the Neo-Assyrian Empire* in advance of publication of the relevant volumes.
[13] Several of nos 293–311 in Hunger 1968.

is worth considering the possibility that those 'K.' tablets were in fact excavated not at Nineveh, but at Kalhu; two fragments of the annals of Tiglath-pileser III in the Kouyunjik collection were clearly found by George Smith in 1873 in the 'S.E. Palace, Nimroud', as written in pencil on the tablets in Smith's handwriting (CTN IV: 4, note 41). But it does seem plausible, also, that tablets were transferred to Nineveh from the Kalhu library, perhaps along with the transfer of personnel.

Other libraries elsewhere, for comparison

It is of interest to compare some other Assyrian libraries. The two libraries (perhaps better described as tablet storage rooms) of the temple of Nabû at Dūr-Šarru-kīn were also housed in rooms directly off the forecourt and central court respectively (on the north-west side, facing south-east). While some aspects of the architecture may have been influenced by the temple of Nabû at Kalhu, the temple at Dūr-Šarru-kīn was much grander. But in the entire building at Dūr-Šarru-kīn, from a total of only 23 tablets (including 5 documents) found, only one tablet (a lexical list) was found in either of its 'library' rooms (Loud and Altman 1938: 46 and pl. 19c, and Conclusion, below).

The library of the family of *āšipū* at Ashur probably dated to about the reign of Sargon II in the seventh century BC, although it contained plenty of earlier tablets. It was housed in a library room off a courtyard with a door 1.5 m wide (facing south-east) (Pedersén 1986: II, 41) exactly as the Kalhu library. It too contained some royal inscriptions, and some documents. In one of the libraries in the temple of Ashur at Ashur, many prisms and barrel cylinders were found in the forecourt together with various tablets; it seems uncertain whether these form a separate group of material archaeologically speaking (Pedersén 1986: II, 13 and n.9).

Conclusions

This should alert us to the conclusion that the physical distinction between first-millennium BC libraries and archives cannot always be maintained. Certainly, closer study of the excavation records from Nimrud has now made this quite clear. The 1996 publication by Wiseman and Black, *Literary texts from the Temple of Nabû*, CTN IV, was slightly misleading in this respect, as it did not include the non-literary material from the temple library room, although it did include some literary finds from other parts of the temple which were not found in the library.

Elsewhere within the temple of Nabû were nine copies of the vassal treaties of Esarhaddon, in the royal suite (evidently that was the repository for these important state

documents). There was also the Shalmaneser III stone tablet (in NTS 17), and a cylinder of the annals of Tiglath-pileser III. A lexical tablet found in the throne room (a palaeographic sign list) actually joins K.8520,[14] incidentally reinforcing the possibility that other K. tablets originated at Kalhu.

But conversely there were some 'historical' records and some administrative or commercial documents found actually in or very close to the library (CTN IV: 4f.). The fact that over 20 documents dated mostly in the 660s (Parker 1957) were found in a later pit above the wall between NT 14 and NT 16 has been thought to indicate 'the use of these rooms for administrative (non-library) activities of the scribes'.[15] But I now doubt that this was the case. There were also three literary tablets found actually on the floors of the same rooms, and two in the pit; eight more on a floor surface in a trench 'west of NT 14'.[16] As stated above, later occupants of the building cleared out tablets from the library and later shovelled them back into pits dug at random across the area. The only realistic conclusion here is that these documents were not a discrete small archive belonging in rooms NT 14–16–17, but that they undoubtedly belonged originally with the other documents, found amongst the literary tablets, that must have come from the library room; in fact they deal with the same subject-matter.

The explanation for this modern confusion is to be found in the very nature of the progressive excavation of a site. Working with the records, it is not always easy to correlate earlier findspots within the area of the temple buildings with the later designations of rooms.[17] The nature of NT loci inevitably changed during successive excavation seasons. What was originally the 'SE edifices' on Felix Jones' map (1852) became the SE Palace for George Smith, 1875; still so for Mallowan in 1950 (Mallowan 1950: pl. XXVI); then the SE Building, as the south-east and north-west ranges of the temple's rooms gradually emerged (so Mallowan, beginning of sixth season, 1955; the cella and front of the temple of Nabû were by then already identified). A sequence of surface trenches across the south-east area yielded many tablets in the sixth season, but it was not clear until later that the pit found in the trench H2 had lain directly over the floor of what was in the seventh season (1956) to be designated as NT 12, the library room. Given this gradually changing picture, I believe the following is a reasonable statement. Roughly there were three concentrations of tablet finds in

---

[14] ND 4311 (CTN IV: 229).

[15] CTN IV: 3; also Oates and Oates 2001: 115.

[16] Floor: CTN IV: 53, 227, 230; pit (probably): CTN IV: 83, 90; eight on floor w. of NT 14: CTN IV: 25, 36, 40, 47, 211, 224, 258, 259.

[17] I am very grateful to Helen MacDonald for elucidating some problems, based on her detailed knowledge of the records.

the south-east area of the temple buildings: (a) the H2 pit, the library room NT 12 and also NT 13; (b) the area of the pit near the door of NT 14; and (c) the area of the pit over and between NT 16/18. All these tablets had originally been stored in the library room NT 12.

The following figures are slightly approximate but demonstrate the mixture of types found in each of these concentrations:

H2/NT 12/NT 13:	literary 187	historical 31	documents 10[18]
NT 14 pit:	literary 42	historical 1	documents 0
NT 16/18 pit:	literary 8	historical 0	documents 30

For comparison:

NT elsewhere:	literary 5	historical 13	documents 5
		+ the 'vassal treaties'	

The greatest concentration is the library room NT 12 and the related pit, where all types are represented. A rough conclusion then is that very roughly 10–20% of the tablets or fragments from this 'library' were in fact historical records or administrative documents. The 'historical' records from in and around the library cover the following reigns: Shalmaneser III (858–824),[19] Adad-nīrārī III (810–783), Tiglath-pileser III (745–727), Sennacherib (704–681), Esarhaddon (680–669) and Ashurbanipal (668–*c.* 631).

I think this gives a more realistic picture of the contents of the temple library. Such libraries regularly contained copies of historical records on prisms, barrel cylinders or tablets. Not infrequently they also contained assorted archival documents and records; but in this particular case it may now be impossible to ascertain the precise connection of these to the library and its personnel.

---

[18] Including an edict in Assyrian dialect: CTN IV: 256=SAA 12 no. 84.

[19] ND 5417 is probably not to be assigned to Shamshi-Adad V (823–822): Grayson 1996: 172 considers Shalmaneser III more likely. Also represented within the temple (not from NT 12) are Aššur-etel-ilāni (≈629–612) (bricks) and Šin-šar-iškun (≈629–612). There are no records of Sargon (721–705).

32 ARAMAIC AT NIMRUD ON CLAY, POTSHERDS, BRICKS AND IVORIES

Alan Millard

About 1,100 BC, Tiglath-pileser I campaigned repeatedly against people he called Aramu, reaching as far west as the Mediterranean Sea. A few decades later Ashur-bel-kala boasted of similar expeditions. Yet neither king won any victory of lasting worth, for by the end of the eleventh century Aramaean tribes had overrun most of Assyria's western provinces and crossed the Tigris to occupy places in the east, confining Assyrian rule to her heartland. It was about a century before Assyria recovered and began to reassert her control over territories she had once ruled in the west. Most of the small states she subdued there were inhabited and ruled by people speaking and, when necessary, writing Aramaic. One of the earliest specimens of that language is preserved on the statue of a local ruler of Guzan (Tell Halaf) from Tell Fekheriyeh, ancient Sikan, probably the Mitannian capital Washshukanni. On the

front of the skirt is an inscription in Assyrian cuneiform, on the back an Aramaic version, written with the twenty-two letter alphabet. The letters have some unusual shapes, perhaps deliberately archaic, and the language has some unexpected forms not previously known earlier than the Persian period. A striking feature of the Aramaic is the inclusion of Assyrian loanwords (*adaguru, gugallu, mātu*), indicating the impact Assyria had on the Aramaic language in eastern Syria. Despite the late Agnès Spycket's arguments for an eighth century date on stylistic grounds and palaeographical preferences for a date about 1000 BC expressed by F.M. Cross, I maintain the statue dates from the reign of Shalmaneser III, the engraver using an archaizing, monumental style of alphabetic script (Abou Assaf *et al.* 1982; Spycket 1985; Cross 1995). It is to Shalmaneser's reign that the earliest examples of Aramaic

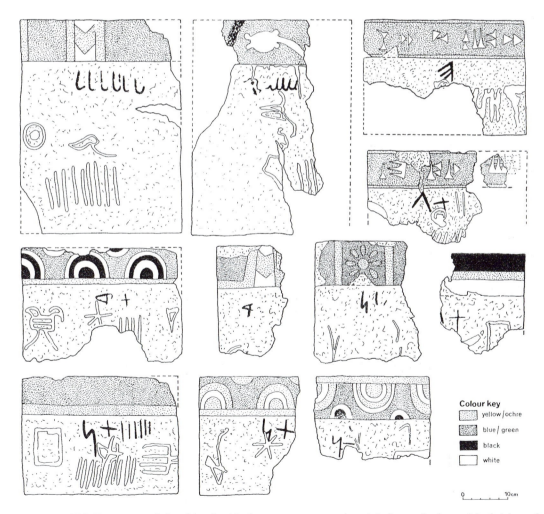

Fig. 32-a. Room T20. Fragments of glazed brick with chevrons, rosettes and semicircles on the front of the bricks and with fitters' marks in black (West Semitic) and white on the top of the bricks.

found at Nimrud belong. The British Museum's excavations in 1989, directed by John Curtis, uncovered almost eighty glazed bricks, whole or fragmentary, originally forming parts of a panel, or panels (Curtis *et al.* 1993), like the one found in Courtyard T of Fort Shalmaneser during David Oates's excavations in 1962 and reconstructed by Julian Reade (Reade 1963). Painted on the edges of some of these bricks are cuneiform signs which give the name and titles of Shalmaneser. On the upper, flat faces are various marks in white paint, including 'groups of up to nine parallel lines, five- or six-pointed stars, a circle with crossed lines, and items that can be recognized as a plough, a mace, a human face, a door, probably a cross-legged table and a cauldron, and possibly a goat. There is also a device of three concentric circles...' (Curtis *et al.* 1993: 27) (fig. 32-a). Such marks had been noted by Layard on bricks he found, by Reade on the 1962 panel and on others at Khorsabad, Ashur, Susa and Babylon. Beside them on these Nimrud bricks there are letters of the West Semitic alphabet in black paint. When the bricks bearing the cuneiform signs were placed in order, the letters on the upper faces were seen to form a sequence in alphabetical order. If we assume the marks belong to the original erection of the panel, although it is possible the bricks were reused, then it is clear that the builders used the letters to ensure they laid the bricks in the correct sequence as they were unable to read the cuneiform script but could read the twenty-two letter alphabet. It seems most reasonable to treat these letters as Aramaic, but they could be Phoenician or even Hebrew; none shows a distinctive characteristic of one script or another, nor do they display any closely datable feature (Millard in Curtis *et al.* 1993: 35–36). They testify to the presence of brick-layers at Nimrud in the mid-ninth century BC who knew the West Semitic abc.

The use of letters of the alphabet as guides for fitting pieces of a composite structure together has long been known from the carved ivories which once decorated wooden furniture (Barnett 1975: 161–62; Röllig 1974: 51–59). One of the magnificent pair of plaques depicting a lioness killing a negro in a papyrus swamp, extracted from Well NN in the North-West Palace, has the letter *aleph* on its upper edge (*Ibid.*: 161, 190, O.1; Mallowan 1966: 140, 142). Although several different letters occur, as yet no carved ivories can be placed in sequence according to the letters on them. From Fort Shalmaneser two small uraei, that might belong together, bear letters far removed from each other, respectively an *h* and a *t* (Herrmann 1992: nos 450, 451). Similarly, a group of nine hemi-cylindrical beadings from Fort Shalmaneser carry a letter and a vertical on the flat base, between dowel sockets, but no effective sequence can be established (*Ibid.*: 59, 60, nos 74–82). The marks appear on the backs, edges and tenons of ivory plaques, many on tenons which have snapped off from the plaques and cannot be reconnected. As on the bricks, the letters are sometimes accompanied by several vertical strokes, apparently numerical. On a few there is a

mark like an inverted horn beside a letter. Its function might be a workshop or a craftsman's mark, a sign for a class or consignment of furniture. It is noteworthy that the same sign also occurs on one ivory found in the provincial palace at Arslan Tash, perhaps implying a common origin for the carvings (Millard 1962: 50). The single letters clearly served as guides for setting the pieces in their right places or order. However, the use of the letters does not necessarily imply that they were placed in sequence, for double-faced stone heads found in the citadel at Amman had eyes of black stone inlaid in them with letters incised on the backs. While one face had the right eye marked *w* and the left, as might be expected, *z* , another had *b* on the right and *s* on the left (Zayadine 1973; Bordreuil 1973). These letters need not indicate that the cabinet makers were literate, as with the brick-layers, they need only have known the alphabetical order of the letters. In passing we note that some ivories bear letters and sketches like those on the Shalmaneser bricks (Herrmann 1986: nos 1137, 1138, see my notes, pp. 44, 45). There are other ivories engraved with several letters spelling names or words. Two griffin plaques appear to have names on the back, one being Elisha ('*lyš*'), the other *sl*' or *zl*' (Millard 1962: 49, ND 10304, ND 10303; Mallowan 1966: 598; Lemaire 1976: 66–68; Teixidor 1977: 268), and another has letters which have been read as 'behind, below' (*b 'ḥr btḥt*) by André Lemaire, although Javier Teixidor disagreed (Mallowan 1966: 597, fig. 581, ND 12049, cf. 598; Lemaire 1976: 65–66; Teixidor 1977: 268). In some cases, letters remain from a previous use of the ivory, and now appear at an odd angle, incomplete and unintelligible (Mallowan 1966: 597, fig. 580, ND 12031, cf. 598; Herrmann 1992: no. 200). Then there are the two pieces bearing place names: Hamath on an otherwise plain plaque and Lu'ash on the back of a horse's nose-piece—the function of the latter is not clear (Millard 1962: 42, 43, ND 10151, ND 10359; Mallowan 1966: 596, fig. 578; 582, fig. 549, cf. 595; Orchard 1967: no. 136). Here is evidence for craftsmen able to recognize more than the order of the letters, but more probably in their Levantine homelands than in Assyria.

Longer texts might be engraved on ivory mounts or labels. Fragments of a curving ivory strip (fig. 32-b) are evidently part of a dedicatory inscription, '...which X gave to...' (...*zy ḥqrb*.., Millard 1962: 43, 44, ND 8184a, b), while the slip of veneer carrying the name Hazael, with the end of 'our lord' before it ([*mr*] '*n ḥz'l*) may surely be treated as part of a longer inscription honouring that king of Damascus, as do the pieces from Arslan Tash (Millard *apud* Mallowan 1966: 598, ND 11310, cf. Thureau-Dangin 1931: 185, pl. xlvii). Although strictly outside the limits of this paper, we should notice the broken plaque inscribed in Hebrew with part of a curse on anyone who might destroy the inscription (Millard 1962: 45–49, ND 10150; Mallowan 1966: 595; Lemaire 1976: 68–69). This plaque gives occasion to note that, while there were people of Israelite and Judaean origin at Nimrud, Stephanie Dalley's

Fig. 32-b. ND 8184. Ivory fragments, upper left with part of a dedicatory inscription.

proposal to identify two of the royal ladies buried together there with such finery as Hebrew princesses is implausible (Dalley 1998: 83–98). The name of one, written *ya-ba-a* (see Plate IVa) can be interpreted equally well as early Arabic or Aramaic as Hebrew (Frahm 2000a; 2000b, cited by Dalley). The name of the other is written *a-tal-ya-a* and *a-ta-li-a*, which Dalley identifies with the Hebrew name Athaliah, born by a daughter of Ahab, king of Israel, who became queen of Judah (2 Kings 8: 18, 26; 11). In neither case does the ending conform to the normal Assyrian way of representing the Hebrew divine name Yahweh at the end of a personal name, which is -*ya-a-u*, -*ya-u* , or -*i-a-u*, indicating the /h/ of the Hebrew by the vowel break (see now Younger 2002: 207–18; previously van der Toorn 1992).

It is likely that all these letters and words were engraved in the ninth and eighth centuries BC. Not until the reign of Tiglath-pileser III is there evidence for the wider use of Aramaic from Nimrud. Among the reliefs decorating his palace is the well-known one showing two scribes, one holding a cuneiform tablet, the other a curling sheet of papyrus or leather on which he writes, presumably in Aramaic. Only a short time afterwards, an artist painted a similar scene on the wall at Til Barsip, giving the colours lost from the stone slab. The presence at Nimrud of people actually speaking Aramaic is implied by the bricklayers' marks in the ninth century presence and attested by personal names in documents of the late eighth and seventh centuries (Fales 1974). It is also shown by the discovery at Khorsabad of a bulla impressed by the seal of one of Sargon's officials, the court having moved from Nimrud to Khorsabad only late in Sargon's reign. The name and title, including the king's name, were inscribed on the seal entirely in Aramaic: [*l*]*pn 'sr*/[*l*]*mr srs z*/[*y*] *srgn*, 'Belonging to Pān-Aššur-Lāmur, *ša rēši* official of Sargon' (Sprengling 1932; Kaufman 1983: 53, 54; Bordreuil 1992: 151; Avigad and Sass 1997: no. 755). Whether he owned

another seal inscribed in Assyrian, or had particular dealings with the west or with Aramaic speakers is unknown. It is noteworthy that inscribed cylinder seals of the Neo-Assyrian period—perhaps six dozen—are only a tiny proportion of the total number of Assyrian cylinder seals, and of those about one dozen are inscribed in Aramaic (Watanabe 1993; 1995). None were found at Nimrud, so far as I am aware, but a tablet from Balawat nearby was sealed with a cylinder whose owner had his name written on it in Aramaic, *brkr*, 'Bar-Kar' (Parker 1963: 97). A stamp seal found at Nimrud had its owner's name engraved in Aramaic below the device, but it is difficult to read from the photograph (Parker 1962: 29, ND 5255; Mallowan 1966: 259, no. 238).

Comparable in many ways to the seals are the alphabetic inscriptions on some of the bronze bowls which Layard recovered and also on the heads of ceremonial staves. The names are West Semitic, e.g. Ba'al-'ezer, Mati'-'el, Semakyaw, although one Assyrian name occurs on two staff heads from Khorsabad, Ashur-shar-usur (Barnett 1967; 1974; Heltzer 1978; 1982; Teixidor 1969: 346–47= 1986:102–3; 1979: 363= 1986: 422; Khorsabad pieces, see Millard 1983:103).

To a different category belong the fine bronze weights cast in the form of seated lions which Layard unearthed (fig. 32-c). Thirteen of them carry inscriptions in Assyrian and in Aramaic, giving their denominations, often qualified as 'of the land' and many stating they are 'royal property' (Mitchell 1990; Fales 1995; Zaccagnini 1999). Mallowan's work yielded another bronze lion weight of different form, with three or four apparently alphabetic, but as yet undeciphered, signs on its base (Mallowan 1966: 170, 172, ND 2163).

Assyrian scribes customarily wrote in cuneiform on clay, so it is no surprise to find Aramaic occasionally written on clay. As yet no examples of Aramaic endorsements on

Fig. 32-c. ME 91226. Bronze lion-weight inscribed in Assyrian 'Palace of Shalmaneser, king of Assyria, 3 royal mina' and in Aramaic '3 mina of the land; three royal mina.'

cuneiform documents nor of legal deeds written wholly in Aramaic on clay have been unearthed at Nimrud as they have at Ashur, Nineveh and sites to the west (Fales 1986). However, there are notes on clay. One triangular clay sealing carries four stamp seal impressions and the Aramaic word 'for the palace' (*lhykl'*), and another one has the word 'for the house', perhaps 'for the house of X' (*lbyt*?[ ]) Two small bullae, each with a stamp seal impression on one face, carry the same text in Assyrian and Aramaic, 'between this side and the centre' (*byn yd z' wlbb'*). Its meaning is unclear. Mario Fales reads one letter differently to give the sense 'between the arms and the heart' (*byn ydy wlbb'*), considering these small lumps of clay to be amulets worn around the neck, the seal impressions including divine emblems with protective value. Being of a more prosaic nature, I prefer to see these notes as instructions for the disposition of the sealed objects (Millard 1972; Fales 1986: 222–24).

Aramaic was written on leather or papyrus rolls, on wooden, wax-covered tablets, like the fine ivory ones found in the well in Room AB and bearing fitters' marks on the hinged edges (Wiseman 1955: 4–5; Howard 1955: 15–16; Mallowan 1966: 152; Röllig 1974: 57–58),

accompanied by very fragmentary wooden ones. The wax on the ivory boards held cuneiform script, but others could as well have held Aramaic, as illustrated by the relief from Zinjirli. All these writing materials cost money; to our delight, ancient scrap paper was free, in the form of potsherds ubiquitous in towns and villages. Nimrud provides one fine example, the Nimrud Ostracon. This is simply a list of names, all West Semitic, originally considered to be Israelite by its editor, J.B. Segal and by W.F. Albright, but recognized by two scholars, P. Bordreuil and J. Naveh, independently, as more likely to be Ammonite, so presumably names of deportees receiving rations or required for work (Segal 1957; Albright 1958; Bordreuil 1979; Naveh 1979–80). Layard found two sherds from jars bearing brief and incomplete Aramaic notes in ink (Rawlinson 1865: 243, nos 19, 20; *Corpus Inscriptionum Semiticarum II: Inscriptiones Aramaicae* 1888: nos 44, 45).

These few examples of Aramaic that survive from Nimrud demonstrate the use of the language in daily life at all levels of society; we can be sure much more existed than we can see today and we may hope that future excavations will expand this store.

THE ARCHIVE OF A PALACE SCRIBE AND OTHER OFFICIALS IN THE QUEEN'S HOUSEHOLD FROM THE NORTH-WEST PALACE AT KALHU (NIMRUD)

Ali Yaseen Ahmad

The excavations of the Department of Antiquities and Heritage headed by Mr M.M. Hussein unearthed in 1989 in Room 57 of the North-West Palace of Ashurnasirpal II a large number of economic and administrative texts. It was under Room 57 that Tomb III was found. The total number of tablets was over 150, dated mainly to the first half of the eighth century BC. The archive is therefore contemporary with the so-called Governor's Palace archive.

I would like to thank Dr M.S. Damerji for his permission to study part of this archive, comprising 54 tablets, but he suggested that Dr Abdulilah Fadhil could share them. Accordingly they chose the best 20 of them and published them from photographs only with Professor K. Deller (Deller and Fadhil 1993).

I copied and transliterated over 34 tablets, while the rest of the archive, i.e. over 100 tablets, was in a very bad condition, fragmentary, with most of the signs erased. As to the dating of this archive, i.e. 54 tablets, it covers the first half of the eighth century BC (800–734 BC) except for IM 132353, dated 844 BC, eponym Aššur-bunaya. This archive therefore covers the reigns of Adad-nirari III, Shalmaneser IV, Assur-dan III, Assur-nirari V, and the first ten years of Tiglath-pileser III. As far as can be judged in the present state of its study, the 54 tablets from the archive cover the following subjects:

sale of fields	18
sale of clear ground	1
sale of house	1
sale of mixed real estate	5
exchange of ground	1
sale of persons	22
uncertain legal documents	3
letter	1
list of oxen	1
harvest labour	1

The sealing practice of the archive illustrates a change which took place within the eighth century. People did not use seals, instead they made fingernail impressions. The phrase ku-um NA₄.KIŠIB-šu supur-šu iškun 'Instead of his seal he placed his fingernail' occurs 36 times in this archive while NA₄.KIŠIB PN 'Seal of PN' occurs only four times. We also have two tablets with space for a seal which was not used—presumably the seal was impressed on the envelope only. Also we have seven tablets which are broken at the beginning where the space for the seal or nail impression would have been. In addition there are five tablets without any seal or finger-nail impressions.

The 54 tablets fall into two main groups or archives:

1. The archive of the palace scribe who is identified as Nabu-tuklatua LÚ.A.BA É.GAL. He appears as a buyer of slaves thirteen times and as a buyer of real estate twice.

From the preserved dates of his texts, it seems that Nabu-tuklatua held the office of Palace Scribe for at least 35 years from 800 to 765. It is worth noting that a person called Nabu-zer-iddina, the son of Nabu-tuklatua's brother (DUMU ŠEŠ-šu ša Nabu-tuklatua) was the buyer of a house (Deller and Fadhil 1993: no. 4).

In a similar case we have 1.d.PA-PAB-AŠ DUMU 1.d.PA-MU-ib-ni LÚ.DUB.SAR as a seller of six persons (ZI.MEŠ) to Nabu-tuklatua, the Palace Scribe (Deller and Fadhil 1993: no. 3).

2. The Queen's Stewards
This group of texts belongs to Stewards of the Queen (LÚ.AGRIG = abarakku or masennu), who were in charge of her commercial activities. Fifteen tablets are classified belonging to different individuals known as PN LÚ.AGRIG ša MÍ.É.GAL. This official appears as a buyer seven times, and a eunuch of his twice as a buyer. These Stewards of the Queen are:

i. Šamaš-issiya (eunuch of steward)			
	buyer of field	IM 132205	762
	buyer of field	IM 132214	[ ]
ii. Nabu-išmanni			
	buyer	IM 132215	779
	buyer	IM 132219	794
	seller	IM 132222	[ ]
iii. Bel-(lu-)duri			
	witness	CTN 2.22	756
	buyer	IM 132383	736
	buyer	IM 132348	736
	buyer	CTN 2.27	743
	witness	CTN 2.26	743
	buyer	IM 132221	[ ]
	list	CTN 2.114	
iv. Ilu-iqbi			
	sealer	IM 132232	762

v. Mannu-ki-belia
    seller   IM 132343
vi. Adad-mušammir
    buyer   IM 132353   844
    eponym 788   CTN 2.52, 94, 103
vii. Gabbi-ilani-Aššur
    buyer   IM 132217   747
    buyer   IM 132209   754
    buyer   IM 132270   734

Except for IM 132353 from 844, these tablets are dated between 800 and 734 BC, covering the reigns of five Assyrian kings from Adad-nirari III to Tiglath-pileser III. So to which queens does this archive belong? It should be possible to divide this archive according to their husband's reign, but the broken dates do not allow for this. Also, the Assyrian scribes used the etymology MÍ.É.GAL for queen, without specifying her name, either because that is how they wrote it to denote the first wife, i.e. the mother of the king's heir, or for taboo reasons. So MÍ.É.GAL here could be the wife of any of the five kings, but that she could be one queen is unlikely, since, as soon as the king died and the crown prince ascended his father's throne, the widowed queen would be described as MÍ.AMA LUGAL 'mother of the king'.

It is worth noting that this archive seems to be contemporary with the royal tomb which was discovered in the same wing of the North-West Palace. We could therefore suggest that parts of this archive belonged to officials of Semiramis, mother of Adad-nirari III, and of Yaba' the wife of Tiglath-pileser III. Whether any of the tablets which are no longer legible came from the time of later queens, like Banitu the wife of Shalmaneser V, and Ataliya the wife of Sargon II, we cannot now tell.

In addition to the Stewards' archives, there are personnel with different occupations, described as LÚ/*ša* MÍ.É.GAL, who were also working in the queen's household. At least 13 of the legal transactions from the archive mention such officials either as seller, buyer, debtor or witness. Those explicitly described as belonging to the queen's household or the palace are listed here:

i. Marduk-ahu-usur
    seller of sister   IM 132215   779
ii. Kulu'u   *karkadinnu*
    witness   IM 132215   779
iii. Bel-lu-dari   [*ša*] UGU É
    witness   IM 132215   779
iv. Abdi-....
    witness   IM 132215   779
v. [ ]   *askāpu*
    witness   IM 132353   779
vi. Iluma-lidgul
    witness   IM 132353   844
vii. [...]-denu   LÚ.GAL URU.MEŠ
    witness   IM 132214   [ ]
viii. Nergal-a-nu   LÚ.GAL URU.MEŠ
    buyer   IM 132355   746
ix. Tab-ahuni   LÚ.SIPA
    buyer   IM 132238   793 ?
    witness   CTN 2.80   775/803
x. (2–4 persons)   LÚ.SIPA.MEŠ
    sellers   IM 132238   793 ?

It is significant that among the witnesses we have at least 19 witnesses identified as LÚ.A.BA. The names of the writers of this archive are also mentioned at the end of each tablet, before the date formula as witness, and written IGI PN LÚ.A.BA *ṣa-bit tup-pi* or *kanīki*.

In conclusion, a full edition of the whole surviving archive has been completed and should appear shortly. It will, it is hoped, shed more light on the royal female household and their officials.

34 THE CHANGING ROLE OF NIMRUD

Joan Oates

I have been asked today to talk about the changing role of Nimrud, but I would like to begin with an entirely personal comment, since Nimrud is a site that has played a pivotal role in the lives of both David and myself, both personally and professionally. It is through Nimrud that we first came to know and love Iraq, and it is for this reason—despite the fact that this is the 'concluding' paper—that I wish personally to say again what others have said before, and that is, what a very great pleasure it is that so many of our Iraqi friends and colleagues are here in London for this conference.

Nimrud was not one of the sites visited by early travellers from the west. That honour of course goes to nearby Nineveh, easily accessible across the Tigris from Mosul, a city which like Nineveh itself lay astride the major routes that passed through Northern Mesopotamia. Nimrud was less centrally situated and, despite its appearance as Biblical Calah, the ancient history of Nineveh was far better known, especially from Classical sources. The first serious visitor to Nimrud was Claudius James Rich who, in 1820, spent four months in the north. But it was Austen Henry Layard who not only first excavated at Nimrud but who provided extraordinarily readable accounts of his travels and explorations, and thus brought ancient Assyria, and in particular Nimrud, not only to the notice of the wider British public but also to the Trustees of the British Museum, who were to sponsor his later work at the site.

Nor is Nimrud the largest of the ancient capitals of Assyria. But it is undoubtedly one of the most beautiful sites in the area, a fact commented on by all its early visitors. In April 1840, Layard travelled from Mosul to Baghdad by *kelek.* In *Nineveh and its Remains* he writes, 'These huge mounds of Assyria made a deeper impression upon me, gave rise to more serious thoughts and more earnest reflection, than the temples of Balbec and the theatres of Ionia….It was evening as we approached Nimrud. The spring rains had clothed the mound with its richest verdure, and the fertile meadows, which stretched around it, were covered with flowers of every hue….My curiosity had been greatly excited, and from that time I formed the design of thoroughly examining, whenever it might be in my power, these singular ruins.' (Layard 1849a: I, 7).

This excitement, even obsession, with the site, was echoed a hundred years later by Mallowan in his memoirs (though perhaps with a degree of hindsight):

'To many travellers there is no more romantic spot than Nimrud, where the bearded heads of protective stone *lamassu,* half man, half beast, stuck out of the ground outside the gates of the ancient palaces, the last of the faithful servants that guarded the warrior-priest kings of Assyria. This is my memory of it as I first saw the place in 1926, after my first season's work with Leonard Woolley at Ur. Here I realized was an archaeological paradise where one day, after I had done my apprenticeship, I might be privileged to enter. And from this intention I never faltered'. (Mallowan 1977: 242–43).

Oddly, one can even credit Leonard Woolley's wife, Katharine, with the initial responsibility for Mallowan's move towards Nimrud. Mallowan left Ur to work with Campbell Thompson at Nineveh when Katharine Woolley refused to let Agatha return to the Woolley excavations. Katharine was not a woman to allow *any* competition, but Agatha was to get her own back many years later by writing *Murder in Mesopotamia,* in which the dig staff at Ur are clearly recognisable and the director murders his wife. Surely the perfect revenge and, perhaps fortunately, the Woolleys never recognized themselves. Thus Katharine Woolley was in a sense responsible for Mallowan's move to Assyria, and therefore literally for the reopening of the twentieth century excavations at Nimrud.

Mallowan moved first to Nineveh, where he worked with Campbell Thompson. Agatha writes of this time:

'On one of our rest days we decided to hire a car and go to find the great mound of Nimrud. Max had some difficulty in getting there, for the roads were very bad. But in the end we arrived and picnicked there—and oh, what a beautiful spot it was then. The Tigris was just a mile away, and on the great acropolis mound big stone Assyrian heads poked out of the soil. In one place there was the enormous wing of a great genie. It was a spectacular stretch of the country—peaceful, romantic, and impregnated with the past. I remember Max saying, 'This is where I would like to dig, but it would have to be on a very big scale. One would have to raise a lot of money but if I could, this is the mound I would choose, out of all the world'. (Christie 1977: 456).

I may seem to have strayed from my assigned topic, but the straying has been deliberate, both in an attempt to give you some idea of the setting of this great site and one of many reasons why we all loved Nimrud and the Iraqi countryside, but also to illustrate the quirks of fate that lead to a choice of archaeological site.

With that background, I move on to examine the work at Nimrud with a view to its changing roles. These seem to me to fall into 5 phases: 1) the initial excavations of Layard, 2) the excavations of his successors, legal and otherwise, in the later nineteenth century, 3) the excavations of Mallowan and David Oates in the mid-twentieth century, 4) the very important Iraqi work at the site, intermittently from 1956 onwards, and 5) the future.

In Phase 1, of course, Layard was successful almost beyond belief, despite his virtually non-existent budget which allowed him initially to employ only 6 workmen, and later a maximum of 31, in extraordinary contrast with Mallowan's 250. The importance of Layard is that with his work at Nimrud and that of Botta at Nineveh and Khorsabad, the foundations not only of Assyrian archaeology but also of Assyriology were laid. Layard's discoveries at Nimrud were not only extraordinarily lucky (on his first day of excavation he chanced upon both the North-West (fig. 34-a) and the South-West Palaces) but owing to his impressively meticulous recording, in itself remarkable in view of his straitened circumstances, they have provided a wealth of material and information that is still attracting the attention of scholars worldwide—a situation of which this conference is but one example (although the British Museum is probably not the place to refer to the degree to which not only Layard, but the site itself, suffered from the parsimony of his English patrons, in marked contrast to the French support of Botta at Nineveh and Khorsabad).

Layard was not unaware of the limitations of his work. He writes,

> 'The smallness of the sum placed at my disposal compelled me to follow the same plan in the excavations that I had hitherto adopted, that is, to dig trenches along the sides of the chambers, and to expose the whole of the slabs, without removing the earth from the centre' (a situation not unknown in later excavations! Though certainly tunnelling was not allowed). 'Thus, few of the chambers were fully explored, and many small objects of great interest may have been left undiscovered. As I was directed to bury the building with earth after I had explored it, to avoid unnecessary expense, I filled up the chambers with the rubbish taken from those subsequently uncovered, having first examined the walls, copied the inscriptions and drawn the sculptures' (Layard 1849a: 332).

Archaeologists should note the consequent problems for later excavators of the same ruins of establishing original contexts for the material recovered.

Layard's workmen were well able to tunnel along the stone-lined walls of the major palaces, but the techniques of excavating unbaked clay, whether *libn* or cuneiform tablet, remained to be perfected. Indeed it was long believed that no cuneiform tablets had been found at Nimrud (though there is more than one join between tablets found by Mallowan in the Nabu Temple in the

Fig. 34-a. Discovery of a colossal human-headed gate figure at the entrance to the Ninurta Temple. Drawing by Austen Henry Layard, 1846.

1950s and those from the nineteenth century Kouyunjik collection in the British Museum, almost certainly recovered during George Smith's slightly later excavations at Nimrud (Oates and Oates 2001: 208; Walker, this volume).

Yet no one can deny that Layard not only laid the foundations for our subject but also served to kindle interest in the ancient history of Mesopotamia in both the then Ottoman and the western worlds. Thus the work of Layard established not only the first of Nimrud's many roles, but undoubtedly one of its most important, especially in focusing world attention on the great antiquity and historical wealth of ancient Assyria.

The second phase of work at Nimrud was less successful, certainly less well executed and, regrettably, barely recorded. In 1851 Layard returned to England, and was succeeded by Loftus of the ivories and his Muslawi assistant, Hormuzd Rassam, who even into the 1880s continued the extensive and essentially *un*recorded looting of a large number of sites, simultaneously, not only in Assyria but also in Babylonia, at a time when other excavators were beginning to act more responsibly. In 1855, the Crimean War put a temporary stop to exploration in Assyria and for almost twenty years no *authorized* excavation took place; yet, as Seton Lloyd aptly wrote, 'at Nimrud the sound of pick and shovel were still not infrequently heard' (Lloyd 1980: 161). Unfortunately, the place of the archaeologists had now been taken by commercial speculators, and during the 1860s at least two consignments of sculpture were dispatched to Europe by Baghdad merchants. Certainly not a happy phase in the excavation of Assyria (*pace* Greene, this volume)

Rassam returned briefly to Nimrud in 1878–80, under the auspices of the British Museum, but thereafter, with the exciting identification of the much earlier Sumerian language, archaeological interest in Assyria waned and attention turned to Babylonia, now emerging as the more ancient cradle of civilization. Thereafter, except for the occasional robbing of stone for purposes of building or the making of lime, Nimrud remained untouched until Mallowan's return in 1949, exactly a century after the publication of Layard's *Nineveh and its Remains*.[1] Thus began Phase 3.

Mallowan's objectives were both simple and straightforward:

> 'We kept before us two primary objectives. First, to discover more ivories, for I was convinced that many more remained to be found. Second, and much more important, to discover cuneiform records, for apart from

the royal standard inscriptions which accompanied the Assyrian reliefs, no clay tablets in the cuneiform script had ever been recorded by Layard, and it seemed incredible to me that so large a city could have been devoid of economic, business, historical and literary texts. I would have staked my life that in the end we would find all these things, and find them we did'. (Mallowan 1977: 251). (Fig. 34-b).

Such 'unscientific' goals, however, would hardly satisfy the awarding committees of modern funding bodies. Mallowan was of course an archaeologist of his time. Indeed, his work at Nimrud has been described as the last of the great nineteenth century excavations, and although he shared an Institute with Gordon Childe, he was little concerned with social or economic questions, except to the extent that these could be understood from the written documents. There was an understandable emphasis on the spectacular, as there was in Layard's time, since impressing the British public was an important part of fund-raising. His London lectures were always highly successful, to say nothing of social, occasions. Moreover, the emphasis on 'finds' in the material sense was understandable, since in the days of the archaeological 'division', that is, the division of the more common antiquities between the expedition and the Iraqi Directorate-General, the expedition's share of the finds provided an important source of funding, museums contributing to the excavations in the hope of receiving in return objects for their collections. The major finds of course went directly to the Iraq Museum.

In this attitude Mallowan was in accord with the distinguished 1950s Director-General (Dr Naji al-Asil), who commented in *Sumer* in 1956 on 'one of the most interesting and fruitful seasons in the long history of Iraq':

> 'With four to five expeditions, both Iraqi and Foreign, working in the field, year after year, one certainly expects remarkable additions to the unique collections of the Iraq Museum. Archaeological activity in the field is never an easy undertaking. It is, indeed, one of the most exacting scientific tasks imaginable. It carries a high sense of responsibility to Science, History, the Antiquities discovered and also to the highest cultural interests of the country in whose soil it undertakes excavations.

> Happily, gone are the days when foreign expeditions working in Iraq had to think only in terms of unearthing antiquities and in shipping them to their respective countries, often at the expense of the ancient sites themselves. The price of ignorance and indifference was colossal for the country in the loss of its great antique treasures. The only excuse and perhaps consolation is that Iraq did not then exist as an independent state' (al-Asil 1956: 3).

A very enlightened comment for 1956.

---

[1] The title of the book reflects Rawlinson's initial misidentification of Nimrud as the site of Nineveh, corrected to ancient Kalhu only in the year of Layard's publication.

Fig. 34-b. The 1953
excavations in the area of the
Town Wall houses. Barbara
Parker, centre, and Agatha
Christie on the extreme left.
(Photograph J. Oates).

These remarks lead us to consider whether the nineteenth century excavation of important sites like Nineveh and Nimrud is to be regretted, even condemned. The parsimony of potential sponsors in England, including both the Government and the British Museum, led Layard to 'obtain the largest possible number of well-preserved objects of art at the least possible outlay of time and money.' It is difficult, however, to judge what would otherwise have been the progress of our knowledge of the culture and history of what was one of the most important areas of the ancient world, and one that provided, by way of the classical world, the foundations of many of our own traditions and institutions.

Certainly one can regret both Layard's lack of funds and his lack of experience. It is clear that large numbers of delicate antiquities were lost 'entire when first exposed to view, it crumbled into dust as soon as touched.... They fell to pieces as soon as exposed'. Thus Layard (1849a: I, 353) writes of ivories and bronze in particular. We doubt, however, that even among modern 'scientific' field archaeologists one could easily find any single individual who has not had at least one such disaster, and one could argue, taking a broader view, that Layard's mistakes are of less account than his meticulous recording and drawing, remarkable for the time, which undoubtedly helped to lay the basis for a more technical and scientific approach to work in the field. Nonetheless, one is aware, especially when working at a vast site like Nimrud, of the enormous amount that was destroyed, not only the objects themselves but, far more seriously, the contexts in which they were found, by far the most important component of archaeological evidence.

At the same time, it must be admitted that there was little interest among Ottoman officials, and stone and other materials were being removed from the ancient sites for reuse with no appreciation of their historical value.

Perhaps it was in this context that the work of those like Layard made its greatest contribution, in demonstrating both to the general public and the academic community, not only in the West but in the Near East as well, the depth and importance of the archaeological information that was there to be found.

Phase 4 began in 1956, with the first restoration work carried out by Iraqi archaeologists at the site, during the time that Mallowan was still digging there. At this time, as we have heard in earlier papers, the Directorate-General in Baghdad together with the Antiquities Office in Mosul began the restoration of the site which continues at the present day. We have heard, too, of the extraordinary discoveries made by Iraqi excavators: the ivories from well AJ (fig. 34-c), of which Mallowan was unable to complete the excavation, significant additions to the plan of the Nabu Temple and the discovery there of more cuneiform tablets and, most recently and most spectacularly, the enormously rich tombs in the North-West Palace. This work continues under the skilled direction of Muzahim Mahmud, and has made Nimrud a site well worthy of a tourist's visit. Both these important investigations and the work of restoration clearly distinguish Phase 4 at Nimrud, and it is most appropriate that these valuable contributions have been made by the Department of Antiquities and Heritage itself. At the same time foreign expeditions have also been generously enabled to work at the site, for example those of the Poles, Italians and the British Museum.

But what of the future (Phase 5)? Clearly the focus of work at the site will and should remain with the State Board of Antiquities and Heritage in Baghdad and Mosul. At the same time we hope that it will continue to be possible for foreign archaeologists, conservators, architects and other specialists to assist when this is thought to be useful.

Fig. 34-c. Ivory bowl from Well AJ. Length 16.3 cm. IM 79511.

But what should be the future goals at a site such as Nimrud?

Despite its long history, in the context of the Late Assyrian kingdom much of Nimrud constitutes essentially a single period site. There are of course numerous Hellenistic tombs and indeed some Hellenistic occupation, especially in the south-eastern corner of the citadel in and south of the area of the Nabu Temple, but Nimrud lacks the heavy overburden of later occupation found at both Ashur and Nineveh. Moreover, at Nimrud, monumental buildings of the ninth century for the most part remained in use until the fall of Assyria in 612 BC. Thus for the archaeologist there is the advantage of relatively simple access to the Late Assyrian levels, and real precision of dating, both for the construction of the buildings themselves and for the destruction of the material remains. The very important distinctions in material culture from one decade to another, however, crucial for wider dating purposes and, *inter alia*, the work of art historians and those interested in social and economic change, are lost in the site's very monumental-

ity. Clean floors and tidy refurbishments are not the archaeologist's bread and butter. In recent years, the important results of rescue operations, often on much smaller sites, have helped not only to increase the chronological precision but also the social and economic scope of Late Assyrian evidence. At Nimrud the life of the ordinary citizen of Assyria remains barely visible. Clearly, the smaller sites have much to offer in this respect. This is not to say that further exploration of the outer town might not be informative of the lives of ordinary people, including the workmen and craftsmen who built the great palaces (some 47,000 according to the banquet stele), an exercise that would almost certainly add to our wider understanding of Nimrud. We already know, however, that at least some of the outer town was occupied by large residences, no doubt of lesser officials than those who occupied the palaces of the citadel, but with the exception perhaps of the barracks and workshops of Fort Shalmaneser, it must be admitted that we have at Nimrud little understanding as yet of the lives of the great majority of those who must have lived there.

Further cuneiform texts would certainly extend our knowledge of Assyrian society and economy, but it seems to me that the enormous value, indeed attraction, of Nimrud for the present generation of archaeologists lies in its essentially single-period archaeology (which means, *inter alia*, that there is no question of which level to restore) and its consequent potential for restoration. Most important of all is the Iraqi programme of conservation and restoration of the monumental buildings of this great city, combined with further exploration of types of building ill-represented at present—for example the Ishtar Temple. Personally, we would hope that someday this programme of restoration could include the *ekal mašarti*, the great arsenal in the outer town, surely one of the major buildings of ancient Assyria, and one that is remarkably well preserved. Certainly the opportunity to recreate one of the great cities of the past constitutes a challenge that is already being effectively addressed, and I would like to close with the hope that it will not be long before Nimrud becomes what it deserves to be, an officially recognized World Heritage Site.

In 1852 Rawlinson wrote off Nimrud as having little further left to offer. His contribution to the decipherment of cuneiform was fundamental, but this conference has certainly confirmed how wrong he was about the potential of the archaeology of Nimrud. Even Mallowan's wife was to write, 'Layard began the work, my husband finished it' (Christie 1977: 456). But we know that this is far from the case, and I hope you will all join me in wishing our Iraqi colleagues many more years of success and achievement at Nimrud.

BIBLIOGRAPHY

List of Abbreviations

AfO	*Archiv für Orientforschung*
AHw	*Akkadisches Handwörterbuch*, 3 vols., by W. von Soden
AMT	*Assyrian Medical Texts*, by R. Campbell Thompson, Oxford 1923
ANET	*Ancient Near Eastern Texts*, edited by James B. Pritchard, Princeton, N.J., 1950
AOAT	Alter Orient und Altes Testament
AoF	*Altorientalische Forschungen*
BAM	*Die babylonisch-assyrische Medizin in Texten und Untersuchungen*
BASOR	*Bulletin of the American Schools of Oriental Research*
CAD	*Chicago Assyrian Dictionary*
CTN	Cuneiform Texts from Nimrud
ILN	*Illustrated London News*
JAOS	*Journal of the American Oriental Society*
JNES	*Journal of Near Eastern Studies*
KAH	*Keilschrifttexte aus Assur historischen Inhalts*
OIP	Oriental Institute Publications
PBS	Publications of the Babylonian Section of the University of Pennsylvania Museum
RLA	*Reallexikon der Assyriologie*
SAA	*State Archives of Assyria*
STT	*The Sultantepe Tablets*
WVDO-G	Wissenschaftliche Veröffentlichungen der Deutschen Orient-Gesellschaft
ZA	*Zeitschrift für Assyriologie*

Abou Assaf, A., Bordreuil, P., and Millard, A., 1982. *La Statue de tell Fekherye et son inscription bilingue assyro-araméenne*, Paris.

Abu es-Soof, B., 1963. 'Further investigations in Ashurnasirpal's Palace', *Sumer* 19: 66–73.

Agha, A.A., 1985–86. 'Notes on the plan of the Nabu Temple, Nimrud', *Sumer* 44: 42–47 (Arabic section).

— and al-Iraqi, M., 1976. *Nimrud*, Baghdad.

Ainachi, M., 1956. 'Reconstruction and preservation of monuments in Northern Iraq', *Sumer* 12: 124–32 (Arabic section).

Ainsworth, W.F., 1844. *Travels in the Track of the Ten Thousand Greeks, being a Geographical and Descriptive Account of the Expedition of Cyrus and the Retreat by Xenophon*, London.

—, 1888. *A Personal Narrative of the Euphrates Expedition*, 2 vols, London.

Akurgal, E., 1962. *The Art of the Hittites*, London and New York.

Al-Asil, Naji, 1956. 'Recent archaeological activity in Iraq', *Sumer* 12: 3–7.

Albenda, P., 1994. 'Assyrian sacred trees in the Brooklyn Museum', *Iraq* LVI: 123–33.

—, 1998. *Monumental Art of the Assyrian Empire: Dynamics of Composition Styles*, Monographs on the Ancient Near East 3/1, Malibu.

Albright, W.F., 1958. 'An ostracon from Calah and the North Israelite diaspora', *BASOR* 149: 33–36.

Al-Gailani Werr, L., 1999. 'Antiquities in Iraq', *Iraq Newsletter* 3: 3–5.

Al-Haik, A.R., 1968. *Key Lists of Archaeological Excavations in Iraq 1842–1965*, Field Research Projects, Study No.l, Coconut Grove, Florida.

Al-Iraqi, M., 1982. 'Bas reliefs from the North-West Palace at Nimrud', *Sumer* 38: 93–102 (Arabic section).

Alizadeh, A., 1985. 'A tomb of the Neo-Elamite period at Arjan, near Behbehan', *Archaeologische Mitteilungen aus Iran* 18: 49–73.

Alvarez-Mon, J., 2004. 'Imago mundi: cosmological and ideological aspects of the Arjan bowl', *Iranica Antiqua* 39: 203–38.

Amirkhiz, A.C. and Harsini, M.R.S., 2002. *A Glance at Iranian Ancient Coffins*, Tehran (in Persian).

Andersen, V., 1999. *Access 2000: The Complete Reference*, Berkeley.

Andrae, W., 1907. 'Aus den Berichten W. Andraes aus Assur', *Mitteilungen der Deutschen Orient-Gesellschaft zu Berlin* 33: 11–23.

—, 1913. *Die Festungswerke von Assur*, 2 vols, WVDO-G 23, Berlin.

—, 1938. *Das Wiedererstandene Assur*, Leipzig.

— and Boehmer, R.M., 1992. *Bilder eines Ausgräbers. Sketches by an Excavator*, 2nd edition, Berlin.

Arnaud, D., 1986. *Recherches au Pays d'Aštata. Emar VI*, Paris.

—, Calvet, Y. and Huot, J.-L., 1979. 'Ilšu-ibni-šu, orfèvre de l'*E.babbar* de Larsa, la jarred 76–7 et son contenu', *Syria* 56: 1–64.

Asher-Greve, J.M. and Selz, G.J., 1980. *Genien und Krieger aus Nimrud. Neuassyrishe Reliefs Assurnasirpals II und Tiglat-Pilesars III*, Zurich.

Avigad, N. and Sass, B., 1997. *Corpus of West Semitic Stamp Seals,* Jerusalem.

Bache, C., 1933. 'First report on the joint excavations at Tepe Gawra and Tell Billa', *BASOR* XLIX: 8–14.

Badger, G.P., 1852. *The Nestorians and Their Rituals,* 2 vols, London.

Baker, H., 1995. 'Neo-Babylonian burials revisted', in Campbell, S. and Green, A.R. (eds), *The Archaeology of Death in the Ancient Near East,* Oxford: 209–20.

Barag, D.P., 1985. *Catalogue of Western Asiatic Glass in the British Museum,* vol. I, London.

Barnett, R.D., 1956. 'The treasure of Ziwiye', *Iraq* XVIII: 111–16.

—, 1967. 'Layard's Nimrud bronzes and their inscriptions', *Eretz Israel* VIII: 1–7.

—, 1970. *Assyrian Palace Reliefs in the British Museum,* London.

—, 1974. 'The Nimrud bowls in the British Museum', *Rivista degli Studi Fenici* II: 11–33.

—, 1975. *A Catalogue of the Nimrud Ivories in the British Museum,* 2nd edition, London.

—, 1976. *Sculptures from the North Palace of Ashurbanipal at Nineveh (668–627 BC),* London.

—, 1978. 'Lady Layard's jewellery', in Moorey, P.R.S. and Parr, P. (eds), *Archaeology in the Levant—Essays for Kathleen Kenyon,* Warminster: 172–79.

—, 1987. 'William Kennett Loftus', *RLA* 7: 102–3.

—, Bleibtreu, E. and Turner, G., 1998. *Sculptures from the Southwest Palace of Sennacherib at Nineveh,* 2 vols, London.

— and Falkner, M., 1962. *The Sculptures of Tiglath-Pileser III (745–727 BC),* London.

Beckman, G., 1978. Review of Bin-Nun 1975 in *Journal of the American Oriental Society* 98: 513–14.

Bernbeck, R., 1993. *Steppe als Kulturlandschaft. Das 'Agig-Gebiet Ostsyriens vom Neolithikum bis zur islamischen Zeit,* Berlin.

—, 1999. 'An empire and its sherds', in Hausleiter, A. and Reiche A. (eds) 1999: 151–72.

Bin-Nun, S.R., 1975. *The Tawananna in the Hittite Kingdom,* Texte der Hethiter 5, Heidelberg.

Birch, S. (ed.), 1875. *Records of the Past, Volume V: Assyrian Texts,* London.

Birot, M., 1980. 'Fragment de ritual de Mari relatif au *kispum*', in Alster, B. (ed.), *Death in Mesopotamia, Papers read at the XXVIe Rencontre Assyriologique Internationale, Copenhagen,* Mesopotamia 8: 139–50.

Black, J.A. and Green, A., 1992. *Gods, Demons and Symbols of Ancient Mesopotamia,* London.

Black, J.A. and Tait, W.J., 1995. 'Archives and libraries in the Ancient Near East', in Sasson, J. (ed.), *Civilizations of the Ancient Near East,* vol. 4, New York: 2197–209.

Boehmer, R.M., 1989. Review of *Archaeologische Mitteilungen aus Iran* 18 (1985) in *ZA* 79: 142–44.

Bohrer, F.N., 1998. 'Inventing Assyria: exoticism and reception in nineteenth-century England and France', *Art Bulletin* 80/2: 337–56.

Bordreuil, P., 1973. 'Inscriptions des têtes à double face', *Annual of the Department of Antiquities of Jordan* 18: 37–39.

—, 1979. 'Les noms propres transjordaniens de l'ostracon de Nimroud', *Revue d'Histoire et de Philosophie Religieuses* 59: 313–17.

—, 1992. 'Sceaux inscrits du pays du Levant', *Dictionnaire de la Bible, Supplément* 12, Paris: cols 86–212.

Borger, R., 1956. *Die Inschriften Asarhaddons Königs von Assyrien,* AFO Beiheft 9, Graz.

Borowski, E., 1952. 'Siegel der Sammlung H.A. Layard', *Orientalia* 21: 168–83.

Bossier, Alfred, 1912. *Notice sur quelques monuments assyriens à l'Université de Zurich,* Geneva.

Botta, P.-E., 1849–50. *Monument de Ninive,* 5 vols, Paris.

Brandes, M.A., 1970. 'La salle dite "G" du palais d'Assurnasirpal II à Kalakh, lieu de cérémonie rituelle', in Finet, A. (ed.), *Actes de la XVIIe Rencontre Assyriologique Internationale,* Ham-sur-Heure, Belgium: 147–54.

Brentjes, B., 1994. 'Selbstverherrlichung oder Legitimätsanspruch? Gedanken zu dem Thronrelief von Nimrud-Kalah', *AoF* 21: 50–64.

Bristowe, W.S., 1976. *Louis and the King of Siam,* London.

British Archaeological Association, 1845. 'Proceedings of the Committee', *Archaeological Journal* 1: 156–68.

Brosius, M., 1996. *Women in Ancient Persia,* Oxford.

Brown, F., Driver, S.R. and Briggs, C.A., 1907. *Hebrew and English Lexicon of the Old Testament,* Oxford (reprinted 1979).

Buchanan, B., 1966. *Catalogue of Ancient Near Eastern Seals in the Ashmolean Museum 1. Cylinder Seals,* Oxford.

— and Moorey, P.R.S., 1988. *Catalogue of Ancient Near Eastern Seals in the Ashmolean Museum III. The Iron Age Stamp Seals,* Oxford.

Buckingham, J.S., 1830. *Travels in Assyria, Media and Persia,* 2 vols, London.

Budge, E.A.W., 1914. *Assyrian Sculptures in the British Museum: Reign of Ashur-nasir-pal,* London.

—, 1920. *By Nile and Tigris. A Narrative of Journeys in Egypt and Mesopotamia on Behalf of the British Museum Between the Years 1886 and 1913,* 2 vols, London.

—, 1925. *The Rise and Progress of Assyriology,* London.

Bunnens, G. (ed.), 2000. *Essays on Syria in the Iron Age,* Ancient Near Eastern Studies 7, Louvain, Paris and Sterling, Virginia.

Canby, J.V., 1971. 'Decorated garments in Ashurnasirpal's sculpture', *Iraq* XXXIII: 31–53.

Cancik-Kirschbaum, E., 1996. *Die Mittelassyrischen Briefe aus Tell Šēh Hamad,* Berlin.

—, 1999. 'Nebenlinien des assyrischen Königshauses', *AOF* 26: 210–22.

Charpin, D. and Durand, J-M., 1985. 'La prise de pouvoir par Zimri-Lim', *Mari, Annales de Recherches Interdisciplinaires* 4: 293–343.

Chesney, F.R., 1850. *The Expedition for the Survey of the Rivers Euphrates and Tigris,* 2 vols, London.

Chevalier, N., 1995. 'Les consuls et l'archéologie', in Caubet, A. (ed.), *Khorsabad, le palais de Sargon II, roi d'Assyrie,* Paris: 81–97.

— and Lavèdrine, B., 1994. 'Débuts de la photographie et fouilles en Assyrie: les calotypes de Gabriel Tranchard', in Fontan, E. and Chevalier, N. (eds), *De Khorsabad à Paris: la découverte des Assyriens,* Paris: 196–213.

Christie, A., 1946. *Come, Tell Me How You Live,* London.

—, 1977. *An Autobiography,* London.

Clive, R.H., 1852. *Sketches between the Persian Gulf and the Black Sea,* London.

Cogan, M., 1974. *Imperialism and Religion: Assyria, Judah and Israel in the Eighth and Seventh Centuries BC*, Missoula, Montana.

Collon, D., 1987a. 'Layard's collection of cylinder seals', in Fales and Hickey 1987: 203–11.

—, 1987b. *First Impressions. Cylinder Seals in the Ancient Near East*, London.

—, 2001. *Catalogue of the Western Asiatic Seals in the British Museum, Cylinder Seals V. Neo-Assyrian and Neo-Babylonian Periods,* London.

Corpus Inscriptionum Semiticarum 1888. *II: Inscriptiones aramaicae*, Paris.

Cowley, A., 1923. *Aramaic Papyri of the Fifth Century BC*, Oxford.

Cross, F.M., 1995. 'Palaeography and the date of the Tell Fahariyeh bilingual inscription,' in Zevit, Z., Gitin, S. and Sokoloff, M. (eds), *Solving Riddles and Untying Knots. Biblical, Epigraphic, and Semitic Studies in Honor of Jonas C. Greenfield*, Grand Rapids, MI: 393–409.

CTN I—see Kinnier-Wilson 1972

CTN II—see Postgate 1973

CTN III—see Dalley and Postgate 1984

CTN IV—see Wiseman and Black 1996

CTN V—see Saggs 2001

Curtis, J.E., 1979. *An Examination of Late Assyrian Metalwork with Special Reference to Material from Nimrud*, unpublished PhD dissertation, University of London.

—, 1983. 'Late Assyrian bronze coffins', *Anatolian Studies* XXXIII: 85–95.

—, 1986. 'Bronze bowls with handles from Nimrud—a note', *Oxford Journal of Archaeology* 5: 109–17 (with Lang, J.R.S., Hughes, M.J. and Leese, M.N.).

—, 1988. 'Assyria as a bronzeworking centre in the Late Assyrian period', in Curtis, J.E. (ed.), *Bronzeworking Centres of Western Asia c.1000–539 BC*, London: 83–96.

—, 1989. *Excavations at Qasrij Cliff and Khirbet Qasrij,* London.

—, 1993. 'William Kennett Loftus and his excavations at Susa', *Iranica Antiqua* XXVIII: 1–55.

—, 1994. 'Assyrian fibulae with figural decoration', in *Altertumskunde des Vorderen Orients* 4 (Festschrift für R. Mayer-Opificius), Münster: 49–62.

—, (ed.). 1995. *Later Mesopotamia and Iran: Tribes and Empires 1600–539 BC*, Proceedings of a Seminar in Memory of Vladimir G. Lukonin, London.

—, 1996. 'Assyrian furniture: the archaeological evidence', in Herrmann, G. (ed.), *The Furniture of Western Asia: Ancient and Traditional,* Mainz: 167–80.

—, 1997a. 'Nimrud', in Mayers, E.M. (ed.), *The Oxford Encyclopedia of Archaeology in the Near East* IV, New York and Oxford: 141–44.

—, 1997b. 'The church at Khirbet Deir Situn', *Al-Rafidan* 18: 368–85.

—, 1999. 'Glass inlays and Nimrud ivories', *Iraq* LXI: 59–69.

—, 2000. 'Animal-headed drinking cups in the Late Assyrian Period', in Dittmann, R. *et al.* (eds), *Variatio Delectat. Iran und der Westen. Gedenkschrift für Peter Calmeyer,* Münster: 193–213.

—, 2005. 'Iron Age Iran and the transition to the Achaemenid period', in Curtis, V.S. and Stewart, S. (eds), *Birth of the Persian Empire,* London: 112–31.

—, Collon, D., Green, A.R. and Searight, A., 1993. 'British Museum excavations at Nimrud and Balawat in 1989', *Iraq* LV: 1–37.

—, and Green, A.R., 1997. *Excavations at Khirbet Khatuniyeh*, Saddam Dam Report 11, London.

—, Green, A.R. and Knight, W., 1987–88. 'Preliminary report on the excavations at Tell Deir Situn and Grai Darki', *Sumer* 45: 49–53.

— and Reade, J.E., (eds), 1995. *Art and Empire: Treasures from Assyria in the British Museum*, London.

— and Tallis, N., (eds), 2005. *Forgotten Empire: the World of Ancient Persia,* London.

Dalley, S., 1998. 'Yaba, Atalya and the foreign policy of Late Assyrian kings', *State Archives of Assyria Bulletin* XII/2: 83–98.

—, 2004. 'Recent evidence from Assyrian sources for Judaean history from Uzziah to Manasseh', *Journal for the Study of the Old Testament* 28: 387–410.

— and Postgate, J.N., 1984. *The Tablets from Fort Shalmaneser,* CTN III, London.

Damerji, M.S., 1987. *The Development of the Architecture of Doors and Gates in Ancient Mesopotamia*, Tokyo (English translation of *Die Entwicklung der Tur- und Torarchitecture in Mesopotamien*, PhD Dissertation, Munich, 1973).

—, 1999. *Gräber assyrischer Königinnen aus Nimrud*, Mainz (reprinted from *Jahrbuch des Römisch-Germanischen Zentralmuseums Mainz* 45: 1–84).

D'Andrea, M.M., 1981. *Letters of Leonard William King 1902–1904; Introduced, Edited and Annotated with Special Reference to the Excavations of Nineveh*, MA Thesis, University of Wisconsin, River Falls.

Deller, K., 1987. 'The sealed burial chamber', *State Archives of Assyria Bulletin* 1/2: 69–71.

— and Fadhil, A., 1993. 'Neue Nimrud-Urkunden des 8. Jahrhunderts v. Chr.', *Baghdader Mitteilungen* 24: 243–70.

De Odorico, M., 1995. *The Use of Numbers and Quantifications in the Assyrian Royal Inscriptions,* Helsinki.

Dowson, V.H.W., 1982. 'Date Production and Protection, with Special Reference to North Africa and the Near East', *Plant Production and Protection Papers,* 35, Rome, Food and Agriculture Organization of the United Nations.

Duistermaat, K., 1999. Review of Pfälzner 1995 in *Bibliotheca Orientalis* 56: 439–46.

Edgü, F. (ed.), 1983. *The Anatolian Civilisations I, The Council of Europe XVIIIth European Art Exhibition, Istanbul 22 May–30 October 1983*, Istanbul.

Englund, K., 2003. 'Nimrud und seine Funde. Der Weg der Reliefs in die Museen und Sammlungen', *Deutsches Archäologisches Institut, Orient-Archäologie* 13, Rahden/Westfalen.

Engstom, C.M.A., 2004. 'The Neo-Assyrians at Tell el-Hesi: a petrographic study of imitation Neo-Assyrian Palace Ware', *BASOR* 333: 69–81.

Fadhil, A., 1990a. 'Die in Nimrud/Kalhu aufgefundene Grabinschrift der Jabâ', *Baghdader Mitteilungen* 21: 461–70.

—, 1990b. 'Die Grabinschrift der Mullissu-mukannišat-Ninua aus Nimrud/Kalhu und andere in dem Grab gefundene Schriftträger', *Baghdader Mitteilunger* 21: 471–82.

Fales, F.M., 1974. 'West Semitic names from the Governor's Palace', *Annali di Ca'Foscari* 13: 179–88.

—, 1986. *Aramaic Epigraphs on Clay Tablets of the Neo-Assyrian Period,* Studi Semitici NS 2, Rome.

—, 1995. 'Assyro-Aramaica: the Assyrian lion-weights', in van Lerberghe, K. and Schoors, A. (eds), *Immigration and Emigration within the Ancient Near East. Festschrift E. Lipinski,* Leuven: 33–55.

— and Hickey, B.J., 1987. *Austen Henry Layard tra l'Oriente e Venezia. Symposium Internazionale, Venezia, 26–28 Ottobre 1983,* Rome.

Fergusson, J., 1851. *The Palaces of Nineveh and Persepolis Restored: an Essay on Ancient Assyrian and Persian Architecture,* London.

Finkel, I., 1983–84. 'Necromancy in ancient Mesopotamia', *AfO* 29/30: 1–17.

—, 2000. 'A new Assyrian queen', *NABU* 2000: 8.

Finkel, I.L. and Reade, J.E., 1996. 'Assyrian hieroglyphs', *ZA* 86: 244–68.

Finkelstein, J.J., 1966. 'The genealogy of the Hammurapi dynasty', *Journal of Cuneiform Studies* 20: 95–118.

Fiorina, P., 1998 'Un braciere da Forte Salmanassar, Nimrud', *Mesopotamia* XXXIII: 167–88.

—, 2001. 'Nimrud: Les coquillages de Fort Salmanassar', in Breniquet, C. and Kepinksi, C. (eds), *Études mésopotamiennes—Receuil de textes offerts à Jean-Louis Huot,* Éditions Recherche sur les Civilisations, Paris: 163–75.

Fischer, S., 2000. '*Inurta-ahia-šukšid?*, in Baker, H.D. (ed.), *The Prosopography of the Neo-Assyrian Empire* 2/1, Helsinki: 545.

Fleming, D., 1989. 'Eggshell ware pottery in Achaemenid Mesopotamia', *Iraq* LI: 165–85.

Fletcher, J.P., 1850. *Notes from Nineveh and Travels in Mesopotamia, Assyria and Syria,* 2 vols, London and Philadelphia.

—, 1853. *The Autobiography of a Missionary,* 2 vols, London.

Frahm, E., 1997. *Einleitung in die Sanherib-Inschriften,* AfO Beiheft 26.

—, 2000a. 'Iabâ', in Baker, H.D. (ed.), *The Prosopography of the Neo-Assyrian Empire* 2/1, Helsinki: 485.

—, 2000b. 'Iapa'', in Baker, H.D. (ed.), *The Prosopography of the Neo-Assyrian Empire* 2/1, Helsinki: 492–93.

—, 2002. 'Sīn-ahhē-erība', in Baker, H.D. (ed.), *The Prosopography of the Neo-Assyrian Empire* 3/1, Helsinki: 1113–27.

Frame, G., 1991. 'Assyrian clay hands', *Baghdader Mitteilungen* 22: 335–81.

Franck, D.S., 1980. 'Missionaries send bas-reliefs to the United States', in Crawford, V.E., Harper, P.O. and Pittman, H., *Assyrian Reliefs of Assurnasirpal II and Ivory Carvings from Nimrud,* New York: 40–46.

Fuchs, A., 1994. *Die Inschriften Sargons II aus Khorsabad,* Göttingen.

Gadd, C.J., 1936. *The Stones of Assyria,* London.

—, 1938. 'A visiting artist at Nineveh in 1850', *Iraq* V: 118–22.

—, 1954. 'Inscribed prisms of Sargon II from Nimrud', *Iraq* XVI: 173–201.

Gallagher, W.R., 1999. *Sennacherib's Campaign to Judah,* Leiden.

Galter, H.D., 1987. 'On beads and curses', *Annual Review of the Royal Inscriptions of Mesopotamia Project* 5: 11–30.

George, A.R., 1990. 'Royal tombs at Nimrud', *Minerva* 1/1: 29–30.

Ghirshman, R., 1950. 'Notes iraniennes IV: Le trésor de Sakkez, les origins de l'art mède et les bronzes du Luristan', *Artibus Asiae* XIII: 181–206.

Gilboa, A., 1996. 'Assyrian-type pottery at Dor and the status of the town during the Assyrian occupation period', *Eretz Israel* 25: 122–35 (in Hebrew).

Godard, A., 1950. *Le Trésor de Ziwiyè (Kurdistan),* Haarlem.

Goff, B.H., 1963. *Symbols of Prehistoric Mesopotamia,* New Haven and London.

Goff, C., 1969. 'Excavations at Baba Jan, 1967: second preliminary report', *Iran* 7: 115–130.

Gonçalves, F.J., 1986. '*L'expedition de Sennachérib en Palestine dans la litérature Hébräique ancienne*', Études Bibliques 7, Paris.

Grayson, A.K., 1972–76. *Assyrian Royal Inscriptions,* 2 vols, Wiesbaden.

—, 1991. *Assyrian Rulers of the Early First Millennium BC,* I, *1114–859 BC,* Royal Inscriptions of Mesopotamia, Assyrian Periods 2, Toronto.

—, 1996. *Assyrian Rulers of the Early First Millennium BC,* II, *858–745 BC,* Royal Inscriptions of Mesopotamia, Assyrian Periods 3, Toronto.

Green, A., 1999. 'The Ninevite countryside. Pots and places of the Eski-Mosul region in the Neo-Assyrian and Post-Assyrian periods', in Hausleiter and Reiche 1999: 91–126.

—, 2000a. 'Botta, Paul-Émile (or Paolo Emilio) (1802–70)', in Bienkowski, P. and Millard, A. (eds), *British Museum Dictionary of the Ancient Near East,* London: 57.

—, 2000b. 'Layard, (Sir) Austen Henry (or Henry Austen) (1817–94)', in Bienkowski, P. and Millard, A. (eds), *British Museum Dictionary of the Ancient Near East,* London: 176–77.

— and Hausleiter, A., 2001. 'Gottheiten in Til Barsip', in Richter, T., Prechel, D. and Klinger, J. (eds), *Kulturgeschichten. Altorientalistische Studien für Volkert Haas zum 65. Geburtstag,* Saarbrücken: 145–70.

Haerinck, E. and Overlaet, B., 1998. *Chamahzi Mumah: an Iron Age III Graveyard,* Luristan Excavations Documents II, Acta Iranica XIX, Louvain.

Haller, A., 1954. *Die Gräber und Grüfte von Assur,* WVDO-G 65, Berlin.

Hallo, W.W. (ed.), 2000. *The Context of Scripture, Vol. 2, Monumental Inscriptions from the Biblical World,* Leiden and Boston.

Hamilton, R.W., 1966. 'A silver bowl in the Ashmolean Museum', *Iraq* XXVIII: 1–17.

Harbottle, S.T.L., 1973. 'W.K. Loftus: an archaeologist from Newcastle', *Archaeologia Aeliana* (Fifth Series) 1: 195–217.

Harding, G.L., 1971. *An Index and Concordance of Pre-Islamic Arabian Names and Inscriptions,* Toronto.

Hausleiter, A., 1997. 'Neuassyrische Keramik—Aspekte der Erforschung', in Waetzoldt and Hauptmann 1997: 271–78.

—, 1999a. 'Neo-Assyrian Pottery from Kalhu/Nimrud—with special reference to the Polish excavations in the "Central Building" (1974–76)', in Hausleiter and Reiche 1999: 17–60.

—, 1999b. 'Graves, chronology and ceramics: some considerations on Neo-Assyrian Assur,' in Hausleiter and Reiche 1999: 127–47.

—, 1999c. 'Neuassyrische Kunstperiode. VI. Keramik', *RLA* 9: 274–77.

—, in preparation. *Neuassyrishe Keramik im Kerngebiet Assyriens: Chronologie und Formen*, (PhD dissertation submitted to University of Munich in 1996).

— and Reiche, A. (eds), 1999. *Iron Age Pottery in Northern Mesopotamia, Northern Syria and South-Eastern Anatolia. Papers Presented at the Meetings of the International "Table Ronde" at Heidelberg (1995) and Nieborów (1997) and Other Contributions,* Münster.

Hawkins, J.D., 1982. 'The Neo-Hittite States in Syria and Anatolia', *Cambridge Ancient History* III/I, Cambridge: 372–441.

—, 2000. *Corpus of Hieroglyphic Luwian Inscriptions. Vol.I, Parts 1–3. Inscriptions of the Iron Age*, Berlin and New York.

Heltzer, M., 1978. 'Eighth century BC inscriptions from Kalakh (Nimrud)', *Palestine Exploration Quarterly* 110: 3–9.

—, 1982.'The inscription on the Nimrud bronze bowl no. 5 (BM 91303)', *Palestine Exploration Quarterly* 114: 1–6.

Herbordt, S., 1992. *Neuassyrische Glyptik des 8.–7. Jh. v. Chr.,* State Archives of Assyria Studies I, Helsinki.

Herrmann, G., 1986. *Ivories from Room SW 37 Fort Shalmaneser*, Ivories from Nimrud IV, 1–2, London.

—, 1989. 'The Nimrud Ivories 1: the flame and frond school', *Iraq* LI: 85–102.

—, 1992. *The Small Collections from Fort Shalmaneser*, Ivories from Nimrud V, London.

—, 1997. 'The Nimrud Ivories 3: the Assyrian tradition', in Waetzoldt and Hauptmann 1997: 285–90.

—, 2002. 'The Nimrud Ivories 5: the ornate group', in al-Gailani Werr, L., Curtis, J.E., Martin, H., McMahon, A., Oates, J. and Reade, J.E. (eds), *Of Pots and Plans: Papers on the Archaeology and History of Mesopotamia and Syria presented to David Oates in Honour of his 75th Birthday,* London: 128–42.

Herrmann, S., 1981. *A History of Israel in Old Testament Times* (revised edition), London.

Hilprecht, H.V., 1903. *Explorations In Bible Lands During the Nineteenth Century,* Philadelphia.

Howard, M., 1955. 'Technical description of the ivory writing-boards from Nimrud', *Iraq* XVII: 14–20.

Howes Smith, P.H.G., 1986. 'A study of the 9th–7th century metal bowls from Western Asia', *Iranica Antiqua* 21:1–88.

Hrouda, B. (ed.), 1962. *Tel Halaf IV. Die Kleinfunde aus historischer Zeit,* Berlin.

—, 1981. *Isin-Išān Bahrīyāt II: Die Ergebnisse der Ausgrabungen 1975–1978,* Munich.

Hunger, H., 1968. *Babylonische und Assyrische Kolophone,* AOAT 2, Neukirchen-Vluyn.

Hussein, M.M., 1985–86. 'Excavation and conservation in the southern and south-east parts of the Nabu Temple, Nimrud', *Sumer* 44: 48–54 (Arabic section).

—, 1995. 'Excavations and restoration work in the Temple of Nabu, Nimrud', *Sumer* 47: 28–34 (Arabic Section).

— and Abdul-Razaq, R., 1997–98. 'Seals from Nimrud', *Sumer* 49: 166–92 (Arabic section).

— and Black, J., 1985–86. 'Recent Work in the Nabu Temple, Nimrud', *Sumer* 44: 135–55.

— and Suleiman, A., 2000. *Nimrud: A City of Golden Treasures,* Baghdad.

Ibrahim, J.K. and Agha, A.A., 1983. 'The Humaidat tombs', *Sumer* 39: 157–71 (Arabic section).

Jamieson, A.S., 2000. 'Identifying room use and vessel function. A case study of Iron Age pottery from the Building C2 at Tell Ahmar, North Syria', in Bunnens 2000: 259–303.

Japhet, S., 1993. *I and II Chronicles*, Old Testament Library, SCM Press, London.

Jastrow, M., 1950. *A Dictionary of the Targumim, the Talmud Babli and Yerushalmi, and the Midrashic Literature*, New York.

Jean, C. and Hoftijzer, J., 1960. *Dictionnaire des Inscriptions Sémitiques de l'Ouest*, Leiden.

Jendritzki, G. and Martin, L., 2001. 'Badewanne oder Sarkophag?, in Meyer, J.-W., Novák, M. and Pruss, A. (eds), *Beiträge zur Vorderasiatischen Archäologie Winfried Orthmann gewidmet,* Frankfurt am Main: 180–95.

Jenkins, I., 1992. *Archaeologists and Aesthetes*, London.

Jones, J.F., 1855. 'Topography of Nineveh.' *Journal of the Royal Asiatic Society* 15: 297–397.

—, 1857. *Memoirs by Commander James Felix Jones, I.N., compiled and edited by R. Hughes Thomas*, Selections from *The Records of the Bombay Government* NS 43, Bombay.

Kamil, A., 1999. 'Inscriptions on objects from Yaba's Tomb in Nimrud', in Damerji 1999: 13–18.

Kaufman, S.A., 1983. 'The history of Aramaic vowel reduction', in Sokoloff, M. (ed.), *Arameans, Aramaic and the Aramaic Literary Tradition*, Ramat Gan: 47–55.

Killick, R., 1988. 'Pottery from the Neo-Assyrian to early Sassanian periods', in Northedge, A., Bamber, A. and Roaf, M. *Excavations at ʿĀna*, Warminster: 54–75.

Kim, Y,. 2001. *A Real-Time Immersive Virtual Environment for an Archaeological Site: The Northwest Palace of Ashur-nasir-pal II (883–859 BC)*, Part of Thesis for Master of Science, Department of Mechanical and Aerospace Engineering, University of Buffalo.

King, L.W., 1912. *Babylonian Boundary Stones and Memorial Tablets in the British Museum*, London.

Kinnier-Wilson, J.V., 1962. 'The Kurba'il statue of Shalmaneser III', *Iraq* XXIV: 90–115.

—, 1972. *The Nimrud Wine Lists*, CTN I, London.

Kletter, R., 1998. *Economic keystones. The weight system of the kingdom of Judah*, Journal for the Society of Old Testament, Supplementary Series 276, Sheffield.

Köcher, F., 1963. *Die babylonisch-assyrische Medizin in Texten und Untersuchungen*, Keilschrifttexte aus Assur 1, Berlin.

Koldewey, R., 1914. *The Excavations at Babylon*, London.

Kooij, A. van der, 1986. 'Das assyrische Heer vor den Mauern Jerusalems im Jahr 701 v. Chr', *Zeitschrift des Deutschen Palästina-Vereins* 102: 93–109.

Kreppner, F.J., 2006. *Die Keramik des 'Roten Hauses' von Tall Šēh Hamad/Dūr-Katlimmu. Eine Betrachtung der Keramik Nordmesopotamiens aus der zweiten Hälfte des 7. und aus dem 6. Jahrhundert v. Chr. mit Beiträgen von Malgorzata Daszkiewicz, Ewa Bobryk und Gerwulf Schneider,* Weisbaden.

Kühne, H., 1993. 'Vier spätbabylonische Tontafeln aus Tall Šēh Hamad, Ost-Syrien', *State Archives of Assyria Bulletin* 7/2: 75–105.

Kwasman, T. and Parpola, S., 1991. *Legal Transactions of the Royal Court of Nineveh, Part I. Tiglath-Pileser III through Esarhaddon*, State Archives of Assyria VI, Helsinki.

Lane-Poole, S., 1888. *The Life of the Right Honourable Stratford Canning*, 2 vols, London.

Larsen, M.T., 1996. *The Conquest of Assyria: Excavations in an Antique Land*, London and New York.

Layard, A.H., 1849a. *Nineveh and Its Remains*, 2 vols, London.

—, 1849b. *The Monuments of Nineveh From Drawings made on the Spot*, London.

—, 1851. *Inscriptions in the Cuneiform Character*, London.

—, 1853a. *Discoveries in the Ruins of Nineveh and Babylon*, London.

—, 1853b. *A Second Series of the Monuments of Nineveh*, London.

—, 1887. *Early Adventures in Persia, Susiana and Babylonia*, 2 vols, London.

Lebeau, M., 1983. *La Céramique de l'âge du Fer II–III à Tell Abou Danne et ses Rapports avec la Céramique Contemporaine en Syrie,* Paris.

Lehmann, G., 1998. 'Trends in local pottery development of the Late Iron Age and Persian period in Syria and Lebanon, *c.* 700 to 300 BC, *BASOR* 311: 7–37.

Lemaire, A., 1976. 'Note sur quelques inscriptions sur ivoire provenant de Nimrud', *Semitica* 26: 65–69.

Lines, J., 1954. 'Late Assyrian pottery from Nimrud', *Iraq* XVI: 164–67.

Loftus, W.K., 1857. *Travels and Researches in Chaldaea and Susiana,* London.

Loud, G., 1936. *Khorsabad, Part I: Excavations in the Palace and at a City Gate*, OIP 38, Chicago.

— and Altman, C.B., 1938. *Khorsabad, Part II: the Citadel and the Town*, OIP 40, Chicago.

Lloyd, S., 1980. *Foundations in the Dust. The Story of Mesopotamian Exploration*, revised and enlarged edition, London.

Luckenbill, D.D., 1924. *The Annals of Sennacherib,* OIP 2, Chicago.

—, 1926–27. *Ancient Records of Assyria and Babylonia*, 2 vols, Chicago.

Lumsden, S., 1999. 'Neo-Assyrian pottery from Nineveh', in Hausleiter and Reiche 1999: 3–15.

Luppert-Barnard, S.M., 1998. 'Adad-šumu-usur', in Radner, K. (ed.), *The Prosopography of the Neo-Assyrian Empire* 1/1, Helsinki: 37–40.

Luschey, H., 1939. *Die Phiale,* Bleicherode am Harz.

MacGinnis, J.D.A., 1987. 'A Neo-Assyrian text describing a royal funeral', *State Archives of Assyria Bulletin* 1: 1–12.

Majidzadeh, Y., 1992. 'The Arjan bowl', *Iran* 30: 131–44.

Mallowan, M.E.L., 1936. 'Excavations at Chagar Bazar and an archaeological survey of the Habur region of North Syria, 1934–5', *Iraq* III: 1–86.

—, 1937. 'Excavations at Chagar Bazar and an archaeological survey of the Habur region, second campaign', *Iraq* IV: 91–177.

—, 1947. 'Excavations at Brak and Chagar Bazar', *Iraq* IX: 1–259.

—, 1950. 'Excavations at Nimrud 1949–1950', *Iraq* XII: 147–83.

—, 1952. 'The Excavations at Nimrud (Kalhu), 1951', *Iraq* XIV: 1–23.

—, 1958. 'The Excavations at Nimrud (Kalhu), 1957', *Iraq* XX: 101–8.

—, 1966. *Nimrud and its Remains*, 2 vols, London.

—, 1977. *Mallowan's Memoirs*, London.

— and Davies, L.G., 1970. *Ivories in Assyrian Style*, Ivories from Nimrud II, London.

— and Rose, J.C., 1933. 'Excavations at Tell Arpachiyah, 1933', *Iraq* II: 1–178.

Matney, T., Roaf, M., MacGinnis, J. and McDonald, H., 2002. 'Archaeological excavations at Ziyaret Tepe, 2000 and 2001', *Anatolica* 28: 47–89.

Matthiae, P., 1999. *Geschichte der Kunst im Alten Orient. Die Großreiche der Assyrer, Neubabylonier und Achämeniden,* Stuttgart.

Maxwell-Hyslop, R., 1971. *Western Asiatic Jewellery c. 3000–612 BC*, London.

McCall, H., 2001. *Max Mallowan—Archaeology and Agatha Christie*, London.

McDonald, H., 1995. Catalogue entries nos 123–52, in Curtis and Reade 1995.

McKay, J., 1973. *Religion in Judah under the Assyrians*, London.

Melville, S.C., 1999. *The Role of Naqia/Zaqutu in Sargonid Politics*, State Archives of Assyria Studies IX, Helsinki.

Meuszyński, J., 1981. *Die Rekonstruktion der Reliefdarstellungen und ihrer Anordnung im Nordwestpalast von Kalhu (Nimrud)*, Baghdader Forschungen 2, Mainz am Rhein.

Ménant, J., 1874. *Annales des Rois d'Assyrie*, Paris.

Miglus, P.A., 2000. 'Assur—Frühjahrskampagne 2000', *Mitteilungen der Deutschen Orient- Gesellschaft* 132: 13–54.

Miho Museum 1997. *South Wing*, Shiga.

Millard, A.R., 1962. 'Alphabetic inscriptions on ivories from Nimrud', *Iraq* XXIV: 41–51.

—, 1972. 'Some Aramaic epigraphs', *Iraq* XXXIV: 131–37.

—, 1983. 'Assyrians and Arameans', *Iraq* XLV: 101–8.

Miller, E., 1973. *That Noble Cabinet: a History of the British Museum*, London.

Mitchell, T.C., 1990. 'The bronze lion-weights from Nimrud', in Gyselen, R. (ed.), *Prix, Salaires, Poids et Mesures,* Res Orientales 2: 129–38.

Moorey, P.R.S., 1971. *Catalogue of the Ancient Persian Bronzes in the Ashmolean Museum*, Oxford.

—, 1980. 'Metal Wine-Sets in the Ancient Near East', *Iranica Antiqua* XV: 181–97.

—, 1994. *Ancient Mesopotamian Materials and Industries: the Archaeological Evidence*, Oxford.

—, 1998. 'Material aspects of Achaemenid polychrome decoration and jewellery', *Iranica Antiqua* 33: 155–57.

Moorgat-Correns, U., 1988. 'Ein Kultbild Ninurtas aus neuassyrischer Zeit', *AfO* 35: 117–35.

Moortgat, A., 1940. *Vorderasiatische Rollsiegel,* Berlin.

Morgan, J., 1984. *Agatha Christie: a Biography*, London.

Müller, K.F., 1937. 'Das assyrische Ritual. Teil 1. Texte zum assyrischen Königsritual. Text II. Dienstanweisun für ein Königsmahl', *Mitteilungen der Vorderasiatisch-Aegyptischen Gesellschaft* 41(3): 59–89.

Muscarella, O.W., 1977. '"Ziweye" and Ziwiye: the forgery of a provenience', *Journal of Field Archaeology* IV: 197–219.

— (ed.), 1981. *Ladders to Heaven, Art Treasures from Lands of the Bible,* Toronto.

Muzahim Mahmud Hussein, see Hussein, M.M.

Na'aman, N. and Thareani-Sussely, Y., 2006. 'Dating the appearance of imitations of Assyrian ware in Southern Palestine', *Tel Aviv* 33: 61–82.

Naveh, J., 1979–80. 'The ostracon from Nimrud: An Ammonite name-list', *Maarav* 2: 163–71.

Oates, D., 1962. 'The excavations at Nimrud (Kalhu), 1961', *Iraq* XXIV: 1–25.

Oates, J., 1959. 'Late Assyrian pottery from Fort Shalmaneser', *Iraq* XXI: 130–46.

— and Oates, D., 2001. *Nimrud: An Assyrian Imperial City Revealed*, London.

Ohtsu, T., 1991. 'Late Assyrian "palace ware"—concerning dimpled goblet', in Mikasa, T. (ed.), *Essays on Ancient Anatolian and Syrian Studies in the Second and First Millennium BC,* Wiesbaden: 131–53.

Olmstead, A.T., 1923. *History of Assyria*, New York and London.

Oppert, J., 1865. *Histoire des Empires de Chaldée et d'Assyrie*, Versailles.

Orchard, J.J., 1967. *Equestrian Bridle-Harness Ornaments*, Ivories from Nimrud I: 2, London.

Orton, C., Tyers, P. and Vince, A., 1993. *Pottery in Archaeology,* Cambridge.

Paley, S.M., 1989. 'The entranceway inscriptions of the "Second House" in the Northwest Palace of Ashurnasirpal II at Nimrūd (Kalhu)', *The Journal of the Ancient Near Eastern Society* 19: 135–47.

—, 1999. 'A winged genius and royal attendant from the Northwest Palace at Nimrud', *Bulletin of the Miho Museum* 2: 17–29.

— and Sobolewski, R.P., 1987. *The Reconstruction of the Relief Representations and their Positions in the Northwest Palace at Kalhu (Nimrūd) II (Rooms I,S,T,Z, West-Wing)*, Baghdader Forschungen 10, Mainz am Rhein.

—, 1992. *The Reconstruction of the Relief Representations and their Positions in the Northwest Palace at Kalhu (Nimrūd) III (The Principal Entrances and Courtyards)*, Baghdader Forschungen 14, Mainz am Rhein.

—, 1997. 'The outer façade of the Throne Room of the Northwest Palace of Ashurnasirpal II at *Nimrūd* (Kalhu)', in Waetzoldt and Hauptmann 1997: 331–35.

Parker, B., 1954. 'The Nimrud tablets, 1952—business documents', *Iraq* XVI: 37–39.

—, 1955. 'Excavations at Nimrud, 1949–53: seals and seal impressions', *Iraq* XVII: 93–125.

—, 1957. 'The Nimrud tablets, 1956—economic and legal texts from the Nabu Temple at Nimrud', *Iraq* XIX: 125–38.

—, 1961. 'Administrative tablets from the North-West Palace, Nimrud', *Iraq* XXIII: 15–67.

—, 1962. 'Seals and seal impressions from the Nimrud excavations, 1955–58', *Iraq* XXIV: 26–40.

—, 1963. 'Economic tablets from the temple of Mamu at Balawat', *Iraq* XXV: 86–103.

—, 1983. 'Magic and Ritual in the Northwest Palace Reliefs', Harper, P.O. and Pittman, H. (eds), *Essays on Near Eastern Archaeology in Honor of Charles Kyrle Wilkinson,* New York: 32–39.

—, 1986. 'The Assyrian tree', *Sumer* 42: 141–45.

Parker, B.J., 2002. 'At the edge of empire. Conceptualizing Assyria's Anatolian frontier *c.* 700 BC, *Journal of Anthropological Archaeology* 21: 371–95.

Parpola, S., 1983. *Letters from Neo-Assyrian Scholars to the Kings Esarhaddon and Assurbanipal, Part II: Commentary and Appendices*, AOAT 5/2, Neukirchen-Vluyn.

—, 1993a. *Letters from Assyrian and Babylonian Scholars*, State Archives of Assyria X, Helsinki.

—, 1993b. 'The Assyrian tree of life: tracing the origins of Jewish monotheism and Greek philosophy', *JNES* 52: 161–208.

Parrot, A., 1952. 'Les fouilles de Mari: septième campagne (hiver 1951–1952)', *Syria* XXIX: 1883–203.

—, 1961. *The Arts of Assyria,* New York.

Pedde, F., 2000. *Vorderasiatische Fibeln von der Levante bis Iran,* Saarbrücken.

Pedersén, O., 1986. *Archives and Libraries in the City of Aššur. A Survey of the Material from the German Excavations,* 2 vols, Uppsala.

—, 1998. *Archives and Libraries of the Ancient Near East,* Bethseda.

Petrie, W.M., 1928. *Gerar,* London.

Pfälzner, P., 1995. *Mittanische und Mittelassyrische Keramik. Eine Chronologische, Funktionale und Produktion-sökonomische Analyse,* Berlin.

—, 1997. 'Keramikproduktion und Provinzverwaltung im mittelassyrischen Reich,' in Waetzold and Hauptmann 1997: 337–45.

Place, V. and Thomas, F., 1867–70. *Ninive et l'Assyrie*, 3 vols, Paris.

Porada, E., 1979. 'Remarks on Mitannian (Hurrian) and Middle Assyrian glyptic art', *Akkadica* 13: 2–15.

Postgate, C., Oates, D. and Oates, J., 1997. *The Excavations at Tell Rimah: The Pottery,* Warminster

Postgate, J.N., 1973. *The Governor's Palace Archive,* CTN II, London.

—, 1974. *Taxation and Conscription in the Assyrian Empire,* Rome.

—, 1976. *Fifty Neo-Assyrian Legal Documents*, Warminster.

—, 1992. 'Trees and timbers in the Assyrian texts', *Bulletin on Sumerian Agriculture* IV: 177–92.

—, 2001. '"Queen" in Middle Assyrian', *Nouvelles Assyriologiques Brèves et Utilitaires* 44–45, note 40.

— and Reade, J.E., 1980. 'Kalhu', *RLA* 5: 303–23, Berlin and New York.

Porter, B.N., 1993. 'Sacred trees, date palms, and the royal persona of Ashurnasirpal II', *JNES* 52: 129–39.

Potts, D.T., 1999. *The Archaeology of Elam,* Cambridge.

—, 2005. 'Cyrus the Great and the kingdom of Anshan', in Curtis, V.S. and Stewart, S. (eds), *Birth of the Persian Empire,* London: 7–28.

Powell, M.A., 1971. *Sumerian Numeration and Metrology,* unpublished PhD thesis, University of Minnesota.

—, 1989–90. 'Maße und Gewichte', *RLA* VII: 457–517.

Radner, K., 1999. 'Banītu', in Radner, K. (ed.), *The Prosopography of the Neo-Assyrian Empire* 1/2, Helsinki: 265.

—, 2003–4. 'Salmanassar V in den Nimrud Letters', *AfO* 50: 95–101.

Rassam, H., 1897. *Asshur and the Land of Nimrod*, New York and Cincinnati.

Rawlinson, H., 1865. 'Bilingual readings—cuneiform and Phoenician: notes on some tablets in the British Museum, containing bilingual legends (Assyrian and Phoenician)', *Journal of the Royal Asiatic Society,* new series 1: 187–246.

Rawson, P.S., 1954. 'Palace wares from Nimrud. Technical observations on selected examples', *Iraq* XVI: 168–72.

Reade, J.E., 1963. 'A glazed-brick panel from Nimrud', *Iraq* XXV: 38–47.

—, 1965. 'Twelve Ashurnasirpal reliefs', *Iraq* XXVII: 119–34.

—, 1979. 'Assyrian architectural decoration: techniques and subject-matter', *Baghdader Mitteilungen* 10: 17–19.

—, 1980. 'The architectural context of Assyrian sculpture', *Baghdader Mitteilungen* 11: 75–87.

—, 1981. 'Fragments of Assyrian monuments', *Iraq* XLIII: 145–56.

—, 1982. 'Nimrud', in Curtis, J.E. (ed.), *Fifty Years of Mesopotamian Discovery,* London: 99–112.

—, 1983. *Assyrian Sculpture,* London.

—, 1986. 'Rassam's Babylonian Collection: the excavations and the archives', in Leichty, E., *Catalogue of the Babylonian Tablets in the British Museum* VI, London: xii–xxxvi.

—, 1993. 'Hormuzd Rassam and his discoveries', *Iraq* LV: 39–62.

—, 2000a. 'The distribution of Assyrian sculptures', *NABU* 2000, no. 4: 88–89.

—, 2000b. 'Restructuring the Assyrian sculptures', in Dittmann, R. *et al.* (eds), *Variatio Delectat. Iran und der Westen. Gedenkschrift für Peter Calmeyer,* Münster: 607–25.

—, 2000c. 'Das Kultrelief aus Assur: Glas, Ziegen, Zapfen und Wasser', *Mitteilungen der Deutschen Orient-Gesellschaft* 132: 105–12.

—, 2002. 'The Ziggurat and temples of Nimrud', *Iraq* LXIV: 135–216.

Reiner, E., 1958. *Šurpu: A collection of Sumerian and Akkadian Incantations,* AfO Beiheft 11, Graz.

Rice, P.M., 1987. *Pottery Analysis. A Sourcebook,* Chicago and London.

Rich, C.J., 1836. *Narrative of a Residence in Koordistan,* 2 vols, London.

Richardson, M.E.J., 1995. 'Nimrud' in *The Encyclopaedia of Islam,* 2nd ed., VIII: 49.

Richardson, S., 1999–2001. 'An Assyrian garden of ancestors: Room I, Northwest Palace, Kalhu', *State Archives of Assyria Bulletin* 13: 145–216.

Roaf, M., 1983. *Sculptures and Sculptors at Persepolis,* Iran 21, London.

—, 1990. *Cultural Atlas of Mesopotamia and the Ancient Near East,* Oxford.

— and Zgoll, A., 2001. 'Assyrian astroglyphs: Lord Aberdeen's black stone and the prisms of Esarhaddon', *ZA* 91: 264–95.

Röllig, W., 1974. 'Alte und neue Elfenbeininschriften', *Neue Ephemeris für Semitische Epigraphik* 2: 37–64.

Rudoe, J., 1987. 'Lady Layard's jewellery and the "Assyrian style" in nineteenth-century jewellery design', in Fales and Hickey 1987: 213–26.

Russell, J.M., 1991. *Sennacherib's Palace without Rival at Nineveh,* Chicago and London.

—, 1997. *From Nineveh to New York,* New Haven and London.

—, 1998. 'The program of the Palace of Assurnasirpal II at Nimrud: Issues in the research and presentation of Assyrian art', *American Journal of Archaeology* 102: 655–715.

—, 1999. 'Some painted bricks from Nineveh, a preliminary report', *Iranica Antiqua* XXXIV: 85–114.

Safar, F. and al-Iraqi, M., 1987. *Ivories from Nimrud,* Baghdad.

Saggs, H.W.F., 1955. 'The Nimrud Letters, 1952—I', *Iraq* XVII: 21–56.

—, 1970. 'Introduction' to reprint of A.H. Layard, *Nineveh and Its Remains,* London: 1–64.

—, 2001. *The Nimrud Letters, 1952,* CTN V, London.

Schneider, E., 1999. '"Assyrische" Schalen aus Tell Sheikh Hassan (Syrien) und ihre Stellung innerhalb der Keramik des assyrischen Einflußgebietes' in Hausleiter and Reiche 1999: 347–75.

Schultz, M. and Kunter, M., 1998. 'Erste Ergebnisse der anthropologischen und paläopathologischen Untersuchungen an den menschlichen Skeletfunden aus den neuassyrischen Königinnengräbern von Nimrud', *Jahrbuch des Römisch-Germanischen Zentralmuseums Mainz* 45: 85–128.

Scurlock, J., 1991. '*Taklimtu:* A Display of Grave Goods?', *NABU* 1991, no.1: 3.

Segal, J. B., 1957. 'An Aramaic ostracon from Nimrud', *Iraq* XIX: 139–45.

Selby, W.B., 1859. *Memoir on the Ruins of Babylon*, Selections from the Records of the Bombay Government, New Series LI, Bombay.

Shukri, A., 1956. 'Conservation and restoration of Assyrian sculpture at Nimrud', *Sumer* 12: 133–34.

Singer, I., 1991. 'The title "Great Princess" in the Hittite empire', *Ugarit-Forchungen* 23: 327–38.

Sinopoli, C.M., 1991. *Approaches to Archaeological Ceramics,* New York and London.

Snyder, A.B. and Paley, S.M., 2001. 'Experiencing an Ancient Assyrian Palace: Methods for a Reconstruction', in Jabri, W. (ed.), *Reinventing the Discourse. How digital tools help bridge and transform research, education and practice in architecture,* Buffalo: 62–75.

Sobolewski, R.P., 1981. 'The Polish work at Nimrud: ten years of excavation and study', *ZA* 71: 248–73.

Sokoloff, M., 1990. *A Dictionary of Jewish Palestinian Aramaic of the Byzantine Period,* Ramat Gan.

Solomon, J., 2001. *The Ancient World in the Cinema,* New Haven.

Speiser, E.A., 1930. 'University of Pennsylvania Museum—Baghdad School expedition at Billa', *BASOR* XL: 11–14.

—, 1932. 'Reports on the Tell Billah and Tepe Gawra Excavations', *BASOR* XLVI: 1–9.

Sprengling, M., 1932. 'An Aramaic Seal Impression from Khorsabad', *American Journal of Semitic Languages* 49: 52–55.

Spycket, A., 1985. 'La statue bilingue de Tell Fekheriye', *Revue d'Assyriologie* 79: 67–68.

Stearns, J.B., 1961. *Reliefs from the Palace of Ashurnasirpal II,* AfO Beiheft XV, Graz.

Stern, E., 2001. *Archaeology of the Land of the Bible, Vol. II: The Assyrian, Babylonian and Persian Periods 732–332 BCE,* New York.

Stierlin, H. and Ziegler, C., 1987. *Tanis—Trésors des Pharaons,* Fribourg.

Stol, M., 1988. 'Greek Deikthrion: the lying-in-state of Adonis', in Kamstra, J.H., Milde, H. and Wagtendonk, K. (eds), *Funerary Symbols and Religion. Essays Dedicated to Professor M.S.H.G. Heerma van Voss,* Kampen, Netherlands: 127–28.

Strickler, G., 1922. *Die Familie Weber aus dem Neubruch Wetzikon,* Zurich.

Strommenger, E., 1964. 'Grabformen in Babylon', *Baghdader Mitteilungen* 3: 157–73.

—, 1971. 'Grab I. Irak und Iran', *RLA* III : 581–93.

Stronach, D.B., 1997. 'The imagery of the wine bowl: wine in Assyria in the early first millennium BC', in McGovern, P.E., Fleming, St.J. and Katz, S.H. (eds), *The Origins and Ancient History of Wine,* Amsterdam: 175–95.

—, 2003. 'The tomb at Arjan and the history of southwestern Iran in the early sixth century BCE', in Miller, N.F. and Abdi, K. (eds), *Yeki bud, yeki nabud : Essays on the Archaeology of Iran in Honor of William M. Sumner,* Los Angeles: 249–59.

—, 2005. 'The Arjan tomb', *Iranica Antiqua* 40: 176–96.

— and Lumsden, S., 1992. 'U.C. Berkeley's excavations at Nineveh', *Biblical Archaeologist* 55: 227–33.

Tadmor, H., 1982. 'The Aramaization of Assyria : aspects of western impact', in Nissen H.-J. and Renger, J. (eds), *Mesopotamien und seine Nachbarn,* XXV. Rencontre Assyriologique Internationale Berlin, vol. 2: 449–70.

—, 1994. *The Inscriptions of Tiglath-Pileser III, King of Assyria,* Jerusalem.

Tallqvist, K.L., 1905. *Neubabylonisches Namenbuch zu den Geschäftsurkunden aus der Zeit Šamaššumukin bis Xerxes,* Helsinki.

Talon, Ph., 1978. 'Les offrandes funéraires à Mari', *Annuaire de l'Institut de Philologie et D'Histoire Orientales et Slaves* 22: 52–75.

Tecoglu, R. and Lemaire, A., 2000. 'La bilingue royale Louvito-Phénicienne de Çineköy', *Comptes Rendus de l'Académie des Inscriptions et Belles Lettres*: 961–1007.

Teixidor, J., 1969. 'Bulletin d'épigraphie sémitique 1969', *Syria* 46: 319–58.

—, 1977. 'Bulletin d'épigraphie sémitique 1977', *Syria* 54: 251–76.

—, 1979. 'Bulletin d'épigraphie sémitique 1978–79', *Syria* 56: 353–405.

—, 1986. *Bulletin d'épigraphie sémitique (1964–1980),* Paris.

Thompson, R.C., 1940. 'A selection from the cuneiform historical texts from Nineveh, 1927–32', *Iraq* VII: 85–131.

— and Hutchinson, R.W., 1931. 'The Site of the palace of Ashurnasirpal at Nineveh, excavated in 1929–30 on behalf of the British Museum', *Liverpool Annals of Archaeology and Anthropology* XVIII: 79–112.

Thureau-Dangin, F., 1931. *Arslan-Tash*, text and plates, Paris.

Tiradritti, F. (ed.), 1998. *Egyptian Treasures from the Egyptian Museum in Cairo,* Vercelli.

Toker, A. and Öztürk, J., 1992. *Museum of Anatolian Civilizations: Metal Vessels,* Ankara.

Tomabechi, Y., 1986. 'Wall paintings from the Northwest Palace at Nimrud', *AfO* 33: 43–54.

Trümpler, C., (ed.) 2001. *Agatha Christie and Archaeology,* London.

Tsukimoto, A., 1985. *Untersuchungen zur Totenpflege (*kispum*) im alten Mesopotamien,* AOAT 216, Neukirchen-Vluyn.

Turner, G., 1970. 'The state apartments of Late Assyrian palaces', *Iraq* XXXII: 177–213.

Uehlinger, C. (ed.), 2000. *Images as Media, Sources for the Cultural History of the Near East and the Eastern Mediterranean (1st Millennium BCE),* Göttingen.

Ussishkin, D. and Woodhead, J., 1997. 'Excavations at Tell Jezreel 1994–1996: third preliminary report', *Tel Aviv* 24: 6–72.

Vallat, F., 1984. 'Kidin-Hutran et l'époque néo-élamite', *Akkadica* 37: 1–17.

Van Buren, E.D., 1954. 'Seals of the second half of the Layard Collection', *Orientalia* N.S. 23: 97–113.

van der Toorn, K., 1992. 'Anat-Yahu, some other deities, and the Jews of Elephantine', *Numen* 39: 80–101.

Veenhof, K.R., 1986. 'Cuneiform archives: an introduction', in Veenhof, K.R. (ed.), *Cuneiform Archives and Libraries, Papers Read at the 30th Rencontre Assyriologique Internationale, Leiden, 4–8 July 1983,* Leiden: 1–36.

Vernier, M. E., 1928. *Catalogue général des antiquités égyptiennes du Musée du Caire, Nos_52001–53855—Bijoux et orfèvreries,* Cairo.

Von Luschan, F., 1943. *Ausgrabungen in Sendschirli V: Die Kleinfunde, Herausgabe und Erganzung besorgt von W. Andrae,* Berlin.

Von Oppenheim, M., 1931. *Der Tell Halaf. Eine Neue Kultur im Ältesten Mesopotamien,* Leipzig.

Von Soden, W., 1958–81. *Akkadisches Handwörterbuch,* 3 vols, Weisbaden.

—, 1969. *Grundriss der Akkadischen Grammatik,* Analecta Orientalia 33, Rome.

Waetzoldt, H. and Hauptmann, H., (eds) 1997. *Assyrien im Wandel der Zeiten. Akten der XXXIX Rencontre Assyriologique Internationale 1992,* Heidelberg.

Walker, C.B.F., 1981. *Cuneiform Brick Inscriptions in the British Museum,* London.

Wartke, R.-B., 2005. *Sama'al: ein aramäischer Stadtstaat des 10. bis 8. Jhs. v. Chr. und die Geschichte seiner Erforschung,* Mainz am Rhein.

Watanabe, K., 1985. 'Die Siegelung der "Vasallenverträge Asarhaddons" durch den Gott Aššur', *Baghdader Mitteilungen* 16: 377–92.

—, 1987. *Die* adê*—Vereidigung anlässlich der Thronfolgeregelung Asarhaddons,* Baghdader Mitteilungen Beiheft 3, Berlin.

—, 1992. 'Nabû-usalla, Statthalter Sargons II. in Tam(a)nūna', *Baghdader Mitteilungen* 23: 357–69.

—, 1993. 'Neuasyrischen Siegellegenden', *Orient* 29: 108–38.

—, 1995. 'Weitere neuassyrische Siegellegenden', *Acta Sumerologica* 17: 291–97.

Waterfield, G., 1963. *Layard of Nineveh,* London.

Weadock, P. N., 1975. 'The *giparu* at Ur', *Iraq* XXXVII: 101–28.

Weissbach, F.H., 1907. 'Uber die babylonischen, assyrischen und altpersischen Gewichte', *Zeitschrift der Deutschen Morganlandischen Gesellschaft* 61: 379–402.

Whiting, R.M., 1977. 'More about dual personal pronouns in Akkadian', *JNES* 36: 209–11.

—, 1987. *Old Babylonian Letters from Tell Asmar,* Assyriological Studies 22, Chicago.

Wicke, D., 2005. '"Roundcheeked and Ringletted"—Gibt es einen Nordwestsyrischen Regionalstil in der altorientalischen Elfenbeinschnitzerei?', in Suter, C.E. and Uehlinger, C. (eds), *Crafts and Images in Contact, Studies on Eastern Mediterranean Art of the First Millennium BCE,* Fribourg: 67–110.

Wiggermann, F.A.M., 1992. *Mesopotamian Protective Spirits: The Ritual Texts*, Cuneiform Monographs 1, Groningen.

Wilcke, C., 1983. 'Ein Gebet an den Mondgott vom 3.IV. des Jahres Ammiditana 33', *ZA* 73: 49–54.

Wilkinson, C.W., 1960. 'More details on Ziwiye', *Iraq* XXII: 213–20.

—, 1975. *Ivories from Ziwiye,* Bern.

Wilkinson, T.J., 2000. 'Regional approaches to Mesopotamian archaeology. The contribution of archaeological surveys', *Journal of Archaeological Research* 8: 219–67.

Williams, D. and Ogden, J., 1994. *Greek Gold Jewellery of the Classical World*, London.

Winnett, F.V. and Reed, W.L., 1970. *Ancient Records from North Arabia,* Toronto.

Winter, I.J., 1981. 'Royal rhetoric and the development of historical narrative in Neo-Assyrian reliefs', *Studies in Visual Communication* 7: 2–38.

—, 1983. 'The program of the throneroom of Assurnasirpal II', in Harper, P.O. and Pittman, H. (eds), *Essays in Near Eastern Art and Archaeology in Honor of Charles Kyle Wilkinson,* New York: 15–31.

—, 1987. 'Art as evidence for interaction. Relations between the Assyrian Empire and North Syria', in Nissen, H.-J. and Renger, J. (eds), *Mesopotamien und seine Nachbarn*, XXV, Rencontre Assyriologique Internationale, Berlin, vol. 1: 355–82.

—, 1992. 'Rituals of the king: royal images as recipients of ritual action in Ancient Mesopotamia', *Journal of Ritual Studies* 6: 13–42.

Wiseman. D.J., 1953. 'The Nimrud Tablets, 1953', *Iraq* XV: 135–60.

—, 1955. 'Assyrian Writing Boards', *Iraq* XVII: 2–13.

—, 1958. 'The Vassal Treaties of Esarhaddon', *Iraq* XX: 1–99.

— and Black, J.A., 1996. *Literary Texts from the temple of Nabû*, CTN IV, London.

Woolley, C.L., 1934. *Ur Excavations II: The Royal Cemetery*, London.

—, 1962. *Ur Excavations IX: The Neo-Babylonian and Persian Periods,* London.

—, 1965. *Ur Excavations VIII: The Kassite Period and the Period of the Assyrian Kings,* London.

Yassine, K., 1984. *Tell el Mazar I. Cemetery A*, University of Jordan, Amman.

Young, R.S., 1981. *Gordion I: Three Great Early Tumuli,* Philadelphia.

Younger, K.L., 2002. 'Yahweh at Ashkelon and Calah? Yahwistic names in Neo-Assyrian', *Vetus Testamentum* 52: 207–18.

Zaccagnini, C., 1999. 'The Assyrian lion weights from Nimrud and the "mina of the land"', in Avishur, Y. and Deutsch, R. (eds), *Michael. Historical, Epigraphical and Biblical Studies in Honor of Prof. Michael Heltzer*, Tel Aviv: 259–65.

—, 1999–2001. 'The mina of Karkemiš and other minas', *State Archives of Assyria Bulletin* 13: 39–56.

Zayadine, F., 1973. 'Recent excavations on the citadel of Amman', *Annual of the Department of Antiquities of Jordan* 18: 17–35.

INDEX

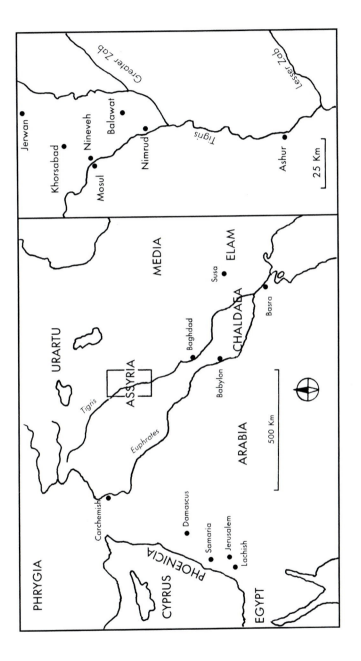

Plan 1. Map showing location of Nimrud (after Reade 1983: fig. 8)

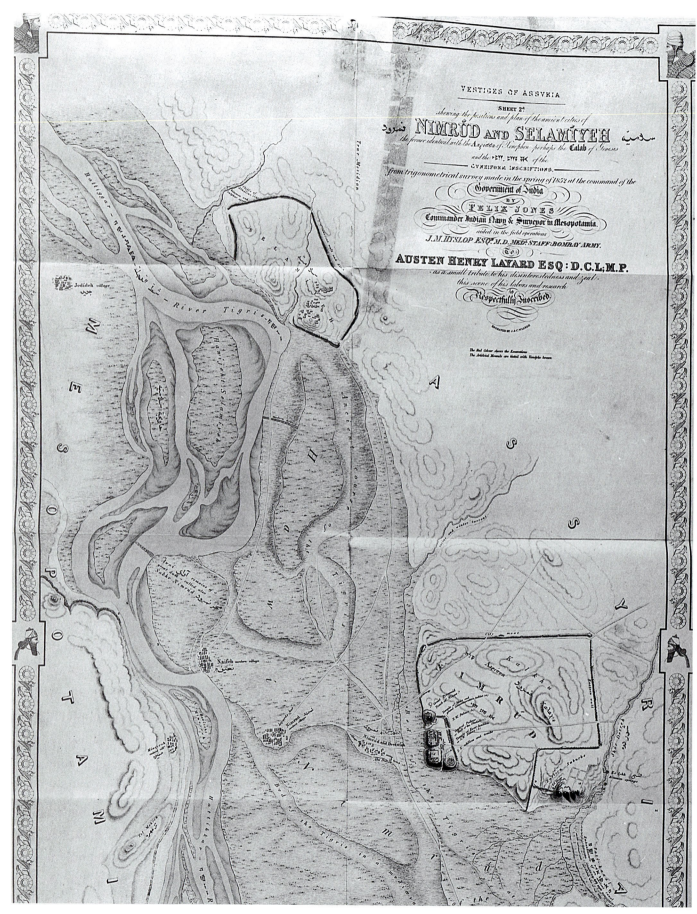

Plan 2. Nimrud, Selamiyeh and Awai: detail from Felix Jones's map, 1852.
(British Museum photograph).

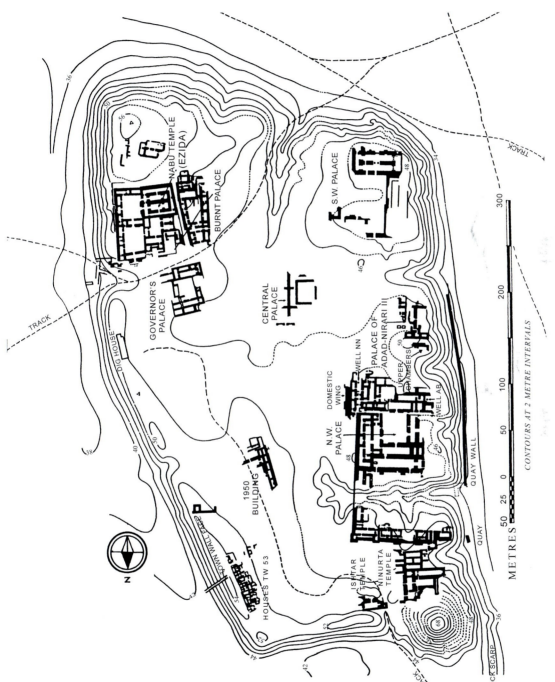

Plan 3. Plan of the citadel mound showing the excavations of the British expedition carried out in the 1950s.

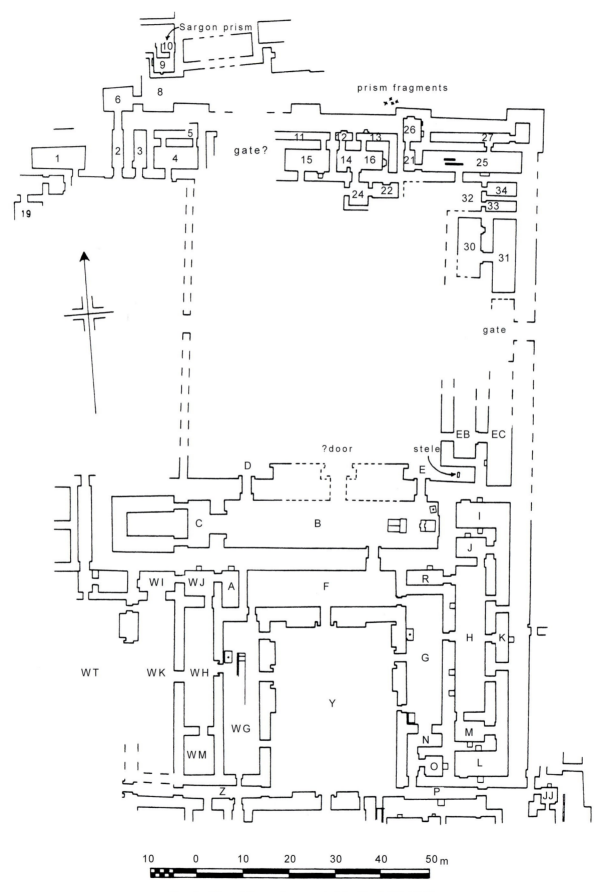

Plan 4a. Plan of the northern part of the North-West Palace.

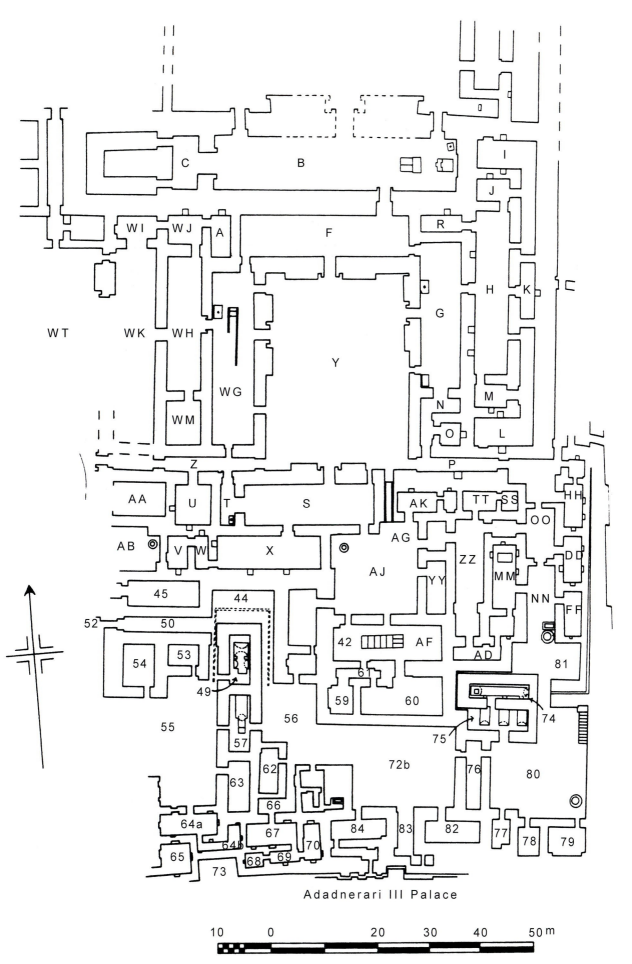

Plan 4b. Plan of the southern part of the North-West Palace.

Plan 5. The southern part of the North-West Palace at Nimrud showing the location of the royal tombs and other recent discoveries.

FORT SHALMANESER

METRES

100   0   100   200   300

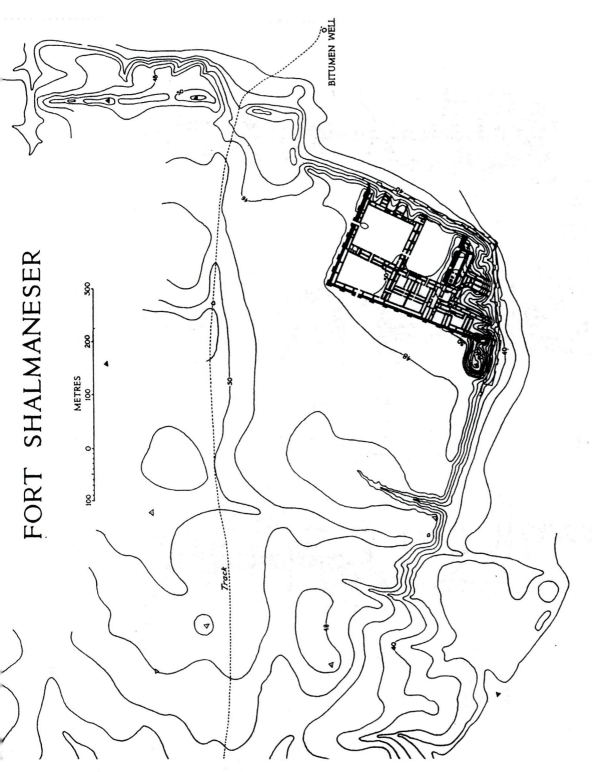

BITUMEN WELL

Track

Plan 6. Contour plan of part of Nimrud showing the location of Fort Shalmaneser

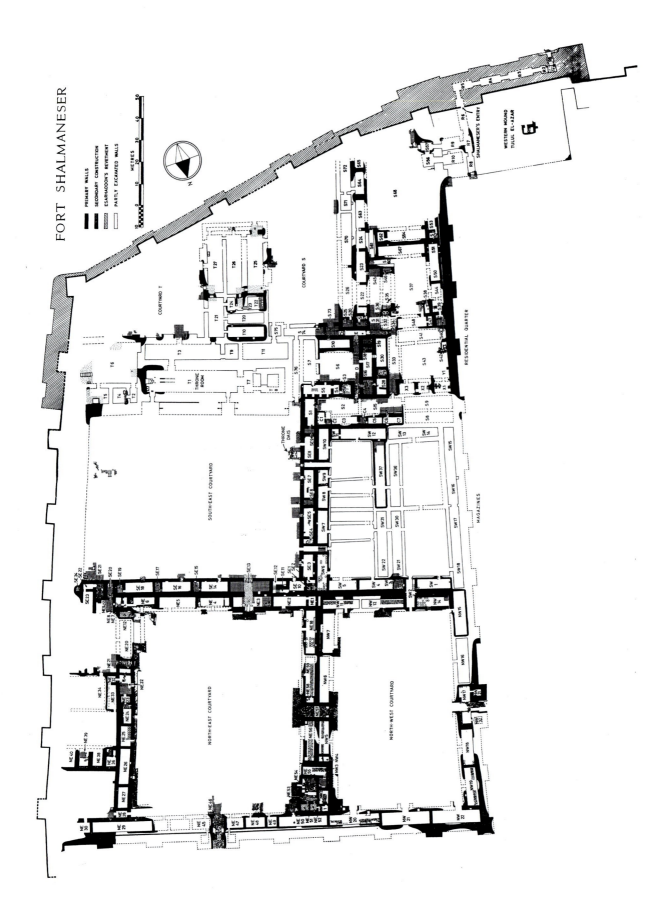

Plan 7. *Plan of the ekal mašarti, Fort Shalmaneser*